The FBI Files:

On The Tainted and The Damned

By: Dempsey J. Travis
Author of *J. Edgar Hoover's FBI Wired The Nation*

Urban Research Press, Inc.

www.urbanresearchpress.com

Copyright 2002 Urban Research Press, Inc.
840 East 87th Street, Chicago, Illinois 60619 USA
Printed in the United States of America
First Edition
ISBN 0-941484-32-7

Library of Congress Cataloging-in-Publication Data.

Dedicated To

My parents, Mittie and Louis Travis

Acknowledgements

A good coach never changes the front line of a winning team. Therefore, with great pride, I salute the following players: Moselynne Travis, *my wife and motivator*, Ruby Davis, *senior researcher*, Pat Scott, *layout designer*, Attorney George N. Leighton, Jewell Diemer, Jasmine Dunning, a student trainee from the University of Illinois at Chicago and the Vivian G. Harsh Research Department of the Carter G. Woodson Regional Public Library.

Prologue
Chicago's Head FBI Agent Marlin Johnson
Pleaded The Fifth Amendment

Through the eyes of J. Edgar Hoover, Director of the Federal Bureau of Investigation, all minorities, foreigners, and left wing thinkers were suspected of being fifth columnists. The same was true of the "Red Squad" Satellites in cities such as New York, Chicago, Seattle, San Francisco, and any other place where individuals were suspected of being affiliated with the National Association for the Advancement of Colored People (NAACP), The Urban League, the Communist Party (Reds), the Mafia, the Black Muslim Organization, the Black Panther Party, and The Rainbow / Push Coalition were baits for surveillance and subjected to investigation by the Federal Bureau of Investigation a subsidiary of the United States Department of Justice in addition to the local "Red Squads". An innocent individual associated with any of the aforementioned groups was grounds for triggering a FBI or "Red Squad" inquiry and thus generate a file that would be maintained by the bureau for the lifetime of an individual and beyond.

The twenty-four hour shadowing of Sam Giancana by the FBI, caused Attorney Anthony Tisei, the son-in-law of Salvatore "Sam" Giancana to recommend that he engage the services of Attorney George Leighton, a prominent civil rights lawyer to protect his constitutional rights. Leighton, a Harvard University Law School graduate had established a reputation for his outstanding work in the civil rights struggle as President of the Chicago Branch of the NAACP. Leighton also had a history of handling controversial legal civil rights matters for the closely monitored Honorable Elijah Muhammad, the spiritual leader of the Nation of Islam.

Attorney George Neves Leighton, agreed to take the Giancana civil rights case on its merits, but only if he was able to convince himself that the FBI agents were indeed depriving Giancana of his constitutional right to privacy. This case represented the first time in the Chicago area that a Black barrister had represented a hoodlum of Giancana's stature, as a matter of fact, the name Giancana was not a household word in Leighton's vocabulary. Leighton was selected to represent Giancana only after Attorney Tisei had been turned down by a number of white Civil Liberties lawyers who would not touch the case because of Giancana's reputation as a mobster.

During the initial meeting between Leighton and Giancana in the latter's basement, Leighton got the feeling that he was as much of a curiosity to Giancana as Giancana was to him. The core of the agreement between the two men was contingent upon Giancana agreeing to swear before an open court that he was a law-abiding citizen. To prove harassment Giancana had to maintain that he was not a reincarnated devil.

To bolster his chances of winning the case, Leighton hired a camera crew to take pictures of FBI agents constantly monitoring Giancana's home, his game on the golf course, and trailing him in heavy traffic as he drove through streets of Oak Park, Illinois. Leighton also brought aboard his team the service of a private detective from the John T. Lynch Detective Agency. Detective Don Ricker was assigned to the case by Lynch and instructed by Leighton to spend a week going wherever Giancana went, and doing exactly what he did. Much of the time that first week was spent lounging around Giancana's Oak Park home or sitting outside on lawn chairs drinking beer under a large tree. Giancana was a very light drinker, whereas Ricker drank multiple glasses of Pryor's beer which Giancana drew for him from a barrel in his basement. For Ricker, Oak Park, Illinois was somewhat of a dull scene in that it mirrored the typical suburban style of living. The exception for the area was the fact that the Giancana homestead had an overpowering presence of FBI agents who parked their cars along the curbs of Wenonach and Fillmore Streets. When the FBI agents Bill Roemer, Marshall Rutland, and John Bassett got out of their vehicles to follow Giancana on foot they always moved in single file like tin soldiers in military lockstep.

Attorney George N. Leighton, could best be described as a 5 feet 11 inch copper colored Negro born on the wrong side of the tracks in New Bedford, Massachusetts on October 12, 1912. His father Antonio N. and his mother Anna Sylvia (Garcia) were people of very meager circumstances. They could ill afford to send both George and his twin sister Georgina to school in proper raiment or encourage them to stay; therefore, George dropped out of school in 7th grade to perform a sundry of odd jobs around his small New England hometown to supplement the family income.

Overriding the poverty that enveloped him in his community was his unquenchable thirst for book learning. His addiction to the library and its wealth of knowledge was stronger than a junky's craving for heroin.

George Leighton's extensive reading enabled him to win a $200 scholarship in a writing contest in 1935 along with another winner who was a junior at a local university. Winning the contest bolstered George's confidence to the point that he got the audacity to lunge from a 7th grade drop out to Howard University in Washington, D.C. and subsequently to Harvard University Law School in Cambridge, Massachusetts from where he was drafted into the military service. He returned to Harvard and graduated after serving three years in the Army as an Infantry Captain in the Pacific Theater during World War II.

Service in a Jim Crow Army instilled the need for religious discipline in Leighton thus he suggested that Don Ricker and Giancana attend church their first Sunday together. The FBI agent learned through observation that attending Mass was alien to this hoodlum in that no one could remember ever seeing Giancana at a church service. Giancana was as much at home in St. Bernadine's Church as he would have been attending a Russian ballet at Samuel Insull's Opera House in Chicago. During Mass he did not know when to kneel, sit down or stand up.

In court before Federal District Judge Richard B. Austin, Giancana had the demeanor of a choirboy. Attorney Leighton filed a petition on behalf of his client demanding that FBI director, J. Edgar Hoover and Chicago's FBI area head Marlin Johnson be enjoined from harassing his client. "Regardless of what Mr. Giancana's reputation may be his civil rights were being violated", Leighton claimed. "No citizen should be subjected to such harassment because it is a violation of his Constitutional rights."

In Judge Richard B. Austin's court, Giancana was spellbound by the rhetoric of his lawyer. Leighton stood ramrod straight in front of the judge and spewed out the legal principle involved. He was methodical without giving the slightest hint that he was attempting to be flamboyant. Leighton had spent most of his legal career defending poor Black folks on the south and west sides of Chicago against racist charges being hurled at them before all white juries. He was by no means a prototype of the typical arrogant, high priced mob barristers. He used the Constitution and not the courtroom technicalities as his springboard. Hence, he was a party to the following:

SAM GIANCANA, Plantiff Appellee,

v.

MARLIN W. JOHNSON,

Agent in Charge, Chicago Office of the Federal Bureau of
Investigation, Defendant Appellant.

In the matter of the Alleged Criminal Contempt of Marlin W. Johnson,
Contemnor Appellant.

No. 14271.
United States Court of Appeals
Seventh Circuit.
June 30, 1964.
Rehearing Denied Aug. 11, 1964.

Defendant agent in charge of the Chicago office of the FBI was called
as an adverse party by the plaintiff. The United States District Court for the
Northern District of Illinois, Eastern Division, Richard B. Austin, J., entered a
judgment finding the agent guilty of contempt for refusing to answer questions
pertaining to exhibits which were never in the files of the Department of
Justice.

Order affirmed.
Kiley, Circuit Judge, dissented.

The contempt charges were based on the following testimony and
behavior, and the fact that the defendant pleaded the Fifth Amendment thirteen
times.

Plaintiff's attorney, George N. Leighton, showed Johnson a copy of a
telegram marked plaintiff's exhibit 5 for identification and asked FBI Agent
Johnson if on June 25, 1963 he had received the original thereof.
The witness replied:
"Your Honor, I respectfully decline to answer the question based on
instructions from the Attorney General of the United States and pursuant
Departmental Order No. 260-62."

Mr. Lulinski (government counsel) stated: "It is a part of the official
file of the Federal Bureau of Investigation, and as such, with respect to that,
Mr. Johnson as a subordinate of the Federal Bureau of Investigation, as a subordinate in the Department of Justice, is, by law, bound by the orders and directions of the Attorney General with respect thereto."

The court instructed the witness to answer the question. His answer was that …

"* * * upon the direction of the Attorney General of the United States, I respectfully submit that I must decline to answer the question under his instructions, pursuant to Departmental Order 260-62."

When Johnson was asked whether he had occasion to call Attorney Leighton at his office on June 25, 1963, he answered:

"Your Honor, again I decline to answer the question, based upon instructions of the Attorney General of the United States under Departmental Order 260-62."

The court asked:

"Will you tell me what his instructions were in regard to a question such as this, that does not require you to consult the files of the FBI?"

The witness answered:

"Your Honor, my instructions are 'not to give any testimony in this matter.'"

The court instructed the witness to answer and the witness replied:

"Your Honor, in accordance with the instructions of the Attorney General, I respectfully decline to answer under Department Order 260-62."

Relying on Order 260-62, the witness declined to answer the following question by Leighton:

"Mr. Johnson, did you not in a conversation with me by telephone in the afternoon of June 25, 1963, tell me that you were not going to remove from the residence of Mr. Sam Giancana the 24-hour surveillance of FBI Agents that you had placed there? Did you not say that to me?"

Johnson based his refusal on an instruction contained in a teletype from the Attorney General addressed to the United States Attorney, Chicago, under date of July 15, 1963, which, as read by the witness; stated:

"Your attention is directed to Department Order No. 260-62 which supersedes Order No. 3229. In connection with the matter under which Special Agent Marlin Johnson is now under subpoena, he is instructed to abide by Order No. 260-62. Johnson is instructed not to produce any of the documents called for nor to give any testimony in this matter."

The court instructed the witness to answer. He refused.

Mr. Johnson was then asked if he was in the courtroom "a moment ago, were you not, when the witness Carmen Skembare displayed to the Court the movie film taken on June 25, 1963, at and around the premise at 1147 South Wenonah Street in the Village of Oak Park?" The witness replied he declined "to answer under Departmental Order 260-62, on instruction of the Attorney General."

He was then asked by the court if he would give the same answer to all further questions asked by Mr. Leighton, and he answered in the affirmative.

The court asked:

"That would also apply to questions as to whether you recognize the faces of anyone you knew on the film you saw?" And Johnson answered, "My answer would have to be the same."

The court then asked:

"Both as to the address on Wenonah Avenue and also in regard to the Fresh Meadows Golf Course?"

The witness answered:

"Your Honor, that is correct on these instructions." As to all other questions Johnson then continued to refuse to make answer.

When the order was entered on July 22, 1963, the court, at Johnson's request, permitted him to make the answer "Yes" to the question asking whether he was in the courtroom when Skembare displayed the aforesaid film to the court.

Johnson testified that he was in the courtroom "a moment ago" when three picture films were exhibited and had a view thereof.

He was then asked:

"Now, did you recognize in those pictures from the first one that we showed, Exhibit 2 to Exhibit 4, any Federal Bureau of Investigation agent under your supervision?"

He replied:

"Your Honor, I respectfully decline to answer under Departmental Order No. 260-62."

The court instructed him to do so and asked for his answer. Johnson said "It will remain the same, your Honor."

The court asked:

"May I ask you, Mr. Johnson whether these films were at anytime in the files of the Department of Justice or in the files of the United States Attorney?"

"Under my instructions, your Honor, from the Attorney General and under Executive - Department Order 260-62, I must decline to answer."

This case represents a landmark decision in that it was the first time that an agent of the FBI had been held in contempt.

The Giancana case was the first of its kind but it certainly will not be the last one because in January 2001 a Federal Court granted the City of Chicago the right to implement the "Red Squad" spying tactics of the 1960s and 70s.

Between 1981 and 2001 the Chicago Police had been restricted in their depth of surveillance on groups that were critics of City Hall and other institutions that were marching to the beat of different drummers or simply exercising their right to freedom of speech.

On January 12, 2001 Mayor Richard M. Daley said: The police won't hurry into spying. The Chicago Police Department will proceed with caution before taking advantage of the relaxed federal restriction on police spying to preserve the First Amendment right and assuage those "paranoid" about a return to the infamous "Red Squad" days.

Dempsey J. Travis
September 2001

Table of Contents

Chapter XIII

Chapter XIV

Chapter XV

Frank Sinatra
XII

Chapter I

Frank Sinatra:
The Life and Times of
A Crooning Waiter

At high noon in Hoboken, New Jersey on December 12, 1915, Natalie "Dollie" Garavante Sinatra gave birth to an oversized 13 ½ pound baby who she named Francis Albert. The young mother had a very rough time in delivering her boy child into this world. The attending physician Doctor C. Anderson had to use forceps to pull the baby out of the womb of this frail 4 feet 8 inch woman. During his tugging and pulling with medical tongs he scarred the baby's right ear, cheek, neck, and also punctured the infant's eardrum.

When the baby was finally delivered out of the dark into the light it was noted that the child was not breathing, his maternal grandmother Rosa Sinatra, an experienced midwife, snatched the deep purple infant out of the doctor's hands and hastily carried him to the kitchen sink where she held his head under cold running water until he gasped for his first breath of air and yelled his very first note.

The delivery had put both the mother and the child in harm's way. Thus a decision was subsequently made by both parents not to ever go through that life threatening ordeal again. Hence, Francis Albert Sinatra was both their Alpha and Omega child.

Frank's father Anthony "Tony" Sinatra was a Sicilian immigrant brought up in the hills of Agrigento, Sicily. Shortly after getting off the boat in America Tony began making his way into the boxing world as a bantamweight prizefighter. He fought under the name "Marty O'Brien", because Hoboken was a town loaded with ethnic tension. He rightly figured his chances of winning a close decision in a boxing match were better if he fought under an Irish name because the referees were usually Irishmen.

On the other hand, his mother Natalie was a strong-minded little woman, born in Italy with good political instincts. She became active in the American political process as an Italian community spokesperson. She was physically small but became a political heavyweight within a relatively short period of time. She was able to get her husband a prestigious patronage job as a captain in the Hoboken Fire Department. Frank inherited his king size ambition and lightning fast emotional temperament from his mother's side of the family.

Anthony Sinatra puts his fireman's hat on his son's head for size.

The building in which Frank Sinatra was born was a four story red brick eight-family coldwater walk up tenement building at 415 Monroe Street in the lions of Hoboken. The structure was located in the tough frontier spirited waterfront section of the New Jersey city and was geographically just across the Hudson River from the spires of lower Manhattan in New York City. The boss of the territory where they lived was a Sicilian born mobster who answered to the Americanized name of "Waxey

Gordon." Northern New Jersey was a sanctuary for the Mafia leaders of New York during both the pre and post Prohibition-eras.

On the other hand, Frank Sinatra was spiritually influenced by his father in that he had a rough and tumble propensity for bare-knuckle street brawling. His skinny 5 feet 8-inch frame did not belie his "boxing to you drop" fisticuff skills or his volcanic temperament. The mean streak in him enabled the kid to battle his way to the top rung of leadership in a local teenage gang of tough Italian corner boys. His crafty and cocky demeanor caused him to be dubbed "Angles" by his friends at the David E. Rue Junior High School.

In 1933, at age 17, Frank dropped out of the Demarest High School in the second semester of his sophomore year, however during the short period of time that he was in attendance at the school he was busy singing and booking jazz bands for teenage Sunday afternoon dances. In the interim while on a hiatus between school and full time employment he was marking time by his own drumbeat on the street corners in his hood. Through the luck of the draw in a nickel blackjack game he managed to hustle up enough money to buy two tickets to see a live Bing Crosby concert at *Loew's Journal Square*, (an old Vaudeville theater in downtown Jersey City). As a result of this one night of inhaling the same air as *Bing the King* he decided he could out croon the crooning star of stage and screen.

Sinatra meets Bing Crosby backstage at Lowes Theater.

As a matter of fact, he emphasized what he could do when he laid his ego on the tabletop and said to his date Nancy Barbato "I can sing that son of a bitch Crosby off the stage any day of the week." Frank made this statement in spite of the fact that Bing Crosby and Russ Columbo the handsome singer and bandleader were his idols. It was generally known in the neighborhood that Bing had always been his hero, because he listened to all of Bing's records for hours at a time in a neighborhood local record shop because he could not afford to buy them.

Seeing Bing perform in person seemed to have a simulated his desire to become a professional singer.

After the Bing Crosby concert Frank shared his innermost thoughts about show business with his childhood sweetheart, Nancy who agreed to come aboard his dreamboat. Miss Barbato was so in love with Frank he could have told her that the moon was made out of white Limburger Cheese and she

would have believed it. The boy did not let too much water pass under their bridge before he convinced the young lady that he would marry her as soon as he could get his hands on enough money, a feat that took some years.

During the next seven years he slept with rocks in his bed as he gigged around the state singing at bars, lodge meetings, small road-houses, social club dances and filling in at local New York City radio stations where the Mutual Broadcasting System paid him a fee of

The Hoboken Four, center is Major Bowes, far right is Frank Sinatra.

70 cents to cover the cost of subway and streetcar fare. On other occasions he worked for as little as a ham sandwich, or a pack of Camel cigarettes. If the bar owner gave him 3 packs of smokes he would sing all night. (Keep in mind that in the 1930s cigarettes were selling for ten cents a pack and a single ciga-rette from an open pack sold for one cent).

In September 1935, Frank Sinatra got his first big break when he and three other Hoboken teenagers who called themselves the *Three Flashes* audi-tioned separately for an appearance on *Major Bowes and His Original*

Amateur Hour, a popular radio show that was broadcast nationwide once a week on Sunday night over *NBC* wire service from the stage of the Capitol Theater on Broadway in New York City. Both Sinatra and the *Three Flashes* tied for first place among those who auditioned for the show, thus Major Bowes decided to have the New Jersey boys work together and he renamed them the *Hoboken Four,* the group's personnel included Sinatra, Pat Prinipe, James Petrozelli, and Fred Tamburro. When they finally went on the air Sunday evening, September 8, 1935, the brash young singer acting as the spokesman for the group introduced himself on the air by saying, "I am Frank, Major Bowes, we are looking for a job. How about it?" Their opening number was *"Shine"* one of the Cecil Mack and Ford Dabney compositions. *"Shine"* had been popularized years earlier by Louis Armstrong at the Sunset Café in Chicago, Illinois and The Four Mills Brothers out of Piqua, Ohio.

The four young entertainers racked up the biggest listener vote in the history of the show with 40,000 people calling in to cast their ballots for them.

Frank Sinatra's mug shot taken in the Bergen County Sheriff's jail.

Major Bowes was so impressed with the group he brought them back as special guest artists for four consecutive weeks. As a result of their popularity Major Bowes arranged for Sinatra and *The Three Flashes* to tour as a team with his road show for three months at a salary of $50, per man a week plus meals. Hotel lodging was only one dollar per night for a double bed. (this was considered big money in the 1930s in that postal clerks who were classed as big time in some communities were only making $1,200 dollars a year.) At the end of three months Frank elected to leave the tour because he became homesick for his girlfriend Nancy and his family.

On November 27, 1938, Frank Sinatra was arrested after he finished singing his closing numbers at the *Rustic Cabin Roadhouse*. The two constables making the arrest were from Hackensack, New Jersey. They handcuffed him like a common criminal and carried him off to the Bergen County Sheriff's office in the county courthouse jail where he was photographed and fingerprinted and given arrest number 42799. He was subsequently released from the holding pen after the Charles Casualty Company, 214 Maine Street, Hackensack, New Jersey put up Sinatra's bond of $1,500. The charge against him was based on a breach of promise suit. According to the FBI files later released under the Freedom of Information Act, the charge read: "On the second and ninth days of November, 1938 under the promise of marriage, Frank Sinatra had a sexual relationship with a female of good repute named Antoinette Della Penta. The complaint was quickly dropped when it was discovered that Della Penta was in fact already married to a man named Edward Franke. Several weeks later the woman filed another complaint on December 22, this time charging Sinatra with committing adultery. Frank posted a bond of $500 and the case was sent to a jury.

On January 4, 1939, the complaint charging adultery was remanded to the jury by order of Judge McIntyre. The Bergen County records reveal that no bill had been returned on January 17, 1939 by the grand jury thus the complaint charging adultery was dismissed in open court. His bride to be Nancy Barbato, in a fit of rage asked Frank, "Was she the first?" Frank replied: "No, but she's the last." Nancy and Frank got married on February 4, 1939 in Jersey City at Our Lady of Sorrows Church. Years later his sexuality would return to haunt him over and over again.

In late 1939 while still working as a singing waiter at the *Rustic Cabin Roadhouse* in Englewood Cliffs, New Jersey he was discovered by Harry

James the star trumpet player who had just organized a new band following a three year gig with Benny "The King of Swing" because of his Black and brilliant musical arranger Fletcher Henderson. Benny Goodman frequently publicly referred to Henderson as a genius. Sinatra toured with the James Orchestra from the summer of 1939 until 1940 when he joined the Tommy Dorsey Orchestra where there was also a talented Black music arranger named Sy Oliver who had been the arranging spark plug for the Jimmy Lunceford Orchestra from 1933 to 1939. The Dorsey band was listed as the top swing orchestra over Duke Ellington and Count Basie in the annual Downbeat Magazine poll in 1940.

"Old Blue Eyes" at his best.

Frank Sinatra rose to enormous popularity in 1942 following the Columbia Recording Company's reissue of his 1939 recording with Harry James of "All or Nothing At All." His popularity had gone through the roof. He had reached what he thought was the top of his pyramid. To break his contract with Dorsey he needed the muscle of some gentlemen of respect from the Chicago and New York mob. They came to his rescue and Frank was able to buy out his contract with Tommy Dorsey for $60,000. His deal with Dorsey had been written in blood and it committed him to a life of Negrotude.

On December 30, 1942, he opened the first of his notoriously successful standing room only engagements at the Paramount Theater on Broadway in New York City. A girl in the audience (who reportedly had not eaten lunch) fainted during his performance. Another girl squealed, and bedlam ensued, and New York's finest in blue had to come to the rescue. From December 30th forward he was called The Voice in the entertainment circles.

An epidemic of Sinatritis swept the nation during the height of World War II. His income jumped to over a million dollars annually, he then moved to Hollywood, California from New Jersey where he commissioned Paul Williams, a Black architect, who was best known for his work among the Hollywood stars, to build a pink mansion for him and his family. He had Williams install a $7,000 electric gadget just to close the drapes on one wall. In keeping with his new lifestyle and wealth he would give his close friends $150 gold cigarette lighters as though they were Baby Ruth candy bars. (During the 40s the average salary was $35.00 per week).

Paul Williams, the architect is just one of many Blacks that Sinatra supported. He opened doors in show business that had been closed to such luminaries as Sammy Davis Jr., Nat "King" Cole, Lena Horne, Ella Fitzgerald, Count Basie, Louis Armstrong and Duke Ellington. A legendary story is told by Steve Bartelestein who said "Sinatra took Lena Horne to Ed Billingsley's Stork Club in New York City at a time when they were not accepting Blacks as patrons. The manager at the reservation desk fumbled around, walked away, and hastily returned and asked, "Who made your reservation because we don't seem to have it." "Who made it?" "Are you serious?" Sinatra snarled, "President Abraham Lincoln made the reservation fool."

Frank Sinatra did not serve in the armed forces during World War II because his ear was punctured doing his delivery at birth and thus he was rendered to be classified as 4-F and not qualified to serve. However, he did make a single United Service Organization trip to Italy to entertain the troops after peace was declared in Europe in the spring of 1945.

In the fall of 1945 he also launched his own campaign to eliminate racial bigotry. He won a special Academy Award for a movie short on racial intolerance called *The House I Live In*. In the same year he impulsively slugged a lunch counter man for refusing to serve a Negro.

Because of Sinatra's position on racism he was accused without a single fact of being a Communist by the House Committee on Un-American Activities.

The conservative Hearst newspaper chain also hinted that Sinatra was a Communist. However, some Mafia connected news brought Sinatra to the center stage when he was discovered in February 1947 by Robert Ruark, a Scripps - Howard columnist hanging out with the recently exiled, Mafia boss Salvatore "Lucky" Luciano in Cuba. Frank's gut reaction to any newspaper reporter's criticism of him or his associates was to use his fist. In April 1947 Lee Mortimer, a writer for the New York Daily Mirror and one of Sinatra's critics was seen in a nearby restaurant booth. When Lee got up to leave the eating establishment he was surrounded by Sinatra and three thugs who beat him up to the tune of a $9,000 damages suit which the reporter won. Up until February 1950 the Sinatras were considered one of Hollywood's ideal couples. It was shortly thereafter that he began showing that he had the heels of clay in that he deserted his wife and three children for Ava Gardner, Hollywood's reigning Femme Fatale.

Frank and Ava

Frank would threaten and sometimes succeed at breaking a photographer's nose for attempting to take a picture of him and his tenderling. He did not simply chase Ava around the bed he literally chased this woman around the world. He dogged her scent like a bloodhound from Hollywood to New York and across the Atlantic Ocean to Madrid, Spain where she had an extracurricular affair almost under his nose with Luis Miguel Dominguin, the famous Spanish matador. He was asked by a Hollywood reporter when he returned to the States from Europe what this affair was costing him and he replied "Six bottles of Coke".

Ava was dubbed an "Avalanche" by some of his close friends in that she was causing Frank Sinatra's image to disintegrate as he tried to hold on to her with his last fingernail. The Voice was dropped from his television spot on *Your Hit Parade List,* his record sales were plunging like the Titanic and his vocal chords were beginning to fray from heavy drinking and smoking. His fans began to jump ship and swim up stream with the singers like Nat "King" Cole, Perry Como, Frankie Laine and Billy Eckstine.

The scrapper from Hoboken had to stop contemplating his navel and find another road back to the top of the hill. To everybody's surprise his road back was James Jones' novel, *From Here To Eternity.* Frank had fallen in love with the character of Angelo Maggio, the tough little soldier who grinned, boozed and fought his way through the pre-Pearl Harbor army in Honolulu, Hawaii. Ruled by violent pride, the gritty Italian American GI character dies rather than allow the brutality of the stockade sergeant played by Ernest Borgnine to break his spirit. Frank felt that this once in a lifetime part could be a new blastoff for his sputtering rocket.

Left to Right: Montgomery Clift, Burt Lancaster and Frank Sinatra.

Sinatra ultimately got the part by default in that Eli Wallach wanted more money than Harry Cohn president of Columbia pictures was willing to pay, and secondly those who saw the film test thought Wallach was too muscular for the part, whereas Frank who was skinny, pathetic and Italian looking was exactly like Jones' character in the book.

The film became the biggest moneymaker in Columbia Studio's history. Frank's newspaper reviews were filled with superlatives. He got the Academy Award Oscar for best supporting actor. All of the leading players in the movie were nominated for Academy Awards. Frank's career had indeed been propelled to new heights. He can thank Ava Gardner who had become his wife in November 1951 and Joan Cohn, a friend of Ava's and the wife of Harry Cohn, President of Columbia Pictures. These two women were the wind under Frank's wings resulting in his getting the role of Maggio.

It was being said on the street that Frank's crime syndicate ties got him the role of Maggio. That was a lie that was started on a broadcast by the British Broadcasting Company. Sinatra made his point by throwing seven the hard way on the crap table when he won the suit against the B.B.C. and also a public retraction.

On the other hand, there was still more than an ounce of truth in the fact the Harry Cohn had organized crime ties and also that Frank had many friends

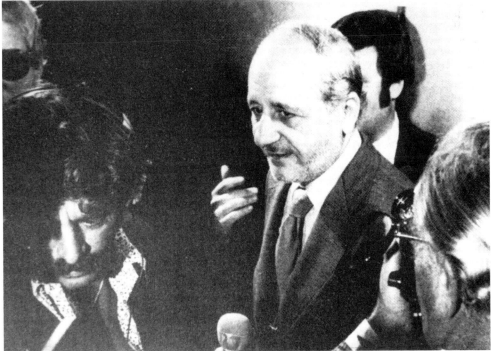

Giancana during recess outside of Judge Richard B. Austin's courtroom.

within the Mafia. It is suggested that Frank Costello spoke to Johnny Roselli on Frank's behalf. It is a fact that Harry Cohn wore a friendship ring from Roselli. And it is also true that years later Frank proposed Roselli for membership in the Friar's Club. Tony "Big Tuna" Accardo and Sam "Momo" Giancana were Sinatra's Chicago connection. Chicago was Frank Sinatra's kind of town.

The Villa Venice located on Milwaukee Avenue near Wheeling, Illinois in a rural section southwest of Chicago was Sam Giancana's joint. During the first month of the grand opening members of the Rat Pack including Dean Martin, Sammy Davis Jr., Eddie Fisher and others plus Frank Sinatra all appeared an entire month gratis, as a personal favor to Frank. This was a way Frank had of saying thanks to "Momo" for his friendship. This activity did not go unnoticed by either the CIA or the FBI.

Frank valued relationships in several worlds. Another prime example of his friendship took place on May 16, 1990 while he was singing to a five night sold out house at Radio City in New YorkCity when he got the news that his friend Sammy Davis Jr., had died. Without saying a word to the audience he cancelled out the four remaining sold out nights, dismissed the 40 piece band that was directed by Frank Jr., got on his private jet and went back to California to console Altovise, Sammy's widow and fill in the gaps where money was needed.

In making out his own will dated September 3, 1991 Frank made cash bequests in the following amounts to each of the following persons who survived him:

1.   To my former wife, Nancy Barbato Sinatra $250,000.
2.   To my wife's son Robert Oliver Marx $100,000.
3.   To my daughter Christina Sinatra $200,000.
4.   To my son Francis Wayne Sinatra $200,000.
5.   To my daughter Nancy Sinatra Lambert $200,000.
6.   To his fourth wife Barbara Marx Sinatra an outright bequest of $3,500,000. And she was also given the real properties owned by Frank located in Beverly Hills, Cathedral City and Malibu, California.

In the opinion of a legal source that was one removed from the Sinatra business affairs said that the 1991 will was not even the frosting on the cake. The real fact is that Sinatra left a fortune estimated to be in the neighborhood of $250 million.

Sinatra had extensive business and property interests. The exact value of his holdings are not really known by anyone other than his lawyer, Harvey Silbert.

Tina Sinatra with the support of her sister Nancy and brother Frank Jr. took control of Sheffield Enterprises, Inc., a corporate entity that was formed to license the Sinatra name and image. Barbara Sinatra and her son Robert Oliver Marx, an entertainment lawyer joined the Sheffield Board and sparks began to fly because Barbara and Robert were opposed to the Sinatra image being cheapened by giving product endorsements to some items.

On the other hand, Barbara gained a fortune from the rights to Sinatra songs before he joined the Reprise Label. This repertoire includes Sinatra's top 40 albums.

Frank Sinatra's obsession with women wrecked 3 of his marriages, but not his last. In 1939 he married Nancy Barbato, and ditto for Ava Gardner in 1951, it lasted only eleven months, and then there was Mia Farrow, whom he married in 1960 when she was only 21 and he was 49. Dean Martin cracked: "I have scotch older than Mia". Lastly he married Barbara Marx, the widow of Zeppo Marx of the Marx Brothers in 1976 that marriage endured to the end of his time for twenty-two years.

First wife Nancy with daughter Nancy greet Frank at train.

Frank Sinatra who once worked as a singing waiter died Thursday night May 14, 1998 at age 82. It can truly be said: "He did it his way."

13

Mia and Frank out on the Town.

**Frank with his bride Barbara Marx
and Nancy and Ronald Reagan.**

Federal Bureau of Investigation

Freedom of Information/Privacy Acts Section

Subject: Frank Sinatra

Freedom of Information

and

Privacy Acts Release of

FRANK SINATRA

File # 28-945

PLEASE FORWARD IN CLOSED ENVELOPE

1- Mr. Rosen

4/10/63

Airtel

To: SACs, Las Vegas (PERSONAL ATTENTION)
      Chicago (PERSONAL ATTENTION)
      Los Angeles (PERSONAL ATTENTION)
      New York (PERSONAL ATTENTION ASAC A. E. Bryant)

From: Director, FBI

JAMES RIDDLE HOFFA
PARK LAKE ENTERPRISES, INC.
DBA, CAL - NEVA LODGE
LAKE TAHOE, NEVADA
FRANK SINATRA; SKINNY D
SANICOLA; SANFORD WATERMAN
MISCELLANEOUS - INFORMATION
CONCERNING
(ACCOUNTING AND FRAUD SECTION)
CO: LAS VEGAS

57D   b7D
       b2

        It has been alleged that the owners of Cal - Neva,
Lake Tahoe, have conducted negotiations to obtain a loan of
approximately $3,000,000 from the Teamsters Union Pension Fund.
It has been reported

57D

        It is noted the Las Vegas Office is origin in a
current investigation captioned "Nevada Gambling Industry,
Cal - Neva Lodge, Crystal Bay, Nevada, AR," Bufile 92-0000,
Las Vegas file 92-000, Chicago file 92-340, Los Angeles file
92-002. A review of this file indicates the present owners
are those identified in the caption of this communication.
During this investigation Frank Sinatra and his attorney,
Milton A. Rudin, were contacted on 1/18/63 by the Los Angeles
Office. Results of these interviews are set forth in report
of SA   dated 1/18/63. During these interviews
it was indicated that the Teamsters Union Pension Fund in Chicago
had been approached by Rudin concerning the possibility of

63 - 8341 -

WAE:raw
(13)

        SEE NOTE PAGE THREE

MAIL ROOM   TELETYPE UNIT

Airtel to SACs, Las Vegas
                    Chicago
                    Los Angeles
                    New York
RE: JAMES RIDDLE HOFFA

securing a loan in connection with a $4,000,000 expansion
program. Rudin further indicated that during the March, 1963,
meeting of the Pension Fund in Chicago, Cal - Neva planned
to apply for a loan in order to achieve the expansion program.
Sinatra and Rudin insisted there were no under-the-table
payments of any kind involved in this loan.

        Las Vegas and Los Angeles Offices are instructed
to immediately review the current investigation of Cal - Neva
and any other pertinent office files for any details concerning
this proposed Pension Fund Loan. The results of this review,
including the interviews with Sinatra and Rudin, are to be
set forth in letterhead memorandum form suitable for dissemination. No open inquiries are to be made outside the Bureau
at this time in connection with this matter.

        The Chicago Office, during the course of making
inquiries in connection with the Teamsters Union Pension Fund
Loan investigation, should be alert to any information relating
to this potential loan. No open inquiries are to be made in
this regard and under no circumstances is this matter to be
discussed with any one outside the Bureau, including Department
attorneys in Chicago. The results of any information coming
to the attention of the Chicago Office are to be set out in
letterhead memorandum form suitable for dissemination.

        New York should recontact the source and attempt
to determine whether any additional developments have occurred.

        Until further information is obtained in this matter
it must be afforded maximum security at all times and no
inquiries made other than set forth herein. Results of these
inquiries are to be set forth in letterhead memorandum form.
New York is to be furnished copies of all communications
marked for the PERSONAL ATTENTION ASAC A. M. Bryant.

- 2 -

UNITED STATES DEPARTMENT OF JUSTICE

FEDERAL BUREAU OF INVESTIGATION
Los Angeles, California
April 17, 1963

In Reply Please Refer to
File No

JAMES RIDDLE HOFFA
PARK LAKE ENTERPRISES, INC.
DBA CAL - NEVA LODGE
LAKE TAHOE, NEVADA
FRANK SINATRA; HENRY W. SANICOLA;
SANFORD WATERMAN
MISCELLANEOUS - INFORMATION CONCERNING
(ACCOUNTING AND FRAUD SECTION)

On January 16, 1963, FRANK SINATRA and MILTON A. RUDIN, Attorney at Law and Financial Advisor to SINATRA, were interviewed at the offices of Essex Productions, 9229 Sunset Boulevard, Suite 512, Los Angeles, California, concerning the Cal - Neva Lodge, Crystal Bay, Nevada.

During the course of this interview Mr. RUDIN, with the consent of Mr. SINATRA, advised that their current plans for the Cal - Neva Lodge included quite a substantial expansion of the hotel which would necessitate the bringing in of some $4,000,000.00 of added capital. RUDIN stated that he found out by checking into the loan situation that banks and insurance companies, in order to make loans, would ask for stock options, which they are not ready to agree to.

Mr. RUDIN advised that he has become familiar with some of the pension fund loans from reading the series of articles run by the "Los Angeles Times" on investigations of loans by the Teamsters to various Nevada casinos and that these are straight forward loans. He advised that he had gone to Chicago and had talked to various Teamster officials in the Chicago area concerning the possibility of securing a loan for Cal - Neva. He advised that the Cal - Neva, at the next meeting of the trustees for the pension fund in March, will, according to their present plans, apply for a loan in order to achieve their expansion program.

Both RUDIN and SINATRA advised they wished to go on record that there were no under-the-table payments of any kind involved, that this was a simple straight forward

0-19 (Rev 10-15—2)

Sinatra Ends His Gambling Ties to Nevada

LAS VEGAS, Oct. 8 (AP) — Frank Sinatra, who surrendered $3.5 million in Nevada gaming interests says he's going to concentrate on the entertainment field from now on

But he wished the gambling industry good luck in parting Casinos he said, make jobs for entertainers and "that's all for them

Mr Sinatra announced yesterday he would not fight an attempt by the Nevada Gaming Commission to revoke his license He said he had been planning to pull out for several months

The commission had been seeking to revoke Mr Sinatra's license on grounds that he entertained underworld figure Sam Giancana at Mr Sinatra's Cal-Neva lodge in Lake Tahoe

Mr Sinatra's attorney Harry Claiborne, asked the gaming commission in a letter yesterday to terminate the singer's license adding that he was withdrawing from the gaming industry

Considered Admission

The singer's withdrawal was expected to end further action by the commission, although technically it still could proceed.

"No useful purpose would be served by my devoting my time and energies convincing the Nevada gaming officials that I should be part of their gambling industry" Mr Sinatra said in a statement issued here yesterday. The singer was in New York

A commission spokesman said Mr Sinatra's failure to respond to the commissions' charges "shall constitute an admission of all matters and facts contained in the complaint

"In such cases," the spokesman said, "the commission may take action based upon such admission or upon any other evidences and without any further notices whatever to respondent (Sinatra)"

Rights Waived

By failing to file a notice of defense Mr Sinatra waives all rights to both a hearing before the commission and any judiciary review of the commission's decision

The gaming commission had asked the gaming Commission, its investigation, to revoke Sinatra's gaming license and to force him to sell his per cent interest in the Hotel in Las Vegas

Mr Sinatra and the Nevada gaming [illegible] his Sands Hotel holding of about $380,000 and the Cal-Neva lodge at about $300,000

The two points were filed in Carson City September 11 Mr Sinatra later was given until yesterday to reply to the charges or risk losing his license without benefit of a hearing

OCT 16 1963

business transaction with sufficient collateral involved.
Mr. RUDIN advised that the person he had contacted regarding
the possibility of such a loan was HAROLD GIBBONS. SINATRA
mentioned that DORIS DAY had secured a similar type loan
from the Teamsters for a motel that she owns, and he had
asked her if she had had to cut anybody in, and she advised
him that it was not necessary, that it was a straight loan.

This document contains neither recommendations nor
conclusions of the FBI. It is the property of the FBI and
is loaned to your agency; it and its contents are not to be
distributed outside your agency.

FE-90. (Rev 3-3-80)

UNITED STATES DEPARTMENT ▬ JUSTICE
FEDERAL BUREAU O▬ INVESTIGATION

CO▬▬NTIAL

Copy to

Report of SA ▬▬▬▬▬▬▬▬▬ b7C   Office· CHICAGO
Date   9/12/60

Field Office File No.   Chicago 92-349   Bureau File No   92-3171-72

Title: SAMUEL M GIANCANA, aka, Sam Flood, Sam Mooney, Momo Salvatore
         Giancana, Gilormo Giangana, Samuél Giancana, Sam Gianaco,
         Sam Gincani, Sam Giancano, Sam Gencani, Sam Gincana,
         Sam Gincanni, Sam Gincanna, Sam Gincina, Sam Ginoina, Sam
         Giacana, Sam Gianana, Sam Ginncana, Albert Manusco, Albert
         Masusco, Anthony De Bendo, J. A. Collins, Russell Paige,
         S. Perry, John De Santos, Morris Simon

Character·ANTI-RACKETEERING

Synopsis   SAMUEL M GIANCANA, FBI No. 58437, age 52, born 6/15 or
           30/08, Chicago, Illinois. GIANCANA, widower, resides
           at 1147 S. Wenonah, Oak Park, Illinois, with his sister-
           in-law, ANNIE TUMMINELLO, and her family. GIANCANA has
           a sixth grade education and his last legitimate employment
           was stated to be in 1943 as a salesman. State of health
           at present is said to be "good." GIANCANA has lengthy
           arrest record dating to 1926, last arrested by Chicago PD
           4/15/57, GP. He has served sentences in Illinois State
           Penitentiary (1929) for attempted burglary, Federal
           Penitentiary Leavenworth (1939) for violation of Internal
           Revenue Service laws. GIANCANA, according to some Chicago
           sources, is the alleged head of organized crime in the
           Chicago area   Other sources place him in the upper echelon
           in the Chicago underworld. His alleged legitimate enterprises
           are, or were, among others, the River Road Motel, The
           American Motel, Forest Lounge, Armory Lounge, Villa Venice
           Restaurant, World Wide Actor's Agency, and others all
           located in Western and Northwest Chicago suburbs. Closer
           associates of GIANCANA in organized crime are MURRAY
           LLEWELYN HUMPHREYS, ANTHONY J. ACCARDO, ▬▬▬▬▬▬▬▬   b7C
           ▬▬▬▬▬▬▬▬▬▬▬▬▬▬ GIANCANA has
           propensity to associating with female show girls and
           entertainers. Sources report GIANCANA to travel extensively,
           primarily between Chicago and Las Vegas and Miami. When
           in Chicago, he usually makes his headquarters at the
           Armory Lounge, Forest Park, Illinois. GIANCANA SHOULD BE
           CONSIDERED ARMED AND DANGEROUS SINCE HE ALLEGEDLY HAS A
           VICIOUS TEMPERAMENT, PSYCHOPATIC PERSONALITY AND HAS BEEN
           KNOWN TO CARRY FIREARMS.

CG 92-349

FRANK SINATRA

b7D _____ advised _____ that during the first part of 1958 when FRANK SINATRA was appearing at the Sands Hotel in Las Vegas, SINATRA was with GIANCANA and accompanied him to the El Rancho Vegas in Las Vegas. _____ described SINATRA as the well-known actor and entertainer.

Among the notes contained in GIANCANA s possession upon being searched by Customs Officers in Chicago on June 15, 1958, mentioned previously, was the name SINATRA, Office 5-4977, home Crestview 4-2368 . Subsequent investigation revealed that Crestview 4-2368 is the private number for FRANK SINATRA in Los Angeles, California.

b7D _____ advised _____ that SAM GIANCANA at that time had been in Las Vegas for two to three weeks and was observed introducing FRANK SINATRA to one BARBARA GROCKE at the Sands Hotel in Las Vegas.

b7D _____ advised _____ that he had received information to the effect that GIANCANA had been in the New Jersey area during the latter part of July or early August, 1959.

b7D

b7D
b7C advised SA _____ and SA _____ that

Upon going to SINATRA's suite at that hotel she noticed among those present were JOSEPH FISCHETTI, JACK ENTRATTA, from Las Vegas and SKINNY D MATO, owner of the 500 Club, Atlantic City, New Jersey. _____ advised she assumes it is common knowledge that FISCHETTI and FRANK SINATRA are close friends and SINATRA has the hoodlum complex .

The Attorney General   November 24, 1961

92-3171-508

REC-75   Director, FBI   1 - Mr. Belmont
EX 110   1 - Mr. Evans
                                                1 - Mr. Stanley
                  SAMUEL M. GIANCANA   1 - Mr. McAndrews
                  ANTI-RACKETEERING   1 - Mr. Leggett

        Information was confidentially received November 23,
1961, concerning the close association between Chicago hoodlum
Samuel M. Giancana and entertainers Frank Sinatra and Tony
Bennett on occasions when Sinatra and Bennett visit Chicago.

        During such visits, according to our information,
Giancana and his associates, John Mattassa, a former Chicago
Police Department Detective, and Dominic "Butch" Blasi,
accompany Sinatra and Bennett on their rounds of various
night clubs reported to be hangouts and possible enterprises
of Giancana. On some past visits, Sinatra and Giancana
have held contests to determine who could spend the most
money buying drinks and trinkets for the party.

        Giancana is one of the individuals selected as a
target for early prosecution. Reports containing the results
of our inquiries into his activities have been furnished to
the Criminal Division.

1 - Mr. Byron R. White
    Deputy Attorney General

1 - Assistant Attorney General
    Herbert J. Miller, Jr.

NOTE   • The confidential source furnishing this information
       was ████████████

JGL-Swb
(10)

MAILED 20
NOV 24 1961
COMM-FBI

50 DEC 6 1961

RE: SAMUEL GIANCANA

Cal-Neva Lounge
Lake Tahoe, Nevada

      This establishment is located in the north end of Lake Tahoe, which borders the States of Nevada and California Located around the lodge, there are approximately 20 cottages which rent from $30.00 to $50 00 a day The lodge has a large dining room and a coffee shop located on the California side of the building Entertainment is provided nightly by known entertainers On the Nevada side of the lodge is located the gambling facility, which there are slot machines and various type table games ɰ

      The following information pertains to the owners of records of Park Lake Entertainment, Incorporated, doing business as Cal-Neva Lodge, Lake Tahoe, Nevada. ɰ

      These are the owners of records of this corporation as of July 30, 1961:

Name	Percent	Address
FRANK A. SINATRA	36.6	2666 Bowmont Drive Los Angeles, California
HENRY W. SANICOLA	24.4	4321 Bellaire North Hollywood, California
BERT GROBER	14 6	Crystal Bay Lake Tahoe, Nevada
IKE BERGER	12 2	2642 Collins Avenue Miami Beach, Florida
SANFORD WATERMAN	12.2	4925 Collins Avenue Miami Beach, Florida.

ɰ

- 221 -

RE: SAMUEL GIANCANA

▓▓▓▓▓▓▓▓ that ▓▓▓▓▓▓▓▓ **b7D**

expressed a desire to become
employed by Frank Sinatra at the Cal-Neva Lodge.

▓▓▓▓▓▓▓▓ according to reliable sources, is
a well known personage of ▓▓▓▓▓▓▓▓ who has
long been associated with Giancana. ▓▓▓▓▓▓▓▓ **b7C**
▓▓▓▓▓▓ Reliable sources have placed
close to Frank Sinatra and Dean Martin

- 222 -

FD-204 (Rev 3-3-59)

UNITED STATES DEPARTMENT OF JUSTICE
FEDERAL BUREAU OF INVESTIGATION

Copy to: **1 - USA, Chicago**

Report of
Date: ████████████████ b7C   Office: **CHICAGO**

          10-11-62

Field Office File #: **92-349**   Bureau File #: **92-3171 -904**

Title: **SAMUEL M. GIANCANA**

Character: **ANTI-RACKETEERING**

Synopsis:
b7C   Information relating to GIANCANA's travels with ████████
          ████████ PHYLLIS MC GUIRE, set forth. GIANCANA observed
          at FRANK SINATRA's residence, Palm Springs, California,
          during September, 1962 Information received that GIANCANA
          has remodeled Villa Venice Supper Club, Wheeling, Illinois,
          into plush night club, which will feature top entertainers.
          Villa Venice scheduled to re-open 10/31/62. GIANCANA
          SHOULD BE CONSIDERED ARMED AND DANGEROUS SINCE HE HAS
          A VICIOUS TEMPERAMENT, A PSYCHOPATHIC PERSONALITY AND
          IS KNOWN TO HAVE CARRIED FIREARMS.
                              (μ)
                      - P -

CG 92-349

FRANK SINATRA

It should be noted that further information pertaining to GIANCANA's relationship with SINATRA will be reflected in that section of this report pertaining to PHYLLIS MC GUIRE. (u)

The Los Angeles Division advised on October 2, 1962, that a physical surveillance reflected that a white Ford Falcon belonging to the Frank Sinatra Enterprises arrived at the Palm Springs Airport at 3.40 AM October 2, 1962, and contained one female and two males FRANK SINATRA's airplane bearing Number N71DE arrived at the Palm Springs Airport at 4:50 AM on October 2, 1962. PHYLLIS MC GUIRE at that time joined the individuals in the Ford Falcon described above. One of the individuals in the Falcon appeared to be SAM GIANCANA. (u)

b7D _____ advised on September 22, 1962, that PHYLLIS MC GUIRE called telephone number 328-2105 in Palm Springs, California. At the time the call was placed, the informant advised that GIANCANA was present with MC GUIRE. (u)

The Los Angeles Office advised on September 23, 1962, that telephone number 328-2105 is the unlisted number of FRANK SINATRA, Tamarisk Country Club, Cathedral City, California. The telephone number is billed to SINATRA's agent, SAM BURK, Suite 419, 9350 Wilshire Boulevard, Los Angeles, California. (u)

b7D _____ advised in August, 1962, that GIANCANA had made plans to be in Atlantic City, New Jersey commencing with the week end of August 25, 1962. (u)

The Newark Office advised on August 22, 1962, that GENE CATENA, brother of GERARDO CATENA and JOSEPH PECORA were in Atlantic City, New Jersey for several days commencing with August 22, 1962. (u)

The Newark Office advised on August 27, 1962, that FRANK SINATRA was due to appear at the 500 Club in Atlantic City to perform with DEAN MARTIN on the last night of MARTIN's singing engagement at that club. (u)

- 4 -

CG 92-349

Surveillances conducted by Agents at the Newark Office indicated that many individuals came to the Atlantic City area for two-fold purposes, that is to attend the wedding of ANGELO BRUNO's daughter on August 26, 1962, and a performance of FRANK SINATRA-DEAN MARTIN-SAMMY DAVIS, JR., at the 500 Club. (U)

FRANK SINATRA arrived in Atlantic City on August 27, 1962, for the above scheduled appearance with DEAN MARTIN and took over the first sleeping floor of the Claridge Hotel, Atlantic City, which consists of approximately 40 rooms SINATRA's representatives allowed no one on the hotel floor, including the hotel management, except by invitation (U)

7D   ████████ advised ████████████████ that SINATRA and MARTIN were appearing at the 500 Club as a personal favor to PAUL D'AMATO, also known as "SKINNY", for which they would receive no money but would have all of their expenses taken care of by D'AMATO. (U)

SINATRA's personal airplane landed at the Atlantic City Airport on August 25, 1962, and departed from the Airport in an unmarked Atlantic City Police car. (U)

SAM GIANCANA in company with ████████████████████████ observed ████████████████ in a private dining room on SINATRA's floor of the Claridge Hotel as of ████████████████████████████

7D   ██
████████████████████████████████████ (U)

- 5 -

CG 92-349

PHYLLIS MC GUIRE   *Arkansas*

1) _____ advised on September 19, 1962, that PHYLLIS
MC GUIRE moved into her temporary residence of 2223 Edgewood,
Las Vegas, Nevada, as of approximately September 15, 1962.
Her residency there was for the period when the MC GUIRE sisters
appeared at the Desert Inn Hotel Night Club. (u)

2) _____ advised on September 22, 1962, that GIANCANA
arrived at the above residence during September 21, 1962. (u)

At this point, refer to that section of this report
relating to FRANK SINATRA whereby MC GUIRE was observed in the
company of an individual believed to be GIANCANA at Palm Springs,
California, on September 25, 1962. (u)

MC GUIRE, according to _____ was in contact with
GIANCANA at the SINATRA residence in Cathedral City, California,
as of October 1, 1962. (u)

Las Vegas Division advised on September 25, 1962,
that GIANCANA had departed Las Vegas on September 25, 1962,
via chartered aircraft to Palm Springs, California. The plane
was identified as a Cessna 310 and the plane was chartered
by GIANCANA under the name of GEORGE GOLDBERG. PHYLLIS MC GUIRE
had chartered an aircraft to depart Las Vegas at 1.45 AM,
September 26, 1962, for Palm Springs. The aircraft and pilot
were to return to Las Vegas at 5·00 PM, September 26, 1962. (u)

Records of the Palm Springs Airport as made available
by _____ to SA _____ on September 25, 1962,
revealed that a chartered plane, described as a Cessna 310
aircraft, number 865, arrived at the Palm Springs, California,
airport at 8·45 AM, September 25, 1962. The plane belongs to
the Alamo Airways and arrived from Las Vegas. (u)

At 3·16 AM, September 26, 1962, PHYLLIS MC GUIRE
was observed departing from a private plane at Palm Springs
Airport and was met by three unknown males in a station wagon
determined to be a 1962 Buick, bearing California License XDP318. (u)

- 6 -

CG 92-349

This wagon is registered to the Essex Productions, 9229 Sunset
Boulevard, Los Angeles, California, an enterprise of FRANK
SINATRA. After Miss MC GUIRE entered this wagon, it proceeded
to the vicinity of the Tamarisk Country Club, Cathedral City,
California, and the vehicle was observed shortly thereafter
parked in the carport of the residence of FRANK SINATRA. (u)

On September 26, 1962, at 4 55 PM, PHYLLIS MC GUIRE
and an unknown male Negro was observed proceeding to a Cessna
310 plane, Registration Number N6848T, belonging to Alamo Airways.
This plane is the same aircraft in which MC GUIRE arrived earlier
that day. After the above plane departed, the Buick Station
which delivered Miss MC GUIRE, proceeded from the airport at
Palm Springs to the FRANK SINATRA residence in Cathedral City,
California. (u)

It would appear from the observation of surveilling
agents at the Palm Springs airport that GIANCANA was one of
the individuals who met Miss MC GUIRE upon her arrival at the
Palm Springs Airport at 3 16 AM, September 26, 1962. (u)

1D ███████ advised ███████████████ that GIANCANA
as of that date was in Hot Springs, Arkansas, with PHYLLIS
MC GUIRE and was scheduled to remain there until August 12,
1962. (u)

It is noted that the MC GUIRE sisters singing team
made an appearance at the Vapors Club, Hot Springs, Arkansas,
on August 4, 1962, and on that date after the completion of
the first show of the MC GUIRE sisters, GIANCANA was observed
by Bureau Agents at Hot Springs, entering an automobile at
the Velda Rose Motel with the MC GUIRE sisters at approximately
9 20 PM on August 4, 1962, and traveled to the Coy's Steakhouse,
in Hot Springs, where this party had dinner. After dinner,
GIANCANA drove the MC GUIRE sisters to the Vapors Club and
then returned to Room 64, Velda Rose Motel, which at the time
was occupied by PHYLLIS and CHRISTINE MC GUIRE. GIANCANA was
not observed from that time until the evening of August 6,
1962, when he departed Room 64 of the Velda Rose Motel and
took a short walk. (u)

– 7 –

CG 92-349
RRH·gaa

II. LEGITIMATE ACTIVITIES

Villa Venice
Wheeling, Illinois

Information has been previously reported relating to the Villa Venice Supper Club in Chicago northwestern suburb of Wheeling, Illinois, with particular reference to the fact that GIANCANA is allegedly in control of this establishment. (U)

Public source information relfects that the Villa Venice has been undergoing extensive remodeling during the past several months and is scheduled for a gala reopening on or about October 31, 1962, and the new Villa Venice will feature as its opening star attraction, EDDIE FISHER. Following FISHER will be such notables as FRANK SINATRA, DEAN MARTIN, SAMMY DAVIS, JR., JIMMY DURANTE, and others of equal stature in the entertainment field. (U)

An article appeared in the "Chicago Tribune" of August 27, 1962, in the "Tower Ticker," a syndicated column of HERB LYONS, and reflected that the "Villa Venice Restaurant of Wheeling, Illinois, is being converted into the area's most plush supper club with a seating capacity of 800 persons." (U)

5D   ▉▉▉▉▉▉▉ advised in September, 1962, that SAM GIANCANA was in the process at the time of making final arrangements for the reopening of the Villa Venice and had scheduled EDDIE FISHER to appear as its first star attraction. It was decided by GIANCANA and others at the time that the seating capacity be 600 persons and that the minimum charge per person which will include one drink and dinner will be $12.50 or $25.00 per couple. (U)

67D   ▉▉▉▉▉▉▉ advised in September, 1962, that the Villa Venice is definitely an operation of the Chicago criminal organization headed by SAMUEL GIANCANA. According to this informant, it appears that a partner of GIANCANA is FRANK SINATRA. SINATRA made the arrangements for GIANCANA concerning the appearance of EDDIE FISHER for the

- 9 -

CG 92-349
RRH gaa

opening act commencing with October 31, 1962. This presented
a problem for the Desert Inn Casina in Las Vegas, Nevada,
in that the scheduled appearance of FISHER conflicts with
his appearance at the Desert Inn during the same period.
Upon the insistence of the GIANCANA group, however, FISHER
is being brought to Chicago for the Villa Venice opening
rather than stay on at the Desert Inn.

b7C

It is noted that information has
been previously reported to the effect that the Cal-Neva
Lodge is jointly owned by GIANCANA and FRANK SINATRA. (u)

b7D   advised in October, 1962, that GIANCANA
and several other individuals made arrangements for other
acts to appear at the Villa Venice and among the performers
that they either have definite commitments for or are
planning to schedule for the Villa Venice are DINAH SHORE,
JIMMY DURANTE, and DANNY THOMAS. (u)

- 48 -

'FD-204 (Rev 3 3-58)

UNITED STATES DEPARTMENT OF JUSTICE
FEDERAL BUREAU OF INVESTIGATION

Copy to: 1 - USA, Chicago

Report of: SA ██████████ b7C   Office: Chicago
Date: 12-20-62

Field Office File # 92-349   Bureau File #   92-3171-947

Title: SAMUEL M. GIANCANA

Character: ANTI RACKETEERING

Synopsis: SAMUEL GIANCANA observed meeting with JOHN D ARCO,
Alderman, 1st Ward, Chicago, 11/29/62, at the Czech
Lodge, North Riverside, Illinois. Informants report
purpose of meeting to replace D ARCO as Alderman with
ANTHONY DE TOLVE, nephew by marriage of GIANCANA.
History and background of 1st Ward set forth. Villa
Venice Club, alleged GIANCANA enterprise, reopened
11/9/62 featuring entertainers EDDIE FISHER, SAMMY
DAVIS, JR., FRANK SINATRA, and DEAN MARTIN. Entertainment
allegedly arranged by GIANCANA. GIANCANA SHOULD BE
CONSIDERED ARMED AND DANGEROUS

(u)

- P -

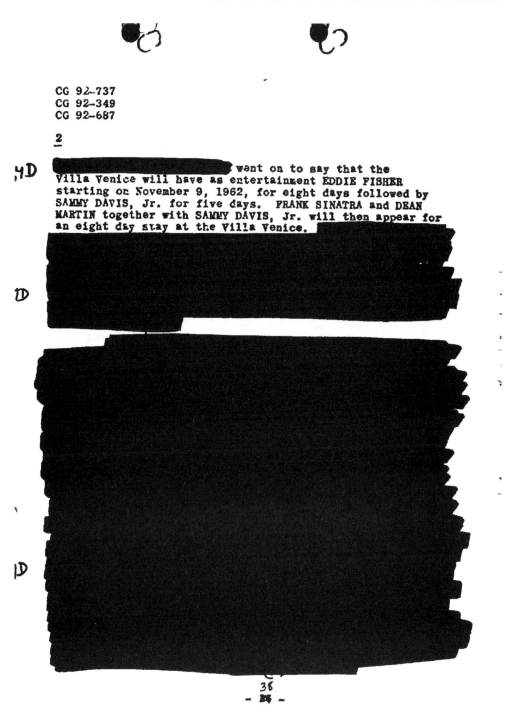

CG 92-737
CG 92-349
CG 92-687

2

went on to say that the Villa Venice will have as entertainment EDDIE FISHER starting on November 9, 1962, for eight days followed by SAMMY DAVIS, Jr. for five days. FRANK SINATRA and DEAN MARTIN together with SAMMY DAVIS, Jr. will then appear for an eight day stay at the Villa Venice.

Ella Fitzgerald
36

Chapter II

Ella Fitzgerald:
The Raggedy Muffin Who Became
America's First Lady of Song

E lla Fitzgerald was born out of wedlock to Tempie Williams, (age 23) and William Fitzgerald, (age 32) on Wednesday April 25, 1918 in the coastal city of Newport News, Virginia.

In December 1918 one month after the end of World War I Fitzgerald deserted his common-law family. Tempie and Ella had been the draft exemption that enabled him to avoid service in Uncle Sam's Army. However, in the shadows of Bill going over the hill was a gentleman by the name of Joseph Du Silva an immigrant from Portuguese, Guinea who readily filled his bunk. Mr. Du Silva, in search of a better life for his ready-made family followed the east coast migration pattern North, thus he moved Tempie and Ella out of Newport News, Virginia to Yonkers in Westchester County, New York.

Ella Fitzgerald began her public school education in Yonkers in September, 1923 at Public School 10. In the same year her mother Tempie gave birth to a second daughter whose given name was Frances and surname was Du Silva. Until Frances' death in 1960, Ella remained very close to her half-sister, which undoubtedly was one of the few enduring relationships that she formed during her lifetime.

Ella was remembered by some of the Yonkers old timers as a shy, tall double jointed loner who displayed flashes of ambition early in her life. When she was in the third grade she started street dancing for pennies in her neighborhood with other kids. She danced with a lot more enthusiasm than the other street dancers. The girl could cut a mean rug with the best of them when she did the Charleston, which was the dance craze of the wild Roaring Twenties. On the other hand, when she was not in a shy mood she could belt out songs with the volume of Sophie Tucker and Bessie Smith without the benefit of a microphone. Her favorite melodies were *Some of These Days* by Shelton Brooks, *My Blue Heaven* by George Whiting and Walter Donaldson, and *Black & Blue* by Thomas "Fats" Waller and Harry Brooks. She sang the songs with a sensitive feeling that was very reminiscent of Louis Armstrong whom she admired. The girl actually considered herself a better dancer than a singer. Her loose dancing style was influenced greatly by Earl "Snake Hips" Tucker the Cotton Club dancing star with the swiveling rubber hips and Bill "Bojangles" Robinson, the world's greatest tap dancer.

Louis Armstrong and Ella Fitzgerald

Although Armstrong was the first singer to leave a permanent footprint on Ella's style, she was also attracted to Bing Crosby, the Crooner and the three Boswell Sisters who had grown up in New Orleans. She specifically wanted to copy the vocal style of Connee Boswell, their lead singer. Tempie, in an effort to help her daughter learn how to sing like Connie bought a Boswell record for little Ella to listen to.

Connee Boswell's talents were not limited to singing she was also a composer and arranger a la Mary Lou Williams the Pittsburgh genius who played the piano, composed and arranged for Andy Kirk and his Twelve Clouds of Joy Orchestra in Kansas City, Missouri. Mary also performed the same musical arrangement task for Benny Goodman, Tommy Dorsey, Earl Hines, Louis Armstrong, Jimmy Lunceford, and many others.

To keep abreast of the dancing trends fourteen year old Ella occasionally would sneak out of the house with Charles Gulliver, who was a next door neighbor and go down to New York City's Savoy Ballroom at 140th and Lenox Avenue to pick up on the latest dance steps. Going to the Savoy was no short trip because they had to take a half hour trolley ride down to the subway station and then catch a subway train to uptown Harlem, where they got off at the 125th Street Station, and then walked an additional 15 blocks north to the Savoy Ballroom at 140th Street. The Savoy ballroom was also known by the real hip cats of that period as the Home of Happy Feet. It was there that Ella learned how to do *The Shuffle Off to Buffalo, Trucking, The Susie Q* and the fast moving finger popping over your head *Lindy Hop* dance steps.

A heavy burden fell on young Ella's shoulders when her mother Tempie dropped dead from overwork with a fatal heart attack at age 38. Ella's school records indicated that she stopped going to Benjamin Franklin Junior High on April 21, 1931. Ella had to move out of the Yonkers apartment shortly after her mother's death because her stepfather began to abuse her. Hence, she moved into her Aunt Virginia's Harlem four story walk-up flat on West 145th Street in New York City.

The next two years for Ella were hell on earth. She skipped school and ran policy numbers door to door for the number kings in Harlem in order to keep skin and bone together. In addition, to being a policy runner she also worked as a lookout girl for a house of prostitution. The warning signal was four hard knocks on the front door of the whorehouse to alert the ladies of evening that the precinct flat feet were in close proximity.

Playing hookey from school to perform her various tasks brought Ella to the attention of the New York School truant authorities. She was apprehended on the street one day by a truant officer and sent to Public School 49, which had formerly been the Colored Orphan Asylum until the Board of

Education took, over the facility in 1911. Since she was determined to get into show business she ran away from that institution early in the fall of 1934 with no intention of ever returning. The poor girl was afflicted with a mild case of claustrophobia, a malady that caused her to panic whenever she was fenced into closet size quarters.

Ella could never return to her Aunt Virginia's apartment because the truant authorities would be able to track her down easily and incarcerate her in a lock down juvenile home. The tall skinny girl's only option was to hangout on Seventh Avenue, the main drag in a section of New York's Harlem known as the "Black Broadway" between 130th and 140th Streets. This ten block stretch along Seventh Avenue was a candy store for every kind of vice known to man in addition to having more than its quota of down on their luck entertainers such as musicians, dancers, singers.

**Fletcher Henderson
"America's Greatest Arranger"**

During the depression years of the 1930s it was possible for a musically gifted person to enter a talent contest every night at some major theater or nightclub. Talent shows were a cheap means of entertainment for show business entrepreneurs who were beating on the walls of hard times themselves. The amateur shows rewarded the winner of the contest with a crisp ten dollar bill. Ten dollars during the 1930s represented seventy-five percent of the average Negro common laborer's weekly wages.

Ella decided she would try her luck for the big bucks at the newly opened Apollo Theater for Colored, which was located at 253 West 125th Street in Harlem. Up until 1934, the theater had been a burlesque house for "Whites Only". One of the Apollo Theater attractions with the change of management was the Wednesday night amateur show which was presided over by the popular Colored movie star Ralph Cooper who also acted as the master of ceremonies.

Miss Fitzgerald actually made her stage debut at the Apollo on Wednesday night, November 21, 1934. Ella's initial intention was to perform a dance number in the contest, that is until she learned that the smooth dancing Edward Sisters would be her competition. The Edwards girls had been trained by their father who was also a professional dancer and they had no juvenile peers on the New York scene other than the Nicholas Brothers during that period. Ella was not stupid, therefore she quickly switched from dancing and entered the contest as a singer. Although her appearance was that of a raggedy muffin her voice and singing style overrode all the negatives and she won the first prize hands down and one week's work in a regular stage show. Her winning song was *The Object Of My Affection* and her encore was *Judy*.

The Nicholas Brothers: Harold and Fayard.

The leader of the backup band for Ella that night at the Apollo was Benny Carter. In the year 2000, Benny at age 93, is still rated among the top musicians. He was impressed by Ella's style to the point that he later took her to meet Fletcher Henderson his former band leading boss in his home on Strivers Row at 110 West 138th Street for a second opinion. Henderson was instantly turned off by Ella's appearance. His opinion was influenced by the fact that he was a Mulatto, and he was partial to high yellow attractive women.

Incidentally, Ella did not get the one week's work she was promised after winning the first prize at the Apollo. Therefore, she was thrown back into the midst of the Seventh Avenue wolves, broke and disgusted but not down hearted. In January, 1935 she started hanging around the Harlem Opera House which was just a short distance from the Apollo, where she finally got a second opportunity to enter another "Amateur Hour". Again, she won first prize hands down. However, this time she got the promised one week gig. Her stage show at the Opera House opened on Friday, February 15, 1935.

Chick Webb and Ella Fitzgerald in 1937.

Others in the show with Ella were Tiny Bradshaw and his band, Mae Alex, the blues singer and several lesser known acts. This engagement marked the first time Ella's name appeared in very small print on a Harlem Opera House poster. A little publicity was the only thing that she got out of that date. The manager refused to pay her after she finished the week. There are several versions of why she was denied a paycheck. The one that appears to hold the most water is told with authority by Frank Schiffman who said the money was used to buy Ella some suitable clothing to wear for her stage appearance. Ella's press people said some years later that Shiffman had lied because the chorus girls had chipped in to buy her a dress, shoes, under garments and a hair treatment.

1935 was Ella's good luck year. Chick Webb was looking for a girl singer to join his band which was opening at the Harlem Opera House. He assigned Charles Linton his male singer the task of finding one. An Italian chorus girl who was a friend of Linton's, recommended Ella Fitzgerald because she had heard her sing at the Apollo Theater the night that she won her first amateur contest.

The problem of getting in touch with Ella was a tough one because she was a street person who could not be reached by telephone and she did not have a permanent street address. The only hope of locating Ella was to scour both 125th Street and also the 10 block area on Seventh Avenue known as the "Black Broadway."

Linton and the Italian girl finally found Ella hanging out in front of Smalls Paradise Night Club at 135th and Seventh Avenue following a forty-eight hour search. Linton rushed Ella over to Chick's dressing room at the Harlem Opera House where he found Chick and Burdu Ali, a part time musical director of the Chick Webb Orchestra shooting the breeze. The first thing Chick said to Linton when he saw Ella was "You are robbing the cradle my man." Chick then asked Ella to step outside of the door. Before the door could hit Ella in the back Chick grabbed Linton by the collar and whispered: "Man, you are not putting that in my band."

Several minutes after Chick regained his cool Charlie Buchanan, the manager of the Savoy Ballroom walked into the room and Chick asked if he had seen that girl standing outside the door. Buchanan nodded in the positive. Chick then said: "That is what Linton wants to put in my band." Buchanan opened the door and took a second look at Ella and said, "No, no, out!" He didn't want her either.

Ella was not aware of all the low tone bickering that was going on about her. Linton said to Buchanan when he was about to leave the room, "If you don't listen to her sing I am going to quit Chick's band!" Buchanan stopped cold in his footsteps and said, "Oh, no. Okay! When you finish the theater gig, you have got a two-week gig at the Savoy Ballroom. Bring her up, let her sing along with the band, and if the public likes her we will keep her and if they don't, out! No pay!"

Chick Webb did not realize that Linton had found a gold mine for him in Ella Fitzgerald. Webb did not pay Ella a regular salary he simply gave her a couple of bucks from time to time. She always wore street clothes when she sang with the band because all she had were two dresses. She wasn't permitted to work formal dances because she could not afford an evening gown.

It wasn't until May, 1935 that Ella began to get some bonifide recognition. A young white writer named George T. Simon from the Metronome Magazine came uptown to the Savoy Ballroom and was figuratively knocked out by her, not only by the way she sang but also by the spirit that she put into a song. Instead of sitting with the band like a canary in a birdcage she exhibited her dance talents on the side of the bandstands. The energetic and rhythmic Ella would also make conductors' arm movements when certain trumpet and sax riffs were being played. She really put additional life in a band that could use a few swift kicks from time to time. Simon gave the Webb Orchestra a B-plus rating in the June edition of Metronome Magazine, and concluded his review by saying that Ella Fitzgerald was going places. This was Ella Fitzgerald's first press mention and one that she would remember for the rest of her life.

George T. Simon made the following comments in predicting Ella's meteoric rise to the top of her profession. As a matter of fact he made the following forecast in Metronome Magazine: *The seventeen-year old girl singing up in Harlem's Savoy Ballroom with Chick Webb's fine band... unheralded and practically unknown right now, but what a future... a great natural flair for singing... extraordinary intonation and figure... As she is right now, she's one of the best femme hot warblers... and there is no reason why she shouldn't be just about the best in time to come.*

On November 10, 1936 Ella appeared on Benny Goodman's coast to coast radio show, "Camel Caravan", then the most popular music show in America. Later Benny offered Webb $5,000.00 to buy out her contract. Ella had truly made the first step on the stairway to stardom. Even the calcified sidemen in Chick Webb's orchestra began to sit back and take notice of this little girl who was now positioned to get into show business big time. Rival orchestra leader, Jimmy Lunceford made her a very attractive offer which included a $2,000.00 advanced bonus. It was for naught, because she was hog tied to a binding contract with the Moe Gale Agency.

In November, 1937 Ella was voted the number one female vocalist in both the Down Beat and Melody Maker Magazine readers' polls, ahead of her main rivals Billie Holiday and Mildred Bailey. On May 2, 1938 Chick and Ella went into the Decca recording studio and recorded, *A-Tisket, A-Tasket!* It was Ella's idea to take, a nursery rhyme and make it a popular song. Actually,

Ella in Chicago, 1950.

Ella in New York City on
December 25,1958.

Ella and Chick Webb on the drums.

the origin of the nursery rhyme dated back to 1879. However, the rhyme had not been copyrighted as a song until 1938. Thus, the credit for the words and music were attributed to Ella Fitzgerald and Al Feldman.

The song went on the music scoreboard as number 10 in June 1938, and zoomed to number 1 weeks later; it stayed on the Musical Hit Parade list for a total of nineteen weeks. It eventually reached the million sales mark in 1950.

The Author Dempsey J. Travis said: *I will always remember the night of nights at Chicago's Savoy Ballroom on July 31, 1938. It was billed as the "Swing Battle of the Century". Oh! But this was a night that this writer will never forget. The marquee in front of the Savoy read: Harlem's Chick Webb, America's Outstanding Swing band versus Bronzeville's Horace Henderson, creator of the Jump Rhythm.*

Ella Fitzgerald was the featured vocalist with the Chick Webb Orchestra and Viola Jefferson was the songbird with the Horace Henderson band. Horace had made an arrangement of "A-Tisket-A Tasket" for Viola that was almost identical to the one Chick Webb had made for Ella Fitzgerald. The Savoy's Bronzeville audience kept yelling for Viola Jefferson to sing "A-Tisket-A-Tasket!" Ella had just finished singing the song during the Chick Webb set. Viola Jefferson appeared to be both scared and reluctant to follow the great Ella Fitzgerald.

However, when Horace Henderson opened his set with "A-Tisket-A-Tasket", Viola had no alternative except to go out there and do her number.When she finished singing the nursery rhyme, the crowd just roared, screamed, and stomped. This writer was standing in front of the bandstand no more than one foot from the stage listening when I noticed my white linen suit was damp with sweat from my own body heat and the heat of the music lovers who were elbowing to get closer to the bandstand. It was hot as the devil's oven in the Savoy Ballroom that evening. In fact, it was so hot that the management stopped the music and moved a portable bandstand to the out-door pavilion which was south and adjacent to the main ballroom. That was probably one of the largest crowds in the Savoy Ballroom's history. I say probably because I had witnessed capacity crowds in that ballroom when Duke Ellington, Cab Calloway, Louis Armstrong and Jimmy Lunceford played gigs there.

On the ninth of June, 1939, Chick Webb was admitted to the Johns

Hopkins Hospital in Baltimore, Maryland with kidney problems that were compounded by the lifelong difficulties he was having with spinal tuberculosis. On June 16th the little drummer man gave up the struggle for life on this planet and died quietly in his mother's arms.

After Webb's death the Moe Gale Agency made Ella Fitzgerald the leader of Webb's all male orchestra. The jazz band was billed as Ella Fitzgerald and the Famous Chick Webb Orchestra. In September of 1939, the Fitzgerald band was booked into Ed Fox's Grand Terrace in Chicago, Illinois. They were the replacement band for the Earl "Fatha" Hines Orchestra which had been booked by Fox to make a four week road trip through the southern part of the country. It was during the Grand Terrace engagement that Chick Webb's name was dropped from his old band. The new orchestra with the Chick Webb personnel was billed as Ella Fitzgerald and her Famous Orchestra. Members of the band such as Lonnie Simmons, Louis Jordan and other old timers, began leaving the band because of personality conflicts with Ella and more importantly because of the extremely low salaries.

Duke Ellington and Ella Fitzgerald.

In August of 1942, the band was totally dissolved because many of the musicians were being drafted into the military service. Ella began working with a smaller group in Philadelphia known as the "Three Keys". By late summer of 1943 the Furness Brothers were claimed by the draft board, forcing the "Keys" to disband. In 1944 Ella Fitzgerald in a joint venture with the Ink Spots made a million-selling hit with *Into Each Life Some Rain Must Fall*, and in 1945 Ella and the Ink Spots struck pay dirt a second time with another million seller with a Duke Ellington creation entitled: *I'm Beginning To See The Light.*

In 1947, Ella married Ray Brown, a bass player from Pittsburgh. Their marriage ended in 1953. Several years earlier on December 26, 1941 Ella married Benjamin Kornegay in St. Louis, Missouri. Moe Gale, her manager was both disappointed and shocked by her sudden rush into marriage. He decided to check out this mysterious man who had married this chick that was laying golden eggs for his agency. His finding revealed that Kornegay had a criminal record. He had been convicted of drug charges in the 1930s and had served time. Based on those facts Moe Gale's lawyers succeeded in getting the marriage annulled. There was evidence that the marriage was motivated for criminal intent and not love. Prior to Kornegay, she was married to a shipyard worker in 1939. That marriage was annulled ten days after it took place.

Among Ella's other brand name suitors were Louis Jordan who worked with her in the Chick Webb Orchestra and later gained fame as the leader of the Tympany Five. Jordan was also the composer of *Five Guys Name Moe, Is You Is Or Is You Ain't My Baby,* and *Choo Choo Boogie.* Joe Jones, the flashy and sharp dressing drummer with the Count Basie Orchestra was also on her known list of lovers. Everlasting love was something Ella never found in her lifetime outside of the lyrics of a song.

During the World War II years Ella's career took a nose dive, in that she slipped from fourth place to thirteenth on the musical popularity chart; however she went into orbit again when she joined forces with impresario Norman Granz and his Jazz at the Philharmonic (JATP) Concerts. With Granz, she toured worldwide with some of America's most prominent jazz instrumentalists such as Willie Smith, Clark Terry, Nat Cole, Oscar Peterson, Illinois Jacquet, Lionel Hampton, Coleman Hawkins and many others.

Norman Granz opened the door of racial equality for Afro-American musicians. He refused to let his group play to any segregated audiences. He had clauses in his contracts that demanded equality in the selling of tickets and seating. If the clause was broken, Granz was legally entitled to have the contracted fee and refused to play. More often than not he prevailed.

The concert halls and nightclubs were not the only places the JATP-ers had problems and the south did not have an exclusive on Jim Crow. On a tour of the Midwest, an Ohio hotel manager refused to allow black and white musicians to share the same room. Europe did not escape the shame of racism either. A German promoter refused to make a private dressing room available for Ella who was the only woman on this particular JATP tour - Granz refused to let his people play for the standing room only audience in an oversold concert hall. He paid the entourage although he gave them the night off.

On another occasion, Ella Fitzgerald and her entourage boarded an airline with the expectation that they would sit in their first-class, reserved seats. To their surprise they were told that they had been bumped in spite of their reservation. Granz won a very large out of court settlement from the airlines. It was Norman Granz's civil rights activity that generated surveillance by the Federal Bureau of Investigation for both he and Ella Fitzgerald.

Ella Fitzgerald was at the apex of her career when she recorded the song books of Cole Porter, Duke Ellington, George and Ira Gershwin and others between 1956 and 1964. She was accompanied by Nelson Riddle, Billy May, Duke Ellington, Count Basie, Oscar Peterson, Joe Pass, Louis Armstrong, et al. Out of the song books she sang dozens of songs by Duke Ellington, Cole Porter, Richard Rodgers, Irving Berlin, Johnny Mercer, Jerome Kern, George and Ira Gershwin, and Harold Arlen. These composers and lyricists represented some of America's elite talents.

In the early 1970s, Ella was plagued with poor health, starting with eye problems related to her diabetes. Because of her high blood pressure she developed a heart condition in the 80s. As a matter of fact she had several heart bypasses. In 1989, she was advised to cut her schedule down to an occasional concert. In 1993 she had both legs amputated below the knee because of complication from her diabetes. Her spokesperson did not release news of the amputations until a year later in 1994 at which time she was confined to a wheelchair. On June 15, 1996, Ella an American Original died at home in Beverly Hills, California. She was surrounded by Ray Brown, Jr. her adopted son and other family members.

Ella Fitzgerald: "The Orchestra Leader" in 1939.

Federal Bureau of Investigation

Freedom of Information/Privacy Acts Section

Subject: Ella Fitzgerald

FEDERAL BUREAU OF INVESTIGATION

FREEDOM OF INFORMATION/PRIVACY ACTS SECTION

COVER SHEET

SUBJECT: <u>ELLA FITZGERALD</u>

UNITED STATES DEPARTMENT OF JUSTICE

FEDERAL BUREAU OF INVESTIGATION

In Reply, Please Refer to
File No.

WASHINGTON 25, D. C.

June 19, 1957

CON~~FIDEN~~TIAL

b7C ▬▬▬▬

     The following information was furnished by a confidential source abroad on June 19, 1957.

1C ▬▬▬▬▬ and his musical orchestra, known as "Jazz at the Philharmonic," performed in Rome, Italy from May 25 to June 6, 1957. The orchestra was composed of nine musicians, among whom was the singer, ELLA FITZGERALD.

    b7C No information was received indicating that ▬ engaged in any political activities while in Italy.

APPROPRIATE ~~AGENCY~~
~~AND~~ FIELD OFFICE
ADVISED BY ROUTING
SLIP(S) OF *CLASSIFICATION*
DATE 9-14-77 *DML / REC*

CON~~FID~~ENTIAL

Classified by 6855 DML/df
Exempt from GDS Category 1
Date of Declassification Indefinate
9-12-77

~~CO~~PIES DESTROYED
11 OCT 24 1963

100-422785-21

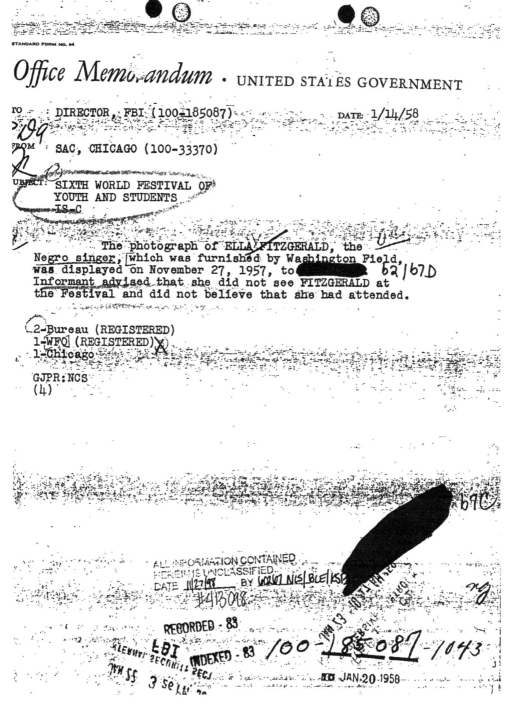

STANDARD FORM NO. 54

Office Memorandum · UNITED STATES GOVERNMENT

TO : DIRECTOR, FBI (100-185087) DATE: 1/14/58

FROM : SAC, CHICAGO (100-33370)

SUBJECT: SIXTH WORLD FESTIVAL OF
YOUTH AND STUDENTS
IS-C

           The photograph of ELLA FITZGERALD, the
Negro singer, which was furnished by Washington Field,
was displayed on November 27, 1957, to ▮▮▮▮▮▮▮ 62/67D
Informant advised that she did not see FITZGERALD at
the Festival and did not believe that she had attended.

2-Bureau (REGISTERED)
1-WFO (REGISTERED)X
1-Chicago

GJPR:NCS
(4)

ALL INFORMATION CONTAINED
HEREIN IS UNCLASSIFIED
DATE 11/27/98   BY ▮▮▮▮▮ NIS/BLE/KSR

#413098

RECORDED - 83

FBI INDEXED - 83   100-185087-1043

JAN 20 1958

February 18, 1970

BY LIAISON

Honorable Alexander P. Butterfield
Deputy Assistant to the President
The White House
Washington, D. C.

Dear Mr. Butterfield:

Reference is made to your name check request
concerning Ella Fitzgerald, ▮▮▮▮▮▮▮▮▮▮

The central files of the FBI reveal no pertinent
information concerning ▮▮▮▮▮▮▮▮

The fingerprint files of the Identification Division
of the FBI contain no arrest data identifiable with ▮▮▮▮▮▮▮
based upon background information submitted in connection with
this name check request.

Attached are separate memoranda concerning
Ella Fitzgerald and ▮▮▮▮▮▮▮▮

Sincerely yours,

ENCLOSURE

Enclosures (2)

Mr. DeLoach (sent direct)
Mr. Gale (sent direct)

CC TO: White Hou
REQ. REC'D 9-12-74
SEP 16 197.
ANS.
BY

REC-33 62-5-35583

17 FEB 20 1970

February 18, 1970

ELLA FITZGERALD

S(DMMNIN()

Ella Fitzgerald, who was born on April 25, 1918, at Newport News, Virginia, has not been the subject of an investigation conducted by the FBI. However, our files reveal the following information concerning her.

7C In June, 1957, it was reported that one ▇▇▇▇▇▇▇ and his musical orchestra performed in Rome, Italy, from May 25 to June 6, 1957. This orchestra was reportedly composed of nine musicians and Ella Fitzgerald, a singer. ▇▇▇▇▇▇▇ was allegedly a member of the Communist Party in the early 1940's. He was interviewed by representatives of the FBI in 1956 and displayed a cooperative attitude. (100-422788-21)

A newspaper article in January, 1957, indicated that Fitzgerald and three other members of her staff had accepted out-of-court settlements on four damage suits they brought against a major air line charging racial discrimination.
(62-101087-A-26)

The fingerprint files of the Identification Division of the FBI contain no arrest data identifiable with captioned individual based upon background information submitted in connection with this name check request.

ALL INFORMATION CONTAINED
HEREIN IS UNCLASSIFIED
DATE 11/27/18 NIS18CE/LCSB
#413098 62164

NOTE: Per request of Alexander P. Butterfield, Deputy Assistant to the President.

ALA:mcb (7)

62-5- 35582

SEE REVERSE SIDE FOR
ADD DISSEMINATION

WFO 100-34373

Height: 5' 5½"
Hair: Black
Eyes: Brown
Occupation: Vocalist

Passport number 266295 was renewed on 3/21/52, and in her renewal application, ELLA BROWN stated she intended to depart from New York City on 3/28/52 for a proposed length of stay abroad of two weeks in order to visit Scandanavian countries, France, Switzerland, Belgium, and Germany for the purpose of performing at jazz concerts.

New York Series passport number 1412 was issued on 2/5/53 to ELLA BROWN, known professionally as ELLA FITZGERALD. In her application for that passport, she indicated she resides at 179-07 Murdock Avenue, St. Albans, L.I., N. Y. She stated her husband, ▮▮▮▮▮▮▮▮▮▮ was residing at ▮▮▮▮▮▮▮▮▮▮▮▮▮▮▮▮▮ N. Y. She stated her maiden name was ELLA FITZGERALD; that she was previously married to ▮▮▮▮▮▮▮▮▮▮ in 1941 at ▮▮▮▮▮▮▮ Missouri, and that this marriage was annulled in 1942. ELLA BROWN stated she would depart from the United States on 2/14/53, for a proposed length of stay abroad of from six to eight weeks in order to visit Sweden, Holland, Belgium, France, Italy, and Denmark for the purpose of performance at concerts.

On 1/20/55, passport number 521063 was issued to "ELLA BROWN, known professionally as ELLA FITZGERALD". In her application for that passport, she stated her marriage to ▮▮▮▮▮▮▮▮▮▮ was terminated by divorce on 8/13/53. She stated her permanent residence was at 179-07 Murdock Avenue, St. Albans, L.I., N. Y. She indicated she would depart from the United States on 2/5/55 for a proposed length of stay abroad of six weeks in order to visit Sweden, Denmark, Norway, Germany, France, and England for the purpose of concert tour with Jazz at the Philharmonic, Inc.

Her passport was renewed on 1/15/57, and in her renewal application she stated she intended to leave the United States on 2/9/57, for a proposed length of stay abroad until April, 1957, in order to visit Norway, Sweden, Denmark, Italy, Germany, and France for the purpose of entertaining.

There was no additional pertinent information set forth in her file.

WFO will forward copies of ELLA FITZGERALD BROWN's passport application photograph to New York. Copies will also be furnished to Chicago for display to ▮▮▮▮▮▮▮ to ascertain if informant can identify same. P.

*if believed ident
w/ Captioned subject
DRL*

- 2 -

Howard Hughes

Chapter III

Howard Hughes:
Played Hardball With The Mob

Allene Gano Hughes gave birth to Howard Hughes Jr. on December 24, 1905 in Houston, Texas. He was the first and only child to be produced by Howard Robard Hughes, a mining engineer, and Allene Gano, the daughter of a very prominent Dallas, Texas judge. Mrs. Hughes was a well educated southern society belle, born with all of the old confederate trappings. Giving birth to the future billionaire Howard Hughes Jr. was such a difficult task, her attending physician Dr. Oscar. L. Norsworthy advised her not to have any more children.

Young Hughes' birth date was somewhat of a mystery, the same as his eventual death in that he did not discover (until he was thirty-six years old), that there was no official evidence of his birth date. This fact came to light when he attempted to register for the military draft following the Japanese bombing of Pearl Harbor on December 7, 1941. The event that sparked the draft was the United States declaration of a retaliatory war against the three

Axis Nations: Japan, Germany and Italy. It was then that it was revealed that there was no official records to validate his birth date except for a personal affidavit signed by his late mother's youngest sister Annette Gano Lumms and Estelle Sharp, the mother of one of his closest childhood friends. There was not even a clue of his having been born at the Houston Board of Health or in the vaults of the Texas Division of Vital Statistics in Austin, Texas the capitol of the state.

The senior Hughes lived a very transient lifestyle during his son's adolescent years. He was busy chasing dollars, women and the smell of oil wells from one oil strike to another. Initially, he and his partner Walter Sharp drilled with a modicum of success with cable tools in their effort to unearth the black liquid gold. However, his wildest dream was to develop a drill bit that would penetrate thick rock formations and hard clay wherever they suspected the topsoil might blanket oil reservoirs.

The original cone bit that launched the Hughes' fortune.

Several years passed before Hughes and his partner Walter Bedford Sharp finally developed a drill that could bore through solid rock. This drill became known as the Hughes Rock Bit, it revolutionized the oil industry and made Hughes and later his son unbelievably filthy rich.

Walter Sharp, Hughes' only partner died on November 28, 1912 at the age of 42. His death came just a few years after the drill was invented. Sharp's widow Estelle claimed that her husband had helped Hughes invent the Hughes Rock Bit. The truth of the matter will never be known because dead men don't talk. However, in fairness to his deceased partner, Hughes divided the stock of the Sharp - Hughes Tool Company equally with Sharp's widow who became the only other stockholder.

One of Mrs. Sharp's first actions as a shareholder was to try and curb

Howard Hughes' extravagant and very expensive promotional appetite. Hughes thought nothing of renting an entire floor in a four star hotel to give a lavish party with all the trimmings, including night crawling women for prospective customers. He was in fact spending more money than their bank balance could cover from time to time, thus causing Mrs. Sharp to panic and have nightmares about the possibility of going bankrupt.

The widow woman relieved her anxieties by selling her interest in the Sharp - Hughes Tool Company to Ed Prather for $65,000 which was actually a handsome sum generated over a short period from an investment that originally cost her husband only $1,500. Prather was a friend of both the Sharp and the Hughes families. However, Prather's ability to control Hughes's wild ways with money was no more successful than Mrs. Sharp's, hence after a relatively short period of time he sold his fifty percent interest in the company back to Hughes.

As the years passed, super salesman Howard Hughes promoted the Sharp - Hughes Tool Company into a national major supplier of drill bits for the entire oil industry and was busy chasing dollars and watching his fortune grow like Topsy in *Uncle Tom's Cabin*. At the same time Allene was smothering Howard Jr. with tender loving care and supervising his every move. Howard Jr. never spent a night away from home until he was eleven years old. In 1916 she gave him permission to spend an abbreviated summer period at Camp Teedyuskung in Pennsylvania. Howard Jr.'s stay at the camp was enjoyable, but aborted by his mother because of a polio scare in the northeast section of the country such as the one that later afflicted President Franklin Delano Roosevelt.

Young Howard and his friend Dudley Sharp returned to Camp Teedyuskung the following summer on July 16, 1917. However, the experience was not the same because the United States army had drafted the most experienced instructors into the service for active duty during World War I.

When Howard and Dudley returned to Houston in late August 1917, the city was engulfed in a race riot that was ignited by the actions of a member of the Houston police force who had manhandled and brutalized a Negro soldier. On the night of August 23, 1917, a group of Negro soldiers stationed at an Army installation on the outskirts of Houston decided to retaliate against the white establishment by arming themselves and marching in formation toward downtown Houston, where it is alleged by some racists that they indiscriminately shot all whites who crossed their path. However, before the gun smoke cleared seventeen Blacks had been shot to death like wild dogs on the streets of Houston by both white civilians and uniformed policemen.   Later, thirteen Black "Doughboys" were court-martialed before a kangaroo military tribunal and hung.

Although the Hughes family lived miles away from the scene where the mass slaughter of Blacks took place, they were brainwashed by rumors and lies about the atrocities allegedly committed by the Black soldiers.. Hughes Jr. was totally catechized by the anti-Black sentiment that swept his city. The propaganda about Blacks instilled in him a lifelong hatred for people of Color in general. As a matter of fact, some fifty years later in 1967 he cited the 1917 riot as the reason his Las Vegas Casinos would not hire Blacks for any jobs above porters and washroom attendants.

In June 1921, Howard graduated from the Fessenden School in West Newton, Massachusetts, an exclusive private school, for youngsters from wealthy families. In lieu of Howard Hughes Sr. sending his son off to a well known secondary eastern prep school, following his graduating from Fessenden he decided to bring the lad back west to the Thacher School in Ojai, California, near Santa Barbara where his mother would be able to visit with him frequently.

Old man Hughes quickly discovered that getting his son enrolled at the Thacher School was more than a notion. He was told by the school's headmaster that the school had filled its quota of sixty students for the forthcoming school year. That explanation did not wear well with Hughes Sr., therefore he figuratively stepped over the headmaster's head and convinced the president and founder of Thacher of the need for the school to make room for his boy. Hughes was not subtle with his offer to build an addition to the school's dormitory. Howard Hughes Jr. was admitted to Thacher in the fall of 1921.

Since Howard Jr. was a loner by nature and shunned group activities whenever possible at the school, his mother thought that a good substitute for that deficiency would be a horse that he could enjoy as he rode alone in the hills near the school. She also believed that it was normal that children without siblings found it difficult to make friends with their contemporaries.

In March, 1922, young Hughes' mother entered the Baptist Hospital in Houston, Texas to have some minor outpatient surgery performed on her uterus to stop what she and doctors considered to be excessive bleeding. Her plan according to her butler was to return home in time for dinner by late afternoon that day. Regrettably, that was not to be because she never regained consciousness from the anesthetic that was used to put her into a twilight zone during the operation. Allene Gano Hughes made her final transition at age 39. Her death devastated her husband. He could not steel up enough courage to share the terrible news with his son who was away at school in Ojai. Thus, he sent the boy a telegram telling him that his mother was ill and that he had better come home immediately.

The pain and anguish that Allene's death caused her son was never articulated by the boy. Grief, like many facets of a loner's life is a very private matter. Whereas Howard Hughes Sr. publicly displayed his lamentations by running away from the scene of his disheartenment. He left his son who was now sixteen years old in the care of Annette, his late wife's youngest sister. The big man attempted to deal with his own despair by creating a multiple of excuses for staying away from Houston, the site of both his success and heartbreaks. Thus, he spent days on end traveling to Chicago, New York, Los Angeles, San Francisco or any other city where an excuse might be contrived, to keep him out of Houston.

In the late afternoon just before sundown on January 14, 1924 Howard Hughes Sr. was having a meeting with S.P. Brown, the Sharp - Hughes Tool Company's sales manager, when he suddenly rose from the swivel chair behind his desk, his eyes mirrored fear and his facial features became distorted from pain as he grabbed his chest and fell rock forward across the center of his desk. The man never uttered a mumbling word. At age fifty-four, Howard Hughes, Sr., died from a heart attack.

On January 16, 1924 Howard Hughes, Sr's funeral was held in his home on Yoakum. The high and mighty of Houston, Texas paid tribute to the man who revolutionized the oil industry with his rock bit. Within twelve months after Hughes senior's death on December 26, 1924 a Houston judge signed orders removing Hughes Jr.'s "disabilities as minor" clause thus eliminating the need for the appointment of a guardian.

The loss of his parents in the prime of their lives had a profound effect on the lonely, withdrawn Howard Hughes Jr. At the age of eighteen Hughes took on all of the manifestation of a hypochondriac, fearful of death and panicky about the possibility of being contaminated by germs. At the same time he was determined to stuff as much life as possible into a very short span of time.

Hughes was a first semester freshman at Rice Institute in Houston at the time of his father's death, although he had never officially graduated from the Thacher Prep School. The teenager decided with the speed of a thunder-bolt to end his formal education and enter the world of business. Moreover, he was not content with inheriting just 75 percent of his father's business assets, therefore, he bought out the other 25 percent that had been dispersed in his father's will among his relatives. The method in which he disendowed his kinfolk was not pretty in that it caused lifelong rifts which were never healed. The fragmentation of the family did not appear to disturb Junior at all. He recognized that taking command of a business meant doing whatever was necessary to accomplish his objective. Playing patty cake with people was not part of his or his father's entrepreneurial equa-tion for success.

On June 1, 1925 to everybody's surprise he mar-ried Ella Rice. She was the beautiful daughter of a wealthy businessman, and the grand-niece of William Marsh Rice, the founder of Rice Institute. In Houston, there was no better name on the Social Register than Rice. Hughes had known Ella since childhood, when both of them had attended Christ Church Cathedral.

Ella Rice Hughes, Howard's first wife.

Hughes performed a very mature act several days prior to getting married, in that at age nineteen with the aid of counsel he wrote his will which read in part as follows: *I give to my friend Dudley C. Sharp... the sum of ten thou-sand dollars; to my uncle Charles Gano, fifteen thousand dollars; to my aunt, Mrs. James P. Houston, twenty-five thousand dollars; to my aunt, Mrs. Fred R. Lumms, one hundred thousand dollars and my home on Yoakum Boulevard... To my wife Ella Rice Hughes, the sum of five hundred thousand dollars in first class, high grade securities, to be delivered to her by my executors as soon after my death as it can be conveniently arranged... To Lily Adams and John*

Farrell (my colored household servants)… A weekly pension of twenty dollars each. The bulk of the Hughes fortune was left to the Hughes Medical Institute. That institute's specialty is principally in the field of medical research and medical education.

Hughes instinctively decided that he did not want to drop dead like his dad from overwork at the Sharp - Hughes tool Company. Therefore he hired men to operate the administrative side of the business with a minimum amount of direction from him. The young man spent the summer of 1925 leisurely playing golf and showing off his trophy bride to his Dallas friends at a time when most of his peers were just finishing their freshman year in college.

In fall of 1925 he and Ella packed their bags and took a train to Los Angeles, California where they holed up at the luxurious Ambassador Hotel. It was the hotel where his father had stayed on his frequent visits to Hollywood. The glamour of Sunset Boulevard, and the beautiful women that attracted him. The glitter of the town made the young man's head twirl the same as it had for his father. Howard Hughes Sr. had been known as a big spender by the Hollywood glamour crowd.

Hughes, like his father did not take advice easily, therefore nothing could keep him from taking the plunge as a movie producer. His first film, *Swell Hogan* was so bad that it was never released. He had better luck with his next two, *Everybody's Acting* (1926), and with *Two Arabian Knights* (1927), directed by Lewis Milestone and starring the strikingly handsome William Boyd. The film brought Milestone an Academy Award for best comedy director. Hughes' success with: *The Mating Call* and *The Racket* (both 1928), inspired him to take on an epic about aviation in World War I namely, *Hell's Angel*, which was two and a half years in production. The October 1929 stock market crash hurt the four star movie at the box office. In the process of making the movie Hughes spent mega bucks buying planes and hiring pilots. The cost of making the film was $4 million which was an astronomical amount of money for that period, and particularly in light of the 1930s economic depression. The movie had a successful run but it took a long time to recoup the investment because in some regions of the country the unemployment rate was hovering at fifty percent and in Detroit and Chicago it reached eighty percent for minorities.

Among Hughes' cost of being a movie producer was the loss of his wife. Ella Rice Hughes left her husband in Los Angeles and returned to

Hughes purchased the Boeing Pursuit from the United States Army in 1933.

Houston because she found it impossible to be married to a man who was seldom home. Her leaving left the mansion door wide open for the Hollywood starlets to crawl in. The first actress to turn the knob on his door was Billie Dove one of the most beautiful stars of the silent film era, she was a former Ziegfeld Follies showgirl and she starred in his next two films, *The Age of Love* and *Cock of the Air,* both were made in 1931 when the unemployment bread lines were extremely long. Neither picture was successful, nor was the love affair. Billie was simply the first in line of what became a very long string of affairs with Hollywood beauties such as Katherine Hepburn, Marian Marsh, Ida Lupino, Lillian Bond, and Mary Rogers, Jeanne Crain, Diana Lynn, Yvonne DeCarlo and Janet Thomas.

Actress Billie Dove

The bevy of women that flocked around the introverted Howard Hughes were generated through the efforts of John William Meyer, who was Hughes' public relations person and procurator. His primary job was to lasso any woman that he thought that Hughes might be interested in knowing intimately.

Katherine Hepburn was the only woman of the bunch who bridged the worlds of society and film. She was born into an aristocratic Connecticut family, she was also among the top ten of Hollywood's great actresses. The romance did not last a year because Hepburn found Howard's expensive gifts and his money to be a bore.

Between 1932 and 1940 Howard Hughes turned his interest from juggling women to juggling various enterprises and fleshless hobbies such as piloting airplanes and race cars. In 1932, Hughes founded the Hughes Aircraft

Katherine Hepburn

Company in Glendale, California. In 1934, he won his first air pilot trophy in Miami, Florida. Hughes followed that feat in 1935 with a new land speed record at Santa Ana, California.

His adventurous appetite had not been fulfilled; therefore in 1936 he established a new transcontinental speed record from Los Angeles to Newark, New Jersey in nine house, and twenty-seven minutes. The man from Houston was still in search of the thrills that would fulfill his appetite, therefore in 1938 with a crew of four men, he established a new record for a round-the-world flight in three days, nineteen hours, and seventeen minutes.

Jane Russell in The Outlaw.

In the spring of 1940, he began filming *The Outlaw* starring Jane Russell. The picture was completed before World War II began in December 1941, but it was not released until 1947. In the meanwhile, Hughes released publicity stills of Jane Russell his star-to-be, that made men salivate. She became a pin-up in footlockers and on barrack walls and in every pup tent in the states and in both the European and Pacific theaters of war during World War II. Hughes's lady Jane's body was world-famous long before she ever appeared on a public movie screen.

A major snag in getting the film released is revealed in a special FBI agent's report dated December 22, 1944. The memorandum stated that: *Hughes Production had used up its quota for raw film and that unless there was a relaxing of the WPB (War Production Board) quota could be obtained, the studio would not be able to release the picture entitled "The Outlaw". The memorandum also pointed out that there was a need to obtain five and one half million feet of .35m raw film.*

Myers is believed to have made some contact with the White House when President Franklin Delano Roosevelt was in office. That connection was made through Elliott Roosevelt, the president's son. Myers, Hughes' aide subsequently also became a spokesman for Elliott Roosevelt in that Myer announced that Roosevelt would go to California to marry Faye Emerson. After the wedding the entire wedding party was flown at Howard Hughes' expense from California to the Grand Canyon as guests on Howard Hughes' Trans World Airline.

If Hughes had one overriding obsession as the director of the movie, *The Outlaw* it was to display Jane Russell's voluptuous breasts. Although the cameras were manipulated to enlarge her naturally endowed bust, Hughes was still not satisfied. It is said that he used his knowledge of aerodynamics and stress to create a king size brassiere that would inflate the moment a string was pulled to accentuate her already impressive boob tubes. There was no doubt that Howard Hughes was truly a nipple man. Some people kept their eyes on the sparrow while Hughes kept his on Jane Russell's breast for over two decades.

In May 1948, Hughes acquired control of RKO (Radio-Keith-Orpheum) one of Hollywood's largest and most prestigious studios. He felt as the single largest stockholder of RKO, that he had a stronger defense in his running, feud with the censor people over exhibiting Jane Russell's breast which, in his opinion, was simply a freedom of expression.

Although Hughes only owned 24 percent of RKO stock he held the undisputed power over operations. As a matter of fact, he ordered RKO to pay Hughes Tool Company $100,000 in 1950 for the right to use Jane Russell in a series of RKO Films. A lawsuit was later filed by an unhappy minority stockholder accusing Hughes of "sitting on both sides of the negotiating table" in many of the company's transactions.

In 1952, Hughes released a film through his RKO Studio entitled *The Las Vegas Story.* It was a flashy, Technicolor melodrama about a former female nightclub singer who returns to the desert city downhearted and blue because of a bad marriage. In Vegas she relights a flame in her heart for her use to be lover.

The movie starred Jane Russell as the singer and dreamy eyed Victor

Jane Russell in Gentlemen Prefer Blonds.

Mature as her exlover. The story line was transparent, and the action was a cousin to naught. Otherwise the movie had all of the trappings that usually made Miss Russell's movies profitable and kept male eyes glued to the screen. Scene after scene showed Jane Russell in suggestive clothing that revealed her 37 ½ "- 24"-36" body. The plunging necklines and strapless gowns made it difficult for the actors and camera-men to keep their minds on their task.

The move did not create the public storm that Hughes expected but the screenwriter Paul Jarrico did. He was subpoenaed to tes-tify before the House Un-American Activities Committee in Washington, D.C. on the subject of Communist infiltration in the motion picture industry. No one was more fearful of creeping Communism than Howard Hughes. He felt that Communism versus free enterprise was a very important issue that must be dealt with and stopped in its tracks. The Junior senator from California Richard Milhouse Nixon, in a speech in Washington, warmly praised Hughes for firing Jarrico a suspected Communist activist.

In September, 1952, Hughes sold his interest in RKO to a syndicate of wealthy businessmen from Chicago. The individual buyers were Abraham L. Koolish, Ralph E. Stolkin, Raymond Ryand, Edward G. Burke, a Texas oil-man, and Sherrill Corwin, the owner of a chain of Los Angeles movie theaters.

Initially, Louella Parsons, the gossip columnist had earlier identified the buyers as a syndicate, whereas The Wall Street Journal exposed their shady past business dealings in a series of reports.

In February, 1953, Stolkin's syndicate surrendered their controlling RKO share to Hughes. Hughes kept the $1.2 million down payment. The money did not afford Hughes a soft bed to lie on considering all the problems that the aborted transaction had caused him.

Hughes lived 24 years after the RKO bump in the road. On April 5, 1946, he died at age 70 fifteen thousand feet in the air, following a long period of both physical and mental detioriation, aboard his private jet which was enroute to a Houston hospital from Acapulco, Mexico.

Howard Hughes out on the town
with Movie Queen Jean Harlow.

Howard Hughes with Marian
Marsh. (1934)

Howard Hughes with Ginger Rogers in New York. (1936)

Federal Bureau of Investigation

Freedom of Information/Privacy Acts Section

Subject: Howard Hughes

FILE DESCRIPTION

SUBJECT — Howard Robard Hughes

FILE NO. — 62-78335

L. 62-2682

10,000, and MEYER said that naturally people like McDONALD resented upstarts like himself, MEYER, coming into the firm in the capacity of public relations director and getting 10,000. MEYER himself suggested that McDONALD should get at least 25,000. MEYER and FRYE appeared agreed that HUGHES had absolutely no sense of proportion in business and it was apparent from this conversation that HUGHES takes very little direct control of the Hughes Corporation and apparently knows very little about its actual operation. It was further indicated that MEYER has better access to HUGHES than perhaps anyone of the executive personnel of Hughes Aircraft.

As indicated in referenced report of Special agent ███████ a memorandum dated December 22, 1944, on the stationery of Hughes Productions was located in the personal papers of Subject, and this memorandum stated that Hughes Productions had used up its quota of raw film and that unless a WPB order relaxing its quota could be obtained, the studio would not be able to release the picture entitled "The Outlaw." The memorandum also pointed out it was necessary to obtain five and one-half million feet of .35 mm. raw film and that unless the film were obtained, United Artists could not release the picture for HUGHES.

It was determined through ████████ on July 2, 1945, that HOWARD HUGHES was ready to release the picture "The Outlaw." ████████ indicated that the raw film stock of .35 mm. must have been obtained by HOWARD HUGHES through some source.

██
██
██ ..vised that in connection with the film, "The Outlaw," JOHN MEYER had circulated rumors through the HUGHES organization that he had obtained four or five million feet of raw film for "The Outlaw" through some secret connections in the motion picture industry in Hollywood. ████████ stated, however, that he personally knew that there were several million feet of old raw .35 mm. film in the HUGHES stockpile at the Romaine Street Plant of Hughes Aircraft, and it was the opinion of ████ ████ that MEYER undoubtedly obtained the film from this old stockpile and then circulated rumors that he had pulled a fast one on the WPB through his underground connections in the motion picture industry. ████████ said that as far as he knew there was no illegal juggling of priorities in connection with the obt. of film for "The Outlaw."

████████ dvised on August 30, 1945, that in his opinion HOWARD HUG' could not have stocked four or five million feet of raw film at the Romaine Street Plant because this is too large an amount of film to have merely accumu-

- 5 -

LA 62-2682

lated from leavings from other pictures, and ███ said that no one was astute enough before the war to store up that much film.

███ pointed out moreover that the Culver City plant of Hughes Aircraft is so constructed that merely by dropping a few partitions it can be converted into an excellent motion picture studio, particularly for television sets. ███ added that ████ ███████████████████ had stated that HUGHES was going to go into television production in the near future, and ███ was of the opinion that this was not mere boasting on Subject's part.

According to ███ Subject's only present connection with HOWARD HUGHES' enterprises is with HUGHES' motion picture work. MEYER has started a lot of wild rumors about what he is going to do for HOWARD HUGHES in connection with motion pictures - that he is going to build an enormous plant in Culver City and that HOWARD HUGHES will have a major studio in the very near future. This has no basis in fact, according to ███ at least as far as he knows. MEYER has never done any work at Hughes Aircraft, at least during the last year and a half, to the direct knowledge of ███ He has appeared at the plant on Romaine Street on rare occasions and allegedly does his work from his home. He has no knowledge, qualifications, or experience in publicity work and has no relationships with the press to qualify him in any way for his title as publicity director. ███ states that MEYER is not even allowed at the Culver City Plant or the main Hughes Aircraft Plant.

- 6 -

LA 62-2682

Subject's Activities in HUGHES Enterprises

By physical surveillance it was determined that on August 20, 1945, JOHN MEYER had lunch with JACK FRYE of TWA and with one DIETRICH of Hughes Aircraft in Houston, Texas, at Romaine's Restaurant in Hollywood. Part of the conversation of these individuals was overheard, and it was noted that MEYER and FRYE discussed changes in the administrative personnel at Hughes Aircraft. It was indicated that the treasurer of the company, one FRANK McDONALD, was quitting and that McDONALD was a very valuable individual. It was also learned that MEYER and FRYE appeared anxious to replace CHARLES PERELLI, executive vice-president of Hughes Aircraft in charge of production. MEYER was particularly insistent that PERELLI be replaced, and discussed an interview of one BUD GILLIES, of Ryan Aircraft, San Diego, who had apparently been interviewed by JACK FRYE as a possible successor to PERELLI. The general trend of this conversation was to the effect that PERELLI was hampering the operation of Hughes Aircraft, at least in the judgment of Subject, and that the Hughes Aircraft needed a complete shake-up. It was also indicated that McDONALD, the treasurer of Hughes, was only getting $13,000 a year, whereas MEYER himself was getting

- 4 -

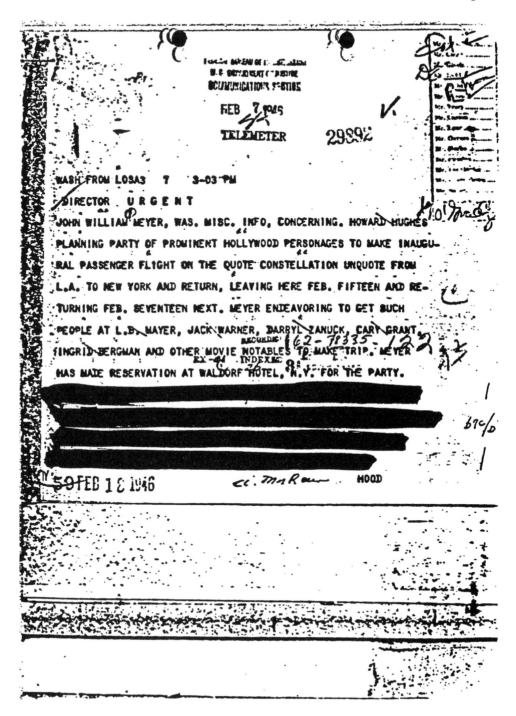

FEDERAL BUREAU OF INVESTIGATION
U. S. DEPARTMENT OF JUSTICE
COMMUNICATIONS SECTION

FEB 7 1946
TELEMETER 29892

WASH FROM LOSA3 7 3-03 PM
DIRECTOR URGENT
JOHN WILLIAM MEYER, WAS. MISC. INFO, CONCERNING. HOWARD HUGHES
PLANNING PARTY OF PROMINENT HOLLYWOOD PERSONAGES TO MAKE INAUGU-
RAL PASSENGER FLIGHT ON THE QUOTE CONSTELLATION UNQUOTE FROM
L.A. TO NEW YORK AND RETURN, LEAVING HERE FEB. FIFTEEN AND RE-
TURNING FEB. SEVENTEEN NEXT. MEYER ENDEAVORING TO GET SUCH
PEOPLE AT L.B. MAYER, JACK WARNER, DARRYL ZANUCK, CARY GRANT,
INGRID BERGMAN AND OTHER MOVIE NOTABLES TO MAKE TRIP. MEYER
HAS MADE RESERVATION AT WALDORF HOTEL, N. Y. FOR THE PARTY.

RECORDED 62-78335-122

50 FEB 18 1946
HOOD

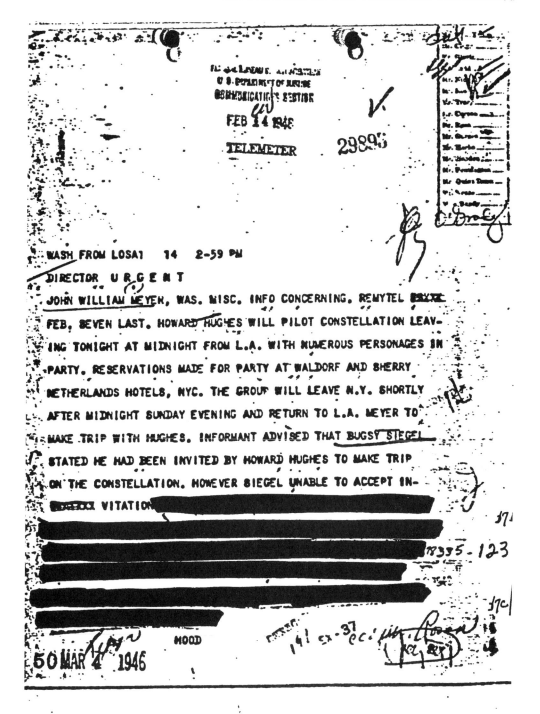

WASH FROM LOSA1   14   2-59 PM

DIRECTOR U R G E N T

JOHN WILLIAM MEYER, WAS. MISC. INFO CONCERNING. REMYTEL

FEB. SEVEN LAST. HOWARD HUGHES WILL PILOT CONSTELLATION LEAV-

ING TONIGHT AT MIDNIGHT FROM L.A. WITH NUMEROUS PERSONAGES IN

PARTY. RESERVATIONS MADE FOR PARTY AT WALDORF AND SHERRY

NETHERLANDS HOTELS, NYC. THE GROUP WILL LEAVE N.Y. SHORTLY

AFTER MIDNIGHT SUNDAY EVENING AND RETURN TO L.A. MEYER TO

MAKE TRIP WITH HUGHES. INFORMANT ADVISED THAT BUGSY SIEGEL

STATED HE HAD BEEN INVITED BY HOWARD HUGHES TO MAKE TRIP

ON THE CONSTELLATION. HOWEVER SIEGEL UNABLE TO ACCEPT IN-

VITATION

HOOD

next day)—Roosevelt dinner par arlo, $163, and Leon and Eddie's, ...

Champagne for Ava

Aug. 23 (next day)—Jack Frye and Elliott Roosevelt party for nine people at Stork Club. $94, and El Morocco, $65; Chic Farmer to stop publicity of Elliott being in New York, $50, and scarce nylon hose gifts, $132.

Sept. 7, 1943—Meyer covered an $83.15 bill of young Roosevelt at Jack and Charlie's.

Sept. 17, 1943—(Back in Hollywood)—Meyer was tabbed for $11 for dinner, drinks and taxi for Faye Emerson, and $116 for liquor from Schwab's drug store for "Doheny Drive," Hughes' home in Hollywood.

Sept. 20, 1943—(Still in Hollywood)—Meyer listed Ava Gardner for champagne charges of $21 at Lamaze and $24 at Macambo.

Elliott stopped at the Beverly Hills Hotel and bungalows in Beverly Hills, Calif., from Nov. 22, to Dec. 8, 1944. The room cost $25 a day. He tallied up a bill during that period totaling $576.83.

The bill was marked "mail to Hughes Aircraft. Culver City, Calif." On it was written "O.K." and signed Col. E. Roosevelt. It was initialled "J. W. M." Johnny Meyer's okay.

A little earlier, the late President's son ran up a huge hotel bill at the Waldorf-Astoria in New York, from Oct. 28 to Nov. 4, 1944. The bill totaled $499.90. Among the charges was a cash C. O. D. for $116.25. This bill similarly was marked "O. K. to pay. Charge H. A. C. (Hughes Aircraft Corporation)" and initialed by Meyer on Nov. 6, 1944.

One of the strange photostats is a check for $159.41 made out on the Bank of America in Hollywood by Hughes Aircraft Corp. payable to a Paul Franklin. It itemized the following:

"Dec. 6, 1944, expenses Col. E. Roosevelt's wedding party, $59.41.

"Four days pilot's time. $100. Net amount, $159.41."

During the time Elliott was at the Beverly Hills Hotel, Johnny Meyer itemized an expense for a weekend trip to Palm Springs. It lasted from Nov. 24 to Nov. 27, 1944. Cost totaled $150, charged to Hughes Aircraft Corp.

Among the items were gas and oil (round trip) $7; maid tip, (4 days at C. Morrison House) $20; bars at Palm Springs, $22; tips to bar maid and phone girl, $10.

Guests were listed by Meyer thus: Col. Elliott Roosevelt, Lt. Col. John Hoover, Faye Emerson, Janet Thomas, Mr. and Mrs. William Powell (Diane Lewis Powell).

Faye Emerson Entertained

After Elliott checked out of the Waldorf and before his trip to Beverly Hills, Johnny Meyer gave a party for Mrs. Anna Roosevelt Boettiger at Elliott's request. It was held in Waldorf-Astoria Towers, apartment 37-C. All the liquor was bought outside and charged to the hotel bill.

The guests included top names in New York's who's who. It was held Nov. 19. Seven days earlier Meyer paid for two public stenographers for Elliott and Mrs. Boettiger, charges being $15.

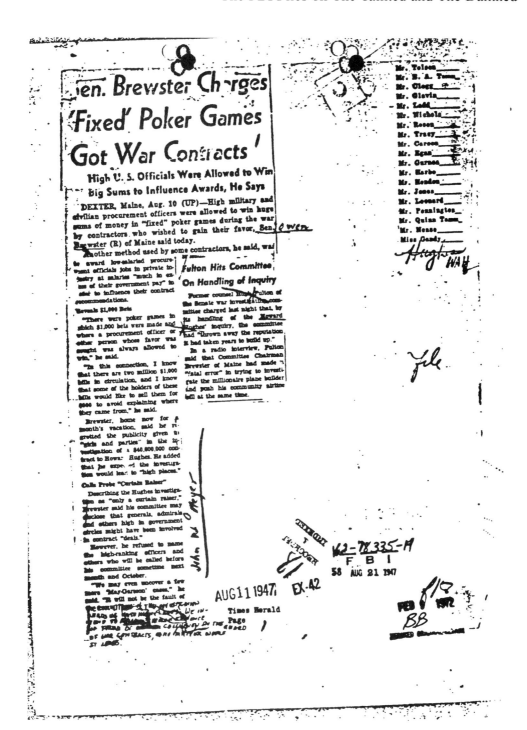

Sen. Brewster Charges 'Fixed' Poker Games Got War Contracts'

High U. S. Officials Were Allowed to Win Big Sums to Influence Awards, He Says

DEXTER, Maine, Aug. 10 (UP)—High military and civilian procurement officers were allowed to win huge sums of money in "fixed" poker games during the war by contractors who wished to gain their favor, Sen. Owen Brewster (R) of Maine said today.

Another method used by some contractors, he said, was to award low-salaried procurement officials jobs in private industry at salaries "much in excess of their government pay" in an effort to influence their contract recommendations.

Reveals $1,000 Bets

"There were poker games in which $1,000 bets were made and where a procurement officer or other person whose favor was sought was always allowed to win," he said.

"In this connection, I know that there are two million $1,000 bills in circulation, and I know that some of the holders of these bills would like to sell them for $900 to avoid explaining where they came from," he said.

Brewster, home now for a month's vacation, said he regretted the publicity given to "girls and parties" in the investigation of a $40,000,000 contract to Howard Hughes. He added that he expected the investigation would lead to "high places."

Calls Probe "Curtain Raiser"

Describing the Hughes investigation as "only a curtain raiser," Brewster said his committee may disclose that generals, admirals and others high in government circles might have been involved in contract "deals."

However, he refused to name the high-ranking officers and others who will be called before his committee sometime next month and October.

"We may even uncover a few more 'May-Garsson' cases," he said. "It will not be the fault of the committee if the investigation...

Fulton Hits Committee On Handling of Inquiry

Former counsel Hugh Fulton of the Senate war investigating committee charged last night that, by its handling of the Howard Hughes' inquiry, the committee had "thrown away the reputation it had taken years to build up."

In a radio interview, Fulton said that Committee Chairman Brewster of Maine had made a "fatal error" in trying to investigate the millionaire plane builder and push his community airline bill at the same time.

Mr. Tolson
Mr. E. A. Tamm
Mr. Clegg
Mr. Glavin
Mr. Ladd
Mr. Nichols
Mr. Rosen
Mr. Tracy
Mr. Carson
Mr. Egan
Mr. Gurnea
Mr. Harbo
Mr. Hendon
Mr. Jones
Mr. Leonard
Mr. Pennington
Mr. Quinn Tamm
Mr. Nease
Miss Gandy

AUG 11 1947
EX-42
Times Herald
Page 1

42-78335-A
F B I
58 AUG 21 1947

LA 62-2662

The New York Field Office, by report dated July 20, 1945, made by Special Agent _____ *37c*/*D*
It was noted that the subject and HOWARD HUGHES were at the Waldorf Astoria on June 14, 1945.

The New York Daily News dated July 6, 1945 featured an article in which Representative SHAFER urged an investigation to determine whether the CAA was under pressure brought by ELLIOTT ROOSEVELT in making its decision to permit the TWA to engage in trans-Atlantic service. Representative SHAFER pointed out when ELLIOTT ROOSEVELT returned to the U. S. from England during the fall of 1944, he was met by JOHN MEYER, a personal representative of HOWARD HUGHES. SHAFER stated MEYER consequently became a spokesman "not only for HUGHES but for ROOSEVELT and made the announcement that ROOSEVELT would go to California to marry FAYE EMERSON."

SHAFER reported MEYER had gone to Hyde Park, where he had conferred with the late President ROOSEVELT. He stated that when ELLIOTT and FAYE were married, the entire wedding party was flown from California to Grand Canyon by JACK FRYE, president of TWA.

The New York office reported that the name of HOWARD HUGHES and JOHN MEYER had appeared occasionally in local newspaper columns as having been observed in various night clubs in New York City.

Bureau letter dated May 10, 1945 reported that an extremely confidential source advised the New York Field Office that on March 30, 1945 HOWARD HUGHES and MEYER had a party at the Waldorf Astoria Hotel in the suite

- 13 -

FEDERAL BUREAU OF INVESTIGATION

Form No. 1				
THIS CASE ORIGINATED AT	LOS ANGELES, CALIFORNIA			NY FILE NO. 62-8491
REPORT MADE AT	DATE WHEN MADE	PERIOD FOR WHICH MADE	REPORT MADE BY	
NEW YORK, NEW YORK	7/20/45	5/3,4,5,19; 6/4,5,21,22,23, 26,28,29;7/2 3,12,13,19/45	███████████	57C
TITLE			CHARACTER OF CASE	
JOHN WILLIAM MEYER, was.			MISCELLANEOUS; INFORMATION CONCERNING	

SYNOPSIS OF FACTS:

Subject registered at Waldorf-Astoria 6/14/45 under own name, and HOWARD HUGHES 6/13/45 under name CRANE GARTZ. Both in different suites.

███████████████████████████████████████

███████████████████████████████████████

- P -

REFERENCE   Bureau letter dated May 10, 1945.
Report of Special Agent ████████████ Los Angeles, 67C
7/6/45.
New York teletype dated July 13, 1945.

DETAILS   Information in this report was received from ████████ 57C
████████████████████████

The subject registered at the Waldorf-Astoria Hotel on June 14, 1945 under the name JOHN WILLIAM MEYER, Howard Hughes Productions, Hollywood, California. He was

APPROVED AND FORWARDED   SPECIAL AGENT IN CHARGE   DO NOT WRITE IN THESE SPACES

62-18335-73

COPIES OF THIS REPORT   RECORDED & INDEXED

5-Bureau
2-Los Angeles (XXXXXXXXXX)
2-New York

AUG 6 1945
COPIES DESTROYED
811 NOV 13 1964

NY 62-8491

assigned Room 3603-4 located in the Waldorf Towers which is a separate unit on the hotel premises, and under different management. All registrations and bills however are handled by the hotel management.

HOWARD HUGHES under the name CRANE GARTZ registered at the hotel on June 13, 1945 and was assigned suite 2635-37 in the hotel proper.

The subject made a side trip to Washington, D.C. which ended June 22, 1945, and he has remained at the Towers since this date. It is noted that in the memorandum received from the Washington Field Division dated June 22, 1945, the subject was actually at the Hotel Statler in Washington, D.C. from June 14th to June 22, 1945.

_____ stated that while MEYER was on this side trip to Washington, D.C., his suite was occupied by HOWARD HUGHES. As of July 19, 1945, subject has incurred a hotel bill in the amount of $1600. which he has informed the hotel management will be paid by the HUGHES AIRCRAFT CORPORATION.

b7c/D

- 2 -

NY 62-8491

57c/D

The New York Daily News dated July 6, 1945 featured an article in which Representative SHAFER urged an investigation to determine whether the CAA was influenced by pressure brought by Brigadier General ELLIOTT ROOSEVELT in making its decision to permit the TWA to engage in Trans-Atlantic service. The article referred to a speech by the Representative which was inserted in the Congressional

- 3 -

NY 62-8491

Record. Among other things Representative SHAFER pointed out that when ELLIOTT ROOSEVELT returned to the United States from England last fall he was met by JOHN MEYER, a personal representative of HOWARD HUGHES, who owns control of TWA. SHAFER stated that MEYER quickly became a spokesman "not only for HUGHES but for ROOSEVELT and made the announcement that ROOSEVELT would go to California to marry FAYE EMERSON". SHAFER stated that later MEYER went to Hyde Park where he conferred with the late President Roosevelt. SHAFER pointed out that when ELLIOTT ROOSEVELT and FAYE EMERSON were married, the entire wedding party was flown from California to the Grand Canyon by JACK FRYE, President of TWA.

The same newspaper on July 13, 1945, featured a story on the loans received by ELLIOTT ROOSEVELT and revealed that he was questioned on July 12, 1945 at the Waldorf Towers by Internal Revenue Agents.

It has been noted that the name of HOWARD HUGHES and JOHNNY MEYER have appeared occasionally in local newspaper columns as having been observed in various night clubs in this city. No physical surveillance has been instituted in this case pursuant to Los Angeles teletype dated June 19, 1945.

- 4 -

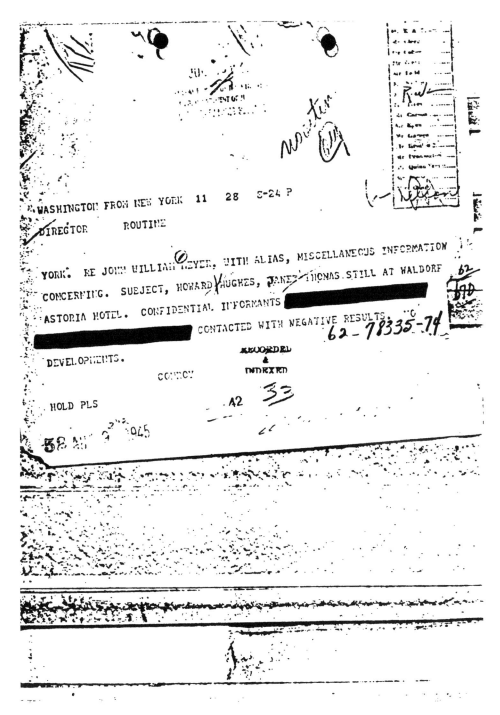

WASHINGTON FROM NEW YORK 11 28 3-24 P

DIRECTOR ROUTINE

YORK. RE JOHN WILLIAM MEYER, WITH ALIAS, MISCELLANEOUS INFORMATION
CONCERNING. SUBJECT, HOWARD HUGHES, JANET THOMAS STILL AT WALDORF
ASTORIA HOTEL. CONFIDENTIAL INFORMANTS ████████████████████
██████████████████████ CONTACTED WITH NEGATIVE RESULTS. NO
DEVELOPMENTS.

62-78335-74

HOLD PLS

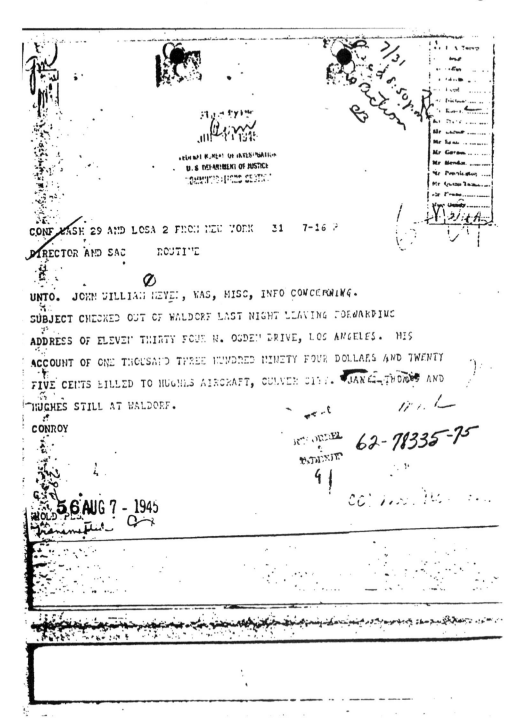

FEDERAL BUREAU OF INVESTIGATION
U. S. DEPARTMENT OF JUSTICE
COMMUNICATIONS SECTION

CONF WASH 29 AND LOSA 2 FROM NEW YORK   31   7-16 P

DIRECTOR AND SAC   ROUTINE

UNTO. JOHN WILLIAM MEYER, WAS, MISC, INFO CONCERNING.

SUBJECT CHECKED OUT OF WALDORF LAST NIGHT LEAVING FORWARDING

ADDRESS OF ELEVEN THIRTY FOUR N. OGDEN DRIVE, LOS ANGELES. HIS

ACCOUNT OF ONE THOUSAND THREE HUNDRED NINETY FOUR DOLLARS AND TWENTY

FIVE CENTS BILLED TO HUGHES AIRCRAFT, CULVER CITY. JANET THOMAS AND

HUGHES STILL AT WALDORF.

CONROY

62-78335-75

56 AUG 7 - 1945

FEDERAL BUREAU OF INVESTIGATION
U S DEPARTMENT OF JUSTICE
COMMUNICATIONS SECTION

SEP 18 1945

TELEMETER

WASH FROM LOSA3 18 1-06 PM

DIRECTOR URGENT

LIKE.

JOHN WILLIAM MEYER, WAS. MISC. INFO. CONCERNING. REBURTEL

SEPT.-THIRTEENTH. SINCE SEPT. FIRST SUBJ HAS BEEN TRAVELING

WITH HOWARD HUGHES. THEY MADE TRIP TO VANCOUVER, BC BY

PRIVATE PLANE OVER LABOR DAY WEEKEND. YVONNE DECARLO,

ACTRESS WHO RECENTLY APPEARED IN MOVIE "SALOME, WHERE

SHE DANCED" WAS WITH GROUP IN VANCOUVER.

RECORDED & INDEXED

62-78335-89

HOOD

END PLS ACK

SEP 28 1945

FEDERAL BUREAU OF INVESTIGATION
U S DEPARTMENT OF JUSTICE
COMMUNICATIONS SECTION

SEP 18 1945

TELEMETER

WASH FROM LOSA3 18 1-06 PM

DIRECTOR URGENT

LIKE.

JOHN WILLIAM MEYER, WAS. MISC. INFO. CONCERNING. REBURTEL

SEPT. THIRTEENTH. SINCE SEPT. FIRST SUBJ HAS BEEN TRAVELING

WITH HOWARD HUGHES. THEY MADE TRIP TO VANCOUVER, BC BY

PRIVATE PLANE OVER LABOR DAY WEEKEND. YVONNE DECARLO,

ACTRESS WHO RECENTLY APPEARED IN MOVIE "SALOME, WHERE

SHE DANCED" WAS WITH GROUP IN VANCOUVER.

RECORDED & INDEXED

62-78335-89

HOOD

END PLS ACK

51 SEP 28 1945

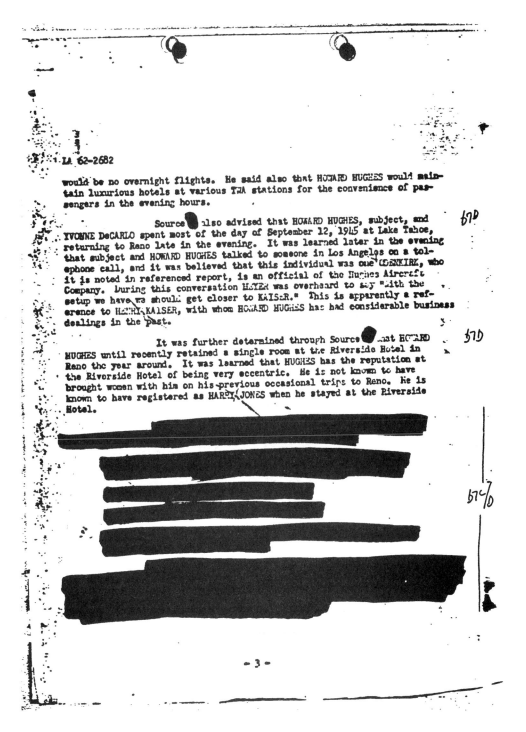

LA 62-2682

would be no overnight flights. He said also that HOWARD HUGHES would maintain luxurious hotels at various TWA stations for the convenience of passengers in the evening hours.

Source [ ] also advised that HOWARD HUGHES, subject, and YVONNE DeCARLO spent most of the day of September 12, 1945 at Lake Tahoe, returning to Reno late in the evening. It was learned later in the evening that subject and HOWARD HUGHES talked to someone in Los Angeles on a telephone call, and it was believed that this individual was one ODEKIRK, who it is noted in referenced report, is an official of the Hughes Aircraft Company. During this conversation HUYER was overheard to say "With the setup we have we should get closer to KAISER." This is apparently a reference to HENRY KAISER, with whom HOWARD HUGHES has had considerable business dealings in the past.

It was further determined through Source [ ] that HOWARD HUGHES until recently retained a single room at the Riverside Hotel in Reno the year around. It was learned that HUGHES has the reputation at the Riverside Hotel of being very eccentric. He is not known to have brought women with him on his previous occasional trips to Reno. He is known to have registered as HARRY JONES when he stayed at the Riverside Hotel.

b7D

b7D

b7C/D

- 3 -

LA 52-2682

Subject, together with HOWARD HUGHES and YVONNE DeCARLO, proceeded to Las Vegas in the early afternoon of September 13, 1945. Subject and HUGHES stayed at the Hotel El Rancho Vegas, but Miss DeCARLO stayed at the Last Frontier Hotel. HUGHES left word at his hotel that his visit there should receive no publicity.

Despite HOWARD HUGHES' request for no publicity, a news-story concerning him appeared in the Las Vegas "Morning Tribune" on September 17, 1945. This story indicated JOHN MEYER accompanied HUGHES to Las Vegas, and that MEYER is his "confidant and assistant for many years".

Subject, together with HOWARD HUGHES and YVONNE DeCARLO, left in HUGHES' plane from Las Vegas September 16, 1945, reportedly for Los Angeles. Subject was first noted again to be in Los Angeles on September 19, 1945. It was learned through a physical surveillance that subject spent considerable time with HOWARD HUGHES who was staying at the Town House in Los Angeles, except for intervals when subject and HUGHES were out of the city.

It was learned through ▮▮▮▮▮ that subject had gone to the home of THOMAS JOYCE in Santa Barbara with HOWARD HUGHES on September 22, 1945

b7c/D
52

Following the return of the subject ▮▮▮▮▮ from Palm Springs on September 25, 1945 subject and HUGHES were together around Los Angeles, HUGHES staying at the Town House, Room 905, under the name J. B. ALEXANDER. On September 29, 1945 subject and HOWARD HUGHES made a trip to San Diego and subject returned alone on the same evening to Los Angeles.

- 4 -

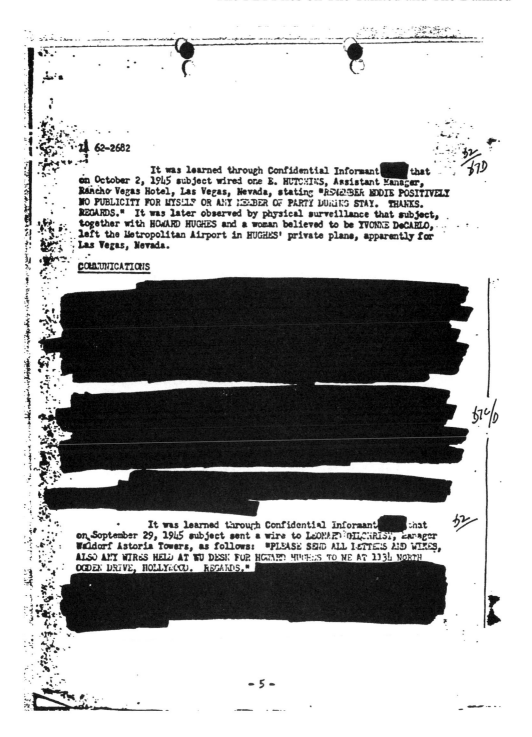

62-2682

It was learned through Confidential Informant ___ that on October 2, 1945 subject wired one E. HUTCHINS, Assistant Manager, Rancho Vegas Hotel, Las Vegas, Nevada, stating "REMEMBER EDDIE POSITIVELY NO PUBLICITY FOR MYSELF OR ANY MEMBER OF PARTY DURING STAY. THANKS. REGARDS." It was later observed by physical surveillance that subject, together with HOWARD HUGHES and a woman believed to be YVONNE DeCARLO, left the Metropolitan Airport in HUGHES' private plane, apparently for Las Vegas, Nevada.

COMMUNICATIONS

It was learned through Confidential Informant ___ that on September 29, 1945 subject sent a wire to LEONARD GILCHRIST, Manager Waldorf Astoria Towers, as follows: "PLEASE SEND ALL LETTERS AND WIRES, ALSO ANY WIRES HELD AT WU DESK FOR HOWARD HUGHES TO ME AT 1134 NORTH OGDEN DRIVE, HOLLYWOOD. REGARDS."

- 5 -

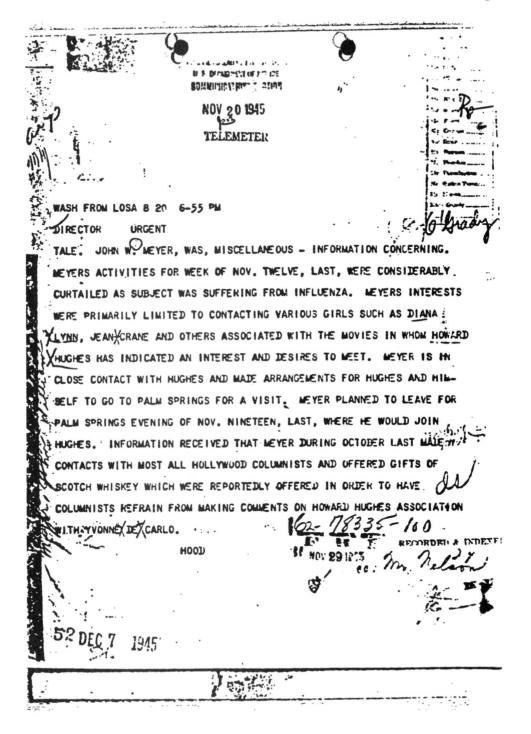

U S DEPARTMENT OF ICE
COMMUNICATION SECTION

NOV 20 1945

TELEMETER

WASH FROM LOSA 8 20 6-55 PM

DIRECTOR   URGENT

TALE. JOHN W. MEYER, WAS, MISCELLANEOUS - INFORMATION CONCERNING.
MEYERS ACTIVITIES FOR WEEK OF NOV. TWELVE, LAST, WERE CONSIDERABLY
CURTAILED AS SUBJECT WAS SUFFERING FROM INFLUENZA. MEYERS INTERESTS
WERE PRIMARILY LIMITED TO CONTACTING VARIOUS GIRLS SUCH AS DIANA
LYNN, JEAN CRANE AND OTHERS ASSOCIATED WITH THE MOVIES IN WHOM HOWARD
HUGHES HAS INDICATED AN INTEREST AND DESIRES TO MEET. MEYER IS IN
CLOSE CONTACT WITH HUGHES AND MADE ARRANGEMENTS FOR HUGHES AND HIM-
SELF TO GO TO PALM SPRINGS FOR A VISIT. MEYER PLANNED TO LEAVE FOR
PALM SPRINGS EVENING OF NOV. NINETEEN, LAST, WHERE HE WOULD JOIN
HUGHES. INFORMATION RECEIVED THAT MEYER DURING OCTOBER LAST MADE
CONTACTS WITH MOST ALL HOLLYWOOD COLUMNISTS AND OFFERED GIFTS OF
SCOTCH WHISKEY WHICH WERE REPORTEDLY OFFERED IN ORDER TO HAVE
COLUMNISTS REFRAIN FROM MAKING COMMENTS ON HOWARD HUGHES ASSOCIATION
WITH YVONNE DE CARLO.

HOOD

62-78335-100

RECORDED & INDEXED
NOV 29 1945

cc: Mr. Nelson

52 DEC 7 1945

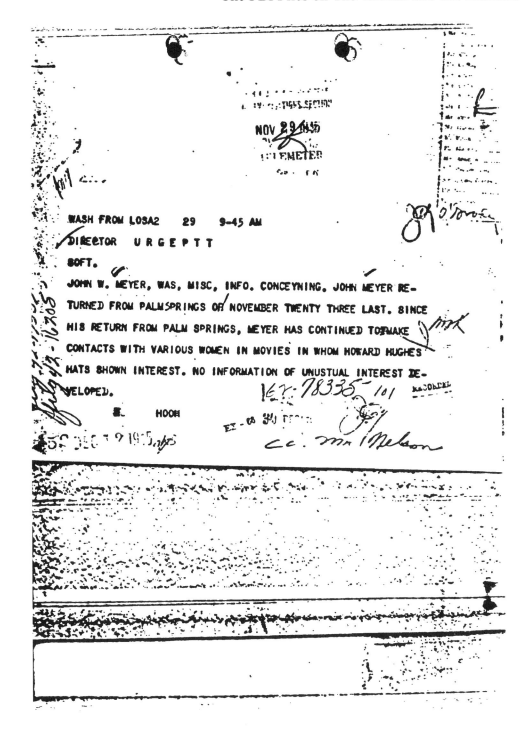

WASH FROM LOSA2   29   9-45 AM

DIRECTOR   U R G E P T T

SOFT.

JOHN W. MEYER, WAS, MISC, INFO. CONCEYNING. JOHN MEYER RE-
TURNED FROM PALMSPRINGS ON NOVEMBER TWENTY THREE LAST. SINCE
HIS RETURN FROM PALM SPRINGS, MEYER HAS CONTINUED TO MAKE
CONTACTS WITH VARIOUS WOMEN IN MOVIES IN WHOM HOWARD HUGHES
HATS SHOWN INTEREST. NO INFORMATION OF UNUSTUAL INTEREST DE-
VELOPED.

                    E.   HOOH

LA 62-2682

SCOTCH and that he was not printing the article simply because it was not news. This informant stated that MEYER had contacted practically every columnist in Hollywood and had sent Scotch all over town in order to attempt to make sure that the item would not leak out in the papers.

MEYER'S Activity in HOWARD HUGHES Productions

Through contacts had with _____ it was learned that HOWARD HUGHES had been able to secure the services of SOL LESSERMAN, United Artists, to handle the release of HOWARD HUGHES' film "The Outlaw"; however, it appeared that some of the terms of the contract were objectionable to LESSERMAN and considerable difficulty ensued. It was reported that MEYER was working on LESSERMAN in order to iron out the difficulties regarding the contract. It was noted on several occasions that MEYER went to the Beverly Hills Hotel where LESSERMAN was staying, and it was thought that MEYER had made contact with LESSERMAN on these occasions for the purpose of endeavoring to straighten out the difficulties. Subsequently it was determined that MEYER was also endeavoring to secure the services of other men well known in the motion picture industry to handle the release of the film instead of LESSERMAN. One of the individuals whose services have been solicited for the position is HARRY GOULD, of United Artists Pictures in New York City.

Through the same source it was reported that MEYER had been keeping himself somewhat busy during the past three or four weeks endeavoring to make contacts with various noted motion picture actresses in whom it was believed that HOWARD HUGHES had indicated an interest. Among those actresses whom MEYER has been contacting are: DIANA LYNN, JOAN LESLIE, GAIL RUSSELL, JEAN CRAIN, and BARBARA BATES.

Trips Made by Meyer

It will be noted in the referenced report it is stated that MEYER, HOWARD HUGHES, and a woman believed to be YVONNE DE CARLO, the noted film actress, had departed from Los Angeles for Las Vegas, Nevada, on October 2, 1945. ████████████████████████████████ ████████████████████████████████ ████████████████████████████████ It was stated that HOWARD HUGHES was to have made the trip to Palm Springs on this occasion; however, his reservations were cancelled ████

- 3 -

Office Memorandum • UNITED STATES GOVERNMENT

DATE: 2/4/46

TO : MR. E. A. TAMM

FROM : R.A. ROSEN

SUBJECT: JOHN WILLIAM MEYER, with aliases;
MISCELLANEOUS - INFORMATION CONCERNING

The purpose of this memorandum is to advise that investigation of
subject Meyer's activities reveals no unusual activity; that he is still making
contact for Howard Hughes with motion picture actresses; that the Howard Hughes
office made reservations which were not used for former Governor John W. Bricker
of Ohio at Palm Springs, California; that the Hughes office endeavored to get
reservations for Edward Flynn, former leader of the Democratic Party; and to call
your attention to other information developed.

MOTION PICTURE ACTRESSES HOWARD HUGHES DESIRES TO KNOW

▓▓▓▓▓▓ advises that subject Meyer has shown considerable interest in
the following actresses:

Jean Crane
Joan Leslie
Dianne Flynn
Gail Russell
Barbara Overton

It is understood that Howard Hughes desires to meet these girls and that Meyer
is making these contacts in his behalf.

RESERVATIONS FOR EDWARD FLYNN AND FORMER GOVERNOR JOHN W. BRICKER

▓▓▓▓▓▓ Racquet Club at Palm Springs,
California, states that reservations were made by the Howard Hughes office during
the month of December in behalf of former Governor John W. Bricker of Ohio. ▓▓▓
▓▓▓▓▓▓ also advises that the Howard
Hughes office during the first part of December, 1945, endeavored to make reservations for Edward Flynn, former National leader of the Democratic Party.

ATTORNEY FRANCIS POULSON OF CLEVELAND, OHIO

▓▓▓▓▓▓ advises that she made reservations for Attorney
Francis Poulson and his son at the request of the Howard Hughes office.

COPIES DESTROYED
211 NOV 13 1964
JO'G:KLW

RECORDED
&
INDEXED

62-78335-121

F B I
30 FEB 6 1946

EX-49

50 FEB 18 1946

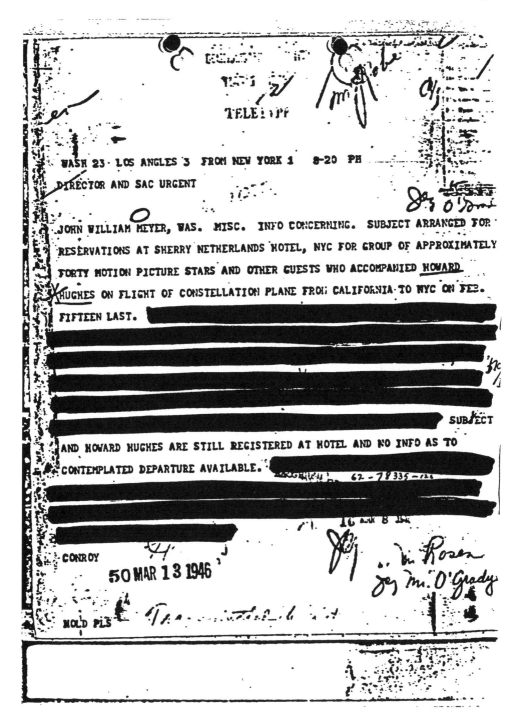

TELETYPE

WASH 23 LOS ANGLES 3 FROM NEW YORK 1   8-20 PM

DIRECTOR AND SAC URGENT

JOHN WILLIAM MEYER, WAS. MISC. INFO CONCERNING. SUBJECT ARRANGED FOR

RESERVATIONS AT SHERRY NETHERLANDS HOTEL, NYC FOR GROUP OF APPROXIMATELY

FORTY MOTION PICTURE STARS AND OTHER GUESTS WHO ACCOMPANIED HOWARD

HUGHES ON FLIGHT OF CONSTELLATION PLANE FROM CALIFORNIA TO NYC ON FEB.

FIFTEEN LAST.

SUBJECT

AND HOWARD HUGHES ARE STILL REGISTERED AT HOTEL AND NO INFO AS TO

CONTEMPLATED DEPARTURE AVAILABLE.   62 - 78335 - 126

CONROY

50 MAR 13 1946

HOLD PLS

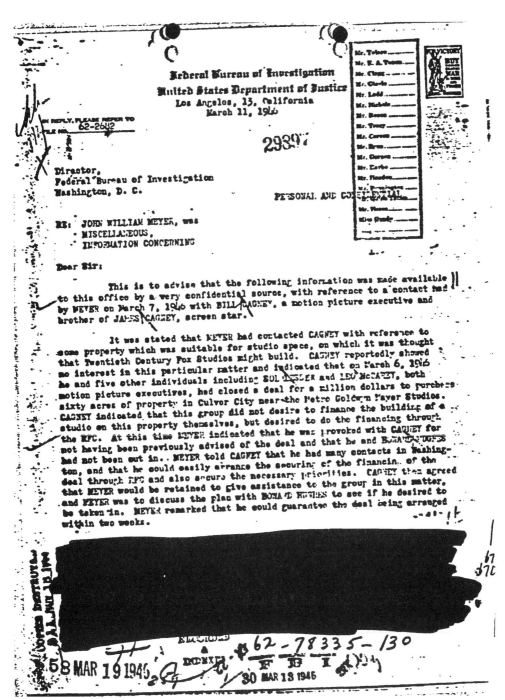

Federal Bureau of Investigation
United States Department of Justice
Los Angeles, 13, California
March 11, 1946

IN REPLY, PLEASE REFER TO
FILE NO. 62-2642

29397

Director,
Federal Bureau of Investigation
Washington, D. C.

PERSONAL AND CONFIDENTIAL

RE: JOHN WILLIAM MEYER, was
MISCELLANEOUS,
INFORMATION CONCERNING

Dear Sir:

This is to advise that the following information was made available
to this office by a very confidential source, with reference to a contact had
by MEYER on March 7, 1946 with BILL CAGNEY, a motion picture executive and
brother of JAMES CAGNEY, screen star.

It was stated that MEYER had contacted CAGNEY with reference to
some property which was suitable for studio space, on which it was thought
that Twentieth Century Fox Studios might build. CAGNEY reportedly showed
no interest in this particular matter and indicated that on March 6, 1946
he and five other individuals including SOL LESSER and LEO McCAREY, both
motion picture executives, had closed a deal for a million dollars to purchase
sixty acres of property in Culver City near the Metro Goldwyn Mayer Studios.
CAGNEY indicated that this group did not desire to finance the building of a
studio on this property, but desired to do the financing through
the RFC. At this time MEYER indicated that he was provoked with CAGNEY for
not having been previously advised of the deal and that he and DONALD HUGHES
had not been cut in.. MEYER told CAGNEY that he had many contacts in Washington,
and that he could easily arrange the securing of the financing of the
deal through RFC and also secure the necessary priorities. CAGNEY then agreed
that MEYER would be retained to give assistance to the group in this matter,
and MEYER was to discuss the plan with DONALD HUGHES to see if he desired to
be taken in. MEYER remarked that he could guarantee the deal being arranged
within two weeks.

62-78335-130

58 MAR 19 1946

30 MAR 13 1946

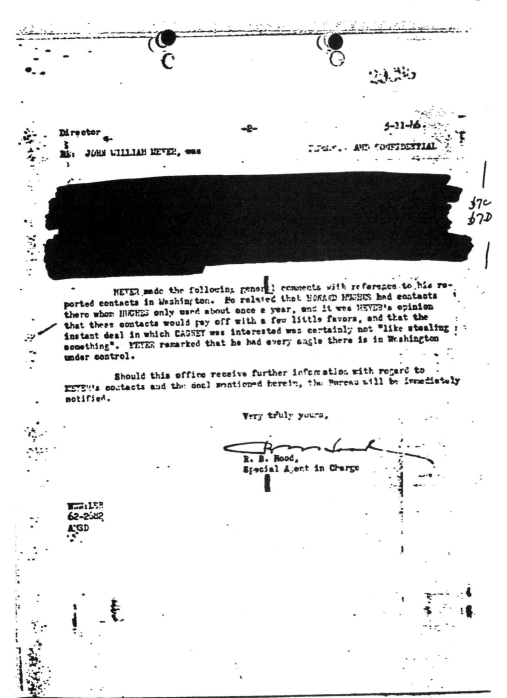

Director

RE: JOHN WILLIAM MEYER, was

5-21-46

-2-

PERSONAL AND CONFIDENTIAL

57C
57D

MEYER made the following general comments with reference to his reported contacts in Washington. He related that HOWARD HUGHES had contacts there whom HUGHES only used about once a year, and it was MEYER's opinion that these contacts would pay off with a few little favors, and that the instant deal in which CAGNEY was interested was certainly not "like stealing something". MEYER remarked that he had every angle there is in Washington under control.

Should this office receive further information with regard to MEYER's contacts and the deal mentioned herein, the Bureau will be immediately notified.

Very truly yours,

R. B. Hood,
Special Agent in Charge

WHH:LES
62-2582
ASD

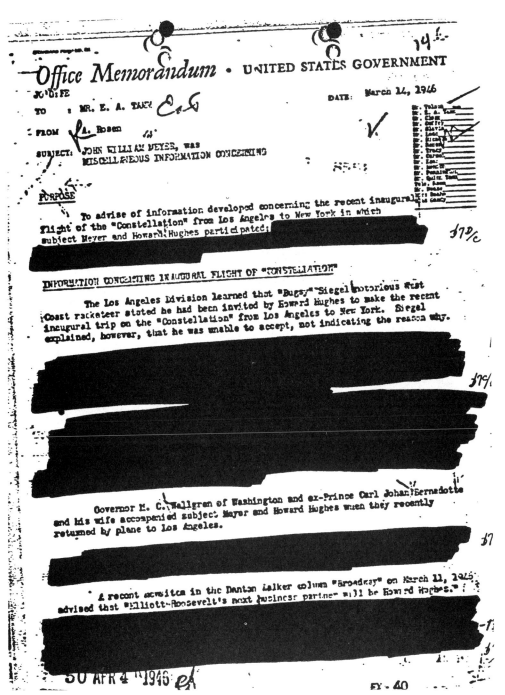

Office Memorandum • UNITED STATES GOVERNMENT

TO : MR. E. A. TAMM

DATE: March 14, 1946

FROM : A. Rosen

SUBJECT: JOHN WILLIAM MEYER, was
MISCELLANEOUS INFORMATION CONCERNING

PURPOSE

To advise of information developed concerning the recent inaugural
flight of the "Constellation" from Los Angeles to New York in which
subject Meyer and Howard Hughes participated.

INFORMATION CONCERNING INAUGURAL FLIGHT OF "CONSTELLATION"

The Los Angeles Division learned that "Bugsy" Siegel notorious West
Coast racketeer stated he had been invited by Howard Hughes to make the recent
inaugural trip on the "Constellation" from Los Angeles to New York. Siegel
explained, however, that he was unable to accept, not indicating the reason why.

Governor M. C. Wallgren of Washington and ex-Prince Carl Johan Bernadotte
and his wife accompanied subject Meyer and Howard Hughes when they recently
returned by plane to Los Angeles.

A recent newsitem in the Danton Walker column "Broadway" on March 11, 1946
advised that "Elliott Roosevelt's next business partner will be Howard Hughes."

30 APR 4 1946

EX - 40

Roy Wilkins

Chapter IV

Roy Wilkins:
The NAACP's Quiet Persuader
With The Big Stick

Roy Wilkins was born in St. Louis, Missouri on August 30, 1901. He was the first child of William DeWitte Wilkins, a third tier minister and Mayfield "Sweetie" Edmundson, a country one room schoolhouse teacher. Roy's parents left Holly Springs, Mississippi under the cover of night for St. Louis soon after they got married on June 7, 1990. The newlyweds caught the Illinois Central Railroad's Louisiana train #3 and sat in the soot filled Jim Crow car which was hooked directly behind the coal tender and locomotive. Riding in the coal, dust-laden coach was not an option but a requirement under the Jim Crow laws of the south. The newlyweds could care less about human degradation because they were headed north in search of freedom from the lynching parties that constantly cast long shadows of fear and death over the heads of the Colored population.

Wilkins' mother made her transition from this life on June 10, 1907 in St. Louis exactly seven years after the family had settled on the west bank of the Mississippi River, a city that W.C. Handy later made internationally famous with his *St. Louis Blues*. Her death was caused by galloping consumption (tuberculosis) shortly before Roy reached his sixth birthday. In addition to Roy, she left behind two younger children Earl and Armeda, in addition to a husband who openly admitted that he could not cope with the notion of raising three small children.

Elizabeth Edmundson Williams, his mother's sister promised while standing at the foot of "Sweetie" Wilkin's deathbed, that she would take care of her three children. Several days after the funeral Aunt Elizabeth fulfilled her promise and carried all three of the youngsters back to St. Paul, Minnesota to live with her and her husband Sam Williams in their home at 906 Galtier Street. The Williams' house was located in an integrated working class neighborhood. Open housing was common until the restrictive covenant ordinances of 1917 outlawed racially mixed communities.

The house that would become their new home was a small, cheaply constructed, clapboard, three-bedroom cottage that was neatly painted white, and attached to a front porch that stretched across the front of the dwelling. The porch was trimmed with Victorian wrought iron and the steps were braced with metal handrailings.

Uncle Sam Williams was a very warm person with a quick, and wide friendly grin that displayed his shiny pearly white front teeth. Sam was employed as a private Pullman sleeping car porter to work exclusively for Mr. Howard Elliot the President of the Great Northern Pacific Railroad. His job description required that he function as both a butler and a cook. The two tasks were performed on the train and at Mr. Elliot's home when they were not on the road. His salary was a hard, hourless earned eighty dollars a month, plus an annual small bonus of twenty-five dollars every Christmas.

Before the September leaves turned from green to brown, Roy entered the first grade at the Whittier Grammar School which was located on the corner of Marion and Wayzata Streets. His Aunt Elizabeth held his hand as she walked and he skipped all the way to school on his first day. The school was only four blocks from their house. His first cultural shock in the State of a Thousand Lakes was discovering that all of his fellow classmates were whiter than freshly drifting snow. On the other hand, the entire student population at the Banneker School which he had attended in St. Louis were Black, brown or beige. The teachers were the exception.

His Aunt Elizabeth's final instructions before leaving him in the hands of the very elderly baldheaded male principal was to remind him that he was to come straight home from school when he heard the school bell ring. When Roy heard the bell go ding! -a-ling! -a-ling! At recess time he took off for home like a racehorse running the last lap in the Kentucky Derby. He leaped up the stairs and ran through the front door of the house which was ajar, he was panting for air and his heart was beating in a 6/8 rhythm as he shouted "Auntie! I am back."

His Aunt Elizabeth greeted him with her outstretched arms and a surprised happy expression on her face.

"What are you doing here, child?" She queried with a full moon smile that appeared to spread from ear to ear.

"You told me to come straight home when the bell rang Auntie," he retorted.

She threw her head back and looked at him with a forgiving twinkle in her eyes because he was right. Before sending him back to school she gave him a peanut butter and jelly sandwich on white toast with a glass of sweet milk and a more definitive explanation of the five school bells: tardy, recess, lunch, fire drill, and dismissal.

Roy Wilkins' best friend at school was a shy, blond, Swedish boy named Herman Anderson. He lived approximately six blocks from Galtier Street on the east side of Race Street. Herman and Roy never talked about Black and white until Herman visited Roy in his 409 Edgecomb apartment on Sugar Hill in New York City. Both men were in their early seventies when Herman finally told Wilkins how he felt about the race question.

Herman said, "I was taught by my mother that skin color didn't make any difference but the thing that really mattered was the kind of person you were."

Following Wilkins' graduation from the George Weitbret Mechanical Arts High School he enrolled in the University of Minnesota where he earned a Bachelor of Arts degree and carried three majors, Journalism, Economics, and Sociology. He supported himself while in college by working as a redcap at the train station, dining car waiter on the Great Northern Pacific Railroad, and as a slaughterhouse laborer at the Swift and Company Packing House. As a result of the journalism courses he had taken while in college he was able to get a job as a part time editor at the *Appeal*, a local Black owned St. Paul weekly newspaper.

After graduating from the University of Minnesota Wilkins began working full time on October 1, 1923 as news editor for the *Kansas City Call*

Wilkins, the train waiter.

a local Black weekly newspaper owned by Chester Arthur Franklin. The newspaper office was located at Eighteenth Street and Vine, the hub of the Kansas City, Missouri's Black business district. He found Black Kansas City, even with all of its problems, to be an exciting 24 hour town where the bars and cabarets jumped all night long with Black and white patrons. They danced to the music of great jazz bands such as Benny Moten, Count Basie, Andy Kirk and the blues shouting of Jimmy "five by five" Rushing , Joe "I am going to Chicago" Turner and countless other entertainers who played the city throughout the third, and fourth decades of the twentieth century.

The white section of Kansas was different, in that it was Jim Crow day and night from the crown of its head to the soles of its feet. It was the racial rigidity on the white side of the city that caused Wilkins to become a fighter for African American rights. He joined the struggle for better schools, and for an end to discrimination in education, and an end to both police profiling and brutality.

Roy Wilkins' first assignment was to cover the NAACP convention which was being held in Kansas City during the first week in October 1923. He turned in his first assignment which was an in-depth story on James Weldon Johnson, the primary speaker at the convention and the Executive Secretary of the NAACP. Mr. Franklin the publisher of the *Kansas Call* flipped through the pages of Wilkins' journalistic efforts and looked up from behind his oversized mahogany desk and said: "You will do." In addition to being a race advocate, Mr. Johnson was the composer of *Lift Every Voice and Sing* which is better known today in the African American community as *The Black National Anthem.*

In 1931 Walter White replaced James Weldon Johnson as Executive Secretary of the National Association for The Advancement of Colored People (NAACP). White, in turn offered his former position as Assistant Secretary to Roy Wilkins, who on August 15, 1931 began a 24 year apprenticeship in the organization's New York City office under White. In his autobiography *Standing Fast* (1982), Wilkins said of his new job, *"My new duties involved a little bit of everything such as: writing, lecturing, organizing new branches, raising money for a treasury that was always Depression dry, in addition to running the national office while Walter White was touring around the country drumming up memberships wherever he could get an audience."* For a

short period Wilkins even reviewed legal cases. He also continued to write a column for the *Kansas City Call* and work with Dr. W.E.B. DuBois, the Harvard educated PhD who was editor for *Crisis* the NAACP membership organ.

Left to right: Roy Wilkins, Walter White and future Supreme Court Judge Thurgood Marshall.

In the fall of 1931, the Scottsboro Boys' incident was on the front burner of the NAACP agenda, when Roy Wilkins joined the organization's staff. Walter White told him that the Scottsboro case was his baby. At this point the Scottsboro Boys' case will be viewed through the eyes and ears of the author and several of his older relatives. The following material about the case appeared in Travis' *An Autobiography of Black Chicago* and it read as follows:

The Communists held mass meetings daily in Washington Park which is located on the east side of South Parkway (now known as Martin Luther King Drive), its north and south boundaries are between 51st and 60th Street in Chicago. In the west section of Washington Park between 51st and 54th there was always one very large crowd listening to a series of prominent left wing speakers, and at the same time there were dozens of smaller groups listening to lesser known soapbox personalities. Late one afternoon after my father returned from the park my mother Mittie Travis asked:

"What subjects did you get an education on today, Sweetheart?"

"The Scottsboro Boys," Dad said.

"Who was the speaker?" Uncle Otis Travis inquired.

"Some white New York lawyer who had been present at the nine boys' first trial in Scottsboro, Alabama."

The nine young Negroes who became internationally famous as the Scottsboro Boys were Charley Weems, Ozzie Powell, Clarence Norris, Olen Montgomery, Willie Roberson, all hard luck cases from Georgia, my father's birth state, and Haywood Patterson, Eugene Williams, Andrew and Leroy Wright, were from Chattanooga. At age twenty, Charley Weems was the oldest of the boys; the youngest boys were Leroy Wright and Eugene Williams, both of them were a few months away from their thirteenth birthday.

"Weren't they arrested on a freight train in Paint Rock, Alabama?" Mrs. Travis asked.

"Yep! But they shipped those boys by open truck to Scottsboro, Alabama the Jackson County seat, because they didn't have a cage big enough for them in Paint Rock," my father replied.

My dad spent the rest of the evening explaining to my mother what the New York lawyer had said to the big crowd in the park. According to the information my dad had, the nine Black boys were arrested for fighting seven white hobos who had been trying to force them to jump from a moving freight train. Instead, the Black boys beat and kicked all of the white hobos off the train except one. They spared the last ofay hobo because the train had picked up too much speed for them to push him off without causing him to get serious injuries or possibly death. The bruised and infuriated white boys who had been kicked off the train hitch-hiked ahead to Scottsboro, where they pressed charges with the sheriff against the Blacks for beating the hell out of them. Deputy Sheriff Charlie Latham put together a posse to capture the Blacks on the freight train. They were arrested at the next scheduled stop, which was Paint Rock. In addition to the nine Blacks and one white boy on the train, two trailer trash white females wearing men's caps and overalls were also aboard.

Only twenty minutes had passed after the arrest had been made when the younger girl, who identified herself as Ruby Bates of Huntsville, had been prompted to accuse the nine Blacks of raping both she and her girlfriend, Victoria Price. The nine boys were arrested on March 25, 1931. They went to trial on April 6, 1931, and three days later, April 9, 1931, eight of the nine were sentenced to die. Roy Wright, who had barely reached his thirteenth birthday, was sentenced to life in prison.

A stony silence fell over the dining room in our home. Everyone at the table was stunned at the severity of Judge Hawkins' sentence and the swiftness of the trial. It seemed like an hour of silence passed before Uncle Joe asked my father, "How did the Washington Park crowd react to this?"

"Shock," Dad answered. "Just plain shock!"

Uncle Otis cut in, "Those boys were lucky they weren't arrested in my home state of Georgia; there they might have been given an instant necktie party. I understand the lynching quota for Coloreds in Georgia was something like eleven a year compared to an average of six annually in Alabama between 1882 and 1930."

Cousin Ralph Crawford gave a grim chuckle. "You fellows have been away from the South so long that you have forgotten 'Uncle Charlie's first commandment, haven't you?" he said. "The first commandment is, 'Don't ogle or touch "Charlie's" ladies unless you have already decided you want to be the centerpiece at a necktie party and are ready to make peace with God.'"

Uncle Joe, jumping from his chair, shouted, "Damn, man! How can any civilized court sentence eight teen-aged boys to die on the word of two white twenty-five cents a trick prostitutes?"

"Easy," Ralph said. "Black men in the white man's scheme of things are a sub-class. Keeping this premise in mind, then you will understand the white man's rage when he discovers that his woman has been violated by a lower order of being."

Uncle Joe "Pretty Boy" Travis smiled. A cynical, streetwise Chicagoan now with a streak of the playboy in him, he was often amused at Ralph's fer-

109

vor in explaining just how White America worked. "Aren't you drawing some pretty broad conclusions from one incident?" he said.

Ralph stared at him seriously and said, "The real issue is not the violation of the white woman, but a systematized program devised by the white man to detour the sub-class from economic and political parity for another two hundred years."

Uncle Joe smiled again. "Those are some pretty strong words, Ralph."

Ralph with a scowl across his forehead screamed. "The Anglo judicial system condones Black genocide by refusing to deal with Black-on-Black killing or crime seriously unless it is directed at him. The legal and social institutions do not see the individual Black man as a personality, but as a blur of an impersonal mass. Therefore, many Blacks have been brainwashed into accepting this indistinctiveness and have adopted a self-defeating
'Nigger ain't nothing' or "a Black man ain't doodlly squat" an attitude fostered by self hate and his social and legal individual invisibility.

"In the absence of individual indistinctiveness, Blacks have taken on a group guilt complex exhibited by such remarks as "We tore up the neighborhoods', or 'Why don't we learn how to act', and 'Why can't we behave like white folks,' or the acceptance of the white man's highest commendation when speaking to Negroes to wit: 'You are not like the others you are different.'"

Everybody let the words hang in the air while they studied each others' faces. Then my mother broke the silence and said, "Sweetheart, you didn't finish telling us what happened to the Scottsboro Boys. Did they try to escape?"

"You have got to be kidding," Dad said.

"Roy Wilkins and his NAACP ain't going to let those boys burn," Dad said.

"They will if they don't dismiss those white New York lawyers hired by the International Labor Defense (ILD). Everybody knows the ILD is a Communist group. As a matter of fact, Walter White, the Executive Secretary of the NAACP, said, "The prejudice against Communism and Blacks combined guaranteed that the Scottsboro Boys were going to the electric chair,'" Dad said.

The ILD attorney, Walter Pullock, defending the Scottsboro boys, took the case to the Supreme Court. On November 7, 1932, the Scottsboro Boys were guaranteed new trials based on the landmark decision in Powell vs. Alabama. The decision of the lower court was reversed on the grounds that their rights under the Fourteenth Amendment had been violated and that they had not received adequate counsel at Scottsboro, Alabama. On April 7, 1933, Ruby Bates took the witness stand and denied she and Victoria Price were raped.

Late in 1937, Alabama agreed to turn loose Eugene Williams, Willie Roberson, Leroy Wright and Olen Montgomery, conceding that the evidence on them had been insufficient. The state turned around and argued that the same evidence justified holding five of them. It took years to obtain their release. Andrew Wright, the last one in custody, wasn't freed until 1950.

The Communists never managed to make a dent in Blacks' loyalty to the party of Abraham Lincoln. In the presidential election of 1932, most of the Blacks stayed with the Republican Party in spite of their disillusionment with President Herbert Hoover and his promise of prosperity with a chicken in every pot and a car in every garage.

In 1940 on the heels of the Scottsboro case World War II became top priority on the NAACP's agenda. The issues were job discrimination in the defense plants and racial violence and segregation within the armed forces.

A you are there view of the Black soldier in World War II is excerpted from Dempsey J. Travis' best selling tome Views From the Back of the Bus During World War II and Beyond. It read as follows:

Negroes comprised 10 percent of the soldier population at huge military installations. Colored soldiers were camouflaged from the white visitor as much as possible. The barracks for the Negroes were about a mile and a half from the main gate, near the edge of the backwoods. The site of the quarters where the Negroes were was an exact replica of the racially segregated cities and mirrored the America from which they had been drafted to die and save a democracy that they had never known.

Living conditions for Negroes on the military post were deplorable. They did not have use of the PX (post exchange) movie houses, or any of the other recreational facilities that were made available to American whites and the German and Italian prisoners of war.

In the Negro section of most Army posts there were no paved roads, just mud, and no movie theaters-just huts. Negroes at Camp Shenango were supposed to efface themselves, stay out of the way of white folks and literally ride in back of the bus when they went to Sharon and Farrel, Pennsylvania or Youngstown, Ohio. Pennsylvania was in the writer's opinion "the Mississippi of the North." The German prisoners of war rode in the front of the bus and Negro soldiers stood or sat in the back of the bus the same as the minority civilian population in Selma, Alabama, Washington, D.C., Jackson, Mississippi, and Atlanta, Georgia. Army food at its best was bad. The chow served in the Colored mess halls was worse. Some parts of each meal were not edible. Bad meat and under cooked watery "shit on a shingle" (powdered eggs) were staples at breakfast. At chow time everyday they were served a new outrage.

One afternoon Private Travis went to the mess hall for dinner and he found soldiers jumping up and down on the tables, and stomping on the food in their trays. Since First Sergeant Hammond had sentenced Travis to a living hell, he knew that he must give serious thought about ways and means to retain his sanity. I couldn't escape through a movie or a 3.2 (alcohol content) beer in the post exchange, because there were no such things in the Colored section of the camp. Blacks were not permitted in the white area except on official daytime business.

Colored soldiers who needed medical attention were suspect if they showed their faces on the "white" side of the camp. Travis went on sick call to the hospital because he had injured his leg on an obstacle course. A white, middle-aged doctor with a southern accent and the rank of full colonel, asked him, without a smile or even a good morning dog: "Boy, what's your problem?" Travis replied: "My right leg and foot are in pain, Sir." "Your what?" The doctor shouted. "My leg and foot have been hurt, Sir," Travis retorted a second time. "Where is the blood nigger?" The doctor asked. "The injury is internal and didn't break the skin, Sir," was Travis' response.

"Boy!" the doctor snarled, glaring at Travis, "a nigger's feet are supposed to hurt. Don't you show your black ass in this infirmary again trying to goldbrick (avoid work) unless you're bleeding, and I don't mean a nosebleed.

To break the spell of daily humiliation some colored soldiers shot craps on doubled blankets spread out over the latrine "bathroom" concrete floor where the lights were on 24 hours a day. Since the lights were turned off in the barracks at 9pm the only place to gamble after bed check was in the john and within an arm's reach of men having bowel movements on a row of unenclosed toilet stools. Sometimes a gambler would shout, "Roll those dice, baby needs a new pair of shoes," or "Daddy needs some money to make honey with Bonnie." Occasionally a kneeling crap shooter would look up after getting a whiff of a soldier sitting on the toilet and growl, "Cut it short and mix some water with that shit."

By the seventh week that Travis was at Camp Shenango, the post authorities had begun to worry about racial conflicts that might result from the large infusion of Colored soldiers being shipped daily into the Replacement Depot. Despite the presence of a makeshift theater, and the absence of a recreation room the sparks hit the fan when the Colored soldiers in large numbers attempted to gain entry to the white post exchanges and the white movie theaters.

Sunday morning July 11, 1943, was hot and dusty in Shenango Valley. Travis said to Norman "Kansas" Taylor, upper bunkmate who had hailed from the Sunflower state, "Let's stay in the barracks and play cards until it's time to go to the movies and see Wuthering Heights, featuring Lawrence Olivier and Merle Oberon." A small, makeshift, totally inadequate theater had just been built, almost overnight, in an effort to calm down the disgruntled Colored soldiers.

"Okay," Kansas replied, "let's play draw poker with a 5-cent limit." Kansas was in good spirits and talked non-stop about his ambitions as they played cards. He already had an undergraduate degree from an Eastern college and planned to go to medical school on the G.I. Bill of Rights when he received his honorable discharge from the Army. Kansas maintained his cheerful composure in spite of all the miseries of life at Camp Shenango. The only thing Travis ever heard him complain about was the white commanding officer who refused to select him for the Army Special Training Program, a program that would have allowed him to enter medical school while still in the service.

The hours passed quickly that Sunday. Travis and Kansas didn't eat lunch because they heard that they were serving a dish that they jokingly called "dear old billy goat" the meat was tough as shoe leather and tasteless. To this day, Travis believes they were being fed horse meat. At 5:30pm they hit the chow line and then went to the small make-shift theater. The line was already too long for them to catch the first show, so they discussed going into Sharon, a small town about 20 miles away.

Kansas was against it. "Let's wait until next Saturday and go into Youngstown (Ohio) where we can really have a ball," he said. They played blackjack while waiting for the second show to start.

When they came out of the movie, a large group of Negroes were milling around in front of the theater. Kansas and Travis were enroute to their barrack which was approximately 300 feet away when they decided to stop to see what was going on. They were told that a Negro soldier had just got both of his eyes kicked out because he tried to buy a beer in the white post exchange.

"A colored soldier's been beat up" someone screamed. "Let's go down there and get those cracker bastards!" Kansas and Travis stared at each other, wondering what course to take. Before they could make a decision, a caravan of Army trucks, filled with white military police carrying M-1 rifles and doubled-barreled shotguns at the ready, pulled up. On signal, the lights in the ghetto section of the post were turned off and the MPs opened fire on unarmed Colored soldiers standing in the middle of the street. Kansas and Travis tried to break for cover, but it was too late. The screams and cries of soldiers who had been shot pierced the hot July night air. Travis was knocked to the ground by a blunt force. He saw Kansas lying near him. Travis didn't realize he had been shot until he felt a warm, sticky substance soaking his pants leg and his shoulder. There was more gunfire, screams and then silence.

Several army ambulances pulled up within minutes after the shooting stopped. Medics with flashlights were applying triage when they stepped over the wounded who were bleeding, moaning and screaming in the middle of the dirt road. The medics were trying to determine who was dead, who was alive, and who warranted a trip to the hospital or the morgue. When they reached Kansas and Travis, they used their flashlights to motion for stretcher-bearers. "Can you walk?" a medic asked Travis. He tried, but Travis was too numb to move. They turned Travis over and one medic said to the other, "This nigger has been shot three times." Then they turned their flashlights on Kansas. "They got this one in the stomach, but he'll be all right."

What did they mean? Did they mean Kansas would be all right and Travis wouldn't? As Travis laid there preparing to die, his thoughts were not of heaven or hell. He was cursing the darkness. The blood that was oozing from his body was polluted with hate.

On the way to the hospital Travis heard the ambulance driver say to the medic, "Why the hell do we shoot our own men?"

"Who said they were men?" The medic replied. "We shoot niggers like rabbits where I come from."

At the hospital, Kansas was rolled into a small room and Travis was left on a cart in the corridor. After a few minutes, a doctor rushed into the little room where Kansas laid motionless. Through the partially opened door, Travis could see the doctor lift Kansas' eyelids. The doctor then put a stethoscope to his chest, then tried without success to straighten Kansas' bent legs. The doctor then turned out the lights and closed the door. Norman "Kansas" Taylor was dead.

Ironically, Travis became the manager of the Main Post Exchange at Aberdeen Proving Ground in Maryland, exactly one year after Taylor was murdered.

The distortion of the Shenango riot by the War Department is on the following pages.

The War Department's Fiction

Despite the alterations to make life more bearable for Negro troops at former Camp Shenango, the official military position regarding the mayhem that had occurred on July 11, 1943 remained one of cover-up and justification, as indicated by the letter reproduced on the following pages. This letter, which was written less than two months after the violence occurred, did not come into Travis' possession until 40 years after the Shenango massacre, despite serious attempts on his part to secure any defining information during the intervening years.

Walter White, Secretary of the National Association for the Advancement of Colored People received the following letter on September 6, 1943:

APPENDIX A

OSA/bc 2 E 924
OCS

WD 221.1   KAR:cib   WAS/ml
(14 Jul 43) OB-C   4371

September 4, 1943.

Mr. Walter White, Secretary
    National Association for the
Advancement of Colored People,
    69 Fifth Avenue,
New York, 3, New York

Dear Mr. White:
    This is in further reply to your letter of July 14, 1943, concerning an incident which occurred at the Shenango Personnel Replacement Depot involving

colored soldiers.

The report of the investigation reveals that on the evening of July 11, 1943, an altercation arose between white and colored soldiers who were present in one of the post exchanges. This altercation expanded until it involved a large number of personnel in that section of the camp. This affray did not reach dangerous proportions, however, and was shortly brought under control by the Military Police which consisted of both white and colored soldiers.

Later the same evening, two colored soldiers were apprehended without proper passes and placed in the guardhouse. Upon arrival at the guardhouse, they harangued the other colored prisoners with exaggerated and lurid statements of the incidents which had occurred earlier in the evening. The colored prisoners subsequently affected a prison break and when joined by other colored soldiers forcefully entered supply rooms where they secured a quantity of firearms and ammunition. In quelling this disturbance, the Military Police, which was again composed of both white and colored soldiers, killed one of the colored rioters and wounded five others.

The Shenango Replacement Depot is, as you know, used to quarter troops who are awaiting shipment overseas. The recreational facilities at the Depot are not as elaborate as those which the men enjoyed when they were undergoing training at their former posts and camps. In this connection definite steps to improve the living conditions and recreational facilities at Shenango have recently been taken.

The investigation discloses that your informant presented an exaggerated and prejudiced picture of what actually occurred and that no colored soldiers was ever handcuffed to a telegraph post as reported by your informant. It is also noted that anonymous informant failed to appear before the Board of Inquiry which was open to all persons having knowledge of the incident. Since the War Department has evidence that Axis-minded agitators are attempting to foment racial disturbances, I would suggest that the disclosure of his name as well as the names of those who supplied him with this information would assist the War Department in its efforts to eradicate the sources of such subversive activities.

The incident, and especially the death of Private Norman Taylor, who appears to have been an unwilling participant in the riotous disturbance, is indeed most regrettable. It may be of interest for you to know that Private Taylor stated before his death that he had been in his barracks and was told to come outside by a colored soldier and fight or he would be killed.

The suggestion contained in your letter for the formation of mixed units has been considered at various times by the War Department and the decision reached was that such action would be inadvisable.

The War Department is doing everything within its power to promote the mutual respect and the common welfare of both white and colored soldiers. I am sure that you will agree with me the mob action is, however, not a proper or efficacious means of promoting any cause.

Your rightful interest in this matter is appreciated and I am certain that you, as a patriotic American, will use your high position to assist in the suppression of unverified rumors which serve to increase racial tension and to impede our war effort.

Yours VeryTruly,
Secretary of War.

COPY FOR: Acting Civilian Aide to the Secretary of War.
Operations Branch, AGO _____ Ext. 2053

Note: Truman K. Gibson, Jr., acting civilian aide to the Secretary of War, during World War II and a friend of Dempsey J. Travis indicated in 1995 during a taped interview with Travis that he had never seen a copy of the afore-mentioned letter.

The racial conflict at Camp Shenango during the summer of 1943 was not isolated in that there were a series of racial outbreaks throughout America taking place in such places as Camp Breckinridge, Kentucky, Camp Claiborne, Louisiana, Camp Davis, North Carolina, Camp Livingston, Louisiana, Camp

McCain, Mississippi, Camp Phillips, Kansas, Camp Luis Obispo, California, Camp Stewart, Georgia, Camp van Dorn, Mississippi, Camp Wallace, Texas, Fort Bliss, Texas Fort Bragg, North Carolina, Fort Dix, New Jersey, Fort Huachuca, Arizona, Fort Jackson, North Carolina, March Field, California, Mitchell Field, California, Tuskegee, Alabama, plus innumerable racial clashes larger and smaller than Shenango in cities and towns throughout America.

Many of the uprisings never saw the light of day in the major newspaper dailies. Such news was thought to have a negative effect on our war efforts. The Negro weeklies, such as the *Chicago Defender* and the *Pittsburgh Courier* carried the message to the Black community. Unfortunately the NAACP did not have the staff or manpower to effectively deal with the mountain of racial problems during World War II.

Picture of the Author and Roy Wilkins taken during a Press Conference at the Waldorf Astoria in New York City in 1968.

The high point of Roy Wilkins' leadership was the 1954 Supreme Court decision in Brown vs. Board of Education. However, the decision was toothless in that it did not order immediate school integration.

Wilkins' real challenge came in 1955 when Dr. Martin Luther King came on the scene marching to the beat of a different drummer. There was the sound of drumbeats coming from the Montgomery, Alabama bus boycott, the lunch counter sit-ins in Greensboro, North Carolina, and the Freedom Ride riders both Black and white brought new leaders, new organizations, and new tactics to the struggle.

The first unified action of the Civil Rights Organization took place in August, 1960 when all of the organizations united by Dr. King, Roy Wilkins, and A. Philip Randolph under the umbrella of the Chicago branch of NAACP, where Dempsey J. Travis was President and coordinator of the March on the Republican Convention. The objective of the March on the Republican Convention in Chicago was to negotiate for a stronger Civil Rights plank in the Republican platform. The 1960 unity of organizations was carried forward in the March on Washington Movement led by King, Wilkins, Randolph and other civil rights leaders when they joined hands in August 1963 not knowing that Dr. Martin Luther King was going to give the *I Have A Dream* speech, which still rings in the ears of those who heard it almost forty years ago.

In 1977 Roy Wilkins, at age 75 handed over the organization he had served for forty-six years to Reverend Benjamin Hooks. Wilkins spent the remaining years of his life in New York City, where he died on August 4, 1981.

Federal Bureau of Investigation

Freedom of Information/Privacy Acts Section

Subject:Roy Wilkins

SECRET

By memo dated 9-10-31 the Department of Justice
referred to the Bureau a letter from Roy Wilkins, Assistant
Secretary of the NAACP, together with correspondence furnished
by Wilkins, concerning alleged peonage conditions existing in
Lincoln County, Georgia. The enclosures transmitted by the
Department included the following correspondence:

A letter from Wilkins, dated 9-9-31 addressed to the
Hon. W. D. Mitchell, U.S. Attorney General, in which Wilkins
requested an investigation of the allegations;

A letter addressed to Walter White of the NAACP,
dated 8-31-31 from the Rev. J. L. Bates of Georgia;

A letter from Rev. J. L. Bates to the Governor of
Georgia, dated 8-10-31, in which Bates made his original
charges concerning the mistreatment of Negro share-croppers
in Lincoln County, Georgia.

Serial described above
50-1049-1
(16)

The name "Roy Wilkins, NAACP" appeared on a list
captioned as follows: "'The High School Student', put out by
high school section of National Student League, 45 N. 30th
St., NYC. Call to Action by the Committee on Negro Student
Problems on April 3, 1933, Number signed by." The list was
contained in miscellaneous material on the National Student
League, which was made available to the WFO from ████████

Photostats of above described
material enclosed with
Bureau memo, 10-5-42
Re: National Student League
61-7497-305
(20)

SECRET

On 10-23-36 the New York Field Office forwarded
a copy of the September 1936 issue of the "Crisis," the official
publication of the NAACP. It was noted that Roy Wilkins was
editor of the magazine. It was also noted that the agent who
had obtained the magazine had contacted the Workers Book Shop,
official part of the CP, and was emphatically informed that
the publication was not handled at that book store, indicating
that it was not classed as a communist publication.

NY letter, 10-23-36
Re: Subversive Activities in
the Steel Industry.
61-7552-76
(20)

This reference was a copy of a letter from the SAC
in New Orleans, dated 10-20-36, to the U.S. Attorney at
Meridian, Miss., enclosing a copy of a letter from Roy Wilkins,
Assistant Secretary of the NAACP, dated 10-6-36. The letter
from Wilkins, which was addressed to Attorney General, Homer
S. Cumming, charged that G. W. Jackson, a colored man in
Sunflower, Miss., was being held in peonage by his employer,
a Mr. Enos of Jackson, Miss. Wilkins asked the Department of
Justice to make an inquiry through the nearest U.S. Attorney.
The SAC advised the U.S. Attorney that the matter would be
investigated.

50-1253-1
(16)

SECRED

The "Daily Worker" on 7-26-37 carried an article
entitled "Harlem Groups Back August 7 Peace March," which
announced plans for a peace march in Harlem, N.Y., called
by the American League Against War and Fascism. The name
of Roy Wilkins, Editor of the "Crisis" and member of the
Executive Board of the NAACP, appeared on a list captioned:
"Endorsers and Participants."

61-7563-34X, "DW", 7-26-37
(20)

This reference was a letter, dated 1-17-38 from
the SAC Little Rock to the SAC in New York, advising that
Roy Wilkins had written to the Attorney General on 9-11-37,
charging that thirty Negroes were being held in virtual
slavery on a farm in Halley, Ark.

It was indicated that a similar case in Arkansas
had been investigated by the Bureau and the report presented
to the U.S. Attorney at Little Rock, who had declined
prosecution.

The New York office was requested to interview Wilkins
for complete information regarding his allegations and to
determine his sources.

50-1324-7X
(16)

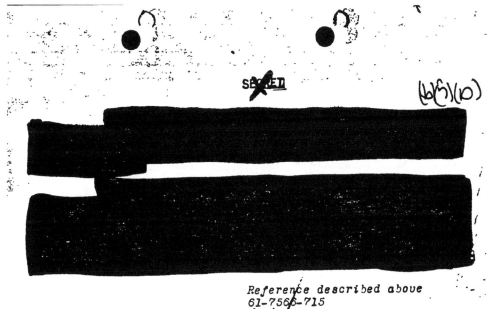

SECRET

(b)(5)(10)

Reference described above
61-7566-715
(21)

The "Daily Worker" on 4-9-38 contained an article
entitled "Negro Leaders Ask End of Rail Union Discrimination."
The article set out a letter addressed to the National
Convention of Railway Employes, Department of the AFL, in
session in Chicago, asking that action be taken to eliminate
discrimination against Negroes. Roy Wilkins, Assistant
Secretary of the NAACP, was listed as one of the signers of
the letter.

61-7563-58X "DW", 4-9-38
(21)

SECRET

By telegram dated 4-20-38, Roy Wilkins, Assistant
Secretary of the NAACP, 69-5th Ave., NYC, advised the
Bureau of the alleged kidnapping of the bride of one,
William Stewart, from their honeymoon residence in Chicago.
Wilkins stated the NAACP urged an investigation by the FBI
of the violation, under the Lindbergh Kidnapping Act.

By letter dated 4-25-38 the Bureau advised Roy
Wilkins that the New York and Chicago Field Offices had
been instructed to conduct an investigation and if the facts
indicated a violation of the Kidnapping Act, a complete
investigation would be made.

Serial described above
7-2301-3X
(2)

The "Daily Worker" on 7-26-38 carried the first of
a series of articles by Will Lawrence entitled: "Max Yergan,
Progressive Leader." It was noted, in the introduction to
the article, that the second in the series would appear the
next week and the subject would be, Roy Wilkins, Assistant
Secretary of the NAACP and Editor of the "Crisis."

61-7568-66X3
(21)

SECRET

This reference was the report of the Hearings before
a Subcommittee of the Committee on Foreign Relations, U.S.
Senate, held March 8 - June 28, 1950. The report, which was
entitled "State Department Employee Loyalty Investigation,"
contained a list of names appearing on a letterhead of the
American Russian Institute, dated 11-16-38. The name of Roy
Wilkins appeared on the list. The letterhead, which was
introduced by Senator McCarthy on 3-8-50, was marked Exhibit
No. 4.

> 121-23278-267X12, encl. Part.
> 1, p.3
> (15)

The HCUA Report entitled "Investigation of Un-American
Propaganda Activities in the U.S., Appendix - Part IX, Communist
Front Organizations," dated 1944, contained the following
information relating to Roy Wilkins:

A letterhead of the Council for Pan-American Democracy,
listed Roy Wilkins as a sponsor for a conference on Pan-American
Democracy to be held on December 10,11, 1938, at Hotel Washington,
Washington, D.C. It was indicated that the Council had been
referred to as a Communist-front organization in previous
reports of the HCUA.

On three undated letterheads of the International
Juridical Association, Roy Wilkins was listed as a member of
the National Committee of the Organization.

A list entitled "United Front for Herndon Grows,"
which appeared in the October 1935 issue of "Labor Defender,"
page 9, set out the public officials who signed a petition for
the freedom of the Negro Communist, Angelo Herndon. The name
of Roy Wilkins appeared among the "prominent individuals" who
had signed the petition as of 9-15-35.

> Documents set out as Exhibits in
> HCUA Report, described above
> 61-7582-1298, Section 2, pp.673,
> 795,809,812; Section 5, p.1643
> (21)

SECRET

The "Daily Worker" on 12-27-38 carried an article entitled "Farm Tenant Convention Begins Dec. 29," which set out plans for the fifth annual convention of the Southern Tenant Farmers' Union to be held at Cotton Plant, Ark. on 12-29-37. Roy Wilkins, Editor of "Crisis" magazine and Associate Secretary of the NAACP, was listed among the nationally known leaders expected to attend the convention.

Reference described above
61-7563-69X67 "DW", 12-27-38
(21)

Photostat of correspondence,
described above.   b7C

Re: Institute of Pacific
Relations-
Owen Lattimore
IS-C
100-64700-271, p.1984
(31)

SECRET

The "Daily Worker" on 2-11-39 contained an article
entitled, "Alliance Weighs Relief March To Washington." The
article was an account of the opening session of the First
State Convention of the Worker Alliance held at Center Hotel,
NYC. Roy Wilkins, Director of the NAACP, was listed among
those who spoke at the meeting.

61-7551-161X11 "DW", 2-11-39
(20)

b7D

Report of _____ enclosing the
6-3-39 issue of the "Amsterdam
News"
61-7565-1566
(21)

b

SECRET

This reference was miscellaneous material relating to the Spanish Refugee Relief Campaign received from an unidentified source. Included in the material was a release dated 1-13-40, containing a statement by the officers of the Spanish Refugee Relief Campaign. Roy Wilkins was listed in the release as a member of the Board.

61-7561-471X1
(20)

On 11-18-41, Walter White, Secretary of the NAACP, wrote to the Director enclosing a statement relating to Civil Rights cases which he referred to as, the "Brownsville, Tennessee case of 1939" and "the Porter Case in Texas in 1938." The statement contained data outlining, in detail, the NAACP's participation in the cases. The statement regarding the Brownsville, Tennessee case indicated that on 7-19-40, Roy Wilkins telegraphed President Roosevelt appealing for action in the case.

Reference described above
44-359-27
(16)

SECRET

The 1941 Annual Report of the NAACP listed Roy
Wilkins as Assistant Secretary and Editor of the "Crisis"
in 1942. The report also indicated that in 1941 Wilkins
had attended 60 meetings and had addressed 23 meetings in
schools, churches, forums, etc. (No evaluation)

MID rpt., 12-19-42
101-3307-16X encl. memo E.
(36)

CONFIDENTIAL

The "Daily Worker" on 4-14-41 carried an article
entitled: "Rap Annapolis Ban on Harvard Negro Athlete." The
article discussed protest made by various groups and individuals
concerning the policy of the U.S. Naval Academy which barred
a Negro star on the Harvard lacrosse team from playing in a
game against the navy. The article quoted a telegram published
in the "Harvard Crimson" which was sent by Roy Wilkins, Assistant
Secretary of the NAACP, condemning the Navy policy.

61-7497-A "DW," 4-14-41
(20)

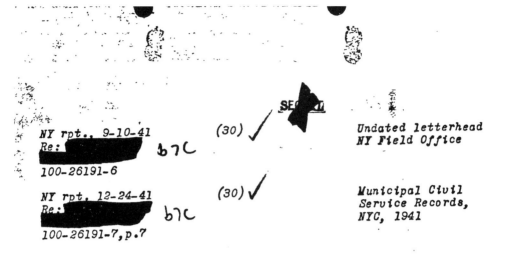

NY rpt., 9-10-41
Re: ██████████ b7C
100-26191-6

(30) ✓

Undated letterhead
NY Field Office

NY rpt. 12-24-41
Re: ██████████ b7C
100-26191-7, p.7

(30) ✓

Municipal Civil
Service Records,
NYC, 1941

    An index of the officers and sponsors of the
International Juridical Association, prepared by the New York
Field Office, contained the following information regarding
Roy Wilkins: "Editor "Crisis", 69 5th Ave., Sponsor 1941
Spanish Refugee Relief Campaign; member, NAACP; is listed on
names and address of American Peoples Mobilization."

NY rpt., 2-11-42
Re: International Juridical
Association;
IS-C
100-25836-14, p.13
(30) ✓

List set out in
NY rpt. 10-23-41 (NY 100-7629)
Re: The NAACP
IS-C
61-3176-18I6
(17)
SI 61-3176-18I5 (List of
officers furnished

(17)

    On 4-1-42 Gloster B. Currant, Executive Secretary
of the NAACP at Detroit, Mich., advised that a committee, known
as the Sojourner Truth Citizens Committee, had been organized
as a result of disputes arising over Negro occupancy of the
Sojourner Truth Housing Project, a Federal Housing Project in
Detroit. He advised that Roy Wilkins, Assistant Secretary of
the NAACP, had come to Detroit from New York City about
3-4-42 and had attended meetings of the Sojourner Truth
Citizens Committee during his visit of a few days.

Detroit rpt., 4-2-42
Re: Sojourner Truth Housing
Project Civil Rights and
Domestic Violence
44-544-23,p.111
(16)

SECRET

According to the 3-5-42 issue of "Sojourner Truth
News"*, Roy Wilkins, Assistant National Secretary of the
NAACP, had pledged full support of the National organization
to the Sojourner Truth Housing Project fight, in progress
at that time in the city of Detroit. It was indicated that
the NAACP had been instrumental in securing the release of
the Negroes who were arrested in connection with the Sojourner
Truth Race Riot on 2-28-42.

Detroit rpt., 3-2-43
Re: ██████████
b7c
100-189566-1, p.8
(33) ✓

*Detroit, Mich.

Detroit rpt., 10-2-42
Re: Civil Rights Federation
IS-C; Espionage
61-10149-122, p.10
(21) ✓
SI 100-189566-5, p.16 ██████ b7D
(33) Copy furnished ██

SECRET

The "Daily Worker" on 7-8-42 contained on page 5,
an article entitled: "Wilkie to Speak at Negro Parley." The
article announced the speakers for the 33rd Annual Conference
of the NAACP in Los Angeles, Calif. It was indicated that
the keynote address on 7-14-42 would be given by Roy Wilkins,
National Assistant Secretary from New York.

61-67??-A "DW", 7-8-42
(20)

The official program of the Thirty-Third Annual
conference of the NAACP, held in Los Angeles, Calif., July
14-19, 1942, contained a list of officers of the organization.
Roy Wilkins was listed as Assistant Secretary and Editor of
the "Crisis."

Roy Wilkins, Assistant Secretary, NAACP, New York,
gave the keynote address at the opening meeting of the NAACP
conference held on Tuesday evening 7-14-42 at the Second
Baptist Church, Los Angeles. Wilkins stated the NAACP would
continue its fight against segregation and discrimination
against Negroes. He declared "We are determined forever to
be through with status quo." Wilkins outlined a number of
the objectives of the organization. (source not given)

Copy of the conference program
enclosed; remarks of Wilkins
quoted in:
LA rpt. 7-27-42
Re: NAACP
IS-R
61-317?-45, pp.2,6,7
(17)
SI as par 2 above
100-135-14 (unidentified report,
dated 7-20-42, re: the NAACP
convention)
(25)

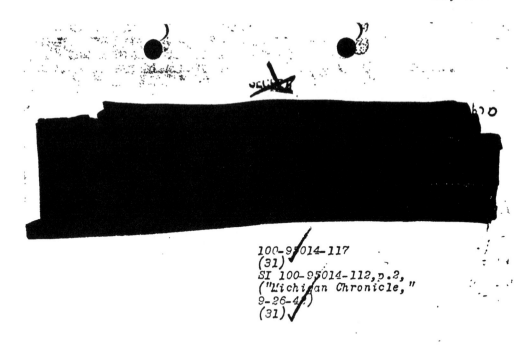

100-95014-117
(31)
SI 100-95014-112,p.2,
("Michigan Chronicle,"
9-26-42)
(31)

An MID report dated 9-9-42 which discussed the Negro
situation in the Kansas City, Mo. area, pointed out that
men like Roy Wilkins of the "Crisis" and columnists for the
"Pittsburgh Courier," the "Chicago Defender" and "Afro-
American," caused racial disturbances by slanting their
stories. According to the report the columnists on the
smaller Negro papers "ape" their style and the editors carry
headlines on derogatory stories involving the Army or Navy.
It was noted that the current (September) issue of the "Crisis"
magazine, official organ of the NAACP was full of Japanese
propaganda.

MID report, 9-9-42
100-135-23-9
(25)

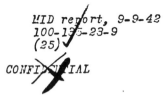

CONFIDENTIAL

SECRET

671

_____ furnished a copy of the "Western Ideal",
Pueblo newspaper, for 11-27-42, which carried an article
entitled: "Roy Wilkins to Speak at Bethlehem Baptist Church
December 9." The article described Wilkins as "Assistant
Secretary of the NAACP and active since the beginning of
America's war effort in seeking wider employment opportunities
for Negroes and better treatment for Negroes in the Armed
Services." It was noted that on the day after Pearl Harbor,
Wilkins was one of twenty Negroes who conferred with officials
of the War Dept. in Washington upon the general policies of
the Department for the use of Negro soldiers and upon the
morale of Negro Americans.

67D

_____ he attended the meeting addressed by Wilkins
and his speech had been in no way subversive or un-American.
He stated Wilkins discussed the anti-poll tax bill and argued
against discrimination against Negro workers but had not
expounded any communist theories.

_____ attended the meeting
which Wilkins addressed and furnished information identical
with that given by _____

67D

67C

Re: Foreign Inspired Agitation
Among the American Negroes in
the Denver Field Division;
Internal Security
100-135-13-4
(25)

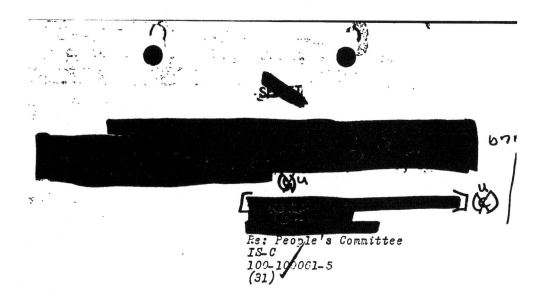

Re: People's Committee
IS-C
100-100061-5
(31)

According to a news item in the "Washington Afro-American" on 2-13-43, on page 1, datelined New York, Feb. 11, Roy Wilkins, Assistant Secretary of the NAACP, had sent a letter to Secretary of War Stimson protesting the exclusive use of Negro troops from Fort Lewis for cleaning snow in downtown Seattle, Washington.

Dept. of Justice memo, 3-2-43
enclosing memo covering the
Negro Press, Feb. 7-13, 1943
100-135-114, encl.
(25)

Re: People's Committee
IS-C
100-100061-5
(31)

According to a news item in the "Washington Afro-
American" on 2-13-43, on page 1, datelined New York, Feb. 11,
Roy Wilkins, Assistant Secretary of the NAACP, had sent a
letter to Secretary of War Stimson protesting the exclusive
use of Negro troops from Fort Lewis for cleaning snow in
downtown Seattle, Washington.

Dept. of Justice memo, 3-2-43
enclosing memo covering the
Negro Press, Feb. 7-13, 1943
100-135-114, encl.
(25)

SECR

SECRET

The "Daily Worker" on 3-10-43 carried an article
by Eugene Gordon entitled "Southern Sheriff Lies - Burrows
Faces Lynch Mob." The article quoted remarks made by Roy
Wilkins regarding the extradition of George A. Burrows from
New York to Mississippi. Wilkins expressed the opinion that
NAACP lawyers, who were supporting Burrows, believed that
Burrows would be lynched if he was returned to Mississippi.

100-136-A "DW" 3-10-43
(27)

Roy Wilkins was listed as Assistant Secretary
of the NAACP, in the files of G-2 as of 3-10-43.

MID rpt., 5-3-43
100-174487-4
(32)

CONFIDENTIAL

SECRET

The Newark Field Division advised in March 1944 that an extensive survey had been conducted by the New York main office of the YWCA on the subject of integration of Negro women into Y.W. work and the method of handling the inter-racial problem. ~~~~~~~~~~~~~~~~~~~~~~~ advised that a young Negro woman by the name of Mary Wilkins, a sister of Roy Wilkins, editor of the NAACP monthly "Crisis," headed the actual survey work.

b70

> Newark letter, 3-10-44
> Re: Foreign Inspired Agitation
> Among the American Negroes in
> the NY Field Division;
> DO-135-31-60
> (26)

The "Baltimore Afro-American" on 3-14-44 page 1, carried an article entitled "NAACP Asks F. D. to End Army, Navy Segregation." The article was datelined New York and discussed a letter signed by Roy Wilkins, acting NAACP Secretary, which had been sent to the President. The letter protested the slurs on colored combat troops made by Secretary of War, Henry L. Stimson, and called upon the President to abolish segregation.

> Excerpts from article quoted
> in
> Baltimore rpt., 3-25-44
> Re: Afro-American Company
> Sedition
> 100-63963-61, p.5
> (30)

SECRET

     This reference was a copy of a portion of an undated report from the New Haven Field Office which was captioned "Negro Activities." According to the report, Roy Wilkins, Assistant Secretary of the NAACP and Editor of the "Crisis," was the main speaker for the membership campaign luncheon rally held by the New Haven, Conn. branch of the NAACP on 4-22-44.

              100-136-32-54
              (26)

advised that Roy Wilkins was the principal speaker on 6-11-44 at the Fifth Annual Meeting of the South Carolina Conference of the NAACP held June 11, 12, 1944 at Sumter, S.C. Wilkins reviewed the history of the Negro, relating how the Negro has always been disregarded as a personality both physically and politically. He stated the day of persecution for the Negro was terminating. He extolled the efforts of the NAACP on behalf of the Negro and criticized political figures of the State of South Carolina for their dogmas on white supremacy. He stressed the fact that the Negro in South Carolina was still practically a slave to the white man. Wilkins emphasized the fact that the Negro did not desire to acquire his lawful rights through revolution but by lawful court procedure.

        (SV 100-3050)
        Re: NAACP
        IS-C
        61-3176-241, pp.1,11
        (17)

SECRET

The 1-20-45 issue of the "New York Age," Negro newspaper, reported that Roy Wilkins of the NAACP, had sent a wire to Chairman Andrew J. May of the Military Affairs Committee, urging that a clause to end discrimination and segregation, be included in proposed legislation for the draft of nurses for military service. Wilkins charged that the War Department policy restricted Negro nurses to nursing Negro soldiers and prisoners of war.

MID Report, Weekly
Intelligence Summary,
January 14-20, 1945
100-7650-2708
(26)

CONFIDENTIAL

advised that Roy Wilkins b and James L. Farmer were the principal speakers for the evening session of the Race Relations Institute on 1-20-45. According to the informant Wilkins spoke on the subject "A Program for Today." Wilkins stated that "America is coming to age on the question of race relations." He also declared "The good neighbor policy does not mean for us to be good to our neighbor but for our neighbor to be good to us."

b7

SECRET

The 1-20-45 issue of the "New York Age," Negro newspaper, reported that Roy Wilkins of the NAACP, had sent a wire to Chairman Andrew J. May of the Military Affairs Committee, urging that a clause to end discrimination and segregation, be included in proposed legislation for the draft of nurses for military service. Wilkins charged that the War Department policy restricted Negro nurses to nursing Negro soldiers and prisoners of war.

MID Report, Weekly
Intelligence Summary,
January 14-20, 1945
100-7650-2708
(28)

CONFIDENTIAL

advised that Roy Wilkins and James L. Farmer were the principal speakers for the evening session of the Race Relations Institute on 1-20-45. According to the informant Wilkins spoke on the subject "A Program for Today." Wilkins stated that "America is coming to age on the question of race relations." He also declared "The good neighbor policy does not mean for us to be good to our neighbor but for our neighbor to be good to us."

SEC[RE]T

b7

Re: Foreign Inspired Agitation
Among the American Negroes in
the Cleveland Field Division;
IS-X
100-135-11-270, pp.6,9
(25)

During the week of Feb. 25 to March 3, 1945, the
Negro press reported that Roy Wilkins, Assistant Secretary of
the NAACP, spoke before members of the Welfare Victory
Committee of Welfare Center 40, 270 Elton Ave., Bronx, N.Y.,
in celebration of Negro History Week (date not given). Wilkins
denounced the treatment of American Negro soldiers in the
South and compared their position with the German and Italian
prisoners of war, who he stated received better treatment
than the Negro soldiers.

MID rpt., Weekly Intelligence
Summary, Feb. 25 - March 3, 1945
100-7560-2787
(28)

CONFIDENTIAL

SECRET

        During the week of May 6-12, 1945, Roy Wilkins of
the NAACP, issued the following statement: "The end of the
war in Europe means that the birthplace of 'Hitler's' and
of racial hatred as a Government policy had been destroyed.
In this destruction, American Negro soldiers, who know what
racial hatred means, have played a valuable and necessary
role, both as combat and service troops. They will press on
with other Americans to the total defeat of Japan, in the
earnest hope that a new world free of racial bigotry, will
be born."   (No evaluation)

                        MID rpt. Weekly Intelligence
                        Summary, May 6-12, 1945
                        100-7860-2979
                        (11)

        According to an ONI report dated 5-31-45, the "Los
Angeles Sentinel" on 5-17-45 carried an article by Roy Wilkins
in which Wilkins made use of minority group propaganda that
had been rather skillfully used in a feature story by Harold
J. Noble in the "Saturday Evening Post." The "Post" article
had appeared under the title, "Give the Devils Their Due"
and Wilkins comments were captioned, "Japan War Must Not
Become 'Race' War." Wilkins stated in the article, "Our
greatest danger lies in our traditional 'white' attitude toward 'colored' people."

                        ONI rpt. 5-31-45
                        105-4822-76, encl. p.2
                        (36)

                CONFIDENTIAL

SECRET

The 7/15/63 issue of "The Plain Dealer," Cleveland daily newspaper, contained an article which revealed that Roy Wilkins was one of the principal speakers at a rally sponsored by the United Freedom Movement (157-933) (UFM) which was held on 7/14/63 at the Cleveland Municipal Stadium in Cleveland, Ohio.

The UFM was reported to be an amalgamation of some thirty organizations interested in desegregation.

157-933-6
(10)
SI 157-933-1 encl. p. 1 (Wilkins
(10)   scheduled to speak according
          to ███████████████████████

b2D

The 7/16/63 issue of the "New York Journal-American" contained an article entitled "The Negro View: 'Now or Never' - Leadership 'Disunity' Grows Graver." This article was the third in a series by Negro author Louis E. Lomax (62-102926) which disclosed the increasing friction among Roy Wilkins, James Farmer and Martin Luther King, leaders of the NAACP, CORE and SCLC, respectively. Who would get the credit for holding mass demonstrations and to whom well-wishers should send their money, were at the root of the "current" crisis. In a speech in Virginia, Wilkins claimed the NAACP was doing all the work and footing the bills while other organizations including CORE and King, were making all the noise and grabbing the headlines. He advised the people not to send money to the CORE and Rev. King but to the NAACP.

62-102926-A "New York Journal
(4)   American" 7/16/63

On 8/22/63 AAG, Burke Marshall, Department of Justice, furnished copies of a telegram dated 7/25/63, and a letter dated 8/14/63, received by the Department from Roy Wilkins, Executive Secretary of the NAACP, regarding the arrest and prosecution of Rev. Harry Blake (44-23130), NAACP Branch President, in Shreveport, La., on c of breach of the peace. Wilkins said that Blake claimed he was warned by the city officials some months before that he would be held respons ible for any demonstrations in Shreveport regardless of whether or not he participated. Wilkins also stated that a warrant was also issued for the arrest of Charles Evers, NAACP Field Secretary for Mississippi because he addressed a public meeting in Shreveport. Wilkins said tha Federal presence and action was badly needed in Shreveport.

(continued on next page)

-9-

Marilyn Monroe

148

Chapter V

Marilyn Monroe:
The It Girl of The 1950's & 60's

Norma Jean Mortensen (also known as Norma Jean Baker) was born on June 1, 1926 in Los Angeles, California. The year of her birth marked the very height of the roaring twenties with its speakeasies, illegal bootleg whiskey, and bathtub gin. Her mother Gladys Monroe Baker Mortensen was an attractive single woman. Gladys was atypical of the Charleston dancing flapper girls of the 1920s at the time she gave birth to Norma Jean. Although the twenties was the (running wild) jazz decade, it was not receptive to women giving birth to bastards. Norma Jean's birth predated DNA testing by seven decades, therefore identifying her father among the several men her mother had been sexually active with eliminated that possibility.

Norma Jean was a big mistake in the life of a philandering and hopeless young woman who chose to put her newborn baby girl in an orphanage two weeks after bringing her into the world. Although her mother held down a full time job as a film cutter at one of the major Hollywood studios Gladys was not considered mentally stable by many of her close friends because shortly before Norma Jean was born, the expecting mother suffered a brief nervous breakdown. To add to her mother's troubles, a crazed neighbor had tried to smother Norma Jean before she was orphanized. Norma Jean's early years were stacked high with a series of nightmarish experiences that included being

tossed around like a basketball from foster homes, guardianships, and orphanages, in addition to being sexually molested by both a female and male guardian. To break the hellish cycle in her life Norma Jean arranged to get married three weeks after her 16th birthday, to a James Dougherty who was five years her senior on June 19, 1942. Dougherty was a patriotic young man who was hellbent on helping to save our imperiled nation following the Japanese bombing of Pearl Harbor on December 7, 1941. The young man joined the Merchant Marines shortly after marrying Miss Baker. He stayed in the service until September, 1945 following the end of World War II. Norma Jean's marriage to Dougherty was a ploy that she used to avoid being thrown back into another series of abysmal orphanage dungeons until she reached maturity at age eighteen.

Norma Jean married James Dougherty after her 16th birthday. He was 21.

While Dougherty was serving in the Merchant Marines, Norma Jean got a job inspecting parachutes at the Radioplane Company (1944-45) in Los Angeles, California. When the Army Signal Corps photographers were assigned the task of taking commercial pictures of female war workers, they zeroed in on Norma Jean in her *"Rosie The Riveter"* overall outfit. These photo shoots were the beginning of the young woman's love affair with the eye of the camera. Cameramen became an integral part of her life's climb up the Hollywood ladder of success. Since there was no room on that ladder for Dougherty she divorced him in 1946.

The Hollywood freelance photographers got their jollies capturing her beauty, her innocence, and her glowing (drugstore-bleached) blond hair. When the 20th Century Fox executives saw the still photographs of this raving young beauty, they immediately arranged for her to have a screen test. After viewing the test, they salivated uncontrollably until they got her signature on a contract in 1946. Following the screen test episode and contract ritual, Norma Jean at the suggestion of a Fox executive, adopted the name Marilyn Monroe in 1946. Ten years later, she legally changed her name because she wanted a moniker that Hollywood could sell. Monroe was her mother's second name.

Marilyn was a sensual tease in front of the camera. Her sexuality, beauty, and her new, moon-shade, dyed blond hair, attributed a great deal to her popularity with both the photographers and filmmakers. She perfected a walk that manipulated her hips and eyes simultaneously. She drove men wild when she peeped through her half closed, baby blue eyes, and spoke in a mellow-pitched voice as she moistened her lips.

In spite of her contract with 20th Century-Fox, roles for Marilyn were not on the front burner. Hence, they did not renew her contract when it expired. The only Fox film she appeared in under the expired contract was a movie of no consequence, entitled *Scudda-Hoo, Scudda-Hay*. Her part consisted of one word, "Hello".

In order for Ms. Monroe to support herself, she engaged in a play for pay game with men that she felt could help her career. High on her list were young eligibles who bore famous names but were one generation removed from the real McCoy to wit: Edward G. Robinson Jr., son of the very famous movie actor, Fred Karger, son of Maxwell Karger who was one of the founders of Metro-Goldwyn-Mayer Studio, and Charlie Chaplin Jr., son of the world class comedian. Chaplin Junior was the same age as Marilyn and his pockets were almost as empty as her purse, in spite of his father's immense wealth.

Young Charlie was so smitten with Marilyn that he would beg, borrow, steal and perhaps die for her. During the first Christmas holidays they spent together, he mysteriously came into a wad of dough with which he purchased a number of expensive stylish dresses to keep his ladylove happy. All went well for the twosome, until Charlie came home early one afternoon and found Marilyn in his brother Sidney's bunk sans Sidney. At that point, their love game vanished like smoke rings in a ventilator although they remained close friends until her death.

Marilyn was at the top of her game when she told stories about how bad life had treated her. Her tall tales about her world got the attention of John Carroll, the movie actor who was very impressed with both her body and her stories. As a matter of fact, the man was so taken with her as a person, he in turn convinced his wife Lucille that they should give this poor little five feet five inch orphan child a hand. His wife, Lucille Ryman, who was casting director for Metro-Goldwyn-Mayer, agreed that they should do something and within a few weeks they were paying Marilyn's room rent and giving her some walking around pocket money.

The arrangement was so comfortable, the Carrolls subsequently let Marilyn move into an apartment that they owned but did not use. Everything was going very smoothly until Marilyn told the Carrolls the story about a man standing on a stepladder and peeping into her bedroom window. Without too much thought, the Carrolls decided that they would put a protective arm around little Marilyn and let her share their oversized apartment.

Soon after Marilyn moved into her benefactor's apartment, John Carroll commenced giving the poor, little pretty girl expensive gifts. Since time was of the essence, Marilyn did not let her bed get too hot before she asked Lucille if she would give her husband a divorce because she could not possibly love him as much as she did. The golden haired one also let Lucille know that she wanted to marry her man. It became self-evident that Lucille accepted the idea of an open triangle affair because the relationship between the three of them became tighter, in that the Carrolls became Marilyn's personal managers. Moreover, Lucille Carroll was singularly instrumental in Marilyn's most important breakthrough in the movies. She got her a small but important role in John Huston's *Asphalt Jungle* in 1950.

After Marilyn strutted her stuff in *Asphalt Jungle,* Twentieth Century Fox re-activated Marilyn's contract at six times her previous salary. She made five pictures that had less than earthshaking consequence in 1953 and 1954, but at the same time those movies propelled her to the head of the box office parade because of the sizzle she brought to the big screen. Sixteen magazines simultaneously selected her as their cover girl. Out of all the hoopla generated by her popularity, a female gossip columnist came up with one juicy bit of gossip: someone had sniffed out the fact that Marilyn had posed in the nude for a calendar. The sale of the calendar vaulted to six million copies worldwide over a period of a few years. "Didn't you have anything on?" quizzed the female writer at the news conference. "Oh! Yes!" Marilyn replied, "I had the radio on."

In December 1953 one of the nude calendar shots was purchased for $500 by a young unknown Chicago boy named Hugh Hefner who had been a former employee of the fashionable Marshall Field's store on State Street, that great street in Chicago. Marilyn's picture graced the pages of the first edition of Hefner's new Playboy magazine. She also appeared, clothed on the Playboy cover. Almost fifty years later, Hugh Hefner can still be heard shouting from the rooftops that she was his first playmate - or sweetheart of the month, and naked as a jaybird center spread.

Joe DiMaggio and Marilyn.

In 1962, a photographer sold, for a record price of $25.00 a second set of Marilyn's nudes to Hugh Hefner, who by this time was the multimillionaire President and CEO of the very successful Playboy magazine. The global sales for the pictures brought a gross dollar amount of more than $500,000.

Marilyn had to work overtime to prove to others that she was not a dizzy, dumb blond broad in a shapely, chiseled shell. She was able from time to time, with proper casting to transcend her negative image. Two good examples, were roles in *Asphalt Jungle* (1950) and *All About Eve* (1950). In those films she worked with two of Hollywood's most lauded directors of the era, namely John Huston and Joseph Mankiewicz. Under their directions, she brought humanity and intelligence to her small roles in those films. She further showcased her dramatic talents in *Clash by Night* (1952), *Don't Bother to Knock* (1952), and *Niagara* (1953). In *Clash by Night* and *Niagara*, Monroe played darker, and more demanding roles. In *Niagara*, as Rose Loomis she was a steamy, two-timing wife, bent on murdering her veteran husband so she could collect his G.I. insurance. In *Don't Bother to Knock,* she portrayed a psychotic babysitter.

On demand, Marilyn's sexuality was frequently played down by wrapping her shapely curves in croker sack. In contrast, she displayed her total sexuality to the 18th hole in the film *Gentlemen Prefer Blonds* (1953), in which

Marilyn standing over a forced air subway grate in New York City.

she played her most famous role as Lorelei Lee, a beautiful but mentally slow - witted gold digger. In the film she sings *Diamonds Are A Girl's Best Friend,* a ditty that became her signature song, the same as it had for actress Carol Channing, who originally played the role in the Broadway production.

Marilyn and Joe DiMaggio (The Yankee Clipper) became public items in June 1952, when she shuffled off from Buffalo, New York as they were in the midst shooting *Niagara.* She joined Joe in the midtown Manhattan section of New York City, where they spent some quiet time and barhopped. The couple went on whirlwind tours of the Manhattan nightclub scene, where the baseball champion showed off his beautiful new trophy to his friends.

Marilyn and Joe got married two years later on January 14, 1954 and got divorced in the ninth month of that year. The straw that broke the camel's back and caused the marriage to dissolve was the dumb blond character that Marilyn portrayed in *The Seven Year Itch.* In this film, she fulfilled the wish of every married man's sexual dreams and every teenage boy's wildest desires. She displayed her own honest and delightful sexuality in the movie as she stood over a subway grate where the forceful cool air lifted her virgin white skirt above her buttocks. (It has been said that Joe physically beat her that night about that scene.) DiMaggio had a love-hate feeling about her career. He loved the idea of other men salivating in solitude over his trophy wife, but at the same time hated any intrusion of their privacy. He was annoyed when anyone asked her for an autograph when they were out on the town dining or drinking in a plush nightclub or restaurant. Marilyn found his mean streak, mean disposition, surly attitude, and his very dirty mind about her attractiveness to other men, a bit too much sugar for a dime.

Marilyn and Arthur Miller, her third husband.

In search of intellectual companionship she latched onto Arthur Miller, the Pulitzer Prize playwright whose works included *Death of a Salesman* (1949) and *The Crucible* (1953). Marilyn married Miller in June, 1956 and divorced him in January, 1961. Between 1956 and 1961 she became a finely tuned political Marilyn Monroe who displayed a sense of morality and astuteness, in that she stood with Arthur Miller when he was being crucified by the House UnAmerican Activites Committee. She risked her reputation and career to combat the committee's unseemly challenges to First Amendment rights in its pursuit of "Communist Corruption" in the arts.

Shortly after Marilyn divorced

Miller, she enrolled herself into a psychiatric clinic in Manhattan. It was assumed that she would receive movie star treatment. Instead, she was pushed around like a welfare person and locked in a padded room with iron bars on the windows to prevent her from breaking out, doing harm to herself, and possibly to others. The crazy scene at this institution caused her to frantically call on Joe DiMaggio for his help in getting her out of that madhouse. He imme-

President John F. Kennedy.

diately responded to her beck and call, got her released and had her transferred to another hospital. She was treated for drug and alcohol addiction, then released when she appeared to have calmed down and seemingly was at peace with the world.

Several weeks thereafter, Marilyn went back to Los Angeles. She purchased a modest house in the Brentwood section of the City of Angels and fell back into the arms of a high roller crowd. This crowd included Frank Sinatra, Dean Martin, Sammy Davis Jr. and Peter Lawford, President John F. Kennedy's brother-in-law. In this group drinking and drugs were at the top of the menu. Joe DiMaggio hated Sinatra and called him a pimp for introducing Marilyn to John F. Kennedy and his brother Robert, both of whom had shared her bed. As a matter of fact, Marilyn played hooky from an important shooting schedule on the *Something's Got To Give* Hollywood lot to appear in Madison Square Garden in New York City and sing Happy Birthday Mr.

Frank Sinatra and Attorney General Robert Kennedy.

President on Kennedy's 45th, which was celebrated on May 19, 1962 although he was born on May 29th 1917 in Brookline, Massachusetts.

When Marilyn Monroe signed her will on January 14, 1961 she had already struck out three husbands, including baseball legend Joe DiMaggio and Pulitzer Prize playwright Arthur Miller. Her first husband was an ordinary Irish stiff named James Dougherty. The magazine pundits had romantically linked Marilyn to both John F. and Robert Kennedy.

None of her three marriages or other liaisons produced any children, but there were reportedly several abortions and miscarriages. The telephone records indicate that Marilyn made several telephone calls to Robert Kennedy's Justice Department office within 48 hours of her death.

Life After The Death of Marilyn

Marilyn Monroe's career was at its lowest ebb at the time of her suicide on August 5, 1962. Her last two films, *Let's Make Love* and *The Misfits* were written by her former husband Arthur Miller and co-starred Clark Gable shortly before his own death. Both films were commercial failures. Monroe had been dismissed because of her unpredictable behavior and excessive absence from the set of *Something's Got to Give* two months before her death.

There is written documentation that both Monroe's mother and grandmother were committed to mental institutions during their lives. Article Five of Monroe's Will established a $100,000 trust for "the maintenance and support of my mother, Gladys Baker," and another relative according to Attorney Herbert E. Nass Esq., book entitled *Wills of the Rich and Famous.*

The remaining portion of that trust and 25 percent of the residuary estate is left to Monroe's psychotherapist, Dr. Marianne Kris, "to be used by her for the furtherance of the work of such psychiatric institutions or groups as she shall elect." When Dr. Kris died in 1980, she left her share of the Monroe estate to an institution that subsequently became the London-based Anna Freud Center for the Psychoanalytic Study and Treatment of Children.

The largest portion of Marilyn Monroe's estate was left to the man she seemed to revere the most shortly before her death, legendary "method" acting teacher Lee Strasberg. Monroe displays her trust and faith in Strasberg by the following bequest of her personal property:

I give and bequeath of all my personal effects and clothing to Lee Strasberg, or if he should predecease me, then to my Executor hereinafter named, it being my desire that he distribute these, in sole discretion among my friends, colleagues and those to whom I am devoted.

Monroe's own devotion to Strasberg is evident from her substantial gift of "the entire remaining balance," or 75 percent, of her estate that Strasberg received under the following residuary clause of her will:

All the rest, residue and remainder of my estate… I give, devise and bequeath as follows:

(a)   to May Reis the sum of $40,000.00 or 25% of the total remainder of my estate, whichever shall be the lesser.

(b)   to Dr. Marianne Kris 25% of the balance thereof, to be used by her as set forth in Article Five (d) of this my Last Will and Testament.

(c)   to Lee Strasberg the entire remaining balance.

It has been reported that the Monroe estate is continuing to earn income in excess of $1 million over twenty-five years after her death, through the licensing of her image on selected products and through film royalties. When Strasberg himself died in 1982, his share of the Monroe estate passed under his will to his surviving widow, Anna Strasberg. Strasberg had married Anna in 1968, six years after the death of Monroe.

As the primary beneficiary of the Monroe estate, Anna was recently named the administrator of it after the death of Monroe's named executor and the draftsman of her Will, Attorney Aaron R. Frosch. One has to wonder whether

Marilyn would truly have wanted her estate to pass to Strasberg's widow or the Anna Freud Center in London. But in the end, Monroe may not have had anyone else whom she wanted to have it.

Monroe's body was finally laid to rest in the "Corridor of Memories" in the Westwood Village, California, Memorial Park Cemetery. According to employees of that cemetery, Monroe's ex-husband Joe DiMaggio placed red roses on Monroe's crypt for many years after her death. However, despite persistent rumors, the unoccupied crypt right next to the one in which Monroe was laid is not owned in the name of Joe DiMaggio and may be available for purchase from the owner at a cost of over $50,000. For that price, one can lie next to the immortal remains of the most illustrious sex goddess of our time for an eternity. That is much longer than any of Monroe's ex-husbands made it.

In 1999 Hugh Hefner announced in a television documentary that he had purchased the crypt next to the one in which Marilyn Monroe was laid. According to Attorney Morris Engelberg, who was at Joe DiMaggio's bedside when he died on March 8, 1999, the "Yankee Clipper's" last words were: 'I'll finally see Marilyn.'

Federal Bureau of Investigation

Freedom of Information/Privacy Acts Section

Subject: Marilyn Monroe

U. DEPARTMENT OF JUSTICE

FEDERAL BUREAU
OF
INVESTIGATION

HEADQUARTERS

Marilyn Moore

FBIHQ INVESTIGATIVE AND ADMINISTRATIVE FILES

105-40018-1

Transfer - Call 3421

M. A. Jones to DeLoach memo
RE: "PHOTOPLAY" ARTICLE CONCERNING MARILYN MONROE'S DEATH

The article alleges the affair between this man and Miss Monroe began during the "worst time of her life and the best time of his." The alleged man was celebrating his good fortune in reaching a height in his career "he never before dreamed" would be possible. The remainder of the article allegedly outlines the end of the romance and Miss Monroe's final efforts to renew the relationship. The article states that she telephoned the man on Sunday night, August 5, 1962, and when he said he would not leave his wife and could not see Miss Monroe "any more," she swallowed a "handful" of sleeping pills. The article claims she later called the man again, implying that she told him of having taken the pills, only to have him hang up on her and states that the last sound she heard was the "buzzing of the receiver in her hand " after the man broke the telephone connection.

The article states that Miss Monroe's housekeeper has "vanished" and that her publicity agent, Pat Newcombe, is now working in Washington, D. C. It says her second husband, Joe DiMaggio, is the only one who remains faithful and that the man who killed Miss Monroe is still at large and can never be arrested. But, the article asserts, "Wherever he goes, whatever he touches, whomever he sees; he thinks of Marilyn. His guilt never leaves him, his fear has become his friend."

RECOMMENDATION:

For information.

V

- 2 -

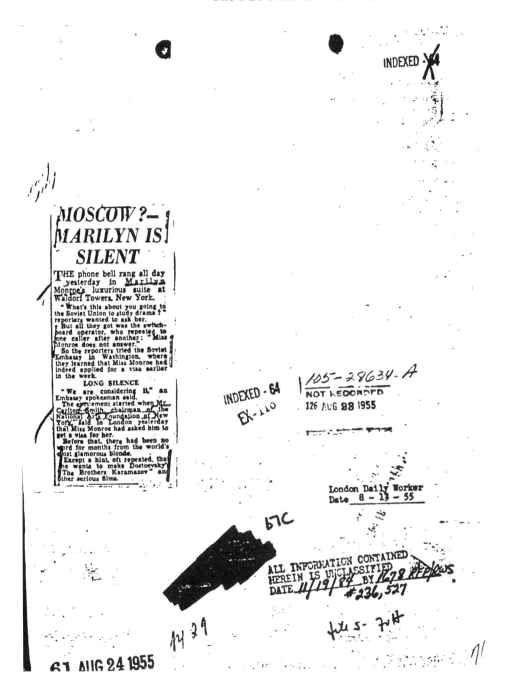

INDEXED - 64

**MOSCOW ?—
MARILYN IS
SILENT**

THE phone bell rang all day
yesterday in Marilyn
Monroe's luxurious suite at
Waldorf Towers, New York.

"What's this about you going to
the Soviet Union to study drama?"
reporters wanted to ask her.

But all they got was the switch-
board operator, who repeated to
one caller after another: "Miss
Monroe does not answer."

So the reporters tried the Soviet
Embassy in Washington, where
they learned that Miss Monroe had
indeed applied for a visa earlier
in the week.

LONG SILENCE

"We are considering it," an
Embassy spokesman said.

The excitement started when Mr.
Carlton Smith, chairman of the
National Arts Foundation of New
York, said in London yesterday
that Miss Monroe had asked him to
get a visa for her.

Before that, there had been no
word for months from the world's
most glamorous blonde.

Except a hint, oft repeated, that
she wants to make Dostoevsky's
"The Brothers Karamazov" and
other serious films.

INDEXED - 64
EX-110

105-28634-A
NOT RECORDED
126 AUG 28 1955

London Daily Worker
Date 8 - 13 - 55

67C

ALL INFORMATION CONTAINED
HEREIN IS UNCLASSIFIED
DATE 4/19/89 BY 1278 REP/ows
#236,527

file s- 7vH

61 AUG 24 1955

Office Mem*um* • UNITED STA* *)VERNMENT

DATE July 2, 1956

TO : L. V. Boardman

FROM : A. H. Be*

SUBJECT: WALTER WINCHELL'S BROADCAST
July 1, 1956

cc Mr. Nichols
cc Mr. Boardman
cc Mr. Belmont
cc Mr. Rosen
cc Mr. Branigan
cc Mr. Bland
cc Mr. Baumgardner
cc Mr. Cromer

Winchell's broadcast was not carried locally on station WWDC due to the broadcast of a baseball game. The following items of interest to the Bureau in Winchell's broadcast off above date were obtained from the New York Office.

WINCHELL SAID:

Playwright Arthur Miller, husband of Marilyn Monroe, refused to disclose names of comrades with whom he once attended Red front meetings. Committee will astonish Miller by telling him those nine names.

COMMENT:

Miller was under communist discipline in the 1930s and was a CP member in 1943, 1946, and 1947. He has been a member of or connected with a number of CP front organizations. Miller testified before HCUA on 6/21/56, and admitted having attended meetings in 1939 or 1940 which he understood were meetings of CP writers, however Miller refused to furnish any names. Miller also admitted having contributed to communist fronts.

WINCHELL SAID:

International news, London – "Time and Tide," British publication, had a remarkable scoop. "Now that the cruel ways of Joe Stalin have been abandoned we hope that Mrs. Khruschev will be released from Siberia. She was arrested and deported in 1938 by Stalin for whom Mr. Khruschev was carrying out mass purges.

COMMENT:

For information.

RECORDED - 30
INDEXED - 30

62-31615- 986

JUL 6 1956

HC:dlj
(9)

JUL 17 1956

Office Memorandum • UNITED STATES GOVERNMENT

DATE July 2, 1956

TO : L. V. Boardman

FROM : A. H. Belmont

SUBJECT: WALTER WINCHELL'S BROADCAST
July 1, 1956

cc Mr. Nichols
cc Mr. Boardman
cc Mr. Belmont
cc Mr. Rosen
cc Mr. Branigan
cc Mr. Bland
cc Mr. Baumgardner
cc Mr. Croner

Winchell's broadcast was not carried locally on station WWDC due to the broadcast of a baseball game. The following items of interest to the Bureau in Winchell's broadcast off above date were obtained from the New York Office.

WINCHELL SAID:

Playwright Arthur Miller, husband of Marilyn Monroe, refused to disclose names of comrades with whom he once attended Red front meetings. Committee will astonish Miller by telling him those nine names.

COMMENT:

Miller was under communist discipline in the 1930s and was a CP member in 1943, 1946, and 1947. He has been a member of or connected with a number of CP front organizations. Miller testified before HCUA on 6/21/56, and admitted having attended meetings in 1939 or 1940 which he understood were meetings of CP writers, however Miller refused to furnish any names. Miller also admitted having contributed to communist fronts.

WINCHELL SAID:

International news, London — "Time and Tide," British publication, had a remarkable scoop. "Now that the cruel ways of Joe Stalin have been abandoned we hope that Mrs. Khruschev will be released from Siberia. She was arrested and deported in 1938 by Stalin for whom Mr. Khruschev was carrying out mass purges.

COMMENT:

For information.

RECORDED - 30   62-31615- 986

INDEXED-30

JUL 6 1956

JUL 17 1956

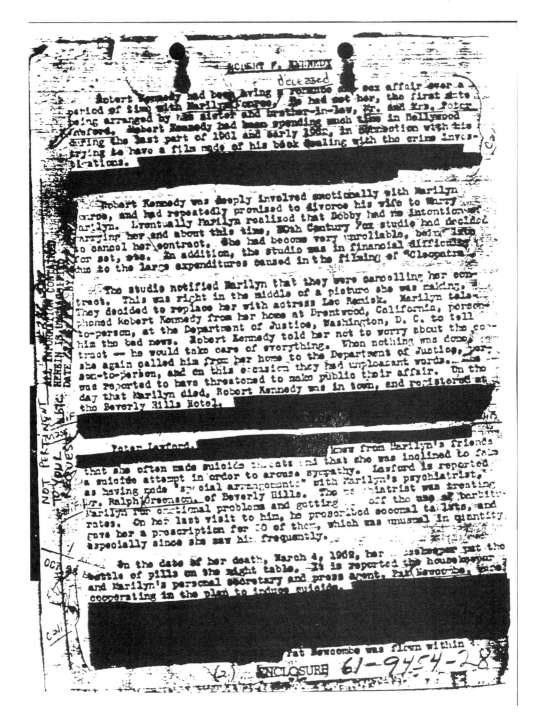

ROBERT F. KENNEDY

deceased

Robert Kennedy had been having ~~romance and~~ sex affair over a period of time with Marilyn Monroe. He had met her, the first date being arranged by his sister and brother-in-law, Mr. and Mrs. Peter Lawford. Robert Kennedy had been spending much time in Hollywood during the last part of 1961 and early 1962, in connection with his trying to have a film made of his book dealing with the crime investigations.

Robert Kennedy was deeply involved emotionally with Marilyn Monroe, and had repeatedly promised to divorce his wife to marry Marilyn. Eventually Marilyn realized that Bobby had no intention of marrying her and about this time, 20th Century Fox studio had decided to cancel her contract. She had become very unreliable, being late or not, etc. In addition, the studio was in financial difficulties due to the large expenditures caused in the filming of "Cleopatra".

The studio notified Marilyn that they were cancelling her contract. This was right in the middle of a picture she was making. They decided to replace her with actress Lee Remick. Marilyn telephoned Robert Kennedy from her home at Brentwood, California, person-to-person, at the Department of Justice, Washington, D. C. to tell him the bad news. Robert Kennedy told her not to worry about the contract -- he would take care of everything. When nothing was done, she again called him from her home to the Department of Justice, person-to-person, and on this occasion they had unpleasant words. She was reported to have threatened to make public their affair. On the day that Marilyn died, Robert Kennedy was in town, and registered at the Beverly Hills Hotel.

Peter Lawford, ... knew from Marilyn's friends that she often made suicide threats and that she was inclined to fake a suicide attempt in order to arouse sympathy. Lawford is reported as having made "special arrangements" with Marilyn's psychiatrist, Dr. Ralph Greenson of Beverly Hills. The psychiatrist was treating Marilyn for emotional problems and getting ... off the use of barbiturates. On her last visit to him, he prescribed seconal tablets, and gave her a prescription for 60 of them, which was unusual in quantity especially since she saw him frequently.

On the date of her death, March 4, 1962, her ... housekeeper put the bottle of pills on the night table. It is reported the housekeeper and Marilyn's personal secretary and press agent, Pat Newcombe, were cooperating in the plan to induce suicide.

Pat Newcombe was flown within 4 ....

(2) ENCLOSURE 61-9454-28

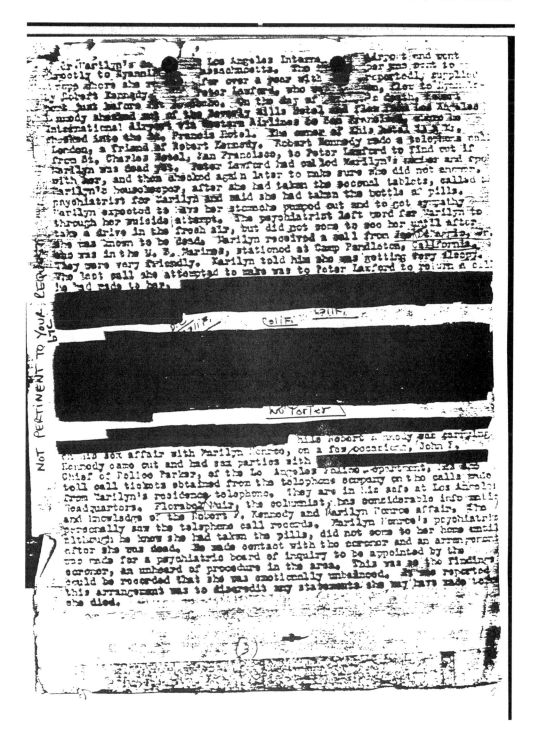

Dr. Marilyn's [...] Los Angeles Interna[...] Airport and went directly to Hyannis[...] Massachusetts. The [...] per was sent to [...] stay where she re[...] for over a year with [...] reportedly supplied by Robert Kennedy. [...] Peter Lawford, who w[...] son, flew to Hyannis Port just before her de[...]ho. On the day of [...]'s death, Robert Kennedy checked out of the Beverly Hills Hotel and flew from Los Angeles international airport via Western Airlines to San Francisco where he checked into the St. Francis Hotel. The owner of this hotel, U.S. X. Lorden, a friend of Robert Kennedy. Robert Kennedy made a telephone call from St. Charles Hotel, San Francisco, to Peter Lawford to find out if Marilyn was dead yet. Peter Lawford had called Marilyn's mother and spo[...] with her, and then checked again later to make sure she did not answer. Marilyn's housekeeper, after she had taken the second tablets, called a psychiatrist for Marilyn and said she had taken the bottle of pills. Marilyn expected to have her stomach pumped out and to get sympathy through her suicide attempt. The psychiatrist left word for Marilyn to take a drive in the fresh air, but did not come to see her until after she was known to be dead. Marilyn received a call from [...]ric, Jr. who was in the U. S. Marines, stationed at Camp Pendleton, California. They were very friendly. Marilyn told him she was getting very sleepy. The last call she attempted to make was to Peter Lawford to return a call he had made to her.

[...] Robert Kennedy was carrying on his sex affair with Marilyn Monroe, on a few occasions, John F. Kennedy came out and had sex parties with [...] Chief of Police Parker, of the Los Angeles Police Department, [...] toll call tickets obtained from the telephone company on the calls made from Marilyn's residence telephone. They are in his safe at Los Angeles headquarters. Florabel Muir, the columnist, has considerable information and knowledge of the Robert F. Kennedy and Marilyn Monroe affair. She personally saw the telephone call records. Marilyn Monroe's psychiatrist, although he knew she had taken the pills, did not come to her home until after she was dead. He made contact with the coroner and an arrangement was made for a psychiatric board of inquiry to be appointed by the coroner, an unheard of procedure in the area. This was so the finding could be recorded that she was emotionally unbalanced. It was reported this arrangement was to discredit any statements she may have made told she died.

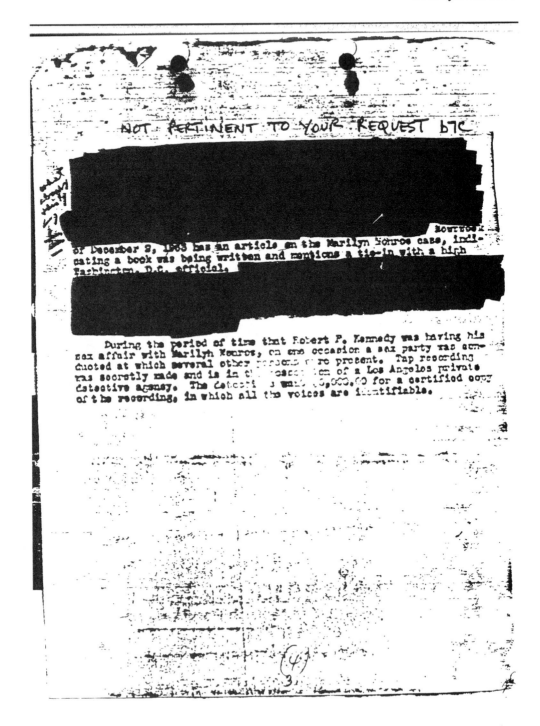

NOT PERTINENT TO YOUR REQUEST b7C

of December 3, 1963 has an article on the Marilyn Monroe case, indicating a book was being written and mentions a tie-in with a high Washington, D.C. official.

During the period of time that Robert F. Kennedy was having his sex affair with Marilyn Monroe, on one occasion a sex party was conducted at which several other persons were present. Tap recording was secretly made and is in the possession of a Los Angeles private detective agency. The detective wants $5,000.00 for a certified copy of the recording, in which all the voices are identifiable.

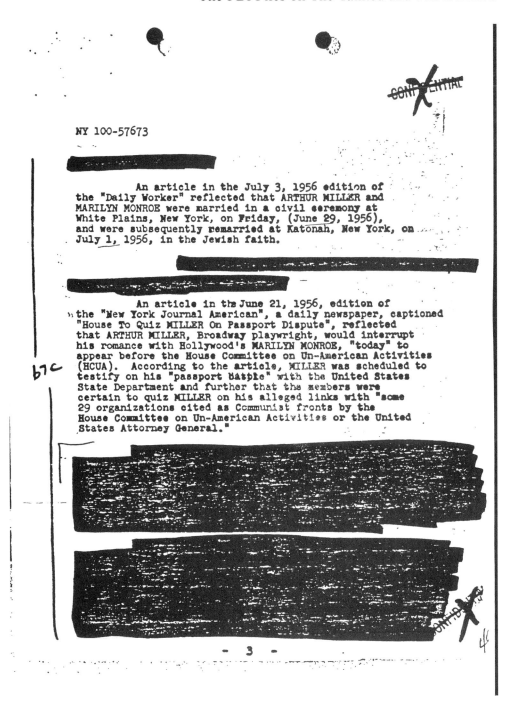

NY 100-57673

An article in the July 3, 1956 edition of the "Daily Worker" reflected that ARTHUR MILLER and MARILYN MONROE were married in a civil ceremony at White Plains, New York, on Friday, (June 29, 1956), and were subsequently remarried at Katonah, New York, on July 1, 1956, in the Jewish faith.

An article in the June 21, 1956, edition of the "New York Journal American", a daily newspaper, captioned "House To Quiz MILLER On Passport Dispute", reflected that ARTHUR MILLER, Broadway playwright, would interrupt his romance with Hollywood's MARILYN MONROE, "today" to appear before the House Committee on Un-American Activities (HCUA). According to the article, MILLER was scheduled to testify on his "passport battle" with the United States State Department and further that the members were certain to quiz MILLER on his alleged links with "some 29 organizations cited as Communist fronts by the House Committee on Un-American Activities or the United States Attorney General."

b7c

- 3 -

NY 100-57673

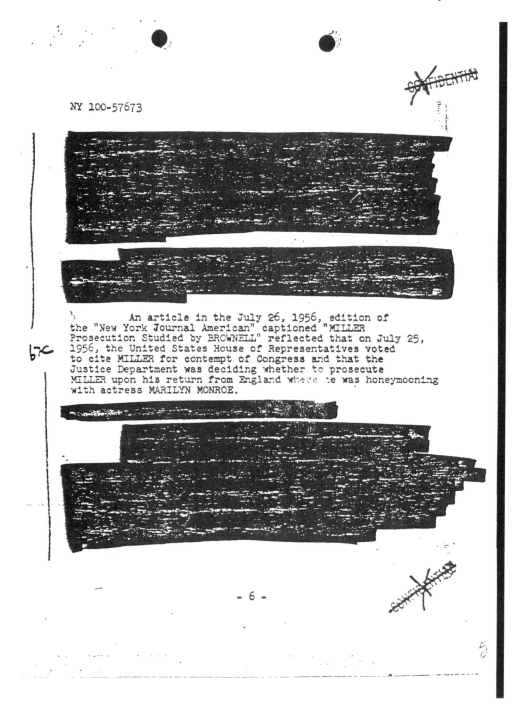

An article in the July 26, 1956, edition of
the "New York Journal American" captioned "MILLER
Prosecution Studied by BROWNELL" reflected that on July 25,
1956, the United States House of Representatives voted
to cite MILLER for contempt of Congress and that the
Justice Department was deciding whether to prosecute
MILLER upon his return from England where he was honeymooning
with actress MARILYN MONROE.

- 6 -

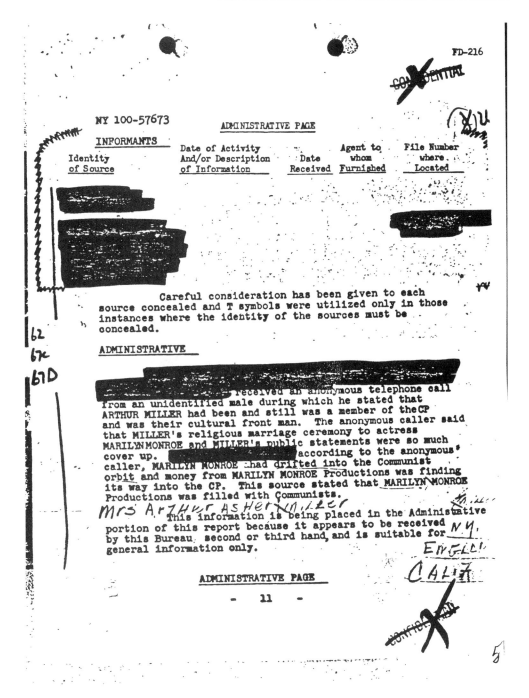

FD-216

CONFIDENTIAL

NY 100-57673

ADMINISTRATIVE PAGE

INFORMANTS

Identity of Source	Date of Activity And/or Description of Information	Date Received	Agent to whom Furnished	File Number where Located

Careful consideration has been given to each source concealed and T symbols were utilized only in those instances where the identity of the sources must be concealed.

ADMINISTRATIVE

received an anonymous telephone call from an unidentified male during which he stated that ARTHUR MILLER had been and still was a member of the CP and was their cultural front man. The anonymous caller said that MILLER's religious marriage ceremony to actress MARILYN MONROE and MILLER's public statements were so much cover up. according to the anonymous caller, MARILYN MONROE had drifted into the Communist orbit and money from MARILYN MONROE Productions was finding its way into the CP. This source stated that MARILYN MONROE Productions was filled with Communists.

Mrs Arthur Asher Miller

This information is being placed in the Administrative portion of this report because it appears to be received by this Bureau second or third hand, and is suitable for general information only.

N.Y.

ENGLL

CALIF

ADMINISTRATIVE PAGE

- 11 -

Sammy Davis Junior
172

Chapter VI

Sammy Davis Junior: Danced Before The Gods

The "Candy Man" was born in a typical 5 story, red brick tenement on Eighth Avenue at 140th Street Harlem in the uptown section of New York City on December 8, 1925. His father Sammy Davis Sr. was a professional Negro buck dancer. His mother Elvera "Baby" Sanchez, a native of Puerto Rico, was an ebony-tinged complexioned, front line chorus girl who was not light skinned enough to qualify for a gig with the top flight, leggy mulatto Cotton Club chorus line. Little Sammy celebrated his first birthday in a specially-made crib in a small, closet size dressing room at New York's famous Hippodrome Theater, where his father and his adopted uncle Will Mastin were performing.

Sammy Davis Jr. first hit the road as a professional dancer at age three, performing with his father in a Will Mastin traveling vaudeville road show production. At the age of seven, the kid was billed as "Silent Sam, the Dancing Midget" in a stage show entitled *Struttin Hannah From Savannah*. In 1933, during the heart of the United States' deepest economic depression, the eight year old made his film debut in a movie short which was entitled *Rufus Jones for President*, featuring the very popular stage and cabaret singer Ethel "Stormy Weather" Waters.

Although young Sammy never had the benefit of a formal public school education, he had an ear for the language, which is evident by his diction in singing such 1930s standards as, *I Will Be Glad When You Are Dead You Rascal You, Chinatown, My Chinatown* and *Lazybones,* in addition to other popular songs of that period. On the other hand, his father was able to route the truant officers away from their backstage dressing room door during the boy's preteen-age years, by falsely claiming that Sammy had a private tutor.

In 1942, Sammy Davis Jr. was drafted into Uncle Sam's Army at age 18 where he entertained World War II troops in camps that stretched across the depth and breadth of the 48 states. In the military service he was slowly weaned from comic books while following an informal, private, remedial reading course given him by a friendly, Black master sergeant. At the same time he was battling racist taunts and insults from whites G.I.s stationed with him at Fort Francis E. Warren, an infantry basic training center in Cheyenne, Wyoming. It was in that almost zero Negro populated state, that his nose was broken when several bigoted white recruits jumped on him and beat him about the face and body until he looked like he had been in a fight with a gorilla. The bloody hurt had been inflicted on Sammy because he had been seen talking to a tall, statuesque, attractive, white WAC officer. The conversation between the female captain and Davis had been about his desire to transfer from his duties as an infantry grunt to the Special Service Branch of the Army for entertainers. No persons other than some dyed-in-the-wool Negro haters would be given a Good Conduct Medal for beating up a diminutive, five feet six, 120 pound, impish looking kid like Sammy Davis Jr.

In addition to beating up the pint size teenager and breaking his nose they ripped off his G.I. fatigues, and painted his bronze, naked body white and then wrote in bold, black letters, the words "Nigger" and "Coon" on the cheeks of his left and right buttocks.

Davis knew that he could not physically beat the racist, white G.I.s, therefore he decided to take them on with a mind game and his showmanship skills. While doing his act, he noted that he had neutralized some of those KKK thugs robed in Army uniforms, in that they were jumping, hollering, and screaming with joy during his performance.

When the young World War II veteran was discharged from the Army in August, 1945, following the Japanese Army's surrender to General Douglas MacArthur in the Pacific Theater of War, Sammy rejoined his father and his adopted uncle Will Mastin.

The first big time break for the Will Mastin Trio came in the Windy City when the Wesson brothers suggested to Mickey *"Andy Hardy"* Rooney, that the unknown Will Mastin Trio would be dynamite as an opening act. The trio was hired, sight unseen and opened the show for Mickey at the Oriental Theater on Randolph near State Street in the downtown section of Chicago, Illinois. They actually performed up and beyond the Wessons' recommendation.

Frank Sinatra and Sammy Davis, Jr. backstage at The Capitol Theater in New York City.

Sammy was thrilled from the crown of his head to the soles of his feet about the opportunity to work on the show with the talented Mickey Rooney for a net five hundred dollars a week. He was so impressed with Mickey, the star of the very popular 1930s *"Andy Hardy"* movie series, he stood in awe in the wings of the stage watching his every move in each of the six shows a day for the entire seven day gig.

The very multi-talented Rooney could do everything: sing, dance do impressions, play drums, trumpet, and act. He could perform vignettes that would break you up in laughter or provoke you into tearing. Mickey Rooney was the performer's performer that Sammy Davis Jr. admired the most. Show after show, Sammy watched as Mickey twisted his audience around his index finger with his excessive energy and talent .

The Will Mastin Trio's next big break came in May, 1947, when Frank Sinatra was contracted to headline a show at the Capitol Theater in New York City. Sidney Fairmont, the theater manager wanted to hire the internationally famous Nicholas Brothers, because they were the undisputed, hottest dance act in show business or in the movies. In spite of the Nicholas Brothers' fame, Sinatra insisted on booking an up and coming dance act known as the Will Mastin Trio. He was fascinated by the young talented fellow who worked with the trio. He could not recall Sammy Davis Jr.'s name, but he remembered seeing him perform, in addition to hearing some mighty good things about him. The trio was hired at a salary of $1,250 per week which was equivalent to $10,000 in the year 2001. As a matter of fact, you could buy a brand name man's suit for $25.00 in 1947.

At the first rehearsal backstage, at the Capitol Theater "The Voice" appeared. Sinatra was super cool when he strolled onto the stage with his top-coat thrown over his left shoulder. He swiveled his head around the perimeter of the stage which was packed with entertainers and hangers-on and said, "Good afternoon everybody". He then walked over to Sammy Jr. who was standing a few feet to his left and said, "My name is Frank Sinatra." Sammy said: "I know. I was the kid in uniform who use to come and see you do your radio show." Frank said, "Wait a minute! Are you the one I used to give the tickets to in Hollywood? You had on an Army uniform. You used to come catch The 'Old Gold Cigarette show." Davis nodded his head in the positive and retorted, "Yes! Sir! I am." Those words marked the beginning of a life-long friendship.

On a later occasion, Sammy Davis Jr. went to the Copacabana Club in New York City to see Sinatra who was performing there and was turned away because he was not wearing the proper skin job. The next afternoon, Sammy dropped a nickel in the phone and told Sinatra how he had been put into a revolving door by the club doorman the night before. On the following night he made another trip to the Copa. This time, he was welcomed with open arms like a long lost brother. From that point forward, Sinata took an interest in Sammy's career and helped him break many of the social barriers. Blacks were confronted daily with racial problems by the bushel from within and outside of the "Black Belt" prior to the Civil Rights campaigns of the 1950s and 60s.

As a result of the Sinatra connection, the Will Mastin Trio, featuring Sammy Davis Jr. was hired in February 1952, as the opening act at Ciro's the reputed home of the movie stars in Hollywood, California. Sammy was able to keep eleven hundred people sitting on the edge of their chairs for almost an hour with his impressions, tap dancing, singing and his ability to display above average proficiency on several musical instruments. Behind that star studded exposure, Sammy Davis Jr. instantly became the talk of the town and shortly thereafter the talk of the nation.

In 1954, he popularized songs like *Hey There, The Birth of the Blues, My Funny Valentine,* and *That Old Black Magic* on Decca Records. In November of that year, he lost his left eye in an automobile accident near San Bernardino, California. For a period of time, he wore a black pirate patch, which was later replaced by his ophthalmologist with a glass eye replica.

In 1956, the very popular Sammy Davis Jr. was selected to play Fletcher Henderson, the great orchestra leader and arranger in a movie entitled *The Benny Goodman Story,* starring Steve Allen, the former T.V. *Tonight Show* host who played Benny Goodman. In the same year, Davis played a character based on his own life in a Broadway production entitled *Mr. Wonderful.* When that show closed in February, 1957, Davis' father and Will Mastin retired.

Shortly thereafter, the very popular Ed Sullivan newspaper columnist and CBS television host extended an invitation for Sammy Davis Jr.'s first national,

Dempsey J. Travis, President of the Chicago Chapter of the NAACP presents Sammy Davis, Jr. with an award. Right is Daddy-O-Daylie.

solo appearance on his Sunday night *Toast of The Town* television variety show.

The activity of Sammy Davis Jr. first surfaced in the FBI files, when he became a fellow traveler on a Freedom Train Rally with Harry Belafonte, the singer, and film star Sidney Poitier, bound for Washington D.C. On May 17, 1957, the three entertainers participated in a program, lobbying for Civil Rights legislation with Dr. Martin Luther King.

The pilgrimage to the capitol marked the third anniversary of the Brown vs. Board of Education Supreme Court decision. A crowd of some thirty thousand people gathered at the Lincoln Memorial for a high-spirited program that lasted for more than three hours. A. Phillip Randolph, the father of the March On Washington Movement, presided and Mahalia Jackson, the first lady of gospel sang. A military helicopter roared overhead as Roy Wilkins, the National Secretary of the National Association for the Advancement of Colored People was speaking, but then instantly vanished when Congressman Adam Clayton Powell spoke. This episode caused some insiders on the platform to joke about the influence Powell had earned by endorsing Eisenhower in the previous election. Most of the other speakers were ministers, such as Dr. Mordecai Johnson, the first Black President of Howard University, William Holmes Borders, and Fred Shuttlesworth, a SCLC (Southern Christian Leadership Conference) board member. The next category of speakers were show business celebrities which included Sammy Davis Jr., Ruby Dee, Sidney Poitier, and Harry Belafonte. Dr. Martin Luther King Jr. made the closing speech that afternoon and put the entire multitude into orbit with his great oratorical skills. When Dr. King bellowed, "Give Us The Ballot" the crowd roared like hometown football fans after a touchdown.

In the following year, on December 16, 1958, a memo was sent to F.B.I. Director J. Edgar Hoover from his agent, Mr. A. Rosen, disclosing that a victory celebration of Governor-elect Edmund G. "Pat" Brown, was held at the Beverly Hilton Hotel in Los Angeles and that Sammy Davis, Jr. and Judy Garland led the entertainers at the victory rally.

When Davis proposed marriage to the shapely Swedish blond actress, Mai Britt in the fall of 1960, J. Edgar Hoover became mentally unhinged. The October 26, 1960 issue of the *Los Angeles Mirror* carried an item captioned, "Mob routs Nazi Group at Davis Show." The article disclosed that four Nazi "Storm Troopers" objected to the forthcoming marriage of caucasian bombshell, Mai Britt and Negro entertainer Sammy Davis, Jr. Therefore, they picketed the theater where Sammy was appearing to make their feelings known;

that is until a counter-integrated mob chased them away.

The *New York Mirror* issue of December 12, 1960, carried a column entitled "*New York Confidential*" by Lee Mortimer. One item in the column commended Sammy Davis Jr., on his show at the Copacabana and his show-

Sammy and Mai Britt, his second wife.

manship and further commented that neither the "Rat Pack" nor Mai Britt were present at his Copa premier. However, a month later on Tuesday January 10, 1961 Mike Wallace interviewed Sammy Davis Jr., and his bride, Mai Britt in the New York CBS Television Studio and briefly discussed their mixed marriage.

Hoover was totally opposed to anything that had the faintest echo of integration. For example, when Sammy Davis Jr. made the following statement at a benefit for the Southern Christian Leadership Conference, indicating that "all races must learn to live together in a peaceful manner," that simple straightforward remark, drew the wrath of FBI Director J. Edgar Hoover. His complexion turned from an ashen gray to a cherry red.

The newly released FBI Freedom of Information Files reveal that Sammy Davis Jr.'s straight from the heart statement was duly entered in the FBI Secret File. The file tagged him as a "Black Nationalist" engaged in questionable activities. His file also revealed that the FBI taped a conversation between Sammy and Dr. Martin Luther King Jr. The tape disclosed that the Civil Rights leader asked Sammy Davis Jr. to organize and participate in a celebrity benefit.

The Los Angeles Times issue of November 17, 1961, contained an article captioned "Entertainers Plan Disarmament Rally." It disclosed that Sammy

Davis Jr. would participate in a demonstration for disarmament, which was organized by a group of Hollywood entertainers and writers under the name Help-Help Establish Lasting Peace. The group planned to hold a rally in front of the Hollywood Palladium in connection with President John F. Kennedy's visit there.

"The Rat Pack"
Left to right: Frank Sinatra, Dean Martin, Sammy Davis, Jr., Peter Lawford and Joey Bishop.

Sammy Davis Jr., was not just an entertainer for the Civil Rights cause, he was a man who believed in putting his money where his mouth was. California Governor Edmond G. Brown sent out invitations for a reception to be held at the home of Burt and Norma Lancaster. A brassy Hollywood lawyer at the reception cut to the chase and announced that it takes $1,000 in hard cash in hand to run the SCLC movement each day. Paul Newman wrote the first $1,000 dollar check, singer Polly Bergen the second, Tony Franciosa the third. Actors John Forsythe and Lloyd Bridges contributed, as did the wife of basketball star Elgin Baylor. Marlon Brando mumbled a warning against "what-we-have-doneism" and bought a week of the movement for $5,000. Sammy Davis Jr., matched the reception total with his own pledge of $20,000. Together with the Wrigley Field contribution of $35,000, the evening brought the SCLC $75,000. Awed by the glitter and money, a *Jet Magazine* reporter who covered the event wrote that "We Shall Overcome" rang out that evening from the Lancasters' Beverly home like the "Wings Over Jordan Choir" on Sunday morning. A $20,000 pledge was peanuts for Sammy Davis Jr., a man who would give millions of dollars to various charitable causes in his lifetime. As a matter of fact, in March, 1990, Sammy Davis Jr., two months before his death, wrote in his Last Will and

Testament the following: I give to Morehouse Teachers College in Atlanta, Georgia one hundred thousand dollars ($100,000) to be used as a scholarship fund. In addition to the scholarship funds, he made bequests of millions of dollars to causes, friends and relatives. However, at the time Sammy Davis Jr. died just two months later on May 16, 1990 it is unclear whether his wife, Altovise received anything (including the house that they lived in) because when her husband made his final transition he was approximately $6,000,000 in debt.

Sammy and his third bride Altovise.

Federal Bureau of Investigation

Freedom of Information/Privacy Acts Section

Subject:Sammy Davis, Jr.

FEDERAL BUREAU OF INVESTIGATION

FREEDOM OF INFORMATION/PRIVACY ACTS SECTION

COVER SHEET

SUBJECT: <u>SAMMY DAVIS, JR.</u>

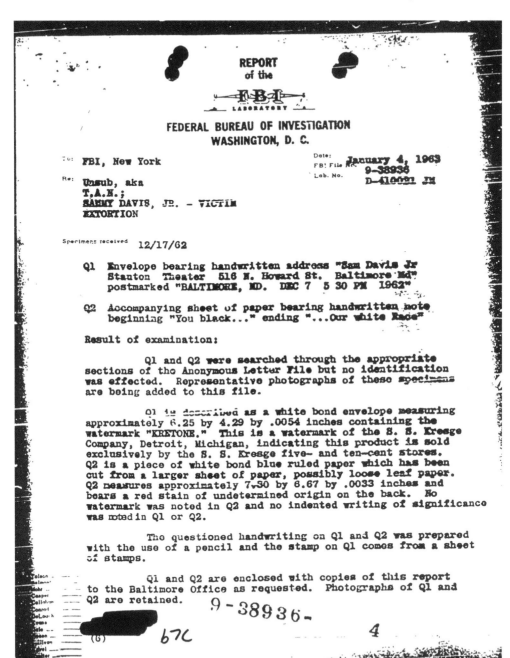

REPORT
of the

FBI
LABORATORY

FEDERAL BUREAU OF INVESTIGATION
WASHINGTON, D. C.

To: FBI, New York

Date: **January 4, 1963**
FBI File No. 9-38936
Lab. No. D-410021 JM

Re: Unsub, aka
T.A.N.;
SAMMY DAVIS, JR. - VICTIM
EXTORTION

Specimens received 12/17/62

Q1 Envelope bearing handwritten address "Sam Davis Jr
Stanton Theater 516 N. Howard St. Baltimore Md"
postmarked "BALTIMORE, MD. DEC 7 5 30 PM 1962"

Q2 Accompanying sheet of paper bearing handwritten note
beginning "You black..." ending "...Our white Race"

Result of examination:

Q1 and Q2 were searched through the appropriate
sections of the Anonymous Letter File but no identification
was effected. Representative photographs of these specimens
are being added to this file.

Q1 is described as a white bond envelope measuring
approximately 6.25 by 4.29 by .0054 inches containing the
watermark "KRETONE." This is a watermark of the S. S. Kresge
Company, Detroit, Michigan, indicating this product is sold
exclusively by the S. S. Kresge five- and ten-cent stores.
Q2 is a piece of white bond blue ruled paper which has been
cut from a larger sheet of paper, possibly loose leaf paper.
Q2 measures approximately 7.30 by 6.67 by .0033 inches and
bears a red stain of undetermined origin on the back. No
watermark was noted in Q2 and no indented writing of significance
was noted in Q1 or Q2.

The questioned handwriting on Q1 and Q2 was prepared
with the use of a pencil and the stamp on Q1 comes from a sheet
of stamps.

Q1 and Q2 are enclosed with copies of this report
to the Baltimore Office as requested. Photographs of Q1 and
Q2 are retained.

9-38936-

67C   4

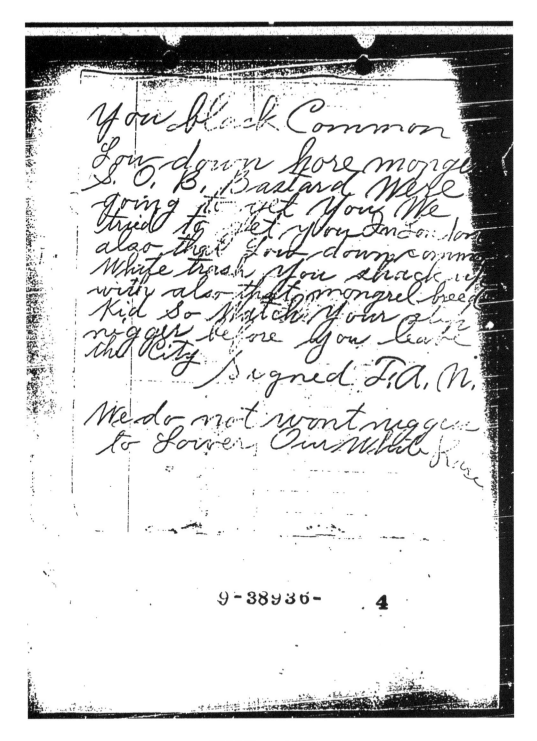

D-36 (Rev. 12-13-56)

FBI

Date: 1/14/63

Transmit the following in _____ PLAIN TEXT
(Type in plain text or code)

Via A I R T E L _____ REGULAR
(Priority or Method of Mailing)

TO: DIRECTOR, FBI (9-38936)

FROM: SAC, BALTIMORE (9-1100)   (P)

SUBJECT: UNSUB; aka T.A.N.
          SAMMIE DAVIS, Jr. - VICTIM
          EXTORTION - RACIAL MATTER
          OO:BALTIMORE

        Re Bureau airtel to New York dated 12/26/62 and Los
Angeles airtel to Director dated 12/27/62.

        New York will submit results of interview with SAMMIE
DAVIS, Jr., currently residing Savoy Hilton Hotel, New York City.
while appearing Copa Cobana until 1/17/63 so that it may be included
in C report being prepared by Baltimore.

9-38936-

109

REC- 13   9- 38936 - 7

17 JAN 15 1963

3 - Bureau   b7C
2 - New York
2 - Baltimore   C. Wick

Approved: _____ Agent in Charge   Sent ___ M ___ Per ___

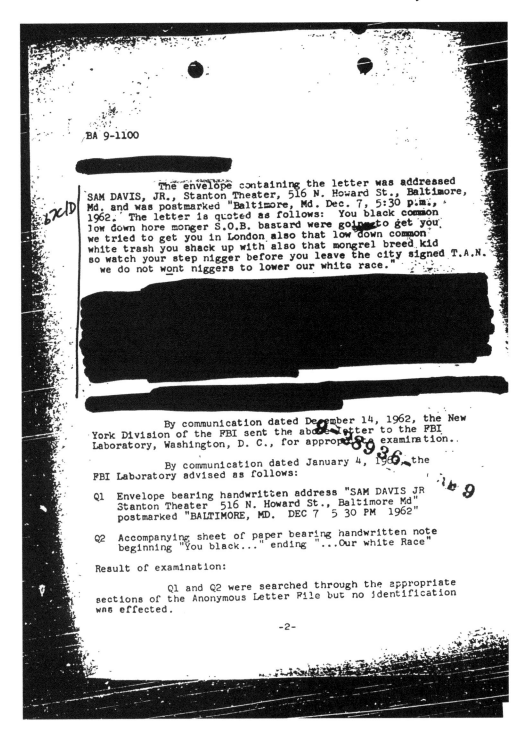

BA 9-1100

The envelope containing the letter was addressed SAM DAVIS, JR., Stanton Theater, 516 N. Howard St., Baltimore, Md. and was postmarked "Baltimore, Md. Dec. 7, 5:30 p.m., 1962. The letter is quoted as follows: You black common low down hore monger S.O.B. bastard were going to get you we tried to get you in London also that low down common white trash you shack up with also that mongrel breed kid so watch your step nigger before you leave the city signed T.A.N. we do not wont niggers to lower our white race."

By communication dated December 14, 1962, the New York Division of the FBI sent the above letter to the FBI Laboratory, Washington, D. C., for appropriate examination.

By communication dated January 4, 1963, the FBI Laboratory advised as follows:

Q1   Envelope bearing handwritten address "SAM DAVIS JR Stanton Theater 516 N. Howard St., Baltimore Md" postmarked "BALTIMORE, MD. DEC 7 5 30 PM 1962"

Q2   Accompanying sheet of paper bearing handwritten note beginning "You black..." ending "...Our white Race"

Result of examination:

Q1 and Q2 were searched through the appropriate sections of the Anonymous Letter File but no identification was effected.

-2-

(Mount Clipping In Space Below)

(Indicate page, name of newspaper, city and state.)

Reveal Sammy Davis Kidnap By Chi Thugs

Sammy Davis Jr. was kidnapped from Las Vegas several years ago by a pair of tough Chicago gangster and quietely released when he was told by them to "forget about any plans you have to wed movie actress Kim Novak" with whom he was carrying on a hot romance at the time.

The snatch of the top entertainer was just disclosed a few days ago following the kidnapping of 19-year-old Frank Sinatra Jr., from a gambling resort at Lake Tahoe in Nevada where he was appearing with members of the late Tommy Dorsey band.

The younger Sinatra's father, Frank, Sr., is one of Davis' closest friends. When he was abducted from his motel room at Harrah's Club in Stateline, Nev., by two men, Frank Jr., was singing with the Dorsey band that features well-known trumpet player Charlie Shavers.

Though it was known by a few of his close associates that he was grabbed by the imported hoods while he was playing at a Las Vegas nite-club, Davis never discussed it at the time and newspapers shied away from the story. A few columnists carried items about the incident but did not identify the principals.

However, Broadway columnist Frank Farrell leaked the news a few days ago that could interest the FBI. It was not known at Courier press time what action the federal authorities might take or whether they would probe into the case.

Reported to be in love with the blonde actress at the time, Davis had planned to wed her.

From a close informant it was learned that a movie contract to play the role of Sporting Life in the "Porgy and Bess" movie had been dangled before him if he forgot about Kim. Even though her friends had told her a marriage with Davis would wreck her career. she elected to ignore them.

As a last resort, "certain people" in show business hit upon the idea of arranging a "friendly kidnapping" with two tough guys with guns to carry it out. This is said to have "shook up" Davis

SAMMY DAVIS JR.
. . They Kidnapped Him, Too

more than many hours of prolonged conversation and caused him to change his mind in a hurry.

Only last week when Davis, Sinatra, Sr., and Dean Martin played a benefit show in Santa Monica, Calif., a death note was left in Davis' dressing room. According to an informed source, this upset him for a while, but his clan friends laughed him out of any fright.

1   CHICAGO COURI
—   CHICAGO, ILLI

Date: 12-21-63
Edition: WEEKLY
Author:
Editor: S. P. FULLE
Title:

Character:
  or
Classification: CHIC.(
Submitting Office: CHIC.(

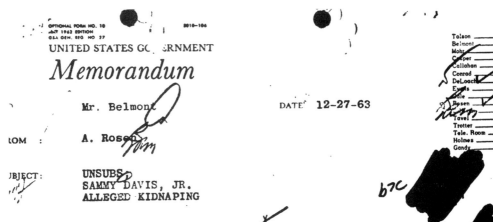

OPTIONAL FORM NO. 10
JULY 1962 EDITION
GSA GEN. REG. NO 27

0010-106

UNITED STATES GOVERNMENT

Memorandum

TO : Mr. Belmont

DATE: 12-27-63

FROM : A. Rosen

SUBJECT: UNSUBS;
SAMMY DAVIS, JR.
ALLEGED KIDNAPING

b7C

Tolson _____
Belmont _____
Mohr _____
Casper _____
Callahan _____
Conrad _____
DeLoach _____
Evans _____
Gale _____
Rosen _____
Tavel _____
Trotter _____
Tele. Room _____
Holmes _____
Gandy _____

This is to advise that the Chicago Courier, a Chicago, Illinois, newspaper on 12-21-63 carried an article alleging that Sammy Davis, Jr., the well-known entertainer and associate of Frank Sinatra, Sr., was kidnaped in Las Vegas several years ago by a pair of tough Chicago gangsters. According to this article, Davis was released when told by his kidnapers to "forget about any plans you have to wed movie actress Kim Novak." The article went on to state that this incident was just disclosed a few days ago following the kidnaping of Frank Sinatra, Jr.

The article states that this incident was known by a few of Sammy Davis, Jr.'s close associates but that Davis did not discuss it at the time. The article alleges that Broadway Columnist Frank Farrell leaked this item a few days ago and that it was not known what action Federal authorities might take in regard to this matter. It is reported that this kidnaping was arranged by certain people in show business as a "friendly kidnaping" to convince Davis not to marry Kim Novak. The article concluded by alleging that a "death note" was left in Davis' dressing room at a benefit show in Santa Monica, California, within the past week.

No information was located in Bureau files concerning the above-mentioned kidnaping or the recent "death note." This story may well be an attempt by Davis to obtain publicity similar to that afforded the Sinatras in the recent kidnaping of Frank Sinatra, Jr.

ACTION RECOMMENDED:

1. In view of the publicity afforded this matter and the likelihood of press inquiry, it is recommended that we interview Sammy Davis, Jr. to determine if this alleged kidnaping or the "death note" recently received by him constitutes a Federal violation. If approved, attached is a teletype instructing our Los Angeles Office to conduct this interview.

REC 27 63- 3475-4

2. This teletype also instructs Los Angeles and Las Vegas to submit any information those Offices may have received concerning this matter.

22 JAN 27 1964 (see addendum page 2)

1 - Mr. DeLoach
Enclosure

Legat, London (100-4528)   September 9, 196[

Director, FBI (157-NEW)   1 - ████████
REC-123 *100-450712-1*   1 - ████████   67C
SAMMY DAVIS, JR.
RACIAL MATTERS - BLACK NATIONALIST

X 109.

      Reurlet 8/14/68, which requested information
concerning any black nationalist activity on the part of
subject ████████████████████████

      Enclosed for Legat, London, are three copies of
a letterhead memorandum (LHM) classified "Confidential"
which contain all the information in Bureau files concerning
black nationalist activity on the part of the subject.
████████████████████████████ You should continue
to keep the Bureau advised of subject's activities relating
to black nationalist matters while he is in England.

Enclosures - 3

1 - Foreign Liaison (Route through for review)

████████ 67C
(6)   ALL INFORMATION CONTAINED   67C
                HEREIN IS UNCLASSIFIED
                DATE ___ BY ___

NOTE: ████████████████████████████████████
██
██   67D
                                                    62

      Information in the attached LHM is contained
in 157-5877-27 and 157-6-34-2417 ████████████████
████████████████████████████████

ENCLOSURE

ALL INFORMATION CONTAINED
HEREIN IS UNCLASSIFIED
DATE _____ BY _____

Sammy Davis Contributes To Black Cultural Center

Sammy Davis, Jr. has become a patron of Chicago's Affro-Arts Theater, the most popular and dynamic Black cultural center in the Midwest.

THE PHARAOHS, a talented group of Black musicians, who both direct and perform in the theater, received a generous gift from Davis recently when they both performed for Black students throughout Chicagoland.

The day started with a performance before an overflow crowd at Marshall High School on the West side. Pretty Patricia Smith, the Pharaohs multi-talented vo-calist who is a Marshall student, welcomed "Golden Boy" and the Pharaohs on behalf of her schoolmates and then proceeded to set the auditorium on fire with a torrid rendition of "Respect."

After the performance, the cast departed and echoes of the Marshall student body's standing ovation had soon set up shop for the Aware Black Students at the University of Illinois' Circle Campus.

It was at this point that Davis, filled with the beauty and power of the Affro-Arts' Pharaohs, presented the group with the very generous donation to aid in the continuation of the theater's vital work in the Black community.

DAVIS ALSO has established a scholarship fund for talented Black youths.

100-450712-A

Bureau memo dated 11/19/56, contained a resume of various items of interest from the Walter Winchell (62-31615) newscast of 11/18/56 and comments related thereto. One item disclosed that the FBI would soon deal with a Miami Beach gangster who had threatened the life of Sammy Davis, Jr. The related comment indicated that the above individual probably referred to ▓▓▓▓▓▓▓▓ of Miami, Fla., and concerned a $7,000 debt which reportedly had been paid by Davis.

no further investigation was contemplated by the Bureau.

62-31615-1013 p.3
(5)

The following reference pertains to ▓▓▓▓▓▓

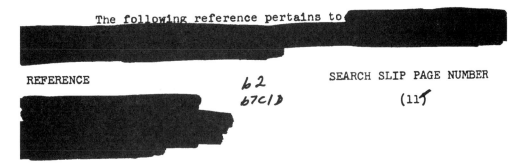

REFERENCE   62   SEARCH SLIP PAGE NUMBER
                   67C/D   (11)

The "Barry Gray" column which appeared in the 5/21/57 issue of the "NY Post" reviewed events of the Pilgrimage for Prayer which was held in Washington, DC, on 5/17/57. The article related that Sammy Davis, Jr., Harry Belafonte and film star Sidney Poitier departed NYC on a special freedom train to attend the ceremonies for civil rights legislation.

The article noted that the Barry Gray show was programmed on WMCA at midnight every night.

62-101087-A "NY Post" 5/21/57
(6)

Bureau memo dated 1/11/58 made reference to ▓▓▓

(continued)

-3-

(continued)

(12)

(6)

"The Southern Patriot," official monthly publication of the SCEF (Southern Conference Educational Fund) (100-10355), published at Nashville, Tenn., issue of December, 1959, carried an article entitled "Noted Californians Supporting SCEF," datelined Los Angeles, Cal. The article disclosed that a group of distinguished Southern California citizens recently sponsored a reception at the home of actor Sammy Davis, Jr., to develop support for SCEF in the area. The guests of honor were Dr. James A. Dombrowski, SCEF executive director, and Bishop Edgar A. Love, SCEF vice-president. (Sponsors of the reception, in addition to Davis, set out.)

100-10355-876 p.34
(10)

Bureau memo dated 4/18/60 made reference to an invitation extended to Mr. W.C. Sullivan to appear on an informal question and answer and general discussion television program of the Columbia Broadcasting System (94-4 sub 925) in Chicago on 4/26/60. ███████ Cunningham and Walsh, Inc., 6 North Michigan Avenue, Chicago, Ill., who extended the invitation, advised that the general subject matter would be "Social Problems of Our Time" and that the other panel members were expected to be ████████████████ of Princeton University; ██████████ movie actress; ████████████ Shakespearean professor, California; ████████████ Michigan; ████████ playwright; and Sammy Davis, Jr., entertainer. The questionable morals of Sammy Davis were called to mind and the invitation was subsequently declined. (Director's Notation.)

94-4-925-451
(9)

65

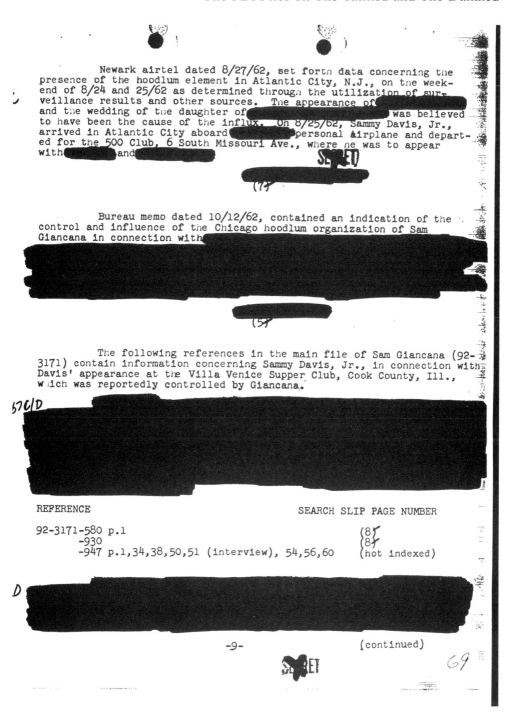

Newark airtel dated 8/27/62, set forth data concerning the presence of the hoodlum element in Atlantic City, N.J., on the week-end of 8/24 and 25/62 as determined through the utilization of sur-veillance results and other sources. The appearance of ███████ and the wedding of the daughter of ███████ was believed to have been the cause of the influx. On 8/25/62, Sammy Davis, Jr., arrived in Atlantic City aboard ███████ personal airplane and depart-ed for the 500 Club, 6 South Missouri Ave., where he was to appear with ███████ and ███████

(7)

Bureau memo dated 10/12/62, contained an indication of the control and influence of the Chicago hoodlum organization of Sam Giancana in connection with ████████████████████████████████████

(5)

The following references in the main file of Sam Giancana (92-3171) contain information concerning Sammy Davis, Jr., in connection with Davis' appearance at the Villa Venice Supper Club, Cook County, Ill., which was reportedly controlled by Giancana.

REFERENCE

92-3171-580 p.1
   -930
   -947 p.1,34,38,50,51 (interview), 54,56,60

SEARCH SLIP PAGE NUMBER

(8)
(8)
(not indexed)

-9-   (continued)

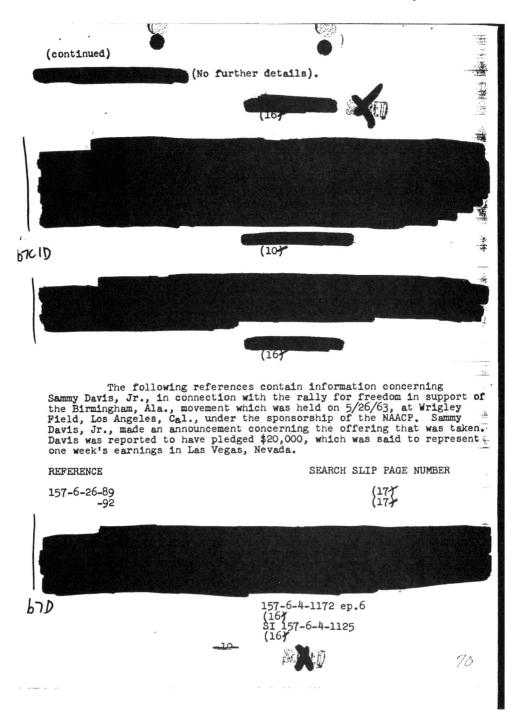

(continued)

(No further details).

(16)

b7c1D

(10)

(16)

The following references contain information concerning Sammy Davis, Jr., in connection with the rally for freedom in support of the Birmingham, Ala., movement which was held on 5/26/63, at Wrigley Field, Los Angeles, Cal., under the sponsorship of the NAACP. Sammy Davis, Jr., made an announcement concerning the offering that was taken. Davis was reported to have pledged $20,000, which was said to represent one week's earnings in Las Vegas, Nevada.

REFERENCE   SEARCH SLIP PAGE NUMBER

157-6-26-89   {17}
        -92   {17}

b7D

157-6-4-1172 ep.6
(16)
SI 157-6-4-1125
(16)

70

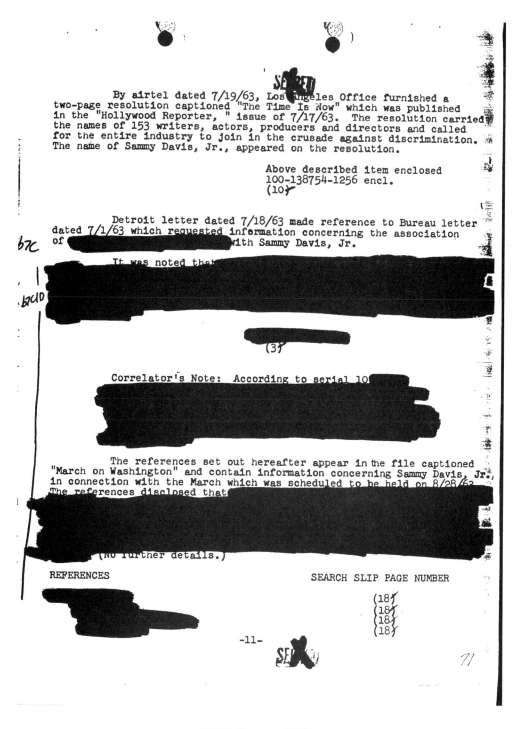

By airtel dated 7/19/63, Los Angeles Office furnished a
two-page resolution captioned "The Time Is Now" which was published
in the "Hollywood Reporter," issue of 7/17/63. The resolution carried
the names of 153 writers, actors, producers and directors and called
for the entire industry to join in the crusade against discrimination.
The name of Sammy Davis, Jr., appeared on the resolution.

> Above described item enclosed
> 100-138754-1256 encl.
> (10)

Detroit letter dated 7/18/63 made reference to Bureau letter
dated 7/1/63 which requested information concerning the association
of ▮▮▮▮▮▮▮▮▮▮▮▮ with Sammy Davis, Jr.

It was noted that ▮▮▮▮▮▮▮▮▮▮▮▮▮▮▮▮▮▮▮▮

▮▮▮▮▮▮▮▮▮▮

(3)

Correlator's Note: According to serial 10▮▮▮▮▮▮▮▮

The references set out hereafter appear in the file captioned
"March on Washington" and contain information concerning Sammy Davis, Jr.,
in connection with the March which was scheduled to be held on 8/28/63.
The references disclosed that ▮▮▮▮▮▮▮▮▮▮▮▮▮▮▮▮▮

(No further details.)

REFERENCES   SEARCH SLIP PAGE NUMBER

                                         (18)
                                         (18)
                                         (18)
                                         (18)

-11-

71

67C

(etails set out.)

92-6667-1x
(9)

62
67D

(No further details.)

The "Los Angeles Sentinel" issue of 10/1/64, identified "Stars for Freedom" as a non-profit organization of outstanding personalities in motion pictures, the arts, science, and public affairs.

105-152164-26 p.3
(15)

The following references in the file captioned "American Nazi Party" (ANP) contain information concerning demonstrations planned by the ANP against Sammy Davis, Jr. On 7/12/60, George Lincoln Rockwell, Organizer and Commander of the ANP, led a group of individuals in picketing The New Lotus, 727 14th Street, NW, Washington, D.C., where Davis had opened an engagement. Davis had reportedly commented during a demonstration at a performance in England, that such an incident could not happen in the US and the ANP intended to prove that it could happen. The ANP planned a demonstration on 7/19/60 at the Black Saddle Restaurant while Davis was being interviewed by radio personality Steve Allison. It was learned, however, that Davis would not appear in order to avoid a disturbance.

(continued)

-12-

72

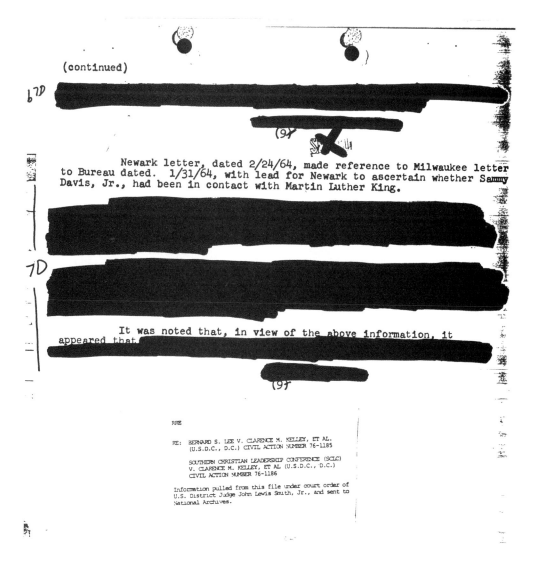

(continued)

Newark letter, dated 2/24/64, made reference to Milwaukee letter to Bureau dated. 1/31/64, with lead for Newark to ascertain whether Sammy Davis, Jr., had been in contact with Martin Luther King.

It was noted that, in view of the above information, it appeared that.

RRE

RE: BERNARD S. LEE V. CLARENCE M. KELLEY, ET AL.
(U.S.D.C., D.C.) CIVIL ACTION NUMBER 76-1185

SOUTHERN CHRISTIAN LEADERSHIP CONFERENCE (SCLC)
V. CLARENCE M. KELLEY, ET AL (U.S.D.C., D.C.)
CIVIL ACTION NUMBER 76-1186

Information pulled from this file under court order of
U.S. District Judge John Lewis Smith, Jr., and sent to
National Archives.

Washington Capital News Service release dated 2/23/64, disclosed that the NAACP announced that comedian Steve Allen and singers Lena Horne and Sammy Davis, Jr., would be co-chairmen of a special civil rights television program to be aired nation-wide on 5/14/64. The

(continued)

-14-

(continued)

snow was scheduled in commemoration of the 10th anniversary of tne US Supreme Court's 1954 decision on school desegregation. Davis was in charge of a working committee in New York for the show.

SECRET 44-O-A, Washington Capital News Service
2/23/64
(3)
SI 61-3176-A Washington Capital News
Service 3/27/64
(4)

On 8/3/64, a source, who had furnished reliable information in the past (source not clear-probably ████████, advised that on 7/27/64, Sammy Davis, Jr., who was appearing in the stage production "Golden Boy" at the Schubert Theatre, Boston, Mass., was interviewed by a member of the news staff of WHDH, T.V., Boston, concerning the racial riots in Harlem and Rochester, NY. Davis indicated that it was his belief that the outside forces, the Nationalists and some of the communists, were the true provocators. Davis indicated that by the term "Nationalists", he meant Black Muslims.

Above Informant advised that as a result of Davis' interview, ████████ Temple II, Dorchester, Mass., requested an opportunity to reply to Davis' statement and was subsequently interviewed on 7/28/64.

25-330971-5-67
(3)

(10)

(Locality not given.)

(10)

The following references appear in the file captioned "National States Rights Party" (NSRP) and contain information of a critical nature relating to Sammy Davis, Jr. During the National Conference of the NSRP held on 11/26/60, in Chattanooga, Tenn. ~~indicated~~ indicated that the Sammy Davis episode was a publicity stunt, as a Negro could not belong to any social group of Jews.

b7C

The references also indicated that alleged members of the NSRP attempted to obtain a permit to picket the Latin Casino, Delaware Township, New Jersey, in the latter part of December, 1960, where Davis was appearing, and their request was denied. A subsequent check on the weekend of 1/20-22/61 disclosed that no incidents developed during Sammy Davis' performance.

"Thunderbolt", self-described as the "Official White Racial Organ" of the NSRP, issues of January 1961 and September 1964, carried articles captioned "Sammy Davis Invited To Inaugural Ball" and "Liz Taylor's Next Husband?", respectively. The articles criticized President Kennedy for extending an invitation to Sammy Davis and furnished a statement to the effect that Liz Taylor had been escorted to a play in NYC by Davis.

REFERENCE   SEARCH SLIP PAGE NUMBER

105-66233-533 p.5,24,33,34   (14)
        -1366 p.7   (14)

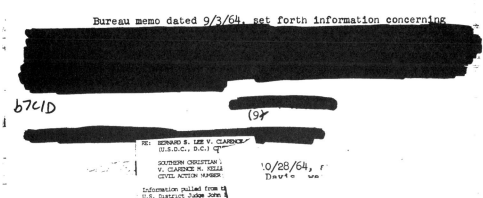

Bureau memo dated 9/3/64, set forth information concerning

b7C1D

(9)

RE: BERNARD S. LEE V. CLARENCE
(U.S.D.C., D.C.)

SOUTHERN CHRISTIAN
V. CLARENCE M. KELLI   10/28/64, f
CIVIL ACTION NUMBER   Davis we

Information pulled from t
U.S. District Judge John
National Archives.

It was noted that Dr. King was President of the SCLC, Atlanta, Ga.

100-442529-293
(13)

-1b-

(continued)

Ala., from Selma, in protest of voter discrimination. Initially, Davis was scheduled to begin the march from Selma on 3/21/65. The references later indicated that he would arrive from Atlanta on 3/24/65 and join other entertainers at the conclusion of the march at Montgomery.

REFERENCE   SEARCH SLIP PAGE NUMBER

Communist Influence In Racial Matters

100-442529-836 ep.1   (13)

March from Selma to Montgomery, Ala.

44-28544-47
        -82 p.2   {4
        -216   {4
                                                       {4

        The "New York Herald Tribune" issue of 4/5/65, carried an article captioned " 'Answer to Selma' Benefit Raises Record $150,000," which reviewed the benefit held at the Majestic Theater, NYC, on 4/4/65. The article related that approximately sixty Broadway performers appeared in the benefit which began with Sammy Davis, Jr., introducing Mayor Wagner. The beneficiaries of the performance included the Voter Education Program of the Southern Christian Leadership Conference and CORE.

100-442529-973 p.115
(13)
SI 100-442529-919 ep.2
(13)

(13)
(13)
(15)

67d/D

-55-   SECRET   (continued)

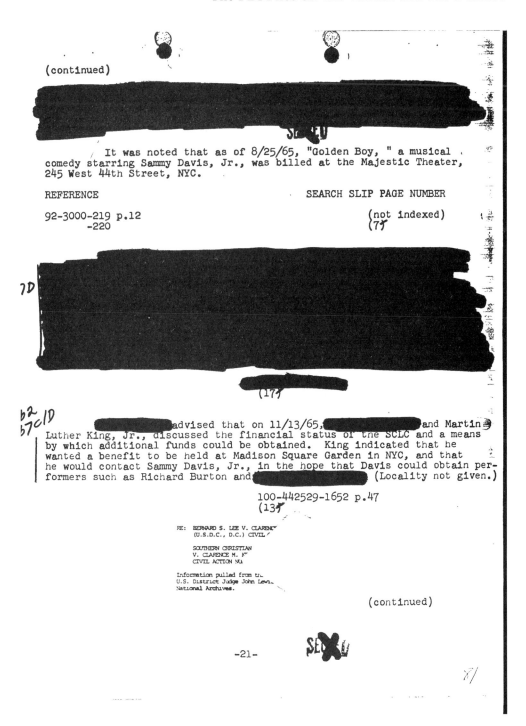

(continued)

It was noted that as of 8/25/65, "Golden Boy," a musical comedy starring Sammy Davis, Jr., was billed at the Majestic Theater, 245 West 44th Street, NYC.

REFERENCE   SEARCH SLIP PAGE NUMBER

92-3000-219 p.12   (not indexed)
       -220   (7)

7D

b2
b7C/D

_____ advised that on 11/13/65, _____ and Martin Luther King, Jr., discussed the financial status of the SCLC and a means by which additional funds could be obtained. King indicated that he wanted a benefit to be held at Madison Square Garden in NYC, and that he would contact Sammy Davis, Jr., in the hope that Davis could obtain performers such as Richard Burton and _____ (Locality not given.)

100-442529-1652 p.47
(13)

RE: BERNARD S. LEE V. CLARENCE
(U.S.D.C., D.C.) CIVIL

SOUTHERN CHRISTIAN
V. CLARENCE M. K
CIVIL ACTION NU

Information pulled from th
U.S. District Judge John Lewi
National Archives.

(continued)

-21-

BERNARD S. LEE V. CLARENCE M. KELLEY, ET AL.
(U.S.D.C., D.C.) CIVIL ACTION NUMBER 76-1185

(continued)

SOUTHERN CHRISTIAN LEADERSHIP CONFERENCE (SCLC)
V. CLARENCE M. KELLEY, ET AL (U.S.D.C., D.C.)
CIVIL ACTION NUMBER 76-1186

Information pulled from this file under court order of
U.S. District Judge John Lewis Smith, Jr., and sent to
National Archives.

Serial indicated that, according to information received on
10/28/58, ████████████ had been a member of the Young Communist
League before coming into prominence as an entertainer.   67C

100-442529-1593
(13)
SI 100-106670-2220 p.14
(10)

The "Chicago Daily Defender," a Negro-owned and operated daily
publication in Chicago, Ill., issue of 4/6/66, carried an article
entitled "Peace Rallies Set For Today and Thursday." The article indicat
ed that grocer ████████ was a source of financial support for the
rallies and had contributed to the successful "Christmas for Mississippi"
project which supplied more than 50,000 turkeys for distribution in
Mississippi. The article also noted that ████████ was instrumental in
bringing Sammy Davis, Jr., to McCormick Place for the climax of the
Christmas fund-raising drive (no further details).   67C

Serial indicated that ████████ had been connected with many
members of the organized crime element in Chicago.

157-6-9-2206 ep.5
(16)

████████ reported on 6/22/66, that ████████ informed
Martin Luther King, Jr.) that he ████ learned from ████
(SCLC, Washington, DC), that several noted entertainers wanted to
join the march*; namely, ████████████████
████ stated that he would instruct his office in Los Angeles, Cal.,
to contact ████ and ████ and inform them that Sammy Davis had invited
them to participate in the march and that he would contact them. ████
stated that a chartered plane would take the group from Los Angeles to
Mississippi.

Serial indicated that ████████████████

100-442529-1870 ep.2
(14)
SI 157-6-54-1457 ep.3
(17)

*Demonstrations Protesting Shooting of James Meredith, 6/26/66, Jackson,
Miss.

The following references in the file captioned "Racial Matters"
contain information concerning the activities of Sammy Davis, Jr., in
connection with the conclusion of the March from Memphis, Tenn., to

(continued)

-22-

(continued)

Jackson, Miss., on 6/25-26/66. The references disclosed that Davis was requested by the SCLC to secure movie and entertainment personalities for the entertainment program for the conclusion of the march. Davis was reportedly engaged in personal appearances in Las Vegas at the time, and it was not determined if Davis had definitely committed himself.

On the evening of 6/25/66, Sammy Davis, Jr., was present to entertain the marchers at Tougaloo College near Jackson, Miss. In addition to Davis, the entertainers included

REFERENCE	SEARCH SLIP PAGE NUMBER
157-6-2-2082	(16)
157-6-26-985	(17)
-996	(17)
157-6-28-1039 ep.2	(17)
157-6-54-1402 p.3	(17)
-1475	(17)
-1480	(18)
-1513 ep.2	(18)

67C

67D

(16)

The following references in the file captioned "Communist Infiltration of the SCLC" contain information concerning Sammy Davis, Jr. During January 1964, a contribution of $16,900 was made to the SCLC by a group of individuals in California through Davis. In February 1964, Davis was identified as Vice President and Treasurer of the Will Master Trio. The references disclosed that from March 1965 to December 1966, Davis was to arrange and/or perform for benefits to raise funds for the SCLC or Martin Luther King, Jr., President of the SCLC.

(continued)

-23-

83

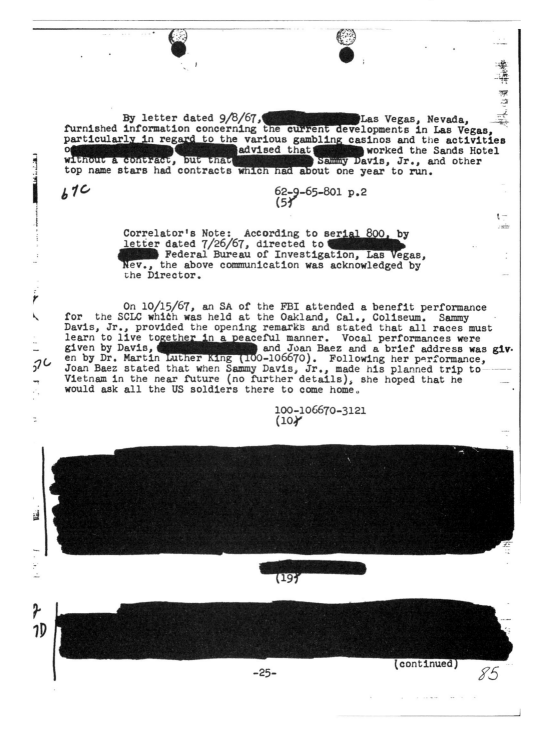

By letter dated 9/8/67, ▓▓▓▓▓▓▓▓▓▓▓▓ Las Vegas, Nevada, furnished information concerning the current developments in Las Vegas, particularly in regard to the various gambling casinos and the activities o▓▓▓▓▓ ▓▓▓▓▓▓▓ advised that ▓▓▓▓▓ worked the Sands Hotel without a contract, but that ▓▓▓▓▓ Sammy Davis, Jr., and other top name stars had contracts which had about one year to run.

b7C

62-9-65-801 p.2
(5)

Correlator's Note: According to serial 800, by letter dated 7/26/67, directed to ▓▓▓▓▓▓▓▓ ▓▓▓▓▓▓ Federal Bureau of Investigation, Las Vegas, Nev., the above communication was acknowledged by the Director.

On 10/15/67, an SA of the FBI attended a benefit performance for the SCLC which was held at the Oakland, Cal., Coliseum. Sammy Davis, Jr., provided the opening remarks and stated that all races must learn to live together in a peaceful manner. Vocal performances were given by Davis, ▓▓▓▓▓▓▓▓▓▓▓▓ and Joan Baez and a brief address was given by Dr. Martin Luther King (100-106670). Following her performance, Joan Baez stated that when Sammy Davis, Jr., made his planned trip to Vietnam in the near future (no further details), she hoped that he would ask all the US soldiers there to come home.

b7C

100-106670-3121
(10)

(19)

7
7D

(continued)

-25-

85

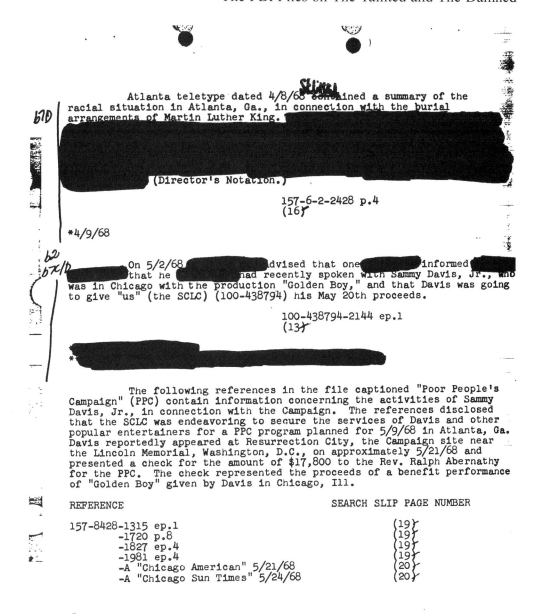

Atlanta teletype dated 4/8/68 contained a summary of the racial situation in Atlanta, Ga., in connection with the burial arrangements of Martin Luther King.

(Director's Notation.)

157-6-2-2428 p.4
(16)

*4/9/68

On 5/2/68 _____ advised that one _____ informed _____ that he _____ had recently spoken with Sammy Davis, Jr., who was in Chicago with the production "Golden Boy," and that Davis was going to give "us" (the SCLC) (100-438794) his May 20th proceeds.

100-438794-2144 ep.1
(13)

The following references in the file captioned "Poor People's Campaign" (PPC) contain information concerning the activities of Sammy Davis, Jr., in connection with the Campaign. The references disclosed that the SCLC was endeavoring to secure the services of Davis and other popular entertainers for a PPC program planned for 5/9/68 in Atlanta, Ga. Davis reportedly appeared at Resurrection City, the Campaign site near the Lincoln Memorial, Washington, D.C., on approximately 5/21/68 and presented a check for the amount of $17,800 to the Rev. Ralph Abernathy for the PPC. The check represented the proceeds of a benefit performance of "Golden Boy" given by Davis in Chicago, Ill.

REFERENCE	SEARCH SLIP PAGE NUMBER
157-8428-1315 ep.1	(19)
-1720 p.8	(19)
-1827 ep.4	(19)
-1981 ep.4	(19)
-A "Chicago American" 5/21/68	(20)
-A "Chicago Sun Times" 5/24/68	(20)

-27-

SECRET

Helen Keller

Chapter VII

The FBI Scruntinized The Deaf, The Dumb and The Blind

Helen (Adams) Keller was born in Tuscumbia, Alabama on June 27, 1880. Her father, Arthur Keller, a successful businessman was 42 years of age at the time of her birth. He was a former Captain in the Confederate Army of General Robert E. Lee. Her mother, Kate Adams was a 23-year-old bonafide Southern "belle" from a well-to-do family that had been classed among the filthy rich in the cotton industry prior to the Civil War between the states. Kate was a tall statuesque, blond beauty with high noon sky blue eyes. Her Cleopatra chiseled shaped pimple free face was covered with an ivory sheen skin.

Helen was the Kellers' first child. She was an alert energetic baby until she became infected with a mysterious illness in her nineteenth month. Doctors misdiagnosed the ailment as scarlet fever. The disease literally blocked the child's eyesight, ears and vocal chords. It has been said that her mental state following the illness was best described as being compared to that of a newborn baby. The tot was declared by all the doctors that examined her as one who would be permanently deaf, dumb, and blind for the rest of her life. In light of the medical prognosis the girl lived an untutored life and was left to her own jigsaw mental devices until she was almost seven years old. She reacted to parental guidance with grunts, groans, kicks, screams, and tantrums as if she were being exorcised. On the other hand, she giggled, chuckled, and smiled when she was at peace with herself.

The environment in the Keller home was mirrored by the mother's concerns for their child's welfare. Thus, Captain Arthur Keller, took his daughter Helen to Baltimore in 1886 to see Dr. Chisholm a famous oculist, only to hear that there was an outside chance of his child being educated. In Baltimore, the good doctor advised the Captain to take his daughter down the road approximately thirty miles to see Dr. Alexander Graham Bell in Washington, D.C. Dr. Bell had earlier demonstrated his telephone and an audiometer before a small group of local businessmen. The large audiometer was an early version of the present day pea size hearing aid.

Hellen Keller and Anne Mansfield Sullivan. The student and her teacher.

Dr. Bell's only advice to Captain Keller was a suggestion that he write to the Perkins Institution for the Blind in Boston, which he promptly did. The response to his missive was immediate, in that Anne Mansfield Sullivan, a beautiful young Irish girl of twenty years of age arrived on his doorstep in Tuscumbia, Alabama on March 3, 1887 prepared to take on the job of educating Helen Keller. Miss Sullivan had been a student at the Perkins Institution and was the product of a world that was almost as barren as Helen Keller's, in that she was partially blind.

Before Anne Sullivan left the Perkins Institution the students gave her a small doll for her new pupil. The doll became the centerpiece of Helen Keller's first lesson. After Helen had had an opportunity to play with the doll for a short period of time, Sullivan spelled into the palm of her new pupil's hand with her finger the word "d-o-l-l." Helen became very interested in the finger and palm game because it tickled. She tried to imitate the teacher without having the foggiest notion of what the word d-o-l-l meant.

In the weeks that followed Helen learned a number of words. However, it was not until she experienced a stream of cold water rolling over her left hand from an open spigot of a hand pump as Anne spelled the word "w-a-t-e-r" into the palm of her right hand that she integrated the language with the act. It was during that finger and palm interplay that Helen began to fully realize that everything had a name and that there was a relationship between the finger language and various objects.

The Pump behind Helen's birthplace in Tuscumbia, Alabama where she learned her first word which was "water".

Anne wrote with her finger in the palm of Helen's hand every task that they had accomplished each day. The teacher had properly assumed that Helen had a normal child's mental capacity to assimilate and imitate, therefore she proceeded to talk with her fingers into the palm of Helen's hand as a mother talks into the ears of a baby. The result was miraculous because after three years Helen knew the alphabet, both manual and Braille, and she had also learned to read and write.

Helen's mother, while in attendance at an afternoon tea party, overheard a conversation between several women about a dumb child in Sweden having learned to talk. As a result of this information Kate did not waste any time arranging for her daughter to take speech lessons. On March 10, 1890 Helen started taking speech lessons with Miss Sarah Fuller, principal of the Horace Mann School for the Deaf in Boston. Her education was on a fast track in that in 1894 she became qualified to enroll in the highly lauded Wright Humason School for the Deaf in New York City where she stayed for two years. That

Helen Keller received her B.A. degree from Radcliffe College with a special mention of her excellence in English Literature.

school had been chosen to give her every possible advantage in vocal culture and in lip reading by placing one's fingers over the speaker's mouth. While there Helen also studied arithmetic, physical geography, French and German.

Helen had a deep thirst for higher education and her ultimate goal was to matriculate at the prestigious Radcliffe College for Girls in Cambridge, Massachusetts. To prepare for the college she went to the Cambridge Prep School and enrolled at a school for Young Ladies in 1896. It was there for the first time in her life that she was able to enjoy the companionship of girls he own age. When she entered Radcliffe, Harvard University's sister school four years later in 1900 she was elected vice president of the freshman class.

Throughout all of her school years Anne Sullivan, her primary teacher was always at Helen's side patiently interpreting all of the material in all her classes, lectures, books and references.

Helen Keller frequently complained about the fact that she never got the opportunity of smelling the old and wise professors, because the students' classes were taught by young instructors while the older seasoned professors were cloistered in the Ivory Tower writing books and learned papers to each other. In June, 1894, Helen Keller received her B.A. degree cum laude from Radcliffe College, with a special mention for her excellence in English Literature.

Helen and Anne met Alexander Graham Bell at a meeting of The American Association To Promote the Teaching of Speech to the Deaf.

A year after Helen graduated from Radcliffe, her teacher, Anne Sullivan married the handsome John A. Macy, the famous literary critic and Harvard University English instructor. John's academic achievements were impeccable, in that he won the coveted Phi Beta Kappa Key; he was also editor in chief of the *Harvard Advocate*, in addition to being the editor of the *Harvard Lampoon*. Anne's marriage to John did not break up the teacher-student relationship between the two women, it simply gave Helen a second teacher and companion. John A. Macy became her adviser and edited her first autobiography, *The Story of My Life*, which was published in 1902 as a serial in the *Ladies Home Journal*. Her personal odyssey was one that the general public had eagerly awaited. She followed her first published work with *The World I Live In* (1908) which was another facet of her life.

Following additional voice lessons Helen Keller's voice improved to the point that she agreed to speak in public in 1913. In that same year she was asked to give a talk in Washington, D.C. It was during her brief stay in the District of Columbia that she was invited to cover the first inaugural of President-elect, Woodrow Wilson for the United Press Service. Many other job offers followed.

In the late summer of 1913, Anne Macy became ill and was advised to have a hysterectomy, her illness was compounded by the fact that her husband had left her for a younger woman. John's actions were possibly stimulated by several things, Anne's hysterectomy and her loss in his eyesight of her vehicle for total womanhood. Moreover he began to think of Helen Keller more as an institution than a woman. He blamed her as much as Annie for the deterioration of their marriage. In his mind's eye, Helen was the president and his wife Anne served as chairman of the board, vice president, secretary, treasurer, janitor, matron and office boy. John questioned his own role in this ménage à trois, in that his wife appeared to be more interested in Helen's welfare and needs than she was in his.

Both Helen and Anne were desperately in need of money after John left, so much so that Helen wrote to her old friend, Andrew Carnegie the philanthropist and steel magnate in Pittsburgh and asked for help. By return mail he sent her check with an offer to give her a lifetime pension. Initially, she objected to the offer of a pension because for a socialist to accept tainted capitalist money, would be an oxymoron. Hunger pains changed her mind and she temporarily shelved her socialist philosophy because a week later she wrote a letter accepting Carnegie's generous offer of a lifetime pension.

Between 1909 and 1924, Helen Keller turned her energies to campaigning for the American Foundation for the Blind. Keller was in the vanguard of the most advanced Progressive thinking and also American left wing causes as well. In 1909, she joined the Socialist Party only to resign just before World War I to protest what she saw as its excessive caution. In 1918, after joining the IWW, she supported the 101 "Wobblies" on trial in Chicago for illegal, antiwar activities. She militantly opposed America's entry into World War I, calling it a "Capitalistic War." She also campaigned for women's suffrage, she assumed the right to vote for women would be a sure cure for killing any future war efforts. Her radicalism hardened in the face of public criticism. She said "I don't object to harsh criticism as long as I am treated like a human being with a mind of my own."

The final two decades of Helen Keller's experience and achievements have been widely circulated in two films, the academy award-winning documentary *The Unconquered* (1953) and the 1962 film *The Miracle Worker*. The latter film was based on a television drama by William Gibson in 1957, then a prize-winning theater production in 1959, *The Miracle Worker* focused on the triumphs of her earliest years, under Anne Sullivan, the teacher who died October 20, 1936. In Keller's last years every living president met or honored her. Lyndon Johnson, in 1964 conferred upon her the nation's most distinguished civilian honor, the Presidential Medal of Freedom.

Keller died at her home in Easton, Connecticut on June 1, 1968. Her epitaph should have been a quote from her book which said:

Few Americans had ever had so far to come, or had come so far "out of the dark."

Helen reading the lips of Eleanor Roosevelt, the wife of President Franklin D. Roosevelt.

Federal Bureau of Investigation

Freedom of Information/Privacy Acts Section

Subject: Helen Keller

FEDERAL BUREAU OF INVESTIGATION

FREEDOM OF INFORMATION/PRIVACY ACTS SECTION

COVER SHEET

SUBJECT: <u>HELEN KELLER</u>

June 24, 1964

HELEN ADAMS KELLER
Born: June 27, 1880
Tuscumbia, Alabama

Name Checks

In response to your request for a check of the files of this Bureau concerning the captioned individual, you are advised that no investigation concerning her has been conducted by the FBI.

There is enclosed herewith one copy of a memorandum dated November 8, 1956, summarizing information in our files concerning captioned individual as of that time. (62-60527-48495)

Our files additionally reveal that an article appeared in the "Daily Worker" former East Coast communist newspaper, on July 18, 1957, indicating that Helen Keller had sent loving birthday greetings to Elizabeth Gurley Flynn, a prominent communist leader, on her 65th birthday. The article indicated that Miss Keller had sent the note to Mrs. Flynn in connection with her 65th birthday on August 7, 1955. Mrs. Flynn, at that time, was confined in the Federal Womens' Prison at Alderson, West Virginia, following her conviction under the Smith Act of 1940. (100-1287-A)

Enclosure

Original & 1 - CSC
Request Received-6-23-64

UN▆▆ STATES CIVIL SERVICE COM▆▆SSION
▆REAU OF PERSONNEL INVESTIGAT▆▆▆
WASHINGTON 25, D.C.

ADDRESS REPLY TO
"CIVIL SERVICE COMMISSION"
AND REFER TO
FILE

AND DATE OF THIS LETTER

KELLER, Helen Adams
BORN: June 27, 1880
Tuscumbia, Alabama

WHO'S WHO IN AMERICA 1960 - 1961
(Volume 31)

KELLER, Helen Adams, counselor on internat, relations Am. Found. for Blind;
b. Tuscumbia, Ala., June 27, 1880; d. Capt. Arthur H. and Katherine (Adams
Keller; deaf and blind since age of 19 mos. as result of illness; ed. under
direction of Anne Sullivan Macy, 1887-1936; A.B. cum laude, Radcliffe Coll.,
1904; D.H.L.., Temple U., 1931; LL.D.,Univ. Glasgow, Scotland, 1932 U.
Witwatersand, Johannesburg, South Africa, 1951; Hon. Yellow Ednl. Inst. of
Scotland; Litt.D., U. Delhi, 1955; M.D. (hon.), Free U. of Berlin, 1955; LL.D.
(honorary), Harvard Univ., 1955. Lectr in behalf of blind throughout U. S.
and in Australia, Can. Egypt, France, Gr. Britain, Greece, Ireland, Israel,
Hashemite Kingdom of the Jordan, Lebanon, Syria, Italy, Japan, Yugoslavia,
Korea, Manchukuo, New Zealand, Scotland, S. Africa, So. Rhodesia, Noe counselor
on nat.and internat. relations Am. Found. for Blind, Inc., N.Y.C. Recipient
Achievement prize Pictorial Rev., 1931; Order of St. Sava Yugoslavia, 1931;
Roosevelt medal, 1936; gold key Nat. Educ. Assn., 1938; Scroll of honor for
pioneer work in relief of handicapped Internat. Fedn. Women's Clubs, 1941;
W.U.S.Achievement Certificate, 1949; award of dir. gen. Lions Internat. 1951;
D.S.M. from Am. Assn. of Workers for the Blind, 1951, Nat. Humanitarian Award
Variety Clubs, Intl., 1951 gold medal Nat. Inst. of Social Scis., 1952,
meritorious service award Nat. Rehabilitation assn., 1952 Medal of Merit
(Lebanon), 1952, Chevalier Medal of Honor (France), 1952 Southern Cross,
(Brazil), 1953, award for best feature length documentary film Nat. Academy
Motion Picture Arts and Scis., 1955; also recipient many other honors and
rewards from fgn. govts. and from civic ednl., welfare organ. throughout
U. S. 1951—;made alumni member Phi. Beta Kappa, Radcliffe Coll., 1933. Member
trustees Am. Hall of Fame, Nat. Inst. Arts and Letters. Author: Story of My
Life, 1902; Optimism (essay), 1903; The World I Live In, 1908; The Song Of
The Stone Wall, 1910; Out of the Dark, 1913; My Religion, 1927; Midstream—
My Later Life, 1930; Helen Keller's Journal, 1938; Let Us Have Faith,1941;
Teacher,1955; The Open Door, 1957; Appeared on TV Program Wide, Wide World,1957.
Home: Arcan Ridge, R.I, Westport, Conn. Address: Care Am. Foundation for the
Blind, Inc., 15 W. 16th St., N.Y.C. 11.

SII INFORMATION -

No Record

62-▆▆▆▆▆▆▆

ENCLOSURE

In response to your request
there are attached ▆▆▆▆ ▆▆▆
reports which appear to relate
to the subject of your inquiry.

b7C

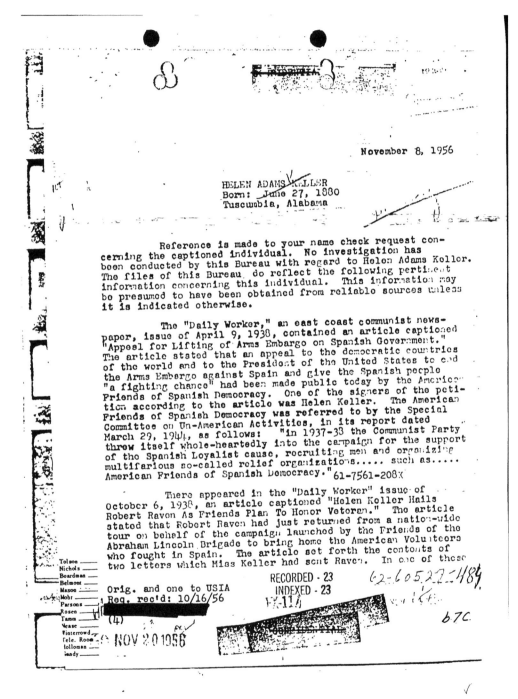

November 8, 1956

HELEN ADAMS KELLER
Born: June 27, 1880
Tuscumbia, Alabama

Reference is made to your name check request concerning the captioned individual. No investigation has been conducted by this Bureau with regard to Helen Adams Keller. The files of this Bureau do reflect the following pertinent information concerning this individual. This information may be presumed to have been obtained from reliable sources unless it is indicated otherwise.

The "Daily Worker," an east coast communist newspaper, issue of April 9, 1938, contained an article captioned "Appeal for Lifting of Arms Embargo on Spanish Government." The article stated that an appeal to the democratic countries of the world and to the President of the United States to end the Arms Embargo against Spain and give the Spanish people "a fighting chance" had been made public today by the American Friends of Spanish Democracy. One of the signers of the petition according to the article was Helen Keller. The American Friends of Spanish Democracy was referred to by the Special Committee on Un-American Activities, in its report dated March 29, 1944, as follows: "in 1937-38 the Communist Party threw itself whole-heartedly into the campaign for the support of the Spanish Loyalist cause, recruiting men and organizing multifarious so-called relief organizations..... such as..... American Friends of Spanish Democracy." 61-7561-208X

There appeared in the "Daily Worker" issue of October 6, 1938, an article captioned "Helen Keller Hails Robert Raven As Friends Plan To Honor Veteran." The article stated that Robert Raven had just returned from a nation-wide tour on behalf of the campaign launched by the Friends of the Abraham Lincoln Brigade to bring home the American Volunteers who fought in Spain. The article set forth the contents of two letters which Miss Keller had sent Raven. In one of these

Tolson
Nichols
Boardman
Belmont
Masoe
Mohr
Parsons
Rosen
Tamm
Nease
Winterrowd
Tele. Room
Holloman
Gandy

Orig. and one to USIA
Req. rec'd: 10/16/56
(4)

RECORDED - 23
INDEXED - 23
FK-117

62-60527-489

b7C

NOV 20 1956

CONFIDENTIAL

November 8, 1956

Helen Adams Keller

According to a reliable source, Helen Keller was a sponsor of the Independent Citizens Committee of the Arts, Sciences and Professions (New York City) in December, 1944. Helen Keller was listed as one of the speakers at a rally at Madison Square Gardens in New York City on December 4, 1945, which was sponsored by the Independent Citizens Committee of the Arts, Sciences and Professions, Incorporated, which organization was cited as a communist front by the Special Committee on Un-American Activities, U. S. House of Representatives. 100-197270-21 page7

There appeared in the New York newspaper "Morning Freiheit" issue of November 10, 1945, information concerning a reception held at the Soviet Consulate in New York on November 8, 1945, commemorating the 28th Anniversary of the Russian Revolution. One of the guests was Helen Keller. When she entered the Consulate, she reportedly said "Finally I am on Soviet Soil." 100-829-713 page 34

Helen Keller was listed as one of a group of individuals who sent messages of greeting to the Eastern Seaboard Conference of the Veterans of the Abraham Lincoln Brigade held in February, 1946, at Manhattan Center in New York City. The Veterans of the Abraham Lincoln Brigade was cited by the Attorney General as a communist organization.

A confidential informant who has furnished reliable information in the past made available to a representative of this Bureau a copy of a letter dated June 1, 1947, from the Communist Party headquarters, 250 South Broad Street, Philadelphia, Pennsylvania, addressed to the membership of the Communist Party in that area. The letter stated that on June 20, 1947, at the Bellevue-Stratford Hotel in Philadelphia, Pennsylvania, the Communist Party and many other individuals would play host to Mother Ella Reeve Bloor. Issued in connection with the occasion was a folder which carried greetings to Mother Bloor by the National Committee of the Communist Party. Included in the Booklet was a statement of greeting signed "Fraternally Yours, Helen Keller." 61-155-93

The Washington, D. C., "Times Herald" issue dated January 24, 1948, carried an article captioned "Plan to Smear

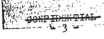

CONFIDENTIAL

- 3 -

Helen Adams Keller   November 8, 1956

Red-Probers Hit By Congressmen" wherein it was reported that
Helen Keller was one of the original sponsors of the Committee
of One Thousand. The Committee of One Thousand was cited by
the California Committee on Un-American Activities in its
report issued in 1948 as "a Communist created and controlled
front organization." 100-353406-A "Times Herald" 1-24-48

     In March, 1948, there was made available to this
Bureau a copy of a letter which was sent to the Speaker of the
House of Representatives in protest against the action of the
Committee on Un-American Activities of the House of Representatives.
Helen Keller was listed as one of the signers of this letter.
61-7582-1502
     A letterhead of the National Council of American-Soviet
Friendship, Incorporated, 114 East 32nd Street, New York City,
dated November 10, 1948, reflected that Helen Keller was a
sponsor of that organization. The National Council of American-
Soviet Friendship, Incorporated, was cited by the Attorney
General as a communist organization. 100-146964-1425 page 5

     It was reported that Helen Keller, blind author and
educator, was one of a group of individuals sending messages
of condolence on the occasion of the funeral of Mother Bloor
well-known Communist Party member on August 14, 1951.
100-3-74-7767
     There appeared in the "Washington Star" Washington, D. C.,
issue of December 13, 1952, an article "Helen Keller Denies
Endorsing Red Parley." The article stated that Helen Keller had
called on a Czechoslovakian newspaper to retract a story in which
it said she endorsed the "Communist-run Vienna 'Peace' Conference." It was indicated that the State Department reported
that Miss Keller had repudiated the story in a Voice of America
broadcast to Czechoslovakia. The article pointed out that the
Prague newspaper "Rude Prazo" reported on December 6, 1952, that
Miss Keller stated "I am with you in your wonderful movement
with all my heart," but that actually Miss Keller, a few days
earlier, had assailed the Vienna Congress as "a mask for the
products of Stalinist propaganda." 100-361031-A

     The foregoing information is being furnished to you
as a result of your request for an FBI file check and is not
to be construed as a clearance or a nonclearance of the
individual involved. This information is furnished for your
use and should not be disseminated outside of your agency.

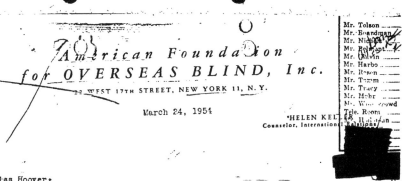

American Foundation

for OVERSEAS BLIND, Inc.

22 WEST 17TH STREET, NEW YORK 11, N. Y.

March 24, 1954

*HELEN KELLER
Counselor, International Relations

Dear Miss Hoover:

We who love peace must recognize our eternal indebtedness to the gallant people of South Korea for their bitter sacrifices during the war so recently ended. My mind turns particularly to the plight of the blind men, women and little children in that unhappy land, and my heart is heavy at the knowledge of the cruel privations they must suffer.

You have doubtless read of Korea's countless war casualties, its ten million refugees and the destruction of seventy-five percent of all its buildings. Yet the most poignant aspect of the total disaster is the tragic fate of so many of Korea's children -- their eyes blinded by war, their only school and training center at Seoul laid in ruins, their sole braille printing machine demolished.

Recognizing that there can be no nobler purpose than to comfort suffering children I have asked the American Foundation for Overseas Blind to launch, as part of its world-wide service, a crusade to aid Korea's blind youngsters. The Foundation has already established a fine school and training center for them outside Pusan. There and at the new Taegu School for the Blind and Deaf 250 handicapped young people, inspired with firm faith and dauntless courage, are learning to break through the barriers of darkness and silence. Bravely they look forward to a brighter future when, skilled and self-reliant, they will return to their communities ready to play a part in the restoration of their homeland.

Yet Korean government records list a total of 50,000 sightless children to provide for their education and training many new centers must be created and the few existing facilities enlarged. The Foundation stands ready to supply the trained staff, the specially designed classroom equipment, braille books and tools for instruction, toys and games for recreation. Funds must also be found to provide food and clothing for their physical necessities.

I have promised the blind children of Korea that my friends in America will ameliorate their terrible needs. Fervently I pray that you will help me keep this pledge by sending a gift today to the American Foundation for Overseas Blind. If you do, you may be sure that it will bring swift and life-giving aid to our young friends across the seas.

Hopefully and sincerely yours,

Helen Keller

2 ENCL.

Coleman A. Young
224

Chapter VIII

The FBI Shadowed Detroit's Mayor Coleman A. Young For 53 Years

Coleman A. Young was born on May 24, 1918 in Tuscaloosa, Alabama. His parents were William C. Young and Ida Reese Young. The senior Young was known as an avid reader, a race man, and a no nonsense doughboy who fought side by side with the French army in the Argonne Forest, the St. Goubain Forest, the Oise-Aisne offensive and the Lorraine offensive. In World War I the Germans (Huns) called the Afro-American Regiment the "Black Devils" because they showed no fear.

In contrast, his mother was soft spoken, prim, proper and a teasing high brown lady of the highest magnitude. She was a graduate of the privately controlled Stillman College for Negroes in Tuscaloosa, Alabama, where she trained to be a public schoolteacher.

In 1923 the Ku Klux Klan in Huntsville, Alabama showered violence upon the heads of Black folks in the former Confederate State. The ruthlessness prompted the Young family to exit from the land of Little Eves without too much deliberation for Detroit, Michigan, where allegedly all the slave chasing bloodhounds had died. The Motor City was considered by many Alabamians to be the land of the free for Negroes and the home of the brave. It was also a mecca for fifty cents per hour job opportunities on Henry Ford's revolutionary automobile assembly line.

The senior Young, who was a tailor by trade, opened a shop in the Detroit area known as the Black Bottom. It was an ethically mixed community in the Motor City where Greeks, Italians, Poles and Negroes lived side by side. It was a cohesive community, with a mixture of working class and middle class people who all got along.

Young Coleman began his public elementary education in Detroit, Michigan at the Capron, and subsequently transferred to the Barstow, Duffield, and the Miller Schools in that order before his parents transferred him to St. Mary's, a private Catholic Academy. He was one of very few Black students in all the five institutions he had attended, public and private. It was in an integrated school environment that he learned early how to compete with white folks in an academic atmosphere.

The lad was a top-flight student in both elementary and junior high school. However, in spite of his high I.Q. and 3.9 grade average, he was denied scholarships to the Catholic operated University of Detroit High School, Catholic Central and LaSalle High School, although his family had converted to Catholicism shortly after moving to Detroit. Young was forced to jump over barriers of Catholic racism in his sophomore year and transfer to Eastern Public High School in the Motor City where he graduated with distinction, and ranked second best in his class of May, 1935, just a few days before his seventeenth birthday.

The race treatment that had umbrellaed Coleman in school, propelled him down a path that caused him to have an adversarial attitude toward the white establishment. His thoughts about racism were further heightened toward the corporate world when he discovered he was caught in a job market that had shrunk dramatically. President Herbert Hoover's depressed economy hit the general population very hard and was doubly hard for Negroes. Even in good times Blacks were the last hired and the first fired. The unemployment rate in Detroit for Colored people during the 1930s reached an unprecedented 80 percent.

After being denied the opportunity of receiving a university scholarship, Coleman jumped in line for what seemed like a golden chance for a position based on his placement test, as an electrical trainee at Henry Ford's River Rouge plant. It did not take him long to discover that the twin brothers, Racism and Jim Crow were ever present on the job, the same as they had been in some of the public schools and all of the Catholic institutions. The white foreman's son got the job in spite of the fact that Young had aced all of the trainees on the final examinations with a perfect grade of 100. Thus, Young found himself bitter and smack dab in the middle of receiving the traditional and historical Negro job on the Ford Motor Company assembly line where he became an underground union organizer.

After several months on the job, a "Company Goon" baited him with racial slurs, then physically attacked him. To defend himself Coleman picked up a thirty-six inch steel bar that he used to unjam the machine and bashed the "goon" on the right side of his head. The "goon" fell like a ton of bricks across the assembly belt, unconscious. Coleman immediately arranged to get some help in carrying the guy out of the plant and dumping him into a boxcar with the steel shavings. Young was fired on the spot.

Young's next job was that of a hospital attendant, emptying bedpans for World War I Vets at the Veterans Administration Hospital at Dearborn, Michigan. As a matter of fact, he was working at the V.A. Hospital when Hitler's storm troopers invaded Poland in September, 1939. This was an early warning sign to Americans of the impending World War II.

In 1940, the job market cracked doors just a wee bit for Negroes because of a labor shortage. In addition, the turbulence in Europe made it necessary to convert manufacturing plants from civilian use to war needs. At the same time a large number of European immigrants were clamoring to return to their homeland in Europe.

Young's next job was not in a war plant but for Uncle Sam as a substitute postal clerk at the Roosevelt Annex Station in Detroit. He worked there from July 2, 1941 until December 31, 1941. As a matter of fact, he was working for the post office when the Japanese bombed Pearl Harbor on December 7, 1941. He was fired as a mail clerk as soon as the Christmas rush was over because his general work habits and his arrogant demeanor rubbed his white supervisors the wrong way. Moreover, when Young initially made application for the post office job he innocently gave the name C. LeBron Simmons, a known local Communist Party member, as a reference.

The FBI files on Young show that on February 15, 1941, Young was present at a meeting of the Executive Board of the Detroit Youth Assembly, which was listed on the FBI files as a Communist front organization. From July 3, through 6, 1941, he was present at the Communist front Seventh American Youth Congress held in Philadelphia, Pennsylvania. A FBI informant's memo dated July 18, 1941, stated that Coleman A. Young was a card carrying member of the Negro Commission of District Seven, which was a radical left wing cell of the Communist Party.

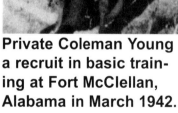

Private Coleman Young a recruit in basic training at Fort McClellan, Alabama in March 1942.

Coleman Young was recruited into the United States Army on February 3, 1942 at Fort Custer, Michigan. The writer was a member of the 1609th Permanent Personnel unit stationed at Fort Custer, Michigan when Buck Private Coleman A. Young was processed into the service.

Following the 3-day processing period he was shipped by troop train from Fort Custer to Fort McClellan, Alabama for an eight-week basic training course. Coleman subsequently became a member of the famed Tuskegee Airmen. After graduating from officer's training school in two months, as opposed to the usual 90 days, he was commissioned a second Lieutenant. When the 477th Bombardment Group was fully staffed, it was transferred from Tuskegee, Alabama to Selfridge Field, outside Detroit, Michigan. The stay at Selfridge was short-lived because of dissension between Blacks and whites over restrictions forbidding Blacks from using the officers' club. The Negro officers were pressing for equal access and white officers took an over-my-dead-body posture. To calm the waters, the military establishment moved the 477th to Godman Field, Kentucky. The move below the Mason-Dixon Line further lowered the morale of the Colored officers. The white officers at Godman were permitted to use the plush decorated officers' club at Fort Knox, which was near the front door of Godman Field, while Negroes were restricted to an inferior facility at Godman Field. Before the bell could ring for the contestants to come out for a third round it was discovered that Godman Field's runways were not suitable for bomber use. When second Lieutenant Coleman A. Young and some of his fellow officers went over to Fort Knox to eat in the small Jim Crow café set aside for them, they could see through the partially open door of the white officers' club across the hall, that the German prisoners of war were in the officers' club enjoying the freedom that Blacks committed to fight against Hitler and his Nazi Army were denied.

To make a bad matter worse, the bomber group was moved again, this time to Freeman Field in Southern Indiana near the town of Seymour, which was reputed to be the birthplace of the Ku Klux Klan. Thus, Seymour was a dangerous place for Negroes and dogs to be caught after sundown. The local whites' blade of hatred for Negroes was sharp enough to amputate an elephant's leg.

Equal but separate facilities were thought by the High Command at Freeman to be the solution to the officers club problem. Negro officers protested and stated loud and clear that piecemeal Jim Crow was not acceptable. The Military Command at Freeman, the First Air Corps Command at Mitchell Field, and the High Command in Washington, were whirling like a merry-go-round with the problem, when the Negro Press stepped into the center of the controversy. The newspaper stories were followed closely by the NAACP and the Urban League. The high profile newsworthiness of the Freeman Field incident heightened because over 100 Colored officers, who symbolized the best and brightest, were involved.

The Freeman incident reached the boiling point when Colonel Robert R. Selway Jr. posted a notice on the bulletin board which essentially said the following: "Negroes could not use facility 123 which was the white officers' club, 124 the swimming pool, and 235, the tennis court".

The Colonel had also denied the families of Negro officers housing, although there were a number of empty buildings within the campground on the officers' row. He further impotized Colored officers by withholding the power to command. Command meant having authority over white junior officers, and that was a situation that President Franklin D. Roosevelt and General Dwight D. Eisenhower were not prepared to accept. No Negro officer could occupy a rank that would put him above a white officer. In other words, there was a gentleman's agreement that prohibited senior Black officers from being in command of lower rank white officers. Negro officers with combat experiences in the European Theater were made junior to white officers with no combat experience.

On April 9, 1945 2nd Lt. Coleman A. Young was called before a panel of nine officers, eight white and one Colored. The Negro officer's name was Nick Roberts. He had attended Chicago's New Wendell Phillips High School in 1935 and 1936 with the author. They were childhood neighbors and fellow morning newspaper delivery boys. Chairing the meeting was Captain Tyson, a friend of 2nd Lieutenant Coleman Young. Captain Tyson asked Coleman if he had read the petition that was posted on the bulletin board. Coleman indicated that he had read the document but would not sign it.

Coleman further stated: "If I don't have the same rights as you as an officer then I should not be one". Tyson bristled and replied: "I am giving you a direct order to sign. If you refuse you are under arrest in your quarters". Coleman was the first officer to be arrested and he was followed by 100 other Negro officers. On April 13, 1945, 101 Negro officers were lined up like convicts and flown back to Godman Field on a DC3. Their actions in attempting to exercise their civil rights were interpreted as a violation of the 69th article of war. The document listing all of the officers under arrest read as follows:

HEADQUATERS
FREEMAN FIELD
Seymour, Indiana

13 April 1945
SUBJECT: Disciplinary Action
TO: All Concerned
1.   Pursuant to authority conferred by the 69th Article of War, the following named commissioned and flight officers were placed under arrest while in transit between Freeman Field, in Seymour, Indiana and to Godman Field, Kentucky, and remain arrested in quarters upon arrival at Godman Field until further notice, effective 0800 hours 13 April 1945:

NAME	RANK	SERIAL NO.	SIGNATURE
Coleman A. Young	**2nd Lt.**	**01297128**	_____

Arthur L. Ward	1st Lt.	0584177	_____
Donald D. Harris	2nd Lt.	02075544	_____
James B. Williams	1st Lt.	0867664	_____
Paul L. White	F/O	T-136700	_____
David A. Smith	2nd Lt.	585809	_____
Charles E. Wilson	F/O	T-62507	_____
William C. Perkins	2nd Lt.	01051725	_____
John E. Wilson	F/O	T-136703	_____
James Whyte, Jr.	2nd Lt.	0339096	_____
Paul W. Scott	F/O	T-1366851	_____
Stephen Hotesse	2nd. Lt.	0207559	_____
McCray Jenkins	F/O	T-136661	_____
Werdell A. Polk	2nd Lt.	0713064	_____
Harris H. Robnett	F/O	T-64629	_____
Robert E. Lee	2nd Lt.	02075548	_____
Donald A. Hawkins	F/O	T-67154	_____
George H. Kydd	2nd Lt.	0828043	_____
Glen W. Pulliam	F/O	T-66410	_____
Eugene L. Woodson	F/O	T-136705	_____
Frank B. Sanders	2nd Lt.	02080926	_____
Charles E. Darnell	2nd Lt.	0824324	_____
Walter M. Miller	F/O	T-141234	_____
James V. Kennedy	2nd Lt.	0841271	_____
Denny C. Jefferson	F/O	T-136714	_____
Glen L. Head	2nd Lt.	02069201	_____
James H. Sheperd	F/O	T-64630	_____
Harry R. Dickenson	F/O	T-140092	_____
Edward R. Lunda	F/O	T-140111	_____
Quentin P. Smith	2nd Lt.	0841269	_____
James P. Jones	2nd Lt.	02075601	_____
Charles J. Dorkins	2nd Lt.	0841269	_____
Sidney H. Marzette	F/O	T-140114	_____
Maurice J. Jackson, Jr.	F/O	T-140105	_____
Leonard A. Altemus	2nd Lt.	02082572	_____
Herdon M. Cummings	2nd Lt.	084127	_____
Howard Storey	F/O	T-036601	_____

Mitchel L. Higginbothan	2nd Lt.	0841164	_____
James C. Warren	F/O	T-131958	_____
Alfred U. McKenzie	F/O	T-68765	_____
Cleophus W. Valentine	2nd Lt.	0841273	_____
Herbert J. Schwing	2nd Lt.	0841273	_____
Ario Dixione	F/O	T-140132	_____
Wendell G. Freeland	F/O	T-141200	_____
Robert B. Johnson	2nd Lt.	02068898	_____
William J. Curtis	F/O	T-68765	_____
Theodore O. Mason	2nd Lt.	0838167	_____
Cyril P. Dyer	2nd Lt.	02080924	_____
Adolphus Lewis Jr.	F/O	T-140136	_____
Victor L. Ranson	2nd Lt.	02080937	_____
Luther L. Oliver	2nd Lt.	0841272	_____
Lloyd W. Godfrey	F/O	T-138243	_____
Edward E. Tillmon	2nd Lt.	02080937	_____
Frank V. Pivalo	F/O	T-136681	_____
Leroy F. Gillead	2nd Lt.	0713060	_____
Leonard E. Williams	2nd Lt.	01054447	_____
Connie Nappier, Jr.	F/O	T-138250	_____
Norman A. Holmes	F/O	T-1412112	_____
Argonne F. Harden	2nd Lt.	0841270	_____
Roy M. Chappell	2nd Lt.	02068895	_____
Robert L. Hunter	2nd Lt.	02082649	_____
Leroy A. Battle	2nd Lt.	02075525	_____
James W. Brown Jr.	2nd Lt.	0838186	_____
Charles E. Malone	F/O	T-138247	_____
Walter R. Ray	2nd Lt.	02068902	_____
Edward W. Woodward	2nd Lt.	02068902	_____
Charles R. Taylor	F/O	T-136723	_____
John R. Perkins, Jr.	F/O	T-64270	_____
Roger Pines	2nd Lt.	02068901	_____
Alvin B. Steele	F/O	T-140140	_____
Roland A. Webber	F/O	T-136696	_____
Hiram E. Little	2nd Lt.	T-140137	_____
Samuel Colbert	F/O	02082500	_____

George W. Prioleau, Jr.	*F/O*	*0713065*	_____
Rudolph A. Berthoud	*F/0*	*02082576*	_____
Marcel Clyne	*2nd Lt.*	*T-131952*	_____
Clifford C. Jarrett	*2nd Lt.*	*02075547*	_____
Arthur O. Fisher	*2nd Lt.*	*02060946*	_____
Marcus E. Clarkson	*F/O*	*T-138615*	_____
Charles E. Jones	*F/O*	*T-140108*	_____
LeRoy H. Freeman	*2nd Lt.*	*02068900*	_____
Charles S. Goldsby	*F/O*	*T-68764*	_____
George H.O. Martin	*2nd Lt.*	*02068900*	_____
Wendell T. Stokes	*F/O*	*T-140123*	_____
Melvin M. Nelson	*2nd Lt.*	*0208653*	_____
William W. Bowie Jr.	*2nd Lt.*	*02080867*	_____
Edward W. Watkins	*2nd Lt.*	*0814209*	_____
Bertram W. Pitts	*F/O*	*T-140119*	_____
Edward R. Tabbanor	*F/O*	*T-131956*	_____
Silas M. Jenkins	*2nd Lt.*	*0838166*	_____
Clarence C. Conway	*F/O*	*T-141193*	_____
Harry S. Lum	*F/O*	*T-141228*	_____
Frederick H. Samuels	*F/O*	*T-66149*	_____
Robert T. McDaniel	*F/O*	*T-140697*	_____
Edward V. Hipps, Jr.	*2nd Lt.*	*02068897*	_____
Haydel J. White	*F/O*	*T-68712*	_____
David J. Murphy, Jr.	*F/O*	*T-66406*	_____
Calvin Smith	*F/O*	*T-136687*	_____
Calvin T. Warrick	*2nd Lt.*	*0841278*	_____
Lewis C. Hubbard, Jr.	*F/O*	*T-136660*	_____
Robert S. Payton, Jr.	*2nd Lt.*	*01174673*	_____

2. It is ordered that each commissioned and flight officer acknowledge receipt of this order, by placing his signature opposite his respective name.
ROBERT R. SELWAY, JR.
Colonel, Air Corps,
Commanding

Between April 10 and April 20, 1945, communications flowed continuously between Freeman, Mitchell Field and Washington. Also during this time communications between the NAACP and the Urban League were sent to Congress, Vice President Harry S. Truman, Truman Gibson Jr. (Civilian Aide on Negro Affairs to Secretary Stimson), Secretary of War, Stimson and President Franklin D. Roosevelt. The McCloy Committee also entered the picture and, following its final decision, published a report that was very distasteful to the military. Basically, the military was upset because McCloy would not undercut the decisions made concerning the officers club incidents at Selfridge, and added some recommendations to clarify the usage of the facilities.

The bottom line to the whole affair was that only the three Negro officers accused of forcing their way into the club were put on trial. Because Lieutenants Shirley R. Clinton and Marsden A. Thompson were base personnel, they were found innocent. The third, Roger Marshal was fined $150.00. In May of 1945, all of the white officers in the 477th were replaced by Negroes.

Second Lieutenant Coleman A. Young was discharged from the United States Army on December 23, 1945, at Maxwell Field, Alabama. The subject's last military assignment was with the 2530 AAF at Selman Field, Louisiana.

Following his discharge from the Army, Coleman Young collected $20.00 per week in unemployment compensation for approximately 26 weeks. He was entitled to collect 52 weeks under the G.I. Bill of Rights.

In July, 1946 he applied for a postal position under his veteran's status and was reinstated as a clerk at the Roosevelt Park Annex. After being reinstated, he requested a six-month leave of absence to clean up his personal business.

In 1950, he was employed for a short time at the Shwayder Brothers Plant in Ecorse, Michigan. Subsequent to this, he washed walls during a period of self-employment and was later fingerprinted for a cab driver's job.

In 1964, Coleman A. Young ran for a seat in the State Senate and won. It was not until 1973 that labor leaders decided to support him following his successful nomination for the office of Mayor of Detroit. Young was known as a quick study in that his political education sifted through his exceptionally quick mind, the same as the truncated officers training course had at Fort Benning, Georgia during World War II.

Mayor Coleman A. Young's nighttime persona, can best be described as a tall, dignified, and imposing smooth-talking man with silver hair and a salt-pepper moustache, who enjoys sports events and the company of beautiful women. In his elected position as Mayor of Detroit he was a tough-talking, streetwise master of negotiation who had a zero tolerance for fools.

Members of The Black Mayor's Forum, Left to Right: Andrew Young of Atlanta, Coleman Young of Detroit, Harold Washington of Chicago, Johnny Coleman of Tuskegee, Alabama and Richard Hatcher of Gary, Indiana.

Federal Bureau of Investigation

Freedom of Information/Privacy Acts Section

Subject: Coleman Young

FEDERAL BUREAU OF INVESTIGATION

FREEDOM OF INFORMATION/PRIVACY ACTS SECTION

SUBJECT: COLEMAN YOUNG

FILE NUMBER: CROSS-REFERENCES

On March 8, 1941 Subject was temporary secretary of the Second National Negro Congress held at Detroit, Michigan.

COLEMAN ALEXANDER YOUNG, Negro, was born May 24, 1918 in Tuscaloosa, Alabama.

Subject himself was employed as Executive Secretary of the National Negro Congress and was also Field Organizer for this organization since April of 1941.

Subject last resided at 2740 Antietam Street but was inducted into the Army on February 3, 1942 and is presently a member of the armed forces.

Subject was present at a Lenin Memorial Meeting and "Rally for Victory" sponsored by the Communist Party of Michigan on January 18, 1942 in the Mirror Ballroom, 2940 Woodward Avenue, Detroit, Michigan. Approximately 1,000 people were present and PAT TOOHEY, State Secretary of the Communist Party of Michigan, was Chairman. Subject was reported as having been present and as having spoken at this meeting, after first being introduced by TOOHEY. The following quotation appears as having been spoken by the Subject:

"Sojourner Truth has been taken away from us by Representative TENEROWICZ and the rest of the Fifth Columnists and I speak to ask your support

- 2 -

"in this great cause. At this very moment several negro organizations are holding protest meetings in the Calvary Baptist Church where letters of protest will be drafted and sent to the Mayor, Governor, and Common Council; that tomorrow at 4:00 p.m. we will picket the Housing Commission. We will never take this lying down. We will fight TENEROWICZ and his Fifth Column who are trying to promote race riots."

At the conclusion of the Subject's statements TOOHEY assured YOUNG that the Communist Party was behind them and would offer assistance as required.

Other speakers at this program were ADELINE KOHL, Acting State Secretary of the Young Communist League, and WILLIAM Z. FOSTER, the main speaker, with ARNOLD JOHNSON, State Secretary of the Communist Party of Ohio, all boosting Lenin.

Subject was at the Second National Conference of the National Negro Congress held March 8, 1941 at the Lucy Thurman Branch of the YWCA; that on January 6, 1941 he was at a meeting of the Ford Negro Unit of the Communist Party and the National Negro Congress held at 1836 Maple Street, Dearborn, Michigan; and that Subject was reported at a Communist Lenin Memorial Meeting held in the Finn Hall, the Communist Party Headquarters at that time, on January 21, 1941.

The "Michigan Chronicle," negro publication, under date of August 1, 1942, set forth under the heading "Fort McClellan, Alabama," a statement to the effect that Corporal COLEMAN A. YOUNG, among others mentioned, will be one of the men moved to the Infantry School at Fort Benning, Georgia, at an early date.

Subject: set forth the following description of the

Race	Negro
Height	6 feet
Weight	160 pounds
Complexion	Brown
Criminal Record	None

- C L O S E D -

190-5953-2

FEDERAL BUREAU OF INVESTIGATION

Form No. 1
THIS CASE ORIGINATED AT DETROIT, MICHIGAN

REPORT MADE AT	DATE WHEN MADE	PERIOD FOR WHICH MADE
DETROIT, MICHIGAN	8/6/46	7/26,27,30/46

TITLE

COLEMAN ALEXANDER YOUNG

SYNOPSIS OF FACTS:
Subject resides at 4034 Harding Avenue, Detroit, Michigan, and is employed by the United States Post Office Department as a Clerk at the Roosevelt Park Annex Station, Detroit, Michigan. Subject holds Communist Party Registration Card #53949 and until recently was assigned to the Nat Turner Communist Party Club. He has now been assigned to a new Communist Party group in the National Negro Congress. Reported to have been in the party for six years.

The Subject is the Regional Vice Commander for this organization and is very active in its activities.

- C -

REFERENCES:
Report of Special Agent dated January 3, 1943, at Detroit, Michigan.

APPROVED AND FORWARDED.	SPECIAL AGENT IN CHARGE	DO NOT WRITE-IN THESE SPACES
COPIES OF THIS REPORT		

Federal Bureau of Investigation
United States Department of Justice
Washington, D. C.

R n T-1

2

he following is the record of FBI number   110 072 A   J. E. Hoover

Director.

CONTRIBUTOR OF FINGERPRINTS	NAME AND NUMBER	ARRESTED OR RECEIVED	CHARGE	DISPOSITION
	Admits: 1936, driving thru stop street; traffic ticket, settled thru Violations Bureau by payment of fine.			
	Admits: 1936, speeding, Violation Bureau, Detroit, Mich; fine $4.			
	Admits: 1936, driving through red light, Violation Bureau, Detroit, Mich; fine $2.			
	Admits: 1937, improper left turn, Violation Bureau, Detroit, Mich; fine $2.			
	Admits: 1937, speeding; traffic ticket, settled thru Violations Bureau by payment of fine.			
	Admits: February 1941, speeding; traffic ticket, settled thru Violations Bureau by payment of fine.			

NATIONAL NEGRO LABOR COUNCIL

Information has been developed indicating that COLEMAN YOUNG, President of the National Negro Labor Council, will appear as guest speaker at a meeting of the National Negro Labor Council to be held at 188 Belmont Ave., Newark, N. J., on Sunday, 3/29/53.

L 1-6-12 7486

UNITED STATES DEPARTMENT OF JUSTICE

FEDERAL BUREAU OF INVESTIGATION

Reply, Please Refer to
No.

Detroit, Michigan
April 4, 1966

Re: Adult Community Movement For Equality
      (ACME), Rally, Detroit Police
      Department Headquarters, Detroit, Michigan,
      April 2, 1966

advised that at approximately 3:15 p.m. on this date, a group
of about 31 individuals led by Alvin Harrison, one of the
leaders of ACME, assembled at Chene and Macomb Streets in
Detroit and from this area, a group of approximately 26 of
these individuals walked to the front of the Detroit PD
Headquarters, 1300 Beaubien, Detroit, where they picketed and
sang "freedom" songs until approximately 6:30 p.m.
       advised their protest concerned the proposed "stop and
frisk" legislation which has been pending in the State of
Michigan. He said that there was not a petition presented as
had been previously indicated concerning this legislation and
Michigan State Senator Coleman Young, who had been scheduled to
appear, was not observed during this demonstration.

                                        the demonstration was
peaceful and no arrests were made.

                        pointed out that
ACME is a small local civil rights
group somewhat active on the East
Side of Detroit which has, in the
past, accused the Detroit PD of
harrassment, police brutality, and
discrimination against the Negroes.

                          , advised on
September 16, 1965, that as of
September 13, 1965, Coleman Young was
a current member of the Freedom Forum
Club, Michigan District Communist Party.

       This document contains neither recommendations nor
conclusions of the Federal Bureau of Investigation. It is the
property of the Federal Bureau of Investigation and is loaned
to your agency; it and its contents are not to be distributed
outside your agency.

UNITED STATES DEPARTMENT OF JUSTICE

FEDERAL BUREAU OF INVESTIGATION

, *Please Refer to*

Detroit, Michigan
March 31, 1966

Re: Adult Community Movement For Equality
(ACME), Rally, Detroit Police
Department Headquarters, Detroit, Michigan,
April 2, 1966

_____, advised that a small local
civil rights group known as ACME is planning to hold a street
rally in the area of Chene and Macomb Streets on the East
Side of Detroit in the late afternoon of Saturday, April 2,
1966. _____ this demonstration is being
held in opposition to a proposed "stop and frisk" ordinance
presently pending in the State Legislature.

_____ advised that today, a permit was being
granted by the City of Detroit for the holding of captioned
rally and also for a march on this same date by this group
from the rally area to the Detroit PD Headquarters at 1300
Beaubien Street, Detroit.

_____ this permit is being
obtained by Alvin Harrison, one of the leaders of ACME who
stated that Michigan State Senator Coleman Young will participat
in the rally and the march to Police Headquarters and that a
petition will be furnished by the ACME group to Young in front
of the Police Headquarters. This petition is a protest to
the proposed "stop and frisk" legislation.

_____ advised that ACME
is a small local civil rights group
somewhat active on the East Side of
Detroit which has, in the past, accused
the Detroit PD of harrassment, police
brutality, and discrimination against
the Negroes.

Re: Adult Community Movement For Equality
    (ACME), Rally, Detroit Police
    Department Headquarters, Detroit, Michigan,
    April 2, 1966

                                                    advised
        on September 16, 1965, that as of
        September 13, 1965, Coleman Young was a
        current member of the Freedom Forum Club,
        Michigan District Communist Party.

        This document contains neither recommendations nor
conclusions of the Federal Bureau of Investigation. It is the
property of the Federal Bureau of Investigation and is loaned
to your agency; it and its contents are not to be distributed
outside your agency.

Dorothy Dandridge

246

Chapter IX

Dorothy Dandridge: The Copper-Colored Bombshell

Dorothy Jean Dandridge was born in Cleveland, Ohio in the City Hospital on November 9,1922. She was the second daughter of Reverend Cyril Dandridge and his wife Ruby Butler, an amateur singer, dancer, and actress. The Dandridge family broke up before Dorothy was born. The disintegration of the marriage was caused by Geneva Williams a very talented piano player and Ruby's lesbian lover.

All of Dorothy's formative years were spent with her sister Vivian, her mother Ruby, and Geneva. Ruby was the household breadwinner and Geneva was the girls' disciplinarian and music teacher. The Dandridge girls in fact had two stage mothers. The four of them traveled on the T.O.B.A. (Theater Owners Booking Association) known in the entertainment business as "Tough On Black Assess".

The Dandridge sisters at age eight and ten were billed as "The Wonder Kids". They sang, danced and performed comedy skits at church and school functions throughout the South and on the vaudeville "Chitterlings Circuit" on the East Coast, and in the Midwest. They primarily attended Negro theaters such as the Regal and Grand in Chicago, the Paradise in Detroit, the Apollo and Lafayette in New York City, the Royal in Baltimore, the Howard in Washington D.C. and the Nixon in Philadelphia and in many smaller and lesser known entertainment houses.

In 1929, Ruby Dandridge saw the William T. Fox Hollywood studio's all Colored film entitled *Hearts in Dixie* starring Bill "Bojangles" Robinson with an all Black cast. It was believed to be the first successful all Colored movie produced by a white man. (One of the early Colored pioneers of all Colored movies was a producer by the name of Oscar Micheaux). After seeing the *Dixie* show Ruby concluded that Hollywood was the place for an aspiring Colored actress to be anchored. The following year marked the beginning of the Great Depression of the 1930s and it was at that time Dandridge chose to board a Greyhound bus destined for Hollywood in Los Angeles, California with her two daughters and her ladylove.

On the West Coast Ruby eventually established herself as a small time comedy actress playing Mammy roles on radio, bit parts of the same character in film and later on television. Although Ruby's daughters were enrolled in school they were absent a great deal of the time doing thumbnail parts in Hollywood films such as *The Big Broadcast of 1936* and the closing sequence in the Marx Brothers comedy, *A Day At The Races* (1937) in addition to dancing and singing in *It Can't Last Forever* (1938) featuring Ralph Bellamy the actor and the dancing Jackson Brothers.

At age fifteen Dorothy, Vivian Dandridge and Etta Jones, a neighborhood friend who they met in dancing school toured the country with their two stage mothers. The Dandridge Sisters became an important act in Jimmy Lunceford's traveling stage show. The show was billed as the *Jazznocracy Express*. Traveling with the popular Lunceford orchestra was the Dandridge Sisters entry to the internationally famous Cotton Club in New York City where they opened to rave reviews. The Cotton Club was the Jazz bastion where the Duke Ellington, Cab Calloway and the Jimmy Lunceford orchestras held fort in the 1930s. It was backstage at the Cotton Club in the spring of 1938 where the sensational dancing Nicholas Brothers were performing, that Harold Nicholas the youngest of the two brothers first laid eyes on Dorothy Dandridge, the sixteen year old beauty. It was also in the same season that

Dorothy first saw her father the Reverend Cyril Dandridge who had moved to New York City to accept a pastorate.

Following their long Cotton Club engagement in May 1939, the Dandridge sisters and Geneva their chaperon and teacher went to London, England to perform at the Palladium. Their reception was a bloody stomp. England loved the dancing and singing dolls. During their stay in Great Britain, Geneva became obsessed with Dorothy's blossoming breasts. She began questioning her about her virginity and after a show one night, threw her across a bed and attempted to pull down her panties and examine her private parts like a gynecologist. Dorothy pushed the much older, and heavier woman off her and then proceeded to knock her to the floor with a series of swift Joe Louis punches. Geneva's behavior with Dorothy was legally tantamount to being raped by a male person.

Dorothy Dandridge and Harold Nicholas her first husband and childhood sweetheart.

Upon returning to the United States, Dorothy decided that Geneva's presence was both obstructing and smothering her creativity. Therefore she decided to perform from that point forward as a single. In 1940, she auditioned and got a role in the Los Angeles *Meet The People* stage production. She was the only person of Color in the cast.

In 1941, she appeared in the Colored segment of the film *Sun Valley Serenade* with the Nicholas Brothers doing a dance routine to the song *Chattanooga Choo Choo*. She looked sensational in a black satin dress that fell just above her slightly knock knees. Harold Nicholas who was engaged to Dorothy at the time had convinced the producers that her talent would add spice to their act, and it did. This marked the first time that a female dancer had hoofed with the brothers in their fast and flashy dance routine. Their dance routine in the film was incongruous, in that it did not relate to any of the other characters in the movie. Therefore, that sequence could be excised by theaters in the south without disturbing the flow of the general theme of the show. On September 6, 1942 four years after they met, Harold and Dorothy took their wedding vows in a very elaborate and celebrated setting.

In November, 1942, Dorothy Dandridge made some musical shorts on "soundies" a gadget made for video jukeboxes in the 1940's. The sound machine made it possible for entertainers to sing and play their popular hits on 10 inch screens. The author was a soldier in the United States Army during World War II, it was then that he first saw and heard Dorothy on a "soundie", dancing and singing to the melody of *Cow Cow Boogie* (1941). The sound machine was actually a prelude to television and was used widely by artists like Thomas "Fats" Waller who performed medleys that included: *Ain't Misbehavin* (1929), *Your Feet's Too Big*, and *The Joint is Jumpin*. Nat "King" Cole used it to sing his, *Is You Is or Is You Ain't My Baby*? *Route 66* and *Straighten Up and Fly Right* (1943). Ditto for the Delta Rhythm Boys- *Don't Get Around Much Any More* (1942), and the Mills Brothers- *Up The Lazy River* (1931). Soldiers housed in isolated military camps could stand around the "soundie" machine in their Post Exchanges or Day Rooms and reminisce about that girl back home and be entertained for ten minutes by their favorite artist for a nickel.

Jumping from being featured in ten minute "soundies" to the big screen was a big leap for Dorothy. She always had a burning desire for developing a movie career. During the nineteen thirties and forties, most Colored women in films were like Hattie McDaniel, who won an Oscar in 1939 in a supporting role as a servant in *Gone With The Wind* or Louise Beavers, who was the jolly pancake cook with the infectious smile in the 1934 film *Imitation of Life*. The dialogue written for Negroes in films during that period was both stereotypical and degrading.

Dorothy wanted to raise the bar several levels above what her mother had achieved as a bit player. To accomplish this feat she bartered her beauty and talent for minor roles in *Drums of the Congo* (1942) and *The Hit Parade*

(1943). These two films were mere appetizers that stimulated her taste buds for the main event.

While struggling to meet her acting goal, she polished her singing talents with the help of the swerve and sophisticated Phil Moore, the Black composer- arranger and piano guru who guided Lena Horne, Frank Sinatra, Marilyn Monroe, Ava Gardner, Lavern Baker, and Ernestine Anderson.

From 1944 forward she was doubling in brass, in that she was in demand both as a singer and an actress. She appeared in the following films, *Atlantic City*, 1944; *Pillow to Post*, 1945; *Tarzan's Peril,* 1951; *The Harlem Globetrotters*, 1951; *Bright Road*, 1953; and *Carmen Jones* in, 1954.

Dorothy Dandridge had become a very disciplined actress. However, director and producer Otto Preminger, discarded her resume after her first interview for the role of *Carmen Jones*. She later learned through her agent Earl Mills, that Preminger saw her as a sophisticated Fifth Avenue model, thus light years away from the sassy, sexy and earthy Carmen that he was searching for to match up with Harry Belafonte.

Earl Mills succeeded in getting Dorothy a second interview with Preminger. This time Dorothy wiggled into his office in a tight fitting skirt that displayed all of her curvatures and an open blouse that partially exposed her breast. She fixed her hair so it would have that windblown look and she lowered her voice to sound as if she were gasping for air. Like a jackrabbit jumps out of a bush Preminger leaped out of his swivel chair and pointed at Dorothy when she sauntered through his office door and shouted, "You are my Carmen"!

Following her success in *Carmen Jones*, Dorothy was nominated for the Academy Award (Oscar) for the best actress in 1954; and later for the Golden Globe Award for her role in *Porgy and Bess*, 1959.

Dorothy was a winner in everything but love. She divorced her first husband Harold Nicholas in 1949 because of his womanizing; Otto Preminger loved her but refused to marry her because he felt that marrying a Black woman would ruin his career; Peter Lawford would not cut the cake because of his ties to the Kennedy money.

In 1959, she married a white nightclub owner John (better known as Jack) Denison. Jack was near the end of the line of her white lovers. At her wedding reception, she fell asleep from drugging and drinking too much. He had hoped that she could help support his failing business and she in turn thought that he would be the wind under her declining career. They both had miscalculated. In March of 1963, Dandridge declared personal bankruptcy and lost everything she owned including her house in the Hollywood Hills. When she died in September 1965, she had $2.14 in her bank account.

Left to Right: Dorothy and her second husband Jack Denison are joined by Nat "King" Cole.

Federal Bureau of Investigation

Freedom of Information/Privacy Acts Section

Subject: Dorothy Dandridge

FEDERAL BUREAU OF INVESTIGATION

FREEDOM OF INFORMATION/PRIVACY ACTS SECTION

SUBJECT: DOROTHY DANDRIDGE

CROSS-REFERENCES

CONFIDENTIAL

```
2 - Orig. & dupl.
1 - Yellow
1 - Mr. Bates
1 - Section Tickler
1 - M. S. Cole
```

August 23, 1956

VIA LIAISON

SUMMARY

DOROTHY DANDRIDGE, also known as
Dorothy D. Nicholas
Born: November 9, 1922
Cleveland, Ohio

No investigation has been conducted by the FBI relative to the captioned individual. However, our records reflect the following information concerning her:

On July 30, 1953, a confidential source furnished a letter dated July 22, 1953, written by Dorothy Dandridge to an official of Loew's, Inc. which pertained to articles which had appeared in the "Daily People's World," west coast communist newspaper. The pertinent portions of the letter follow:

"Certain newspaper reports have been brought to my attention which I would like to comment on.

"1. PW 3/14/47 - One Dorothy Dandridge will appear at a party Saturday night, March 22nd at 2118 Hobart Street, Los Angeles, auspices National Negro Congress.

"I appeared at this party believing that the National Negro Congress was associated with the National Association for the Advancement of Colored People (NAACP), a well recognized organization. I went with my husband, Harold Nicholas. I went for social reasons and because I was interested in the Negro community. I honestly can't remember who asked us to attend.

"2. PW 6/30/47 Dorothy Dandridge among those who spoke at a series of rallies sponsored by the Progressive Citizens of America protesting the Taft-Hartley bill.

ENCLOSURE
- M.S.Cole:men
  (6)

RECORDED-41
INDEXED-41   62-6527-47987

delivered 8-23-56

CONFIDENTIAL

my knowledge the Lab was no longer in existence at this date.
I recall one incident regarding Hedda Hopper while I was a
student at the Lab. What Hedda Hopper said did affect me and
I did express concern. However, the exact wording of this
particular quotation is not the kind of language I use but
I'm sure no one could object to my expressing concern.

"I would like to close by saying that I am not now
nor ever have been a member of the Communist Party or Communist
Party Political Association nor have I ever made any donations
to these parties. Had I known that any of the above organizations
would later be cited as Communistic and or subversive, I would
never have participated. I have at no time been active
politically. My sole interests are towards having a successful
career and aiding my people." (Letter among many by various individ.
furnished by James F. O'Neil, Director of Publications, American *

In reference to item 5 quoted above, our records
reflect an article which appeared in the "Daily Worker," east
coast communist newspaper dated September 22, 1948, captioned
"Hedda Hopper Rapped for Anti-Negro Bias" which relates to the
incident referred to by Miss Dandridge. (100-294936-A)

Regarding the organizations referred to by Miss Dandridge
the National Negro Congress has been designated by the Attorney
General of the United States pursuant to Executive Order 10450.
The Progressive Citizens of America was cited by the California
Committee on Un-American Activities in its 1947 and 1948 reports.
An informant who has furnished reliable information in the past
advised on May 15, 1956, that until January 3, 1956, the Hollywood
Arts, Sciences and Professions Council (HASP) was the California
Chapter of the National Council of the Arts, Sciences and Professio.
(NCASP) in New York City and consistently followed the programs
and policies of the parent organization. On January 3, 1956, the
HASP officially dissolved by action of its executive committee and
vote of its membership. The NCASP was cited as a "Communist front"
by the Congressional Committee on Un-American Activities in its
1950 report. Actors Laboratory was cited as a "Communist venture"
by the California Committee on Un-American Activities in its 1947
report.

An informant who has furnished reliable information
in the past reported on February 21, 1955, that an employee of
the Sands Hotel, Las Vegas, Nevada, who was a gambler from the
east coast, had advised the informant that Jack Entratter, part
owner of the Sands Hotel and who was in charge of the Sands'
Copa Room, found Nat King Cole and Dorothy Dandridge together
in Cole's room at the hotel. Cole was appearing as a star in
the Copa Room at the time. The informant stated that Entratter
became furious with Cole for having an "affair" with Dorothy
Dandridge and threatened him. Dandridge reportedly told

*Legion, which he asked be treated confidentially: 100-138754-977)

CONFIDENTIAL

Entratter to forget the whole matter as she was Cole's color,
too. The informant further advised that Entratter was formerly
manager and part owner of the Copacabana in New York City and
has reportedly spent a great deal of time and money promoting
Dandridge's career and that Entratter considered her his girl
friend. (CI SU-283-C; 62-75147-44-591)

On May 10, 1955, Agents of the FBI arrested Louis Arlan
Kerr at New Orleans, Louisiana, on a federal warrant charging a
violation of the Interstate Transportation of Stolen Property Statut
while being interviewed concerning the federal charge on which he
was arrested, Kerr volunteered information that he was a homosexual.
He furnished the names of 45 individuals with whom he claimed to
have had homosexual relations since 1951. Kerr also stated that he
had a long standing friendship with Dorothy Dandridge, Negro movie
actress. However, he added that she was in no way a sex deviate.
The reliability of Kerr is unknown. It is to be noted that he had
previously been arrested on fraudulent check charges and had admitte
receiving psychiatric treatment of an unknown nature in the past.
(105-34074-1210X)

The foregoing information is furnished to you as a
result of your request for an FBI file check and is not to be
construed as a clearance or nonclearance of the individual
involved. This information is furnished for your use and should
not be disseminated outside of your agency.

LA 100-35836

b1

FOREIGN TRAVEL

The "Los Angeles Tribune", a weekly Negro newspaper, pages 1 and 3, for June 5, 1957, carried an article reflecting that LEO BRANTON, Jr., left Los Angeles via TWA for Paris, France, arriving on June 5, 1957. The article stated that the trip was for the purpose of BRANTON consulting with his client, actress DOROTHY DANDRIDGE, who was then on the French Riviera. The article stated BRANTON's trip was for two weeks.

b7C

b7C
b7D

6 (Rev. 12-13-56)

F B I

Date: 5/24/63

CONFIDENTIAL

smit the following in _____
(Type in plain text or code)

AIRTEL   AIR MAIL
(Priority or Method of Mailing)

- -

ALL INFORMATION CONTAINED
HEREIN IS UNCLASSIFIED
EXCEPT WHERE SHOWN
OTHERWISE

TO: DIRECTOR, FBI

FROM: SAC, LOS ANGELES (157-630)

SUBJECT: RALLY AT WRIGLEY FIELD, SPONSORED
         BY NATIONAL ASSOCIATION FOR THE
         ADVANCEMENT OF COLORED PEOPLE, ET AL
         LOS ANGELES, CALIFORNIA
         5/26/63
         RACIAL MATTERS
         OO: LOS ANGELES

b7C

         Re Los Angeles airtel to Bureau dated 5/21/63.

         Enclosed herewith are eight copies of a LHM setting
forth additional information concerning captioned subject
matter.

         One copy of the LHM is being furnished to the 115th
INTC, Region II, U.S. Army, Pasadena, California.

         The LAPD is covering the rally. Arrangements have
been made for the Los Angeles Office to be advised of what
transpires at the rally and the Bureau will be advised immediately.

b7

         The LHM is designated as confidential to protect a
confidential source of continuing value.

③ - Bureau (Encl.-8) (REGISTERED)
1 - Los Angeles

(4)   G-2, ONI, CSI, CRD   REC-62 157-6-26-90

Date Forw. 6-3-63   15   11 MAY 27 1963

How Forw.   Classified by 98C9
                                                       Declassify on: OADR
By   b7C

Approved: _____   Sent _____ M   Per _____

FD-36 (Rev. 12-13-56)

F B I

Date: 5/27/63

Transmit the following in _____
(Type in plain text or code)

Via AIRTEL _____ AIR MAIL _____
(Priority or Method of Mailing)

TO: DIRECTOR, FBI

FROM: SAC, LOS ANGELES (157-630)

RE: RALLY AT WRIGLEY FIELD,
         SPONSORED BY NATIONAL
         ASSOCIATION FOR THE ADVANCEMENT
         OF COLORED PEOPLE, ET AL
         LOS ANGELES, CALIFORNIA
         5/26/63
         RACIAL MATTERS
         OO: LOS ANGELES

Re Los Angeles airtels to the Bureau dated 5/21 and 24/63 and teletype dated 5/26/63.

There are enclosed for the Bureau 8 copies of a letterhead memorandum setting forth information regarding the captioned rally. One copy of this memorandum is being furnished to the 115th INTC, Region II, U. S. Army, Pasadena, California.

3-Bureau (AM)(RM)(Enc. 8)
1-Los Angeles
(4)

Agency G-2, ONI, OSI, CRD

Date Forw. 6-4-63

How Forw. 6-9

MAY 29 1963

ENCLOSURE

UNITED STATES DEPARTMENT OF JUSTICE

FEDERAL BUREAU OF INVESTIGATION

Los Angeles, California
May 27, 1963

Reply, Please Refer to
ile No.

RALLY AT WRIGLEY FIELD, SPONSORED BY THE
NATIONAL ASSOCIATION FOR THE ADVANCEMENT
OF COLORED PEOPLE, ET AL, LOS ANGELES
May 26, 1963

All of the sources used in this document have
furnished reliable information in the past.

Sources advised that the rally for freedom in support
of the Birmingham, Alabama movement filled Wrigley Field to
near the capacity and that approximately 30,000 persons were
in attendance. The meeting lasted from about 3:00 p. m.
until 5:30 p. m. and it was described as the largest rally of
its sort ever to be held in Los Angeles, California. The
featured speaker was Reverend Martin Luther King, President
of the Southern Christian Leadership Conference, who spoke in
support of the Birmingham non-violence movement. He commented
on events in Birmingham and remarked that they would be
helped by getting rid of segregation and discrimination in Los
Angeles, California. King also stated that President Kennedy
should personally escort Negro students into the University
of Alabama and issue an executive order declaring that segregation is unconstitutional under the 14th Amendment.

There were numerous introductions and comments by
people in the entertainment world. One of the more celebrated
was Sammy Davis, Jr., who was reported to have pledged $20,000.00,
which was said to represent one week's earnings in Las Vegas,
Nevada. There were also various donations from individuals,
churches, unions, and other organizations, and a collection
was taken from the audience. These proceeds were requested for
the Birmingham demonstrators. The other celebrities who
participated were actresses Dorothy Dandridge, Joanne Woodward,
Rita Moreno, and Davis's wife, May Britt. The actors included
Tony Franciosa, Mel Ferrer, and Miss Woodward's husband, Paul
Newman. Comedian Dick Gregory also spoke at the rally.
California Governor Brown sent a message supporting the meeting
which was read at the rally.

#348488

LL INFORMATION CONTAINED
REIN IS UNCLASSIFIED

Groucho Marx

262

Chapter X

Groucho Marx: You Can Bet Your Life He Was Funny

F.B.I. Director J. Edgar Hoover, thought Groucho Marx was funny until the comedian was quoted as coming to the defense of the nine Negro Scottsboro boys in a trial involving the alleged rape of two white female hoboes. Groucho made the following statement: "The battle of the Communists for the lives of those colored boys in Alabama is one that will be taught in Soviet America as the most courageous battle ever fought. It will be a red letter day on the calendar. It will be what Bunker Hill in Boston is to the modern American textbooks."

Julius Henry Marx, publicly known as Groucho, was born in New York City on October 2, 1890. His parents were Minnie and Simon Marx. The couple initially met on the lower east side of New York City, although both of them were immigrants from Alsace-Lorraine, Western France's heaviest populated Jewish territory. The French surrendered that section of their country to Germany after they were defeated in the 1871 war.

In addition to Groucho, Minnie and Simon had three other sons who were musically gifted, namely Leonard (Chico), Arthur (Harpo) and Zeppo Marx. Although Groucho began his career as a soprano singer at age 13 with the Leroy Trio for $5 a week, it was shortly thereafter that the talented four brothers were collectively introduced to the stage by their mother and her sister Hannah in a vaudeville act that was known as the "Six Musical Mascots".

Groucho Marx at age 13.

In 1909, the young men toured as the "Four Nightingales" and finally as the "Four Marx Brothers". Their mother Minnie, was their road manager and chaperon. All of the boys were extremely competent professional musicians. Groucho Marx was reputed to be one of the top guitar players in the United States. He also played some mean piano, mandolin, and harp. Arthur's nickname was Harpo. He got his name because he played the harp, and also played piano, flute, trombone. Whereas, Chico played jazz piano with the flair of a great concert artist, he too was an accomplished instrumentalist with the cornet, zither, and violin. Brother Zeppo who was God's gift to the ladies, played the saxophone, piano, cello, and flute.

In addition to their mother and aunt, the boys were influenced a great deal by Adolph Shoenberg their maternal uncle who, in addition to being a professional singer was a member of the Manhattan Comedy Four. His weekly salary was $250.00, which was a very handsome sum of money during the first four decades of the twentieth-century. On the other hand, their father as a tailor only made $25.00 per week sweating over a sewing machine 10 hours a day, 6 days a week in the lower Manhattan east side garment district.

Top to bottom: Chico, Harpo, Groucho and Zeppo clown backstage.

The four Marx brothers became so successful on the Gotham stage they accepted an offer to take their act "On The Mezzanine" to the Coliseum Theater in London, England in the summer of 1922. There they quickly learned the pains of how it felt to flop big time. Undaunted, they got up from the sawdust covered floor and brushed themselves off and revived one of their old and tested productions entitled "Home Again", which was a glove tight fit for an English music hall audience. Through perseverance, and talent the boys were able to turn their near disastrous trip into a transatlantic triumph.

When they returned to the states from England, they hooked up with a small time booking agent-producer, Joseph M. Gaites, who decided to build a musical comedy around them and use some of his old discarded theatrical scenery as a backdrop. The Marx Brothers opened the *I'll Say She Is* production at the Walnut Street Theater in downtown Philadelphia. The play was a smash hit with the theatergoers in the City of Brotherly Love, and Sisterly Affection. However, in spite of their success, the brothers were still fearful of the New York critics. Therefore, they took the low road and dodged the "Big Apple" and toured the country with *I'll Say She Is*. It enjoyed a very successful run for over a year.

During the twelve plus months they were on the road, they literally exhausted the available supply of large legitimate theater houses where they could perform in major cities. Since there was no place else to go except home, the Marx Brothers decided to bite the worm-threaded "Big Apple" and take their chances with the New York critics. On May 19, 1924, the Marx Brothers opened at the Casino Theater on Broadway. Alexander Woollcott one of New York's most highly respected entertainment critics wrote a glowing review about their performance and suggested that his readers go and see the show and be prepared to figuratively laugh their heads off.

The Marx Family home at 4512 So. Grand Boulevard (Dr. Martin Luther King Drive) in Chicago, Illinois.

Mother Minnie Marx was aware that on the business side of theater, popular silent movies had encroached on their venue to the point that it was absorbing more than fifty percent of the theater patron's entertainment dollars. Therefore, she could reach a larger and more stable market if the family moved west to Chicago. Chicago, which was known through Carl Sandburg's poems as the "Hog Butcher Of The

World", the railroad hub of the United States and the Windy City was also the headquarters of three major vaudeville booking agencies headed by Gus Sun, Pantages, and Consodine and Sullivan.

Following the east wind and the strong animal odor of Chicago's stockyards, the matriarch and her brood found themselves living in a three story brownstone home at 4512 South Grand Boulevard (Dr. Martin Luther King

Drive), which in the early 1920s was an upper middle class Jewish section of Chicago, the toddling town that Reverend Billy Sunday could not shut down. Mrs. Marx purchased the $21,000 home with a $1,000 down payment from a grumpy old mortgage banker named Sidney Greenbaum. The down payment had been borrowed from Al Shean, a family friend in New York City.

The Marx boys spent their first summer in Abraham Lincoln's City by the Lake, explor-

Groucho Marx and Al Shean an old family friend.

ing the sites and going to see the Chicago White Sox baseball team play at Comiskey Park which was just a short walking distance from their new home. "Shoeless" Joe Jackson had been one of Groucho's favorite baseball heroes, until he was kicked out of the American Baseball League because of his alleged role in the 1919 Black Sox scandal.

Groucho Marx first saw Charlie Chaplin perform onstage in Winnipeg, Canada. The English comedian made such a deep impression on the young entertainer, he told his brothers that Chaplin just might be "the greatest comedian in the world". As Groucho and Chaplin matured, they became mutual admirers of each other's contribution to the theater. They both were undisputed geniuses. Groucho worked overtime trying to emulate and befriend Chaplin.

When Groucho ran into Chaplin again in Salt Lake City, he attempted to tighten up their friendship by inviting him to join the four brothers in a visit to a lavishly-adorned whorehouse for upper crust gentlemen. The quartet made their selections from a group of ladies-in-waiting, in a spacious living room complete with a white grand piano surrounded by several musicians playing

Groucho with his second car, a 1928 Cord.

mood music. After enjoying several glasses of champagne, the brothers retired to the upstairs bedchambers with their ladies of the evening. Chaplin was too shy to participate in the *I Am In The Mood For Love* game, thus he stayed downstairs in the parlor listening to the music and exchanging niceties with the Madam of the house.

For female companionship, Groucho usually relied on houses of joy or on Chico's uncanny ability to attract beautiful women by simply sitting down on a piano stool and whipping up some popular girl catching tunes on the keyboard. Among the female piano groupies, Groucho was usually lucky enough to get a date. If that failed, he could certainly depend on one of Chico's hand-me-down old flames.

Although Groucho was in his thirties, he was not as aggressive with women as his younger brothers. However when he met Ruth Johnson one of Zeppo's hand-me-downs a bulb went off in his head and he flipped. He proposed marriage to this stunning blond actress and dancer without adhering to the customary courting period. The wedding took place in Chicago in the home of the bride's parents. Nobody was happy with this union other than the bride and groom. Groucho describes his mother-in-law as a small-town bigot. She was extremely displeased with the notion of having a Jew as a son-in-law. On the other hand his mother looked upon her new daughter-in-law as an interloper without dowry, humor, or style. Minnie's dislike for Ruth was blatantly displayed by her attitude and speech. She made certain that her Wasp daughter-in-law remained an outsider.

Groucho's son, Arthur J. and his daughter, Miriam Ruth, were the off-springs of a marriage that was made in hell and ended in divorce in 1942. His daugher later said, "My father and Ruth really were not meant for each other from the start, and they should have never married in the first place."

Where women were concerned, Groucho was more interested in the kill than in the chase. (Nobody ever told him that the fun was in the chase and not the kill). He depended on getting female companions via love couriers like his brothers Chico and Zeppo. In one instance however, it was his daughter Miriam who introduced him to the woman who would become his second wife. She was a married woman by the name of Kay Gorcey, a petite beautiful actress who was harnessed to a wife-beating, jealous radio broadcaster. Miriam felt sorry enough for her new friend to persuade her father to give the young woman the use of the guest room in their Westwood home. Mariam discovered after a very short period of time, that the female houseguest was not sleeping in the guestroom but with her father. In 1945, Kay divorced Leo Gorcey and married Groucho and thereby became Mariam's stepmother. This marriage also ended in divorce five years later.

In 1954 Groucho got the hots for a 24 year old, leggy brunet model named Eden Hartford. Eden was beautiful wide-eyed girl with a physical shape that would put Marilyn Monroe's body to shame. Groucho was ashamed to tell his son and daughter face to face that he was fixing to jump the broom again. Thus, he wired them from Sun Valley, Idaho and informed them that they had a new mother named Eden. The new Mrs. Marx was only seven years older than his daughter. This marriage ended in 1969, when Eden was hitting 40 years of age and Groucho was looking in the mirror at 80.

After three strikes, Groucho never remarried. However, in 1972 he began publicly appearing with his attractive "secretary-companion", Erin Fleming. In Groucho's twilight years, his mental competence came into question, and he became the object of a messy conservatorship proceeding, involving Miss Fleming and Groucho's family. Ultimately, Groucho's grandson, Andrew, was named Groucho's permanent conservator until Groucho's death.

Groucho married Kay Gorcey in 1945.

Last Will and Testament

As his Will makes evident, comedian Groucho (Julius) Marx was the self-appointed victim of three ex-wives. The second article of Grouco's will states:

I declare that I am not married; that I have had three former wives, to wit, Ruth Garrity (formerly Ruth Marx), Catherine Marie Marx (formerly know as Kay Marie Marx), and Edna Marie Marx (formerly known as Edna Marie Higgins and also as Eden Hartford), from whom I have been divorced by final decree. I have three children, namely my son, Arthur J. Marx, my daughter Miriam Ruth Marx, and my daughter Melinda Marx… Except as above specified, I have never been married and have no additional children.

Later in the Will, Marx reiterates, "I have, except as otherwise stated in this will, intentionally and with full knowledge omitted to provide for my heirs living at the time of my decease. Moreover, except for the trust established in Article SIX, I expressly disinherit my ex-wives." The trust referred to was

$25,000 for the benefit of his ex-wife Catherine Marie Marx, and provides for the payment to her, the grand sum of $100 per week.

Gorucho's Will makes the following interesting provisions for the disposition of some of his personal property.

A.   I give and bequeath to the Smithsonian Institution, Washington, D.C. all of my memorabilia, including items such as scrapbooks, still pictures, scripts and film materials (but not the intangible property rights therein), my Academy Award statuette, my French medal, and such other items as Erin Fleming determines to constitute the collection of memorabilia; provided, however, that prior to the gift to the Smithsonian Institution, subject to approval of Erin Fleming, each of my children may select from among the memorabilia such items as each desires, and I hereby give to each of them the items so selected, as tokens of my affection.

B.   I give to Erin Fleming... the Boutonniere of the Commander des Arts et Lettres presented to me by the French government.

C.   I give to Goddard Lieberson, if he survives me, that painting in my home depicting myself and my brothers, painted by John Decker.

D.   I direct my executors to sell as soon as reasonably convenient all remaining items of jewelry, books, pictures, paintings, works of art, furniture, furnishing, fixtures and personal effects, together with my home at 1083 Hillcrest Road, Beverly Hills, California...

Despite the foregoing bequests and a cash bequest to Miss Fleming of $150,000, she filed a claim against the estate for approximately $75,000, according to papers filed with the court. The Bank of America National Trust and Savings Association, which was named as the sole executor of the Groucho Marx estate, rejected Miss Fleming's claim. There was additional legal skirmishing over the estate between Marx's children and Miss Fleming, which was widely reported by the press.

Marx was generous with others named in his Will. He gave $50,000 to each of his brothers who survived him (only Zeppo), and $5,000 to each of his grandchildren living at the time of his death. He rewarded a cousin of one of his ex-wives with a bequest in the amount of $3,500 "because she has been so kind to my daughter Melinda."

Despite his apparent generosity, Marx's Will also utilized the feared in terrorem clause. Pursuant to the provisions of the will, if a bequest was forfeited by any beneficiary, it was to be paid instead to the Jewish Federation Council of Greater Los Angeles.

Finally, for the man who once remarked that he would not want to be a member of any club that would accept him as a member, Groucho specifically bequeathed his membership in the Hillcrest Country Club to his son, Arthur. According to papers filed by the estate with the Los Angeles County court, that Hillcrest Country Club membership had an appraised value of $20,000 in Marx's estate, which had a market value of almost $2 million. Apparently, Groucho said the magic words many times.

/s/ Julius H. Marx

/s/ Groucho Marx

The will was dated September 24, 1974 and signed in Beverly Hills, California.

Grouch Marx died on August 19, 1977 at the age of 87 at the Cedars Sinai Medical Center in Los Angeles, California.

Federal Bureau of Investigation

Freedom of Information/Privacy Acts Section

Subject: Groucho Marx

FEDERAL BUREAU OF INVESTIGATION

FREEDOM OF INFORMATION/PRIVACY ACTS SECTION

COVER SHEET

SUBJECT: <u>GROUCHO MARX</u>

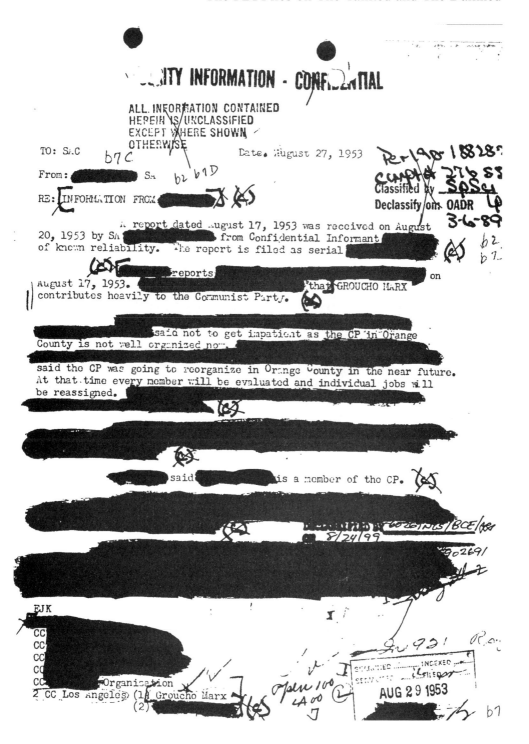

SECURITY INFORMATION - CONFIDENTIAL

ALL INFORMATION CONTAINED
HEREIN IS UNCLASSIFIED
EXCEPT WHERE SHOWN
OTHERWISE

TO: SAC

From: ▓▓▓▓▓ SA

RE: INFORMATION FROM ▓▓▓▓▓

Date. August 27, 1953

A report dated August 17, 1953 was received on August 20, 1953 by SA ▓▓▓▓▓ from Confidential Informant ▓▓▓ of known reliability. The report is filed as serial ▓▓▓▓▓

▓▓▓▓▓ reports ▓▓▓▓▓▓▓▓▓▓▓▓▓ on August 17, 1953. ▓▓▓▓▓▓▓▓▓ that GROUCHO MARX contributes heavily to the Communist Party.

▓▓▓▓▓▓▓▓▓▓ said not to get impatient as the CP in Orange County is not well organized now. ▓▓▓▓▓ said the CP was going to reorganize in Orange County in the near future. At that time every member will be evaluated and individual jobs will be reassigned.

▓▓▓▓▓ said ▓▓▓▓▓▓ is a member of the CP.

EJK
CC
CC
CC
CC
CC ▓▓▓▓▓ Organization
2 CC Los Angeles (1 Groucho Marx)
(2)

AUG 29 1953

SAC, SAN DIEGO

September 21, 1

SAC, LOS ANGELES (100-46665)

GROUCHO MARX
SECURITY MATTER -

C O N F I D E N T I A L

ALL INFORMATION CONTAINED
HEREIN IS UNCLASSIFIED
EXCEPT WHERE SHOWN
OTHERWISE

Classified by
Declassify on: OADR

Re memo of SA ▓▓▓▓▓ San Diego, dated August 27,
1953, captioned "Info from ▓▓▓▓▓" b2 b7D

▓▓▓▓▓ noted that during a ▓▓▓▓▓
▓▓▓▓▓ on August 17, 1953, the latter said GROUCHO MARX
contributes heavily to the Communist Party. ▓▓▓▓▓ apparently
referred to GROUCHO MARX, the film and T-V star, but no further
elaboration is indicated in referenced memo.

You are requested to furnish your evaluation of the informant in this matter as well as the information received. If further
elaboration was made by ▓▓▓▓▓ or the informant in connection
with this particular allegation, it should be furnished, along with
available details concerning the basis upon which ▓▓▓▓▓ statement was made. If you deem it necessary, it is suggested that
▓▓▓▓▓ be recontacted specifically in reference to this matter.

b2
b7D

902691
DECLASSIFIED BY 60267NW5/BCE/
ON 8/24/95

Reg.

MMB:aem

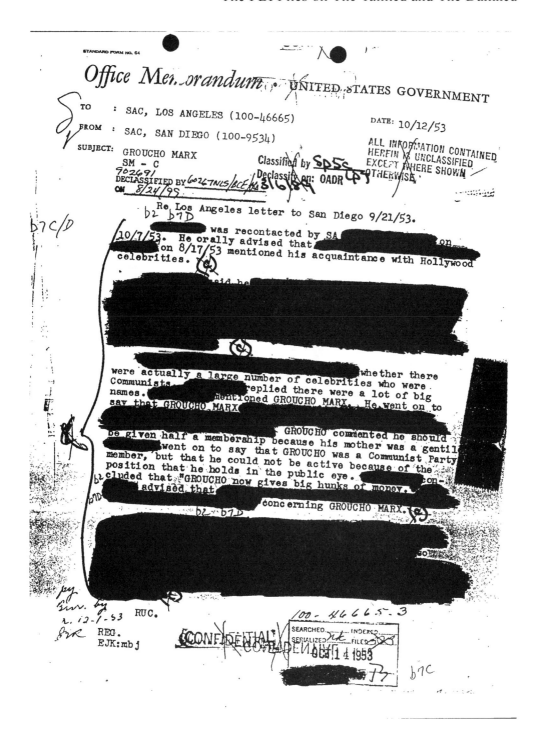

STANDARD FORM NO. 64

Office Memorandum • UNITED STATES GOVERNMENT

TO : SAC, LOS ANGELES (100-46665)

FROM : SAC, SAN DIEGO (100-9534)

DATE: 10/12/53

SUBJECT: GROUCHO MARX
SM - C
902691

Classified by SP5C

Declassify on: OADR

ALL INFORMATION CONTAINED
HEREIN IS UNCLASSIFIED
EXCEPT WHERE SHOWN
OTHERWISE

DECLASSIFIED BY 6026 7N15/BCE/4316/84
ON 8/24/95

Re Los Angeles letter to San Diego 9/21/53.

_____ was recontacted by SA _____ on 10/7/53. He orally advised that _____ on 8/17/53 mentioned his acquaintance with Hollywood celebrities.

_____ were actually a large number of celebrities who were Communists. _____ replied there were a lot of big names. _____ mentioned GROUCHO MARX. He went on to say that GROUCHO MARX _____ be given half a membership because his mother was a gentil _____ GROUCHO commented he should member, but that GROUCHO was a Communist Party member, but that he could not be active because of the position that he holds in the public eye. _____ con-cluded that "GROUCHO now gives big hunks of money. _____ advised that _____

_____ concerning GROUCHO MARX.

RUC.

REG.
EJK:mbj

CONFIDENTIAL

SEARCHED _____ INDEXED _____
SERIALIZED _____ FILED _____
OCT 14 1953

100-46665-3

FEDERAL BUREAU OF INVESTIGATION

SECURITY INFORMATION - CONFIDENTIAL

FORM No. 1
THIS CASE ORIGINATED AT LOS ANGELES   FILE NO.

REPORT MADE AT	DATE WHEN MADE	PERIOD FOR WHICH MADE	REPORT MADE BY
LOS ANGELES	12/1/63	9/21;10/30;11/9 13,14,16,17/53	JER b7C

TITLE		CHARACTER OF CASE
JULIUS H. MARX, wa. Groucho Marx	ALL INFORMATION CONTAINED HEREIN IS UNCLASSIFIED EXCEPT WHERE SHOWN OTHERWISE	SECURITY MATTER - C

Classified by SDS1
Declassify on: OADR

SYNOPSIS OF FACTS:

Subject is radio and TV comedian currently starring in TV show "You Bet Your Life" sponsored by DeSoto-Plymouth Dealers over NBC ~~███~~ recently remarked to confidential informant that GRAUCHO MARX contributes heavily to CP; however, original source gave no basis for this allegation. Los Angeles informants familiar with CP activity in Hollywood motion picture and radio industry throughout 1940's state MARX was never affiliated with CP and never a contributor so far as informants are aware. ~~███~~ on subject's TV program, is reported CP member, however. In 1934 the Daily Worker quoted MARX as saying, "The battle of the Communists for the lives of these boys (Scottsboro defendants) is one that will be taught in Soviet America as the most inspiring and courageous battle ever fought." Subject reported to have been affiliated or otherwise interested in varying degrees during 1940's with a number of Communist front or influenced organizations, including League of American Writers, American Council of Soviet Friendship, Hollywood Democratic Committee, Joint Anti-Fascist Refugee Committee, and others. MARX was indicted and convicted for violation of Copyright law in 1937. (U)

DECLASSIFIED BY 60267NLS/BCE/GH - C -
ON 8/25/99

DETAILS:

AT LOS ANGELES, CALIFORNIA

CLASSIFIED AND
EXTENDED BY
REASON FOR EXTENSION
FCIM II, 1 2.4.2
DATE OF REVIEW FOR
DECLASSIFICATION 4/26/89

100-46665-6

COPIES OF THIS REPORT

5 - Bureau (REG.)

3 - Los Angeles (100-46665)

9/11/64

U. S. GOVERNMENT PRINTING OFFICE

LA 100-46665

        Confidential sources, for whom T symbols are designated.
hereinafter, are of known reliability unless otherwise stated.

        The 1950 issue of the International Motion Picture
Almanac identifies subject as JULIUS MARX, professional name
GRAUCHO MARX, one of the well known Marx Brothers, all of whom
were born in New York City. GRAUCHO MARX, as he is best known
to the public, was born in New York on October 2, 1895. His
brothers are LEONARD (CHICO), ARTHUR (HARPO), and ZEPPO MARX.
Their first stage experience was in a vaudeville with their
mother and aunt, and were known as "Six Musical Mascots." Later
they toured as the "Four Nightingales," and finally as the "Four
Marx Brothers." They are all musicians of note. GRAUCHO MARX
is rated as one of the best guitar players in the country and
also plays the piano, mandolin, and harp. HARPO gets his name
from playing the harp, and also plays the piano, flute, and
trombone. CHICO is an artist at the piano, but he is also
accomplished with cornet, zither, and violin. Brother ZEPPO
plays the saxaphone, piano, cello, and flute.

        GRAUCHO MARX, together with his brothers, has starred
in a number of motion picture productions including Paramount
films, "The Coconuts," "Animal Crackers," "Monkey Business"
(1932), "Horse Feathers" (1933), and "Duck Soup" (1935).

        Brother ZEPPO quit acting and opened the Zeppo Marx
Agency in Hollywood during the 1930's; and thereafter, GRAUCHO,
CHICO, and HARPO appeared in "A Night at the Opera" produced by
MGM. In 1937 GRAUCHO collaborated on a screen play entitled
"The King and the Chorus Girl" produced by Warner Brothers.
In 1936 GRAUCHO, CHICO, and HARPO made a film "A Day at the
Races" for MGM. Other film productions in which the Marx
Brothers have appeared have been "Room Service" for RKO in 1938,
and "At The Circus" for MGM in 1938. In 1940 they made "Go West"
for MGM. More recent pictures have been "Night in Casablanca,"
"Love Happy," and "Copacabana."

        In regard to GRAUCHO MARX's background, the following
appears in the Daily Worker, an East Coast Communist newspaper,
issue of May 23, 1934, in a column about MARX by EMANUEL
EISENBERG:

        "GRAUCHO MARX is of working class origin: His
father was an Eastside tailor, and his mother sewed in

- 2 -

LA 100-46665

be sympathetic thereto. Informant bases this on the recollection that MARX was an avid reader of such publications as "New
Republic" and "The Nation," and tried to get informant interested
in such reading material. Informant had no information that
MARX ever contributed money to the Communist Party.

_____ who is not a member of the Communist Party but
is active in the _____ in
Hollywood at the present time, advises that GRAUCHO MARX is not
a member of this organization and has never been referred to by
the leaders of the organization in such a way as to indicate that
he is a friend of or sympathetic to this group.

_____ advises that he has no evidence that GRAUCHO MARX
is or ever has been a member of the Communist Party, but that
radio and television program "You Bet Your Life," is or has been
a member of the Party, according to information which _____
considers reliable. Informant had no information, however, as to
whether GRAUCHO MARX is aware of _____ affiliations.

b7C

ACTIVITIES

NATIONAL COMMITTEE FOR DEFENSE
OF POLITICAL PRISONERS (NCFDPP)

The NCFDPP has been designated by the Attorney General
of the United States pursuant to Executive Order 10450.

The Daily Worker, Communist news organ in New York City,
in its issue of May 23, 1934, page 5, carried a column by
EMANUEL EISENBERG under the caption "GRAUCHO MARX on MOONEY,
USSR, and Political Prisoners."

The write-up was the result of the author's having
visited GRAUCHO MARX in New York to ask him to appear at the
June Jamboree which the NCFDPP was to hold on June 1 (1934) at
138th Street and 7th Avenue, New York City. The Jamboree was
being held for the benefit of the organization's campaign for
recognition of the status of political prisoners. It stated
that MARX immediately accepted the invitation to appear at the
Jamboree to help in the campaign.

- 7 -

LA 100-46665

CONFIDENTIAL

be sympathetic thereto. Informant bases this on the recollection that MARX was an avid reader of such publications as "New Republic" and "The Nation," and tried to get informant interested in such reading material. Informant had no information that MARX ever contributed money to the Communist Party.

████████ who is not a member of the Communist Party but is active in the ███████████████████████████████████ in Hollywood at the present time, advises that GRAUCHO MARX is not a member of this organization and has never been referred to by the leaders of the organization in such a way as to indicate that he is a friend of or sympathetic to this group.

████████ advises that he has no evidence that GRAUCHO MARX is or ever has been a member of the Communist Party, but that radio and television program "You Bet Your Life," is or has been a member of the Party, according to information which considers reliable. Informant had no information, however, as to whether GRAUCHO MARX is aware of ██████████ affiliations.

b7C

ACTIVITIES

NATIONAL COMMITTEE FOR DEFENSE
OF POLITICAL PRISONERS (NCFDPP)

The NCFDPP has been designated by the Attorney General of the United States pursuant to Executive Order 10450.

The Daily Worker, Communist news organ in New York City, in its issue of May 23, 1934, page 5, carried a column by EMANUEL EISENBERG under the caption "GRAUCHO MARX on MOONEY, USSR, and Political Prisoners."

The write-up was the result of the author's having visited GRAUCHO MARX in New York to ask him to appear at the June Jamboree which the NCFDPP was to hold on June 1 (1934) at 138th Street and 7th Avenue, New York City. The Jamboree was being held for the benefit of the organization's campaign for recognition of the status of political prisoners. It stated that MARX immediately accepted the invitation to appear at the jamboree to help in the campaign.

- 7 -

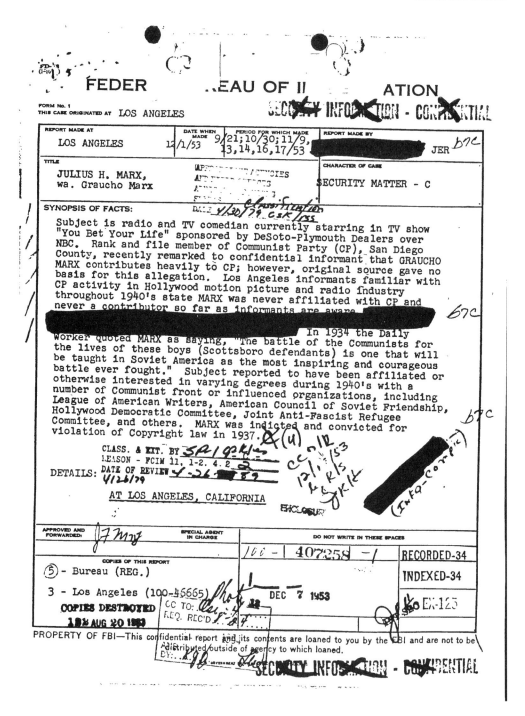

FEDER ... EAU OF II ... ATION

SECURITY INFORMATION - CONFIDENTIAL

FORM No. 1
THIS CASE ORIGINATED AT LOS ANGELES

REPORT MADE AT	DATE WHEN MADE	PERIOD FOR WHICH MADE	REPORT MADE BY
LOS ANGELES	12/1/53	9/21;10/30;11/9, 13,14,16,17/53	JER

TITLE

JULIUS H. MARX,
wa. Graucho Marx

CHARACTER OF CASE

SECURITY MATTER - C

SYNOPSIS OF FACTS:

Subject is radio and TV comedian currently starring in TV show
"You Bet Your Life" sponsored by DeSoto-Plymouth Dealers over
NBC. Rank and file member of Communist Party (CP), San Diego
County, recently remarked to confidential informant that GRAUCHO
MARX contributes heavily to CP; however, original source gave no
basis for this allegation. Los Angeles informants familiar with
CP activity in Hollywood motion picture and radio industry
throughout 1940's state MARX was never affiliated with CP and
never a contributor so far as informants are aware.

In 1934 the Daily
worker quoted MARX as saying, "The battle of the Communists for
the lives of these boys (Scottsboro defendants) is one that will
be taught in Soviet America as the most inspiring and courageous
battle ever fought." Subject reported to have been affiliated or
otherwise interested in varying degrees during 1940's with a
number of Communist front or influenced organizations, including
League of American Writers, American Council of Soviet Friendship,
Hollywood Democratic Committee, Joint Anti-Fascist Refugee
Committee, and others. MARX was indicted and convicted for
violation of Copyright law in 1937.

CLASS. & EXT. BY
LEASON - FCIM 11, 1-2. 4.2
DETAILS: DATE OF REVIEW

AT LOS ANGELES, CALIFORNIA

APPROVED AND FORWARDED:

SPECIAL AGENT IN CHARGE

DO NOT WRITE IN THESE SPACES

100 - 407258 - 1

RECORDED-34

INDEXED-34

COPIES OF THIS REPORT

(5) - Bureau (REG.)

3 - Los Angeles (100-46665)

COPIES DESTROYED
AUG 20 19

CC TO:
REQ. REC'D

DEC 7 1953

EX-125

SECURITY INFORMATION - CONFIDENTIAL

LA 100-46665

CONF:

The book thereafter lists a large number of Hollywood personalities including GRAUCHO MARX who allegedly signed the "New Declaration of Independence."

LEAGUE OF AMERICAN WRITERS

The League of American Writers has been designated by the Attorney General of the United States pursuant to Executive Order 10450.

In June, 1942, the Hollywood Chapter of League of American Writers issued a card advertising a function to be sponsored by this organization at the Hotel Roosevelt in Hollywood on June 12, 1942. This announcement card stated that the program would include an analysis of humor and the war, and that among the speakers would be GRAUCHO MARX.

RUSSIAN WAR RELIEF

The Fourth Report (1948) of the California Legislative Committee on Un-American Activities, on page 357, characterizes the Russian War Relief as "in every respect a satellite front of the Communist Party and....not an organization similar to the American Red Cross."

"News Letter," Volume 1, No. 3, published by the Southern California Division of Russian War Relief, Inc., dated August 1, 1942, carried an article advertising that the Music Committee of the Hollywood Committee of Russian War Relief held a Shostakovich Concert on Sunday, July 19, 1942, and that among those present were GRAUCHO MARX among other motion picture film personalities.

NATIONAL COUNCIL OF AMERICAN-
SOVIET FRIENDSHIP (NCASF)

The NCASF has been designated by the Attorney General of the United States pursuant to Executive Order 10450, as has also been its predecessor organization American Council on Soviet Relations.

bl

- 9 -

LA 100-45665

COMMITTEE FOR THE FIRST AMENDMENT

The California Committee on Un-American Activities, in its 1948 Report on page 210, identifies the Committee for the First Amendment as "a recently created Communist front in the defense of Communists and Communist fellow travelers. Its immediate purpose is to create favorable public opinion for the Communists who refuse to testify (in October, 1947) before the House Committee on Un-American Activities in Washington, D. C."

The "Peoples World," Communist news organ for the West Coast, in its Los Angeles edition for October 29, 1947, page 3, column 1, carries an article under the caption, "More Celebrities Join Defense Group, Denounce Film Industry Inquisition." The article thereafter stated that GRAUCHO MARX was among an expanded list of actors, writers, directors, and others in the Hollywood film industry released by the Committee for First Amendment; that the Committee condemned the attempt by the House Committee on Un-American Activities to smear the motion picture industry, and that "any investigation into political beliefs of the individual is contrary to the basic principles of democracy."

CIVIL RIGHTS CONGRESS (CRC)

The Civil Rights Congress has been designated by the Attorney General of the United States pursuant to Executive Order 10450.

- 12 -

LA 100-46665

AMERICAN YOUTH FOR DEMOCRACY (AYD)

The AYD has been designated by the Attorney General of the United States pursuant to Executive Order 10450.

MISCELLANEOUS

The "Daily Worker," Communist news organ on the East Coast, in its issue of February 9, 1939, carried an article under the caption "Lift Embargo Say Screen Stars." The article thereafter includes the photographs of a number of motion picture actors and actresses, including that of GRAUCHO MARX. According to the article, all of these were for lifting the embargo on the Spanish Government.

The "Peoples World," Communist periodical for the West Coast, in its issue of April 25, 1945, page 2, column 4, carried a news item from San Francisco, California, under the caption "Anti Franco Forces Open Office in SF." GRAUCHO MARX was indicated in the article as active in a new committee called Friends of the Spanish Republic, which had been formed to insure that no recognition should be accorded to the Franco Government at the United Nations Conference.

- C -

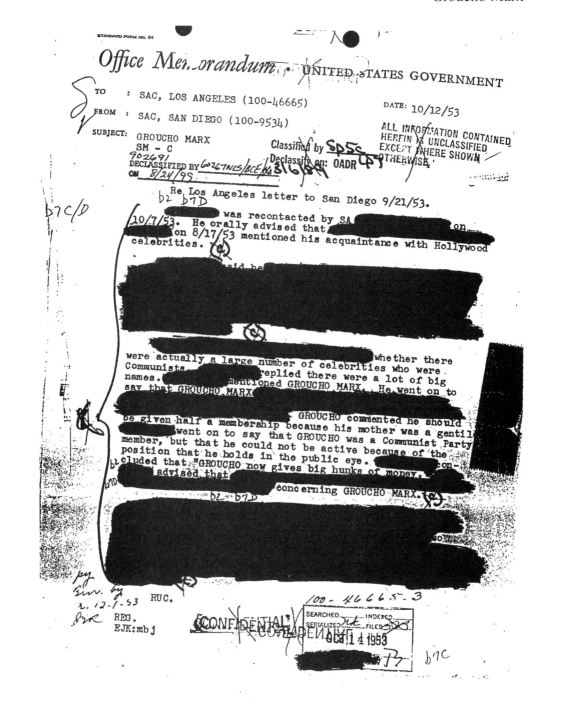

STANDARD FORM NO. 64

Office Memorandum · UNITED STATES GOVERNMENT

TO : SAC, LOS ANGELES (100-46665)

FROM : SAC, SAN DIEGO (100-9534)

DATE: 10/12/53

SUBJECT: GROUCHO MARX
SM - C
702691
DECLASSIFIED BY 60267NLS/BCE/KS 31689
ON 8/24/95

Classified by SP5C
Declassify on: OADR

ALL INFORMATION CONTAINED
HEREIN IS UNCLASSIFIED
EXCEPT WHERE SHOWN
OTHERWISE.

b7C/D

b2 b7D

Re Los Angeles letter to San Diego 9/21/53.

10/7/53.   was recontacted by SA   on
He orally advised that   on 8/17/53 mentioned his acquaintance with Hollywood
celebrities.

were actually a large number of celebrities   whether there
Communists   replied there were a lot of big
names.   mentioned GROUCHO MARX. He went on to
say that GROUCHO MARX

GROUCHO commented he should
be given half a membership because his mother was a gentile
                   went on to say that GROUCHO was a Communist Party
member, but that he could not be active because of the
position that he holds in the public eye.   concluded that "GROUCHO now gives big hunks of money.
                   advised that

b2 b7D   concerning GROUCHO MARX.

RUC.

100 - 46665-3

REG.
EJK:mbj

CONFIDENTIAL

SEARCHED   INDEXED
SERIALIZED   FILED
OCT 14 1953

b7C

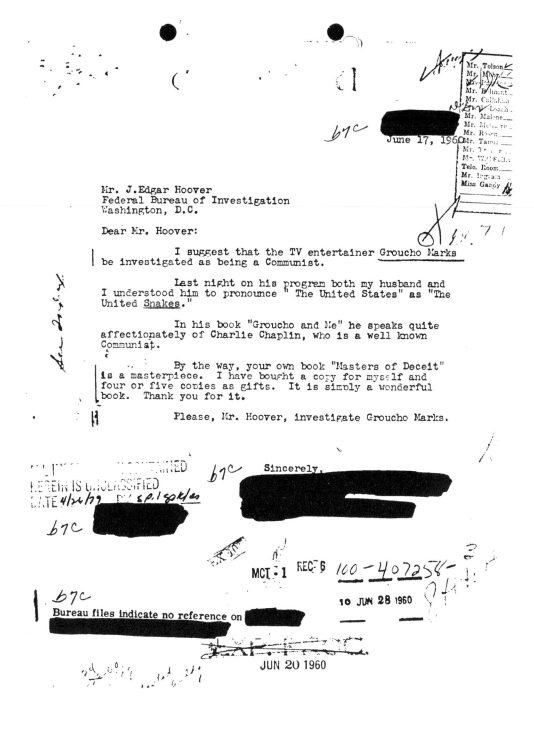

Mr. Tolson
Mr. Mohr
Mr. _____
Mr. Belmont
Mr. Callahan
Mr. ___ Loach
Mr. Malone
Mr. McGuire
Mr. Rosen
Mr. Tamm
Mr. _____
Mr. W.C. Sullivan
Tele. Room
Mr. Ingram
Miss Gandy

June 17, 1960

Mr. J. Edgar Hoover
Federal Bureau of Investigation
Washington, D.C.

Dear Mr. Hoover:

        I suggest that the TV entertainer Groucho Marks be investigated as being a Communist.

        Last night on his program both my husband and I understood him to pronounce " The United States" as "The United Snakes."

        In his book "Groucho and Me" he speaks quite affectionately of Charlie Chaplin, who is a well known Communist.

        By the way, your own book "Masters of Deceit" is a masterpiece. I have bought a copy for myself and four or five copies as gifts. It is simply a wonderful book. Thank you for it.

        Please, Mr. Hoover, investigate Groucho Marks.

Sincerely,

ALL INFORMATION CONTAINED
HEREIN IS UNCLASSIFIED
DATE 4/24/79 BY sp.lgpk/ao

Bureau files indicate no reference on ▮▮▮▮▮

MCT-1 REC-6 100-407258-

10 JUN 28 1960

JUN 20 1960

Marian Anderson

Chapter XI

Marian Anderson: The 20th Century's Unforgettable Contralto

Marian Anderson was born in a rented one-room kitchenette on Webster Street in South Philadelphia, Pennsylvania on February 17, 1897. Her father John Berkley Anderson was a common day laborer at the Reading Railroad Terminal Market. He supplemented his meager salary by moonlighting the evenings and on weekends as a bootleg barber. Her mother, Annie was a domestic day worker who did general cleaning and laundry for upper middle class white folks.

Mr. Anderson was a very religious person who took a great deal of pride in performing various duties in his neighborhood Union Baptist Church. His main task at the Church was that of a senior deacon in charge of the white glove-wearing ushers. The ushers always snapped to attention like tin soldiers when he gave them their final general orders just before the regular Sunday church service which began at 11:00A.M. Several months before Marian reached her sixth birthday her father began shepherding her to church every

Sabbath morning. When she was six and a half years old her father encouraged her to join the children's choir. Shortly thereafter, she became a member of the Junior Chorus where the music director took note of her beautiful voice and the fact that she could sing in all registers of the hymns. Mr. Alexander Robinson, the choirmaster subsequently selected Miss Anderson and Viola Johnson her friend and neighbor to sing a hymn as a duet for the Sunday school class. The favorite hymn was *"Dear To the Heart of the Shepherd"*, which they later sang at the regular 11A.M. church service. The latter function marked her first genuine appearance as a singer before the general public.

Miss Anderson was exhibiting a natural musical talent before she reached the age of eight. It was at this point that her father bought an old upright piano for the family from his brother. In a heartbeat and without the aid of a music teacher she taught herself the ways of the keyboard and thus became proficient enough with the instrument to accompany herself and others. When Marian reached the age of thirteen she was asked to join the senior choir at the church and was also recruited to sing in the high school glee club.

While still in high school she attempted to enroll at a local music school in downtown Philadelphia where a white receptionist greeted her with a patented racist remark: "We don't accept colored people here".

In spite of the racial put down, Marian Anderson was vocally prepared by an interracial bouquet of teachers beginning with Mrs. Mary Saunders Patterson an African-American woman who was both a voice teacher and per-former, Agnes Reifsnyder a German- Jew who was also a contralto, Giuseppe Boghetti an Italian vocal teacher who she met while still in high school, and Frank La Forge an American of French ancestry. She was also coached by Michael Rauchersen and Raimond Von Zur Mublen. She also worked briefly on her middle register in London, England with Amanda Aldridge, the daugh-ter of the famous Black Shakespearean actor Ira F. Aldridge. In Miss Anderson's opinion Giuseppe Boghetti was her greatest pedological influence. In spite of all the coaching by many talented teachers, Ms. Anderson still felt a void in her training for not having been able to attend the Julliard School of Music in New York City or the Yale University Music School in New Haven Connecticut.

In 1921, while in Chicago on summer vacation she got an opportunity to get a music scholarship to a school of her choice. She was invited as a young aspiring musician to sing a song in the National Association of Negro

Musicians Competitive contest. When she finished her rendition of *Ave Maria*, someone in the back of the hall made a motion for the Association to help the talented young lady get a formal musical education. The motion was seconded. Individuals throughout the Masonic Hall began raising their hands frantically and showcasing by volunteering to pledge money they did not have in various denominations up to one hundred dollars. According to one of the Association officials who was taking a head count the pledges which had exceeded more than one thousand dollars. The National Association of Negro

Miss Anderson greeted in Moscow.

Musicians in committee agreed that the young singer should try to enroll in the Yale University School of Music. Thus, when she returned to Philadelphia from Chicago she was bubbling with hope as she filled out the proper papers and forwarded them back to the treasurer of the National Association who had been designated to complete the arrangement. The Yale University School of Music accepted Miss Anderson's application to become a student but the pledges fell short of the monies in that the pledges had not been fulfilled. However, the amount of money that had been collected was turned over to Mr. Boghetti, who in fact had been selected by Miss Marian Anderson to be her musical guardian.

In 1925, she competed against 300 other singers in the National Music League Competition in New York City. This time the prize was a small monetary stipend, plus a rare opportunity to appear with the New York Philharmonic at the Lewisohn Stadium. The following year she received financial assistance fron the Julius Rosenwald Foundation. The monies enabled Miss Anderson to go to Europe for further musical study. Before returning to the United States, she gave her first European concert in Berlin, and toured the Scandinavian countries. While in Europe during the 1930s she appeared at Mozarteum in Salzburg, where the renowned conductor Arturo Toscanini was overheard uttering to Miss Anderson the following memorable line, "Yours is a voice such as one hears once in a hundred years." Another plaudit of equal thought-fulness took place in the home of noted composer Jean Sibelius in Finland. After hearing Miss Anderson sing, he uttered, "My roof is too low for you", he then cancelled the previously ordered coffee and requested that his butler bring champagne. Sibelius also honored Miss Anderson by dedicating his composition *Solitude* to her. Paul Robeson heard Marian Anderson again at what he described as a "glorious" concert at Wigmore Hall in London, England where she was accompanied on piano by Sir Roger Quilter.

From 1935 forward for the remainder of her life she was booked and managed by the great New York City impresario Sol Hurok. In 1938, Anderson did seventy U.S. concerts. At that time it was clocked as the longest and most extensive tour in concert history for a singer. Being a person of Color in America made traveling on the road extremely difficult and humiliating. Being stranded at the Atlanta Airport for hours was not cracker jacks for Marian Anderson, particularly when she was cold, hungry, and denied the use of a taxi-cab because she was Black. Langston Hughes, the renowned poet made the following observation about Atlanta: *With mingled feelings of delight and disgust I sat through that concert given by Miss Marian Anderson in Atlanta in a segregated audience. Anderson and her white accompanist held hands when they took their bows at the end of their performance, on the other hand, if a white person and a Colored person in the audience had had the audacity to hold hands across the rope that separated the Colored from the whites, they would have been put in jail because it was against Georgia laws for Blacks and whites to be within a breaths throw of each other.*

Hughes further notes, in Salt Lake City, Utah when he personally was barred from the Hotel Utah, its objection was a bit old fashion; in that the manager said: The only socially acceptable Blacks at the hotel were Paul Robeson and Marian Anderson.

In 1939, when Howard University a predominately Black populated school of higher learning approached the Daughters of the American Revolution to arrange for the use of the Constitution Hall, the only hall in the

District of Columbia large enough to accommodate the capacity audience that they had projected would want to see Miss Anderson, the DAR refused to consider the request and its president said that no Negro artist would be permitted to appear in their hall today, tomorrow or ever. The DAR's ban on Negroes was a public matter from the beginning of time. They had openly proclaimed and held their lily white policy close to their bosoms.

The DAR's defense of racism posed the same public challenge that the Atlanta, Georgia enforcement of its segregation laws. People were stupefied and Miss Anderson and her fellow-musicians were outraged, however Eleanor Roosevelt's decision to resign from the DAR turned a Potomac episode of bigotry into a world wide cause celebre.

Walter White, National Secretary of The NAACP and Marian Anderson's manager, Sol Hurok ruminated with the idea of a free open-air concert by Marian Anderson on the steps of the

Mrs. Eleanor Roosevelt makes a presentation to Miss Anderson.

Lincoln Memorial. White shared his idea with his friend Oscar Chapman, the Assistant Secretary of the Interior who was as excited as all get out and thus, he in turn bounced the idea off of his boss who was Harold L. Ickes, the Secretary of the Interior. Ickes' response to the idea was one of exhilaration. With cyclone speed, Ickes took the idea to President Franklin D. Roosevelt to get his stamp of approval before the President left town for his regular polio treatment in Warm Springs, Georgia. President Roosevelt in concert with his wife Eleanor gave the idea thumbs up and their private blessings. Neither of the Roosevelts attended the concert because of the ongoing political problems with the Dixiecrats.

The concert took place on Easter Sunday April 9, 1939. Secretary of

the Interior Ickes presided over the event, and estimated along with the District of Columbia Police Department the 75,000 people standing en masse at the base of the Lincoln Memorial. The crowd stretched in a great semicircle from the Lincoln Memorial around the reflecting pool the same as 200,000 people did

Marian Anderson sings on the steps of the Lincoln Memorial on Sunday March 9,1939.

for Dr. Martin Luther King thirty-eight years later on August 28,1963 when he made his famous *I Have A Dream* speech at the climax of the March On Washington Rally.

According to the *Washington Post* and the *New York Times*, the Marian Anderson concert began with her singing "*America*" and then she proceeded to sing an Italia aria "*O mio Fernando*", Schubert's, "*Ave Maria*", and four Negro Spirituals- "*Gospel Train*", "*Trampin*", "*My Soul Is Anchored In The Lord*", and she closed the concert singing "*Nobody Knows The Trouble I've Seen*" cheering and thunderous applause filled the air.

Commemorating the 1939 Lincoln Memorial Concert is a mural at the Interior Department. It was formally unveiled in 1943. Miss Anderson was invited by the Secretary of the Interior to witness the event. In that same year Miss Anderson made her first appearance in Constitution Hall, at the request of the Daughters of the American Revolution; the occasion was a benefit for the United China Relief.

Marian Anderson made the following statement about the concert in her autobiography "*My Lord, What A Morning:*"

I can not forget that demonstration of public emotion or my own strong feelings. In the years that have passed I have constant reminders of that Easter

Sunday. It is not at all uncommon to have people come backstage after a concert even now and remark, "You know, I was at that Easter Concert." In my travels abroad I have met countless people who heard and remembered that Easter Sunday concert.

Following the Constitutional Hall concert in Washington D.C. in 1943 twelve years passed before Miss Anderson was invited to make her premier performance on the stage of the Metropolitan Opera House in New York City

as a principal in a major production. On January 7, 1955 she became the first African-American to enjoy that honor. She debuted in that legendary Opera House as Ulrica in Verdi's *Un Ballo in Maschen (The Masked Ball).* The January 17 edition of *Time Magazine* reported that she and the cast received eight curtain calls. "She acted with the dignity and reserve that she has always presented to the public... *Her unique voice is black velvet that can be at once soft and dramatic, menacing and mourning and stirring the heart as always."* Langston Hughes, the master poet was present at that historic event, he made the following observation: "Her performance, broke the unspoken barrier excluding Blacks from the most prominent operatic company in the United States, the tickets had sold out swiftly with the announcement that the great contralto was coming, she was

On January 7,1955 Marian Anderson returns for one of many curtain calls following her successful debut as Ulrica in The Masked Ball at the Metropolitian Opera House in New York City.

then fifty-eight years old. Her singing role of the sorceress Ulrica was written for a younger person, the other members were Richard Tucker, Roberta Peters and Zinka Milano. All of them were younger than Miss Anderson by at least twenty years. The fact that Miss Anderson was fifty-eight and clearly past her prime only added to the pathos of the evening. A tremendous ovation greeted her appearance in the second scene of the opera and another standing ovation was awarded her at the end of the Act. When Milano embraced and kissed her, the house responded wildly, and some members of the audience's eyes were flooded with tears."

The Grand Lady from Philadelphia died April 8,1993 at age of 96 in Portland, Oregon where she moved to live with her nephew who was her only living relative.

Federal Bureau of Investigation

Freedom of Information/Privacy Acts Section

Subject: Marian Anderson

FEDERAL BUREAU OF INVESTIGATION

FREEDOM OF INFORMATION/PRIVACY ACTS SECTION

SUBJECT: <u>MARIAN ANDERSON</u>

FILE NUMBER: <u>77-HQ-78164</u>

F B I

Date: May 9, 1958

Transmit the following in _____
(Type in plain text or code)

Via ___AIRTEL_____
(Priority or Method of Mailing)

- -

TO: DIRECTOR, FBI

FROM: SAC, NEW HAVEN (77-3643)

SUBJECT: MARIAN ANDERSON, aka Mrs. Orpheus
           Hodge Fisher, Marian Elina Blanche Anderson
           SPI

           Re Bureau Airtel dated 5/2/58.

           Dept. of State requested investigation of above captioned
individual who is being recommended to the President for appointment for a top
level position in the State Dept.

           Applicant resides "Marianni Farms", Joes Hill Road, R. D. #1,
Danbury, Conn.

           In report of SA ▇▇▇▇▇▇▇▇ dated 11/18/48, at New
Orleans, captioned "SOUTHERN CONFERENCE FOR HUMAN WELFARE (SCHW); SOUTHERN
CONFERENCE EDUCATIONAL FUND, INC. (SCEF); IS-C", New Orleans file #100-759,
on page 39 of this report, ▇▇▇ who is identified as ▇▇▇▇▇▇▇▇,
Barnard Printing Co., New Orleans, advised that the name MARIAN ANDERSON, R.F.D.
#1, Danbury, Conn., appears on the mailing list of the "Southern Patriot", a
monthly publication of the SCEF.

           New Orleans requested to furnish complete documentation of
SCEF, SCHW and "Southern Patriot". Also advise if identity of ▇▇ mentioned
in this report should be concealed.

           If so, furnish characterization. Expedite as report must
reach Bureau by 5/16/58 without fail.

③ - Bureau
2 - New Orleans
1 - New Haven
EHG:ra
(6)

ALL INFORMATION CONTAINED
HEREIN IS UNCLASSIFIED
DATE 12/15/97 BY SP5 JC/LS
#373638

77-78164 - 9
NOT RECORDED
8 MAY 10 1958

NO

67C

Approved: _Amb_____   Sent _____ M   Per _____
         Special Agent in Charge

Report Form
FD-263 (5-12-55.)

FEDERAL BUREAU OF INVESTIGATION

Reporting Office	Office of Origin	Date	Investigative Period
PHILADELPHIA	BUREAU	5/27/58	5/7,9,10,12,13,22,23/58

TITLE CF CASE	Report made by	Typed By:
	67C	cpc

MARIAN ANDERSON

CHARACTER OF CASE

SPECIAL INQUIRY

Synopsis:

No birth record located for ANDERSON at Philadelphia. Education, South Philadelphia High School, verified. ▮▮▮▮▮▮▮▮▮▮▮▮▮▮▮▮▮▮▮, Temple University, who does not know ANDERSON personally, believes ANDERSON should not be placed in high level Government position because he is under impression she is a "typical temperamental musician." ▮▮▮▮▮▮▮▮▮▮ critical of her former accompanist, WILLIAM KING, and ▮▮▮▮▮▮ Philadelphia Orchestra ▮▮▮▮▮▮▮▮▮▮▮▮ and other associates recommend highly. ▮▮▮▮▮ Credit and arrest negative at Philadelphia. ANDERSON listed as one of national sponsors of Women's International League for Peace and Freedom in 1955. ANDERSON's name appeared on a special mailing of the Philadelphia Chapter of the American Council for a Democratic Greece. ▮▮▮▮▮

- RUC -

Approved	Special Agent in Charge	Do not write in spaces below

Copies made:

2 - Bureau (77-78164)

1 - Philadelphia (77-9562)

ALL ▮▮▮▮
HER▮▮ IS UNCLASSIFIED
DATE 12/15/92 BY SPS JCRS
#373638

Property of FBI — This report is loaned to you by the FBI, and neither it nor its contents are to be distributed outside the agency to which loaned.

☆ U. S. GOVERNMENT PRINTING OFFICE: 1956 O—388319

PH 77-9562

_____, Temple University, advised on May 7, 1958, that he is not personally acquainted with ANDERSON; therefore, he does not know much about her. He said his ..._ession of her, which he has obtained second-hand from other people whose names he did not recall at the time, is that she, like many other musical people, is not temperamentally well balanced. He said he believes she is a "typical temperamental musician." He said for that reason he does not believe she is suited for any high level position in the Government.

_____ Temple University, advised on May 7, 1958, that he is acquainted with ANDERSON, but is not a close personal friend. He said he admires her greatly as a singer and a person. He said she is a noble and dignified person who in the eyes of the entire music profession has been admired as an artist and an exceptionally fine person.

_____ said that she has a great social consciousness and pointed out that many white, as well as Negro singers, have benefited from the Marion Anderson Award. He said this award is made annually to deserving young people coming up in the music world.

_____ said that _____ has known ANDERSON well since her childhood and is one of her close friends. He said ANDERSON has suffered many indignities throughout her lifetime and has never shown any cynicism as a result. He said she has remained aloof and dignified.

_____ He said there is no question in his mind concerning her ability, her loyalty, or her patriotism. _____ recommended her for a high level Government position.

_____ said he does not believe there was any close relationship between PAUL ROBESON and ANDERSON. He said their abilities in the music world were far apart and that while ROBESON undoubtedly admired ANDERSON greatly, he does not believe this admiration was returned by ANDERSON.

- 3 -

Orson Welles

Chapter XII

Orson Welles:
The Sire of Citizen Kane

Orson Welles made his first onstage theater appearance at age 2, in 1917. He was born in Kenosha, Wisconsin on May 6,1915, two years before the United States entered World War I, the war that President Woodrow Wilson declared was the war to end all wars.

George Orson Welles was the second son of Richard Head Welles and Beatrice Ives Welles. Orson's father was an inventor and promoter, his mother was a talented pianist. The senior Welles was a tall handsome man with roving eyes for the ladies and they in turn had eyes for him; he was also known as a lover of bootleg booze.

Poppa Welles' excessive drinking and absence from the home created space for a third parent. The perfect candidate to fill the vacuum was the family doctor Maurice Bernstein, an orthopedist who was more than pleased to fill his shoes, in as much as he had very warm feelings that were deeper than an above board platonic interest in the delightful, delicious and lovable Mrs.

Welles

Welles. The icing that sweetened the layers of the love cake for Beatrice was Bernstein's genuine interest in baby Orson. As a matter of fact, when he first laid eyes on the child at age eighteen months he declared without any reservation that little Orson was a genius. Hence, he commenced showering the baby with a variety of educational toys and the mother with a daily bouquet of freshly cut flowers. The jury never reached a unanimous decision on whether or not his obsession for the baby paralleled or perhaps surpassed his love for Beatrice. Both the child and his mother were in constant need of medical attention. Therefore, their delicate physical condition gave the doctor professional reasons to visit the Welles' home almost on a daily basis. The physician's fatherly affection for the little boy was so passionate that little Orson started calling Doctor Bernstein "Dadda".

The love-triangle became so entangled, that Orson's father decided to move his brood 64 miles south as the crow flies to Chicago, Illinois in an attempt to escape the hot hands of Dr. Bernstein. The move by the Welles family to Chicago was futile in that the good doctor packed his bags and closed his medical office in Kenosha in less than 30 days after they left town and followed the powerful aroma of Beatrice's body to Abraham Lincoln's city by the lake.

Orson's musically talented mother's social connections opened doors that enabled her extremely bright child to touch the hem of the garments of Chicago's musical society. The show business contacts laid open an opportunity for Orson's first professional walk-on stage part in the Chicago Opera Production of *Samson and Delilah*. His next theatrical exposure was a role in *Madame Butterfly*. In this classic opera, he was the mixed breed love child of a young American naval officer and an Asian beauty. Following the *Madame Butterfly* engagement, he got a temporary job wearing a rabbit costume at Marshall Field's and Company on Chicago's State Street, where he directed customers to the long underwear department on the eighth floor. Childlike bashfulness was a word that was never identified with young Orson.

In 1921, shortly after Orson's sixth birthday the emotional ties of the love triangle between Doctor Bernstein, Beatrice, and his father caused the Welles family to legally separate. Following the separation, Maurice and Beatrice became full time common-law lovers. Orson's up and down flares with various physical maladies such as chronic myoditis and arizinal syndrome arthritis in addition to bronchial asthma kept him out of school until he was ten years old. However, he received superior basic education and cultural grounding at home from his mother and the good doctor. The kid had read all of Shakespeare's works and was proficient in the belles lettres, and from time to time amused himself by critically analyzing the work of Zoroaster, the Sixth Century B.C. Persian prophet. In spite of his reading and linguistic skills, he literally could not master simple elementary addition and subtraction. (It has been said that counting nickels, dimes, and quarters would never be Orson's lot.)

After Orson's mother died from cancer at the age of 43, Dr. Bernstein enrolled him in the Todd High School in Woodstock, Illinois, largely because it specialized in drama. The boy wonder revolutionized the school, in that Skipper Hill the school master reorganized the drama department with a more progressive curriculum in order to keep up with Orson, who by this time was being quietly tagged a bonafide young genius.

Skipper Hill recognized that in Orson they did not have an ordinary youthful drama pupil. The boy was twelve-years old going on thirty. The people that knew him best were adult artistic professionals and they always treated him as if he were a peer. His conversation and baritone voice was four octaves lower that the high pitch voices of most pre-teenage children. It has been said that he did not have any juvenile friends (including his brother Richard) among his contemporaries at the Todd School or anyplace else. As a young person he was in a class among those considered to be without category.

Orson Welles was one of the lead actors in the Todd School production of *Julius Caesar* when it was entered into the Annual Chicago Drama League contest. The play failed to win the first prize because the judges were convinced that the actors playing Cassius and Anthony were professional adults. Thus the Todd School production was disqualified. The judges were wrong in that all of the actors were teenagers. Orson, at the time was only fourteen years old and the other lead actor was also fourteen.

Three weeks after his sixteenth birthday, Orson graduated from the Todd School. As opposed to enrolling into President Robert Maynard Hutchin's revolutionary accelerated two year Bachelor of Arts program at the University of Chicago, he opted to become a professional actor. He selected Europe as his venue to seek his fortune by breaking into big time show business. He hitchhiked around Great Britain for several months before stumbling into Hilton Edward and Michael MacLiammoir. Both were directors at the famous Gate Theater in Dublin, Ireland. The two men had performed stateside as actors with the New York Theater Guild.

Orson, at age seventeen, was six feet plus, tall with an athletic heft, a chubby round baby face, disconcerting Chinese shaped eyes, a Negroid lower lip, large flat feet, shocking thick black hair, and a Churchillian speaking voice that could convince one into believing that the moon was made out of ripe lemons. He proved himself to be very persuasive, in that he talked both Edward and MacLiammoir into giving him the role of Duke Alexander in a play entitled *Jew Suss* being cast at the famous Gate Theatre in Dublin, Ireland.

Orson Welles' portrayal of Duke Alexander was a howling, bloody success. He overshadowed Hilton Edward's lead role as the Jew, according to the local newspaper critics. Thus, Orson's ability as a professional actor was confirmed on the stage of the Gate Theater.

Following his engagement at the Gate Theater in Ireland the kid was lost in a fog on what and where he should make his next move. He tried to get work in London's Piccadilly Circle, but was turned away at the door because he could not get the mandatory British work permit. His next stop was New York City, where he was rejected by the booking agents because he was an unknown, quantity in his own country. Orson decided to follow the evening sun and go west to Illinois, where in spite of his youth he enjoyed some niggardly amount of recognition.

Upon his return to Woodstock, Illinois Orson learned that his mentor, Skipper Hill, was now the headmaster at the Todd School replacing his father, the founder of the school. In the speed of a heartbeat Hill hired Welles as the drama coach and director for the school. During Orson's tenure in his new positions, the Todd School was awarded first place in the Chicago Drama Festival for its edited rendition of the *Twelfth Night*, in 1932.

Skipper Hill was so pleased with Orson's contribution to the school he rented an apartment for him in Old Town, on the Near North Side of Chicago where he could work without disturbance on the first four volumes of a series entitled, *Everybody's Shakespeare*, which was edited by Skipper's brother Roger Hill and Orson Welles.

Between 1932 and 1934, Welles wiled away his time performing in a national tour company directed by Guthrie McClintic, producer-director and husband of Katherine Cornell, who was known for her Broadway role in a *Bill of Divorcement* (1921). The plays that he appeared in during the tour were: *The Barretts of Wimpole Street*, *Romeo and Juliet* and *Candida*. In *The Barretts of Wimpole Street*, he played a minor role as the stuttering brother Octavius; he was Mercutio in *Romeo and Juliet* (a short but showy role) and in *Candida*, he got the lead role of Marchbanks opposite actress Katherine Cornell, the great lady of Broadway.

Orson became disappointed when he learned that the tour was not going to play on New York's Great White Way as he had been told. In deep disillusion he left the tour and started looking around for another venture. One night while sitting alone in his dimly lit bedroom a bright light went off in his head and he hastily went directly to his friend Skipper Hill in Woodstock and shared his notion about putting on a summer festival in Woodstock. Skipper thought it was a top cabin idea and thus agreed to underwrite the event.

Following the successful Woodstock Summer Festival, Orson rejoined the Katherine Cornell Company, hoping to play Browning in *The Barretts of Wimpole Street*. This time the play had a firm, written commitment to open on Broadway during the 1934 season. To his disappointment, Brian Aherne, the movie star had been signed to play the role. Welles was given the role of Tybalt, which was a minor part. In addition he was given a groupie role in the play's opening scene as a member of the chorus. The role in the choir was a put-down for Welles. However, he was happy because he was on the brink of accomplishing one of his life long ambitions, that was to star in a play on Broadway. The play opened at the Martin Beck Theater on the Great White Way, on Thursday, December 20,1934. He was adequate in the character Tybalt on opening night, but on Friday, the second night he was absolutely brilliant. In the audience on that Friday night, was none other than the great John Houseman, the director, producer, teacher, autobiographer and a man of all seasons who later became an actor, in both the movies and television productions. John Houseman subsequently became the father figure for Orson and replaced "Dadda", Skipper Hill and his birth father Richard Head Welles. This great man was fascinated with Orson and the nineteen year old kid was bewitched by him. He saw in Orson something that placed him just on th eedge of being a demonic genius. Through Welles' lens he saw Houseman as the essence of a cosmopolitan man, in that he was Romanian-born, with the demeanor of an European aristocrat, educated in the English public schools, where he learned to speak the English language in a Churchillian style that exuded an aura of confidence dripping from his every word.

Houseman wanted to work with Welles. He actually had a concrete offer in mind for this giant size boy. It specifically was a role in Archibald MacLeish's *Panic*. Houseman had failed to get movie star Paul Muni or any other known actor to sign on to his three night presentation. However, he had seen in the unknown Orson Welles, while playing the role of Tybalt, the talent needed to achieve his objective. Welles, whose ego was as large as Houseman's, agreed with the big man's assessment of him, but attempted to hide his anxiety for the part in *Panic* behind a cool façade.

The summer of 1935 found Orson Welles back in Woodstock participating in the Woodstock Dramatic Festival, where he both acted and directed. On his return trip home, he married the pretty 18-year old Virginia Nicholson, who was an actress in the Woodstock Company. In the fall of 1935, the young couple journeyed to New York City in search of job opportunities at a time when the nation's economy had hit rock bottom, and the soup and breadlines for the unemployed had reached untold millions.

In light of the economic hard times the Federal Government asked Welles and Houseman to help launch a Federal Theatre to be operated under the wings of President Franklin Delano Roosevelt's Work Progress Administration for unemployed actors, writers, dancers, and musicians. Welles' first attempt in the Federal Theater program was *Macbeth* staged in Haiti. With an all Negro cast, he used a generous sprinkling of voodoo-doctors to take the place of Shakepeare's three witches. The next production was Marlowe's *Dr. Faustus*. For his performance, Welles made up his face to appear more grotesque than Boris Karloff in *Frankenstein*, his booming voice was amplified to sound spooky like an organ being played in the bass clef on a minor key. In that eerie mode he proceeded to wander around the stage like a ghost in search of its lost soul among the gigantic shadows in a shifting shaft of light. Critics hailed the staging as revolutionary.

The White House overseers of the Work Progress Administration wanted Houseman and Welles to present theatrical performances that were considered serious, and socially responsible but politically center stage. In Marc Blitzstein's *The Cradle Will Rock*, the message of the work was unionization which Washington considered left wing.

After completing the production of *The Cradle Will Rock*, the association between Houseman, Welles and the WPA came to an abrupt end. Welles and Houseman left the WPA and *The Cradle* went on to become a landmark production in the history of the Federal Theatre.

After leaving the WPA Theatre Project Welles and Houseman founded a radio program entitled the *Mercury Theatre of the Air*, in 1938. Its national broadcast wire was the Columbia Broadcasting System. From the early 1920s through the late 1940s, radio was the primary source of family home enter-

Orson Welles in the CBS Studio on Sunday night October 30,1938 narrating H.G. Wells' " *War of the Worlds*".

tainment before the advent of television. Sunday nights were particularly popular because you could hear such stars as Jack Benny, Bob Hope, Bing Crosby, Edgar Bergen and Charlie McCarthy, Kate Smith, Hollywood Playhouse, Walter Winchell, Harriett Hilliard, the canary with the Ozzie Nelson Orchestra.

Orson Welles was busy at the Mercury Theatre writing, editing and directing the sketches and frequently playing in them. He decided that for Halloween night Sunday, October 30, 1938, he would produce a spectacular diversion to go up against Edgar Bergen and Charlie McCarthy who had the unbeatable top rated Sunday night program which aired at 8:00p.m. over the National Broadcasting Company wire.

The super kid's secret weapon was a script based on H.G. Wells' *War of the Worlds*. In his opinion, the script was a bit dull. Therefore, he put some spice in it by creating an invasion of the Martians at Grover Hill, New Jersey. In order to make people believe that what they were hearing was actually happening, he formatted the program with dance music from the Meridian Room in the Hotel Park Plaza on Central Park South in midtown Manhattan, where-as they were being entertained by the music of Ramon Raquello and his orchestra. Without skipping a beat, the band fades into an interruption of another phony news flash. Orson Welles the announcer is describing a battle between the citizens of Grove Hill, New Jersey and the invading Martians. Thousands of people in the New Jersey area believed that what they heard was an authentic news report and took the hills. There was a panic rush for shelter, there were heart attacks, and suicide attempts, and numerous miscarriages, which were subsequently validated. The hoax caused Welles and CBS to be deluged with threats.

When Orson Welles awakened Monday morning October 31, 1938 he found that he had become internationally famous (or notorious) overnight. What had happened was certainly beyond his wildest dreams. His original idea going into the radio show was: 'Let's do something impossible, make them believe it, then show them it's only radio.'

The success of Orson's treatment of H.B. Wells' *War of the Worlds* brought him to the attention of the R.K.O. Movie Studio executives in Hollywood, California. His agent, Arnold Weissburger was able to negotiate an unheard of spectacular four-way contract for him. He wrote, acted, direct-ed and produced. Welles' contract tied him into making two movies, paying him $100,000 for the first movie and $125,000 for the second, plus twenty-five percent of the profits after the initial $500,000 nut was recovered. In the jeal-ous eyes of his Hollywood contemporaries, Welles had not proved anything except that his interplanetary radio high jinks had scared the hell out of thou-sands of people.

Orson Welles flew to Hollywood in August, 1940, with members of the Mercury Theater and a freshly grown beard to age himself and prepare for his work as an actor.

Welles hit the ground in Hollywood running. He wrote two scripts *The Heart of Darkness* and *The Smiles With a Knife*. Both of them were rejected by the studio executives. *Citizen Kane,* in which he played the lead was accepted. It took him exactly 10 furious weeks to shoot the film.

Orson Welles' *Citizen Kane* was a very thin take-off on the life and times of the newspaper publishing magnate, William Randolph Hearst. The movie was denounced, sight unseen by Louella O. Parsons, the famous gossip columnist for the far-flung Hearst Newspaper chains. The Hearst papers refused to accept any advertising for the picture. Mr. William Randolph Hearst's reaction to the film created a wide blitz of unexpected publicity. The magazine and competitive newspaper reviews, for the most part, were four stars. In this writer's opinion, the lighting, composition, direction, dialogue, acting, makeup, music, sound, editing, and construction were unparalleled. I sat through the movie three times one afternoon, shortly after it was released at the Metropolitan Theater on 46th and South Park Boulevard in Chicago, Illinois.

As D.W. Griffith's *Birth of A Nation* marked the beginning of spectacular films in the Twentieth Century, the rambunctious Orson Welles' *Citizen Kane* was both Alpha and Omega. *Kane*, sixty years later in 2001 still stimulates its viewer's cultural taste buds like a cool mint julep on a summer's eve in Mississippi.

Orson Welles played the role of *Citizen Kane* in a movie on the life of William Randolph Hearst, the newspaper tycoon.

The Last Will and Testimony of a Genius: Radio broadcaster, actor, and film director Orson Welles was a source of controversy from the time of his faked broadcast of a Martian invasion of New Jersey in 1938, through his tour de force film *Citizen Kane* and until the day he died October 10,1985. Welles' will was also controversial because it included substantial gifts to a woman who was not Welles' wife.

In his 1982 will, Welles makes the following bequests and devise of real property to a woman who had been his companion for several years: I hereby give to Olga Palinkas (also known as Oja Kodar), whose address is Post Restante Primosten, Republic of Yugoslavia, the house located at 1717 North Stanley Avenue, Los Angeles, California... and all of the improvements and household furniture, furnishings, pictures, books, silver, paintings, works of art and other personal effects therein... All taxes

Orson Welles with Rita Hayworth, his second wife and one of Hollywood's most glamorous movie stars.

attributable to this bequest shall be paid from the residue of my estate. Welles left his residuary estate to his third wife the Italian actress Paolo Mori Welles, whom he had married in 1955. If Mrs. Welles had not survived her husband then Welles' residuary estate was to be left entirely to Olga Palinkas.

To each of his three daughters, Rebecca, Christopher, and Beatrice, Welles made a $10,000 bequest. Daughter Christopher was the issue of his first marriage, to Virginia Nicholson. Daughter Rebecca was Welles' child with his second wife, Rita Hayworth, the very glamorous movie star. And daughter Beatrice was Welles' child with his third and final wife, Paola. Although Welles had been divorced from his first two wives, he treated all of his daughters equally under his will.

As the executor of his will, Welles named producer Greg Garrison, whom Welles had first met in 1946 and with whom Welles collaborated often in his later years. Apparently, Welles felt that neither his wife Paola nor friend Olga were appropriate for the role of his executor.

Finally, the will contains this unusual section excerpted from the in terorem clause:

If any benficiary under this Will in any manner directly or indirectly contests or attacks this Will or any of its provisions, including paragraph B or Article Four hereof giving the entire house to Olga Palinkas, any share interest in my Estate given to such beneficiary under this Will is revoked and shall be disposed of in the same manner provided herein as if such beneficiary had predeceased me leaving no living lawful descendants.

By specifically referring to the gift to his companion Olga, Welles obviously wanted to prevent his wife from contesting the gift of his California home to his beautiful companion. Although Welles maintained a home in Los Angeles, California, he was a legal resident of Nevada when he died. It was, however, in his Los Angeles home that Welles suffered the fatal heart attack that killed him.

One Friends Opinion

Richard Wright the author of the classic *Native Son* said, "One Orson Welles on earth is enough. Two of them would no doubt bring civilization itself almost to an end. If there were 10,000 Orson Welles, society would fly apart like an exploding bomb. Orson was a noisy, expansive, jovial young man who called everybody "Loveboat".

Orson Welles and one of his many "Loveboats".

Federal Bureau of Investigation

Freedom of Information/Privacy Acts Section

Subject: Orson Welles

FEDERAL BUREAU OF INVESTIGATION

FREEDOM OF INFORMATION/PRIVACY ACTS SECTION

SUBJECT: ORSON WELLES

FILE NUMBER: 100-23438

71753

DETAILS:

Information came to the Los Angeles Division Office from █████

████████████████████████. The Group Theatre was an organization then similar to the Theatre Guild. █████ advised █████ the ORSON WELLES Company █████ produced such plays as "Pins and Needles". █████ stated █████ the ORSON WELLES Radio Program █████ was sponsored by the Campbell Soup Company. █████ ORSON WELLES was employed by R.K.O. to produce some pictures █████ was under the impression that R.K.O. did not complete any pictures for ORSON WELLES as the subject matter at that time was considered too far "leftist" to be used by the studio. █████ that it would be interesting to find out █████ why they never finished any pictures for ORSON WELLES █████ stated that it is reported that ORSON WELLES and █████ in the past few years received payments from R.K.O. in the neighborhood of $100,000.

██
██
██
██

█████ is now under extensive investigation in the Los Angeles Origin File entitled, █████ ETAL. INTERNAL SECURITY (R)" Los Angeles File █████ and no further effort will be made to identify him in this report other than to show his past connection with Subject ORSON WELLES. The recent investigation on █████ has failed to show any present connection with ORSON WELLES.

██
██
██

-2-

Subject ORSON WELLES is not registered as a voter in Los Angeles County.

The Los Angeles Examiner newspaper of April 29, 1941, with a New York date line of April 28, 1941, reflected the founding of the "Citizens' Committee for HARRY BRIDGES". This article reflects that Subject ORSON WELLES as well as JOHN HENRY HAMMOND, JR., and Professor F. O. MATTHIESSEN had founded this committee. In the article WELLES was listed as a playwright-producer; HAMMOND as a music patron and art critic; and MATTHIESSEN as an English professor at Harvard University. This committee was formed in New York City and the article states that more than 65 persons became sponsors of the committee. The article states that in the letter of invitation from ORSON WELLES and the aforementioned individuals to the sponsors, it is stated, "Mr. BRIDGES is now on trial in a second deportation hearing, the only man in the United States ever to be tried twice in this manner. On the pretext of a new law passed after an exhaustive hearing and acquittal by Dean JAMES M. LANDIS, he is being tried anew on essentially the same charge. - - - - We join in an attempt to inform public opinion as to the realities behind Mr. BRIDGES' second trial, which we consider an attack on all organized labor, on the rights of minorities and a focal point of the entire current attack on civil liberties." The sponsors of this committee are listed in the news article and include HUGH DE LACY, president of the Washington Commonwealth Federation and president of the American Committee for the Protection of Foreign Born; RUSSELL N. CHASE, chairman of the Cleveland Committee of the American Civil Liberties Union; DONALD OGDEN STEWART; and I. F. STONE, Washington editor of "The Nation".

The Los Angeles Herald Express of May 7, 1941 carried an article under the caption, "Gold Star Mothers Head Hits Radicals". In this article Mrs. MAE CUSHMAN, national president of the American Gold Star Mothers stated that she had listened to a number of the "Free Company" Sunday morning broadcasts starring ORSON WELLES and others and that she is definitely against such programs as they appear subversive. In this article Mrs. J. HENRY ORME, president of the Americanism Defense League, stated that she heartily endorsed the action taken by the American Legion against some of the plays broadcast recently by the "Free Company - ORSON WELLES group". The article states that definite action condemning such programs was being considered by the American Legion, by the Americanism Defense League, the California State Daughters of the American Colonists, and by the Kennesaw Mountain Chapter of the National Society of Daughters of the Union.

The Los Angeles Herald Express of May 27, 1941 had an article stating that ORSON WELLES' actions were being probed by the American Legion and by the state executives of the American Legion. This article states that the American Legion officials claim this right is based on the fact that WELLES is a leader of a movement opposed to the deportation of HARRY BRIDGES. The article stated that investigation was being made regarding the military service of ORSON WELLES or his exemption from military service. The article states that there has been a nation-wide storm of protest led by the American Legion against the radio broadcasts of the "Free Company" in which WELLES was starred as these plays were considered radical. The article states that the national committee of the American Legion at Indianapolis had taken similar action. The article states that ORSON WELLES, age 25, was due for

-3-

classification before Selective Service Board 245 in Westwood, where his
order number was 1027. It appeared that a questionnaire had been mailed
ORSON WELLES on April 1, 1941, and WELLES did not return the questionnaire
until April 30, 1941 as he had been given extended time. The article
states when ORSON WELLES appeared before the classification board, he had
informed the board that he was willing to serve if passed, but declared
that he suffered from "inverted flat feet" and that his "spine was not in
good shape either". The article states that after his appearance before
the board, ORSON WELLES visited several bone specialists and that the report
of these specialists would be made known to the Selective Service Board.
This article states that ORSON WELLES sought and obtained permission from
the Draft Authorities to make a trip to Mexico.

An article in the "News Week" of August 4, 1941 reflects that
Subject ORSON WELLES had announced the week before in Hollywood that he had
taken over the Columbia Broadcasting System's Lady Esther Serenade program
beginning early in September, 1941 and that this broadcast, a dramatic show,
would originate from Hollywood on Mondays at 10:00 to 10:30 P.M., Eastern
Daylight Saving Time. This new program will replace the light music program
of the Lady Esther Company.

On the night of October 6, 1941, at 7:00 P.M., over radio station
K.N.X. at Los Angeles, ORSON WELLES put on his third radio program for the
sponsor, "Lady Esther Cosmetics Company". On this particular program, he
dramatized a program by NORMAN FOSTER, which had nothing of a subversive
character. Radio station K.N.X. is located at 6121 Hollywood Boulevard,
Hollywood, California, telephone HOllywood 1212.

Extensive biographies appear on ORSON WELLES and for the information of the interested offices and the Bureau, some biographical history on
ORSON WELLES is being reported herein.

"Who's Who" in America, in the 1940 and 1941 issue states that
GEORGE ORSON WELLES, known as ORSON WELLES, is an actor, radio, and theatrical
producer and that he was born at Kenosha, Wisconsin, May 6, 1915, the son of
RICHARD HEAD and BEATRICE IVES. The education of WELLES included attendance
at the Todd Schools, Woodstock, Illinois, from 1927 to 1930. ORSON WELLES
married VIRGINIA NICHOLSON in December, 1934 and a divorce was granted in
1940. He has one daughter, CHRISTOPHER. ORSON WELLES was described as an
actor with the Gate Theatre in Dublin, Ireland, from 1931 to 1932. He toured
with KATHARINE CORNELL in 1933. He directed the Woodstock Festival in 1934.
He played the lead in "Panic" in 1935. He directed a Negro "Macbeth" and
"Horse Eats Hat" in 1936. He directed "Dr. Faustus" and "The Cradle Will
Rock" in 1937. He founded the Mercury Theatre and directed "Julius Caesar"
in 1937. He directed and produced "Shoemakers Holiday", "Heartbreak House",
and "Daubins Death" in 1938. He directed and was an artist on radio programs
since 1938. He made recordings of Shakespeare's plays for the Columbia
Recording Company in 1939. He has been a producer, writer, and director for
R. K. O. Radio Pictures in 1939 and 1940. He is a member of the Actors
Equity League, American Federation of Radio Artists, and was awarded the
CLAIRE M. SENIE Award for the foremost achievement in the American Theatre
in 1938. He belongs to the Lotus Club in New York. He was the editor of

-4-

71756

"Everybody's Shakespeare" with ROGER HILL in 1933 and was editor of the "Mercury Shakespeare" with ROGER HILL in 1939. In "Who's Who", WELLES gave his address as 1430 Broadway, New York City.

The Columbia Broadcasting System, Columbia Square, Hollywood, California, puts out several biographical releases on ORSON WELLES, which further identify him. The release of September 8, 1941 stated that ORSON WELLES would begin a new series of broadcasts Monday, September 15, 1941 and that he starts on the first of four new films for R.K.O. on September 16, 1941. ORSON WELLES also plans new Shakespearean recordings; also to appear as a magician at the California State Fair; to make a lecture tour in the Fall of 1941; and to broadcast for the Defense Program.

The C.B.S. Hollywood release of September 8, 1941 states that ORSON WELLES makes his home, office, and work shop on the studio grounds of R.K.O. at Culver City, California. This release states that he has a bungalow which houses his office and living quarters. This release states that his play "Native Son" was one of the hits of Broadway last season.

The C.B.S. Hollywood, California release of February 11, 1939 reflects that Subject as GEORGE ORSON WELLES was born in Kenosha, Wisconsin, May 6, 1915 and was named after GEORGE ADE and a man named ORSON WELLS, both friends of his father. Subject's mother is described as a pianist and composer. Subject's father is described as a manufacturer of automobiles, who turned to the development of a bicycle lantern. The release states that his father objected to Subject ORSON WELLES' desire to be an orchestra leader or a magician and that Subject was sent to BORIS ANISFELD to study painting and cartooning. The release states that the mother of ORSON WELLES died when he was six years of age and that his father took him on a trip abroad, shortly after which Subject's father died. On this occasion a Dr. MAURICE BERNSTEIN was made the legal guardian of ORSON WELLES. He then entered the Todd School at Woodstock, Illinois. At the age of 13, ORSON WELLES was directing the Todd Troupers and arranged a production of "Julius Caesar" and other Shakespearean historical plays.

The C.B.S. release of February 11, 1939 states that in 1931 ORSON WELLES suffered a hay fever attack and that he went to Scotland and Ireland. While abroad he became an actor at the Gate Theatre in Dublin, Ireland, appearing in 40 plays, and made occasional guest appearances at the Abbey Theatre. This release states that he returned to Woodstock, Illinois in 1932 and wrote a few plays in conjunction with ROGER HILL. The release states that being unable to find a backer for these plays, Subject sailed for Africa and while in Morocco he met "The Glaoui", a chieftain he had previously met in Paris. While in a Moroccan retreat, he completed a volume of "Everybody's Shakespeare". The Release states that he met and married a Chicago debutant that he met at Woodstock, Illinois, VIRGINIA NICOLSON; that JOHN HOUSEMAN, an ex-grain magnate, invited WELLES to be co-producer of theatre presentations.

Another release of September 8, 1941 of C.B.S., Hollywood, reflects that Subject's father took him to China when he was six years of age. This release reflects that when WELLES was associated with JOHN HOUSEMAN, they produced hit plays at the Federal Theatres in New York.

-5-

April 16, 1943

RE: GEORGE ORSON WELLES
also known as ORSON WELLES

ALL INFORMATION CONTAINED
HEREIN IS UNCLASSIFIED
DATE 5-27-86 BY SP 6BIJ/CCL

B2C

4-15-43

Personal History

George Orson Welles was born on May 6, 1915, the son of
Richard Head and Beatrice (Ives) Welles, in Kenosha, Wisconsin. His
father is stated to have been an inventor, while his mother was a
talented musician. From an early date Welles is stated to have moved
in a field of talented personalities. He attended Todd High School in
Woodstock, Illinois, from 1927 to 1930, where he specialized in art
and dramatics. It is stated that at the age of 13 Welles was directing the Todd Troopers in various arrangements of Shakespeare's plays.

Upon graduation from high school, Welles had a desire to go
into the theater; however, he was discouraged in this regard by his
guardian. (Welles' father died when he was 13 years of age). His
guardian in 1931 persuaded him to take a sketching tour through Ireland.
While there he identified himself with the Gate Theater in Dublin and
appeared in some forty plays. In 1932 he returned to this country, at
which time he reportedly went to Woodstock, Illinois, where he engaged
in the writing of a few plays which he is stated to have had little
success in selling. In 1933 he is reported to have toured this country
with Katherine Cornell in "Candida."

In 1934 he played the leading role in "Panic." During the
summer of 1935 he participated in the Woodstock Dramatic Festival in
which he both acted and directed. In 1936 he directed "Macbeth" with
an all-Negro cast, and in the same year he directed "Horse Eats Hat."
In 1937 he was associated with the Federal Workers Theater of the WPA
and during that time directed "Doctor Faustus" and "The Cradle Will
Rock." He also founded the Mercury Theater in that year, its first production being "Julius Caesar." In 1938 he directed and produced "Shoe-
maker's Holiday," "Heart Break House" and "Danton's Death."

In 1938 the Mercury Theater of the Air came into being, with
Welles acting, writing and directing practically all of the skits. In
1939 Welles signed a four-year contract with RKO pictures as a writer,
actor, director and producer. In 1940 he went to Hollywood, California,
at which time he wrote a few scripts which were rejected. In 1941 Welles
wrote, directed and acted in "Citizen Kane" which has been hailed by
many as the "most sensational production of the moving picture industry."
This production was violently attacked by the Hearst Syndicate, and the
question of its actual release to the public was questionable for many
months.

INDEXED
RECORDED
ENCLOSURE
100-23428-16

Mr. Tolson
Mr. E. A. Tamm
Mr. Clegg
Mr. Coffey
Mr. Glavin
Mr. Ladd
Mr. Nichols
Mr. Rosen
Mr. Tracy
Mr. Carson
Mr. Harbo
Mr. Hendon
Mr. McGuire
Mr. Mumford
Mr. Piper
Mr. Quinn Tamm
Mr. Nease
Miss Gandy

COPIES DESTROYED 6-26-58

- 2 -

In 1942 Welles went to South America for the RKO pictures with the approval of the Motion Picture Section of the Coordinator of Inter-American Affairs, at which time he engaged in a motion picture project, one of the purposes of which was to develop good will between the United States and the various South American countries.

Welles in December, 1934, married Virginia Nicholson, which marriage resulted in a divorce in 1940. There was one child born of this marriage, namely Christopher, a daughter.

Welles presently has an international reputation as an actor, writer, director and producer in the legitimate theater, motion pictures and radio.

(94-3-4-115-3X)

Activities

An article appearing in the "Daily Worker" for May 6, 1938, reflects Welles as a member of the Negro Cultural Committee. The committee is stated to have contemplated producing a review for the benefit of the New York Chapter of the National Negro Congress, which organization is a known Communist front group. The Negro Cultural Committee was reportedly a group organized by the Communist Party for the purpose of agitating in favor of anti-lynching bills. Many of the other members of this committee were either known Communist Party members or sympathizers. (100-23438-X)

A "Daily Worker" article in the April 15, 1938, issue reflects that Welles delivered a series of speeches at the Workers Bookshop Symposium for the Workers Bookshop Mural Fund. Some of these speeches carried such titles as "Culture and the People's Front" and "Theater and the People's Front." This bookshop at the time was reported to be under the direct management of the Communist Party in New York City. (100-23438-X)

The letterhead of the Medical Bureau and North American Committee to Aid Spanish Democracy in July, 1938, reflects Orson Welles as a member of the Theater Art Committee of this organization. This committee was a reported Communist front organization at that time and has since then changed its name to the United American Spanish Aid Committee and is presently known as the Joint Anti-Fascist Refugee Committee, both of which are known Communist front organizations. (100-23438-X)

The name of Orson Welles appears in a pamphlet published by the Coordinating Committee to Lift the Embargo Against Republican Spain. This group is reported to have been organized at the instigation of the

—18

Federal Bureau of Investigation

United States Department of Justice

Portland, Oregon
December 10, 1943

Personal and Confidential

Director, FBI

DECLASSIFIED FROM SP2BTJCAL
ON 5-27-86

Dear Sir:

I thought that you might be interested in information which has recently come to the attention of this office as a result of inquiries made after a report was received that ORSON WELLES was to deliver an address in Portland on the evening of December 17, 1943, under the auspices of the American Free World Association. It was announced in the press that the appearance of WELLES had been announced by Mrs. NAN WOOD HONEYMAN.

You may recall that Mrs. HONEYMAN is a former U. S. Congresswoman from the state of Oregon and is reportedly intimately acquainted with Mrs. ROOSEVELT. During Mrs. ROOSEVELT's visit to the Pacific Northwest last summer she contacted Mrs. HONEYMAN and I am also informed that Mrs. HONEYMAN was one of the bridesmaids at the ROOSEVELT wedding.

A discreet inquiry disclosed that the American Free World Association is a branch or an affiliate of the United Nations Association. More complete and definite information concerning these two organizations is not available in the Portland office at the present time. However, it is known that both of the organizations are under the active sponsorship of Mrs. STUART STRONG, who, in turn, is known to have been connected in the past with a number of extremely liberal groups.

The United Nations Association is reportedly the successor to an old League of Nations group and is endowed by the Carnegie Fund for International Peace.

advised that Mrs. NAN WOOD HONEYMAN is regarded as a "well-known leftist group follower". Mrs. HONEYMAN is also alleged to have had close ties with the Oregon Commonwealth Federation.

It is planned that the public appearance of ORSON WELLES

COPIES DESTROYED 6-26-58
R-34

RECORDED & 100-23438-1
29 DEC 1943

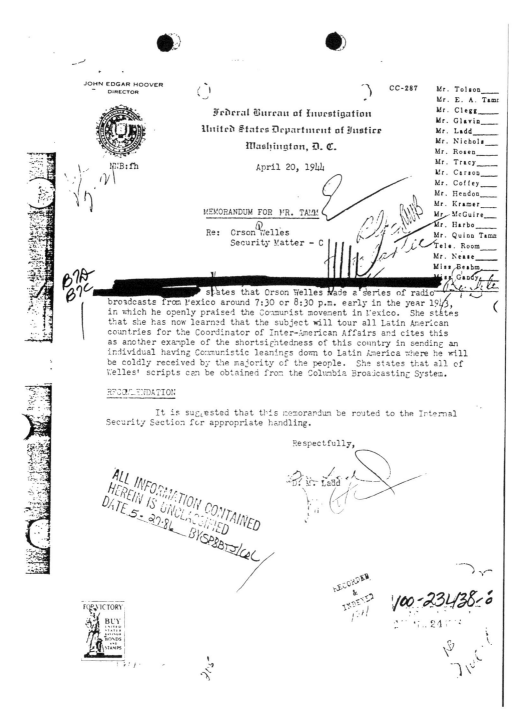

JOHN EDGAR HOOVER
DIRECTOR

CC-287

Mr. Tolson____
Mr. E. A. Tamm
Mr. Clegg____
Mr. Glavin____
Mr. Ladd____
Mr. Nichols____
Mr. Rosen____
Mr. Tracy____
Mr. Carson____
Mr. Coffey____
Mr. Hendon____
Mr. Kramer____
Mr. McGuire____
Mr. Harbo____
Mr. Quinn Tamm
Tele. Room____
Mr. Nease____
Miss Beahm____
Miss Gandy____

Federal Bureau of Investigation
United States Department of Justice
Washington, D. C.

NNB:fh

April 20, 1944

MEMORANDUM FOR MR. TAMM

Re: Orson Welles
     Security Matter - C

states that Orson Welles made a series of radio
broadcasts from Mexico around 7:30 or 8:30 p.m. early in the year 1943,
in which he openly praised the Communist movement in Mexico. She states
that she has now learned that the subject will tour all Latin American
countries for the Coordinator of Inter-American Affairs and cites this
as another example of the shortsightedness of this country in sending an
individual having Communistic leanings down to Latin America where he will
be coldly received by the majority of the people. She states that all of
Welles' scripts can be obtained from the Columbia Broadcasting System.

RECOMMENDATION

It is suggested that this memorandum be routed to the Internal
Security Section for appropriate handling.

Respectfully,

D. M. Ladd

ALL INFORMATION CONTAINED
HEREIN IS UNCLASSIFIED
DATE 5-22-86 BYSP8BT/col

FOR VICTORY
BUY
UNITED
STATES
SAVINGS
BONDS
AND
STAMPS

RECORDED
&
INDEXED

100-23438-6

Office Memo____ um • UNITED S   GOVERNMENT

TO : Director, FBI

FROM : SAC, Los Angeles

SUBJECT: RE: ORSON WELLES, WA
SECURITY MATTER – C

DATE: November 3, 1944

Reference is made to the report of Special Agent [redacted]
Los Angeles, dated November 3, 1944.

On August 28, 1944, there appeared in HEDDA HOPPER'S column an
article that the President had called the Subject's wife, RITA HAYWORTH, and
explained that ORSON WELLES was doing some special work for him.

Special Agent [redacted] interviewed HEDDA HOPPER regarding
this item and she stated she did not know exactly what the President was
having WELLES do but she did know that he was on some kind of mission for
the President.

According to the September 22, 1944, issue of the Los Angeles
Daily News, the Subject appeared at a rally in Madison Square Garden on
September 21, 1944, where he introduced Vice-President WALLACE who made a
speech on behalf of the President.

100-5440   B7C

100-23438—2

6 1 NOV 28 1944

EX-33

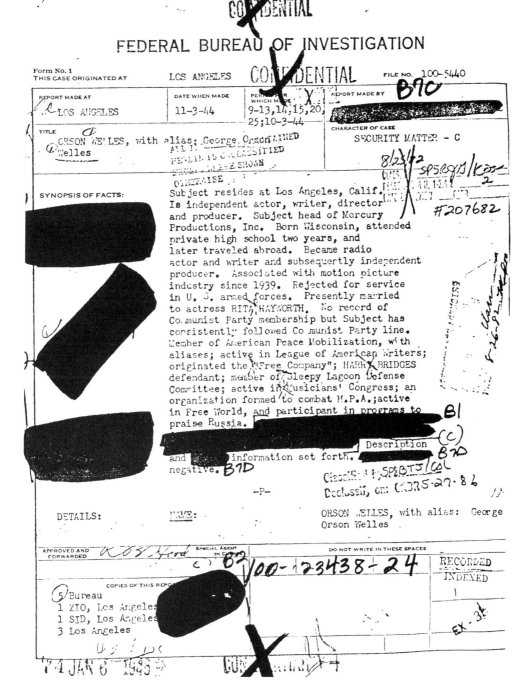

CONFIDENTIAL

FEDERAL BUREAU OF INVESTIGATION

CONFIDENTIAL

Form No. 1
THIS CASE ORIGINATED AT   LOS ANGELES   FILE NO. 100-5440

REPORT MADE AT	DATE WHEN MADE	PERIOD FOR WHICH MADE	REPORT MADE BY
LOS ANGELES	11-3-44	9-13,14,15,20, 25;10-3-44	B7C

TITLE
ORSON WELLES, with alias: George Orson Welles

CHARACTER OF CASE
SECURITY MATTER - C

#207682

SYNOPSIS OF FACTS:

Subject resides at Los Angeles, Calif. Is independent actor, writer, director and producer. Subject head of Mercury Productions, Inc. Born Wisconsin, attended private high school two years, and later traveled abroad. Became radio actor and writer and subsequently independent producer. Associated with motion picture industry since 1939. Rejected for service in U. S. armed forces. Presently married to actress RITA HAYWORTH. No record of Communist Party membership but Subject has consistently followed Communist Party line. Member of American Peace Mobilization, with aliases; active in League of American Writers; originated the "Free Company"; HARRY BRIDGES defendant; member of Sleepy Lagoon Defense Committee; active in Musicians' Congress; an organization formed to combat M.P.A.; active in Free World, and participant in programs to praise Russia. and information set forth. negative.

Description

-P-

DETAILS: NAME: ORSON WELLES, with alias: George Orson Welles

APPROVED AND FORWARDED   SPECIAL AGENT IN CHARGE   DO NOT WRITE IN THESE SPACES

100-123438-24

RECORDED
INDEXED

COPIES OF THIS REPORT
5 Bureau
1 ZIO, Los Angeles
1 SID, Los Angeles
3 Los Angeles

EX-34

74 JAN 6 1945

CONFIDENTIAL

LA - 100-5440

CONFIDENTIAL

RESIDENCE:

136 S. Carmelina, Brentwood, Los Angeles, California. Telephone number (unlisted) Arizona 39668.

BUSINESS ADDRESS:

Mercury Productions, Inc., 427 N. Canon Drive, Beverly Hills, California. Telephone CR 51108.

EMPLOYMENT:

The Subject is self-employed as an independent actor, writer, director and producer. The Subject releases his productions through the Mercury Productions, Inc.

CITIZENSHIP:

The Subject is a United States citizen inasmuch as he was born in this country.

BACKGROUND INFORMATION:

B2 _____ advised the writer that the Subject was born May 6, 1915 in Kenosha, Wisconsin, and according to a release by the Columbia Broadcasting System in Hollywood, the Subject was named after GEORGE ADE, noted humorist and a friend of the Subject's father, ORSON, but he has always been known as ORSON WELLES.

According to B2 _____ the Subject attended eight years of elementary grammar school in Kenosha, Wisconsin, following which he went to a private high school, the Todd School, in Woodstock, Illinois, where he was enrolled for two years. According to "Who's Who", the Subject's father died when the Subject was six years of age and a Doctor BERNSTEIN became his guardian. The Subject became ill while at the Todd School and was taken abroad by his guardian. Later, according to "Who's Who", he became a member of the Gate Theater in Dublin, Ireland, 1931-32, after which time he returned to Woodstock, Illinois, and began to produce plays. In the following year the Subject appeared on the stage with KATHERINE CORNELL and in 1934 was married to VIRGINIA LEDERER. Subject subsequently separated from this wife and went to Africa where he appeared in a few plays and compiled a book known as "Everyone's Shakespeare".

In 1937 he returned to this country and became a radio actor and writer. It was during this period that he made a sensational broadcast and was brought to the attention of the motion picture industry, and subsequently was employed by R.K.O. Studios and associated with B7C _____ prominent member of the Northwest Section of the Los Angeles County Communist Party.

-2-

CONFIDENTIAL

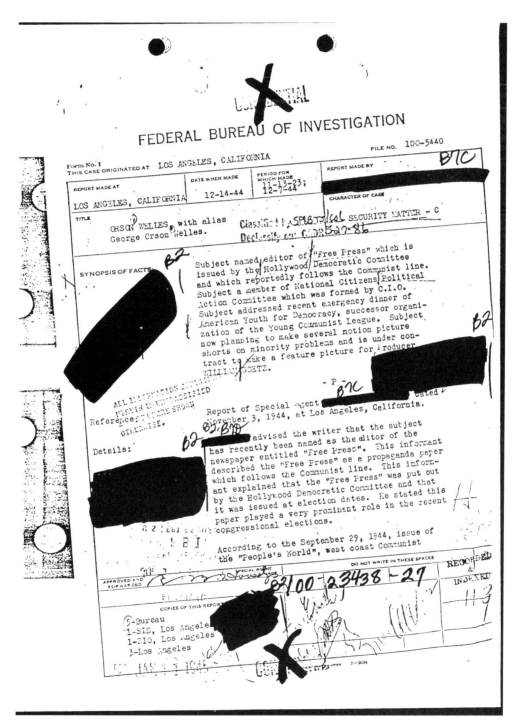

FEDERAL BUREAU OF INVESTIGATION

FILE NO. 100-5440

Form No. 1
THIS CASE ORIGINATED AT LOS ANGELES, CALIFORNIA

REPORT MADE AT	DATE WHEN MADE	PERIOD FOR WHICH MADE	REPORT MADE BY
LOS ANGELES, CALIFORNIA	12-14-44	12-13-23; 12-7-44	

TITLE
ORSON WELLES, with alias
George Orson Welles.

CHARACTER OF CASE
SECURITY MATTER - C

Classified SPECIFICAL
Declassify on OADR

SYNOPSIS OF FACTS:

Subject named editor of "Free Press" which is
issued by the Hollywood Democratic Committee
and which reportedly follows the Communist line.
Subject a member of National Citizens Political
Action Committee which was formed by C.I.O.
Subject addressed recent emergency dinner of
American Youth for Democracy, successor organization of the Young Communist League. Subject
now planning to make several motion picture
shorts on minority problems and is under contract to make a feature picture for Producer
WILLIAM GOETZ.

- P -

ALL INFORMATION CONTAINED
HEREIN IS UNCLASSIFIED
Reference:
OTHERWISE.

Details:

Report of Special Agent dated
November 3, 1944, at Los Angeles, California.

advised the writer that the subject
has recently been named as the editor of the
newspaper entitled "Free Press". This informant
described the "Free Press" as a propaganda paper
which follows the Communist line. This informant explained that the "Free Press" was put out
by the Hollywood Democratic Committee and that
it was issued at election dates. He stated this
paper played a very prominent role in the recent
congressional elections.

According to the September 29, 1944, issue of
the "People's World", west coast Communist

APPROVED AND FORWARDED	SPECIAL AGENT IN CHARGE	DO NOT WRITE IN THESE SPACES	RECORDED & INDEXED

COPIES OF THIS REPORT
6-Bureau
1-SID, Los Angeles
1-ZIO, Los Angeles
3-Los Angeles

L.A. F.D. 100-5440

publication, the subject has been named to the National Citizens Political
Action Committee as a representative from the state of California. This
Political Action Committee was formed by the C.I.O. Political Action Committee and is designed to include and to influence people who are not members
of any particular labor organization. According to this article, the members
from California were ORSON WELLES, Screen Writer BEN HECHT and Screen Actor
EDWARD G. ROBINSON.

_____ stated that _____ of the American Youth for
Democracy in Los Angeles, which is the successor organization to the Young
Communist League, had recently told him that he had gone to considerable
trouble to secure ORSON WELLES as a speaker for the emergency dinner that
was to be held on December 1, 1944. He stated that he felt WELLES would be
an excellent choice as a master of ceremonies and that his second choice would
be ALBERT DEKKER, who was recently elected to the California State Legislature.

On December 1, 1944, the "Salute to Young American Dinner" was
held by the AYD at the Hollywood Roosevelt Hotel in Hollywood, at which time
ORSON WELLES analyzed the G-I Bill of Rights and strongly condemned the
"money interests and money lenders". WELLES stated he felt the lobbyists,
the powerful interests in wall street, had corrupted the G-I Bill of Rights
and had written it largely to make it appear that this country was interested
in providing for the welfare of the returning soldier, but that in reality
they had written in provisions which would prevent the returning soldier from
securing any real benefits under the act. WELLES concluded his remarks by
stating that Fascism in the United States was still possible until all the
greedy people in this country had been killed.

In the November 10th issue of "Now" magazine which is published in
Los Angeles there appeared on the cover a picture of WELLS together with the
prominent negro actor REX INGRAM. In this issue there was an article about WELLES, and
it was stated that he would soon begin to make a series of short subjects
on minority problems and that he hoped that these would be released for showing in schools throughout the country. It should be pointed out that the
magazine "Now" is published semi-monthly in Los Angeles and appears faithfully
to carry out the Communist line.

According to the November 20th issue of "Hollywood Reporter",
Hollywood trade publication, subject has been signed by Producer WILLIAM
GOETZ to star in a picture produced by International Pictures with CLAUDETTE
COLBERT in "Tomorrow is Forever". This article pointed out that GOETZ looked
upon the signing of WELLES as one of the most important casting assignments
in the history of his company.

-2-

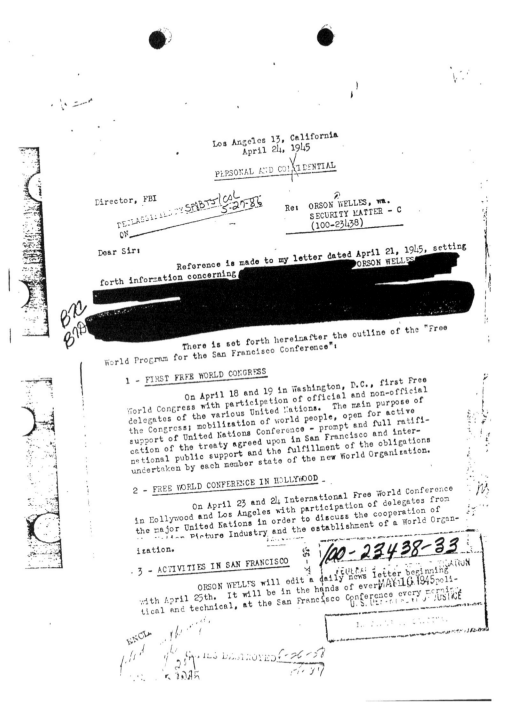

Los Angeles 13, California
April 24, 1945

PERSONAL AND CONFIDENTIAL

Director, FBI

DECLASSIFIED SPABTS/CoL 5-27-86
ON

Re: ORSON WELLES, was.
SECURITY MATTER - C
(100-23438)

Dear Sir:

Reference is made to my letter dated April 21, 1945, setting forth information concerning ~~ORSON WELLES~~

There is set forth hereinafter the outline of the "Free World Program for the San Francisco Conference":

1 - FIRST FREE WORLD CONGRESS

On April 18 and 19 in Washington, D.C., first Free World Congress with participation of official and non-official delegates of the various United Nations. The main purpose of the Congress; mobilization of world people, open for active support of United Nations Conference - prompt and full ratification of the treaty agreed upon in San Francisco and international public support and the fulfillment of the obligations undertaken by each member state of the new World Organization.

2 - FREE WORLD CONFERENCE IN HOLLYWOOD -

On April 23 and 24 International Free World Conference in Hollywood and Los Angeles with participation of delegates from the major United Nations in order to discuss the cooperation of ... Picture Industry and the establishment of a World Organization.

3 - ACTIVITIES IN SAN FRANCISCO

ORSON WELLES will edit a daily news letter beginning with April 25th. It will be in the hands of every ... MAY 10 1945 political and technical, at the San Francisco Conference every morning.

100-23438-33

FEDERAL BUREAU OF INVESTIGATION
MAY 10 1945
U.S. DEPARTMENT OF JUSTICE

ENCL
COPIES DESTROYED 1-26-50

Jackie Robinson

Chapter XIII

Jackie Robinson:
Never Had It Made,
He Was Born Too Soon

Jack Roosevelt Robinson was born on January 31,1919 in Cairo, Georgia. He was the son of Jerry Robinson (a farm worker and sharecropper) and Mallie McGriff (a maid, cook, and washer woman). Six months after Robinson was born, his father deserted his family and left town with a neighbor's wife. In the face of severe financial difficulties following World War I, his mother at age thirty moved with her five children to Pasadena, California to be near her eldest brother Burton McGriff. There she had hoped to find a better life. At the time that she decided to make the move, Jackie was one year old, the youngest of the five kids. He had three brothers- Edgar, 11; Frank, 9; Mack, 7; and one sister Willa Mae who was 5. Mrs. Robinson could not earn enough money working as a domestic to support a family of six, therefore she went to a private charity organization and enrolled the children and herself into a Dole Plan. Although the extra money and food from the Dole was a godsend she still had to struggle to make ends meet. The majority of the days the kids were able to

333

eat two meals a day, however on some days they did not get any food at all except the leftovers that Mrs. Robinson brought home from her white employer's kitchen table.

During the hours that Mrs. Robinson was at work Jackie's little sister Willa Mae assumed the little mother's role and took her baby brother to school with her. He was too young to be enrolled in kindergarten, therefore his mother asked the principal to let him play in the sandbox during school hours. However, on rainy days he was permitted to sit in the back of the room in Miss Mary Green's kindergarten class. When Jackie reached the age of 5 he was enrolled in school where he joined his siblings as a full time student.

In grammar school Jackie exhibited a multiplicity of talents for sports. As a matter of fact, some of his classmates would share their lunch money with him, provided he agreed to play on their team. When he went to John Muir Technical High School, he earned letters in football, baseball, basketball, and track. His brother Frank was his cheerleader and greatest fan. His brother Mack was a great track star in spite of a mild heart ailment, Mack set a fast pace for Jackie to follow when he ran second to World Champion Jessie Owens in the 200 meter race during the 1936 Olympic games in Berlin, Germany.

When Jackie graduated from Muir Technical High School in 1937, he was one of the most celebrated

Jackie Robinson as a track star at UCLA in 1939.

athletes in Pasadena, the City of Roses. In 1938, at Pasadena Junior College, he made local history in two different events, and in two different cities on the same day. In the morning in Pomona, he set a new running broad jump record of 25 feet 6 ½ inches. In the afternoon, in Glendale, he played shortstop with the Pasadena team when they won the championship.

Jackie's athletic prowess received a great deal of media print and the publicity brought him to the attention of a large number of local and midwestern colleges and universities who sought his service by offering him extremely attractive athletic scholarships. In 1939, he opted to go to the University of California at Los Angeles because he wanted to stay near home where he would get the constant benefit of his mother's daily prayers and his brother Frank's constant encouragement. As fate would have it, shortly after he made the decision to play for UCLA, his brother Frank was killed in a freak motorcycle accident.

In 1941, Robinson dropped out of the University, because he reasoned that no amount of education could help a Black man get a job above the backbreaking pick and shovel level. Through Pat Ahern, one of his ardent white fans and the athletic director from the National Youth Administrators, Robinson was offered a position as assistant director at a work camp in Atascadero, California. The NYA was one of President Franklin Delano Roosevelt's alphabet depression-proof programs, designed to get young men off the street corners under the National Recovery Act. The NYA job was short lived after World War II broke out in Europe in September 1939. Several months after the war started, our government closed down all the NYA projects, although at the time the United States had not become overtly involved in the war between Adolph Hitler's Germany and Winston Churchill's Great Britain.

In 1941, America entered the war against Japan following their bombing of Pearl Harbor on December 7th. Japan was an Axis Nation in alliance with Germany and Italy. In May 1942, the war with the Axis powers caught up with Jackie Robinson and he was drafted into the service of the United States Army and sent off to Fort Riley, Kansas, for basic military training in a Calvary outfit. After he completed the 120 day basic training program, he applied for Officer Candidate School. It was at this point that his eyes and mind were really opened wide to the fate of a Black man in a Jim Crow Army. He and other Colored office candidates had to sit around playing poker, tonk, and shooting craps for nickels in the barracks for months before they were given orders to enter the Officer Candidate School; whereas, qualified white boys were sucked into the officers program within days after they completed their basic training.

The Black soldiers at Fort Riley didn't get any orders or special orders for starting their training as Officer Candidates, until Sergeant Joe Louis, the

World's Heavyweight Boxing Champion was transferred to Fort Riley. After Sergeant Joe Louis heard Robinson's story, he made a telephone call to the top brass in the War Department in Washington, D.C. Louis' call literally got action overnight, in that within 24 hours Robinson and the other Colored O.C.S. Candidates were whisked into an officers training program like a Kansas tornado.

Jackie Robinson received his second lieutenant bars in January, 1943. There were some other 90 day wonders who graduated with Robinson who were gung-ho, in that they demanded respect from their white superiors in the Army even when the odds and racial climate indicated that favorable results would not be forthcoming. Jackie Robinson, the future baseball hero and legend, really broke the mold in the Army in that he did not believe that rice was white and that fat meat was greasy. A case in point took place while Robinson was in training at the Officer Candidate School in Fort Riley, Kansas. Robinson was completing the last phase of

Jackie Robinson became a Second Lieutenant at Fort Riley, Kansas in January 1943.

his training, when a drill officer referred to a Negro O.C.S. candidate as a stupid black son of a bitch. Jackie intervened and said: "Sir, that man is a soldier in the United States Army." The officer retorted: "Nigger that goes for you too." Wham! Bam! Jackie hit the drillmaster in the mouth and knocked out all his front pearly whites. Before anybody could come to the officer's defense Jackie had the man on the ground preparing to do some major surgery on his face.

Thank God! Joe Louis, who was still stationed at Fort Riley at the time, upon hearing about the incident, got on the telephone when he heard about the incident and called a friend of the writer's Truman K. Gibson Jr. Civilian Aide to the Secretary of War, Henry L. Stimson in Washington, D.C. Joe Louis said: "Man! Jackie is in trouble; you better get out here right away." General B.O. Davis, the U.S. Army first Colored general, Truman K. Gibson Jr. and Joe Louis, met with the Fort Riley Post Commanding General. Joe Louis reportedly gave the general some pacifiers which included a case of Roederer Crystal Champagne and a Piaget watch. (The gifts from Joe Louis saved Jackie Robinson's ass from being kicked out of the OCS school and thrown into the stockade or maybe something worse like Federal prison.)

Jackie's reprieve was short lived, in that the Army shipped him to Camp Swift, Texas after he graduated from O.C.S. where white folks had a reputation of being meaner to colored people than they were in Fort Riley, Kansas. The Mayor of the town bordering Camp Swift, had earlier told his congressman to inform President Franklin Delano Roosevelt that he would personally shoot the first nigger who came to his town.

During World War II Southern bus drivers were deputized and permitted to carry side arms for the primary purpose of keeping all colored soldiers in their place at the back of the bus. Jackie, a spanking brand new second lieutenant, was standing on the corner waiting for a bus. A bus pulled up and the driver said: "Alright nigger get on the bus Gus." Jackie snapped: "You talking to me?" The driver recoiled: "Yes! Nigger I am talking to you." Jackie lowered his voice and said: " I think you are making a mistake. I will get on the bus when I am damn fucking ready." The driver jumped off the bus and pulled out his gun. Jackie took the gun and commenced pistol whipping the driver with his own weapon.

Behind this second major confrontation, the top Washington brass viewed Robinson as a hothead and troublemaker and thought he could better serve his country as a civilian. In November 1944, Jackie was transferred to the separation center at Camp Breckinridge, Kentucky where he received an honorable discharge. While waiting to be discharged, Jackie met a brother named Alexander who had been a member of the Kansas City Monarchs, which was one of the few Black professional baseball teams in the world. Alex told Robinson that the Monarchs were recruiting players.

In the process of looking for a job after becoming a civilian, he wrote to the Monarchs Baseball Organization. They checked his references and quickly agreed to accept him on a tryout basis for spring training. As a matter of fact, two days after he sent in his resume he received a telegram from the organization instructing him to report to Houston, Texas. They offered to pay him $400.00 per month which was considered a lot of bread for a Black in 1945.

The Monarch teams baseball circuit included playing in Kansas City and throughout the Midwest, Atlanta and Birmingham, in the south and in the east at Pittsburgh and Philadelphia. Finding some place to eat, sleep and the use of public toilet facilities was a daily problem, in that they were not welcome in white restaurants, hotels, or the use of the gasoline filling station restrooms in some places in the north and all the filling stations in the south. The boys of summer thought that they were eating high on the hog when they could get a plate of cold cuts and a hunk of bread that they could consume in peace on the bus. Robinson spent the spring and summer of 1945 playing shortstop for the Monarchs.

Pressure to integrate baseball was being whispered in some underground white circles but was not really expected to happen. During the early 40s, a few major league teams gave tryouts to Black players, but no team actually signed one.

As the baseball world slept Branch Rickey, President of the Brooklyn Dodgers baseball team, was doing the math on the gate attraction that Black players might add to his bottom line. Rickey sent his scouts out to scour the Negro American and National Leagues, plus those in the Caribbean. His search was in depth for the most talented Black baseball players on the surface of the earth, during the spring and summer seasons of 1945. Rickey was looking for a Black Babe Ruth who would break the Cotton Curtain and open the gates for Blacks to walk through.

Branch Rickey eventually settled on Jackie Robinson although Robinson was not the best Black baseball player. On the other hand, Robinson was college educated, had experience competing in interracial settings at UCLA, plus he was known for his competitive fire. The latter quality tipped the scale in Jackie's favor.

In August, 1945, Branch Rickey offered Robinson an opportunity to play in the Dodger Organization, but warned him that he would have to undergo a great deal of pressure and abuse. On the other hand, he extracted from Jackie a promise not to respond in kind to personal abuse in his first three years.

Robinson agreed to be cool and was offered and signed a contract in August, 1945 for a $3,500 bonus and a salary of $600.00 a month. He became an official member of the Montreal team which was the Brooklyn Dodgers' top

Jackie Robinson signed a contract in August 1945 with Branch Rickey (on the extreme Left) to play with a Montreal Team which was a Brooklyn Dodgers Farm Club.

minor league farm club. Many naysayers believed in their heart of hearts that the integration experiment would not work. Robinson had enough faith and confidence in the Rickey Plan to get married to Rachael Isum his college sweetheart and start a family in Los Angeles in 1946.

Fighting against racism was not something new to Branch Rickey. In the late 1930s and early 40s when he was a front office executive in St. Louis, he had fought behind doors, against the custom that assigned Black spectators to the Jim Crow section of Sportsmen's Park, which later became Busch (the beer people) Memorial Stadium. His pleas to change the rules fell on deaf ears. The counter argument from the establishment was that an open choice of seating would cause whites to stay away from the park.

Robinson spent the 1946 baseball season with the top Dodgers minor league club located in Montreal, Canada. After leading the Montreal Royals to the International League Championship and winning the league batting championship with a .349 average, he joined the Dodgers the following spring. Several of the Dodgers players objected to Robinson's presence and circulated a petition in which they threatened not to play with a Negro on the team. Rickey threw a wrench into the boycott efforts by making it crystal clear that any renegade would be traded or released if he refused to play.

Jackie Robinson stormed into 1947 as the Dodgers' starting first baseman, hence breaking down the long standing barricade that had barred Negro players from the Major Leagues. During the first year he was umbrellaed with abuse from opposing teams as well as spectators. Pitchers threw balls at his head and opposing base runners cut him with their spikes at every opportunity when they slid into first base. Disgruntled fans sent death threats that triggered FBI investigations on at least a half dozen occasions. Although Robinson innately had a fiery temper and enormous pride, he smothered them in the small bowels of his stomach in keeping with the initial agreement he made with Branch Rickey of not retaliating to the mountains of abuse. Off the field, Jackie was blanketed with the indignities of Jim Crow accommodations while on the road with the team in both the North and the South.

Robinson's aggressive style of playing won games for the Dodgers, earning him the loyalty of his teammates and the Brooklyn fans. Despite the enormous pressures that year, he led the Dodgers to their first National League Championship in six years and a berth in the World Series. Robinson, also led the league in stolen bases and batted 297, plus he was named the Rookie of the Year. Overnight, he captured the heart of Black America. In a relatively short time he became one of the biggest gate attractions in baseball since the Babe Ruth era. He was to baseball in the 1940s what Jim Brown was to football in the 1950s, what Michael Jordan was to basketball in the 1990s and what Tiger Woods is to golf in the new millennium.

As Branch Rickey had calculated, Robinson attracted thousands of Negro spectators to Major League games. Five major league teams set new attendance records in 1947 because of Robinson's presence. By the end of the

1947 season, two major league teams, the Cleveland Indians and the St. Louis Browns, added Negro players to their roster. By the late 1950s most of the other major league teams had hired Negro ballplayers.

In the spring of 1949, Jackie's tolerance cup runneth over and he began to blow his stack because he had fulfilled his pledge of silence to Mr. Branch Rickey. Thus he began to confront opposing players who taunted him and stepped on him as if he was a roach. On a positive side, he enjoyed the best year of his life, in that he led the Dodgers to another national league pennant and he also captured the league's batting championship, with a .342 mark, in addition to receiving the Most Valuable Player of the Year Award.

Jackie's civil rights vocality against racism inside and outside of baseball brought him the attention of J. Edgar Hoover's FBI and the House Committee on Un-American Activities, where he was questioned extensively about Paul Robeson's alleged statement in reference to Negroes not being willing to

Jackie Robinson supported Dr. Martin Luther King in the Civil Rights Struggle.

fight against the Soviet Union, America's ally during World War II.

Robeson's own reaction to Robinson's testimony was muted. He assailed the HUAC proceedings in general terms as "an insult to the Negro people" and an incitement to terrorist groups like the Klan to step up their reign of mob violence; he also challenged the loyalty of HUAC to the ideals of the republic, because it maintained an "Ominous Silence" in the face of the continued lynching of Black citizens. Robeson refused to be drawn into any conflict dividing him and his brothers who were victims of terror.

In 1962, Robinson became the first Black player to be inducted into the National Baseball Hall of Fame. He used his celebrity status as a spokesman for civil rights issues. He served as an active and highly successful fundraiser for the National Association for the Advancement of Colored People. It can be safely said that no other athlete has had a greater sociological impact on American sports than Robinson.

Chronology of Events in Jackie Robinson's Life

January 31, 1919	Born Jack Roosevelt Robinson in Cairo, GA
May, 1920	Robinson family moves to Pasadena, California
September, 1933	Robinson enrolls at John Muir Technical High
September, 1937	Enrolls at Pasadena Junior College
September, 1939	Enrolls at UCLA
1942-44	Serves in the Army
1945	Plays Negro League baseball for the Kansas City Monarchs
August 28, 1945	First meeting with Branch Rickey; signs contract to play for the Montreal Royals in the Brooklyn Dodger's organization
April 18, 1946	Plays first game for the Montreal Royals
1946	Marries Rachel Isum; Royals win the Little World Series championship.
November 1946	Jackie Robinson, Jr. is born
April, 15 1947	Robinson plays first game for the Brooklyn Dodgers
1947	Named National League Rookie of the Year; leads National League in stolen bases.
July 1949	Testifies before the House Un-American Activities Committee
1949	Wins National League Most Valuable Player Award; leads National League in batting average and stolen bases
January 1950	Sharon Robinson is born
1950	Stars in film biography, The Jackie Robinson Story; Robinson family moves to St. Albans, New York; Branch Rickey resigns as president of the Dodgers
May 1952	David Robinson is born

On April 18,1946 Jackie married Rachael Isum.

1955 Robinson family moves to Stamford, Connecticuit; Brooklyn Dodgers win World Series

1956 Ebbets Field sold; Dodgers announce move to Los Angeles; Robinson traded to the New York Giants

January 1957 Announces retirement from baseball

1957 Joins Chock Full O'Nuts as Vice President of Community Relations; Chairs NAACP fund drive

1960 Campaigns for Richard M. Nixon

January 23, 1962 Elected into the Baseball Hall of fame

1965 Campaigns for Nelson Rockefeller; helps establish the Freedom National Bank

1968 Robinson's mother Mallie, dies

June 1971 Robinson's son Jackie, Jr., killed in automobile accident

October 24, 1972 Robinson dies in Stanford, Connecticut

Robinson on the picket line in New York City.

Federal Bureau of Investigation

Freedom of Information/Privacy Acts Section

Subject: Jackie Robinson

RE: "JACKIE" ROBINSON

CONFIDENTIAL

in the courts, police brutality,
and lynching when it happens
doesn't change the truth of his
charges. Just because communists
kick up a big fuss over racial
discrimination when it suits their
purposes, a lot of people try to
pretend that the whole issue is a
creation of communist imagination.

"But they are not fooling anyone
with this kind of pretense, and
talk about communists stirring up
Negroes to protest,' only makes
present misunderstanding worse than
ever. Negroes were stirred up long
before there was a Communist Party,
and they'll stay stirred up long
after the Party has disappeared--
unless JIM CROW has disappeared by
then as well.

"I've been asked to express my views
on PAUL ROBESON's statement in Paris
to the effect that American Negroes
would refuse to fight in any war
against Russia because we love Russia
so much. I haven't any comment to
make on that statement except that if
Mr. ROBESON actually made it, it
sounds very silly to me. But he has
a right to his personal views, and if
he wants to sound silly when he
expresses them in public, that is his
business and not mine. He's still a
famous ex-athlete and a great singer
and actor.

"I understand that there are some
few Negroes who are members of the
Communist Party, and in the event of
war with Russia they'd probably act
just as any other communist would.
So would members of other minority
and majority groups. There are some
colored pacifists, and they'd act

100-428850-1

CONFIDENTIAL

5

just like pacifists of any color.
And most Negroes--and Italians and
Irish and Jews and Swedes and Slavs
and other Americans--would act just
as all these groups did in the last
war. They'd do their best to keep
their country out of war; if successful,
they'd do their best to help their
country win the war--against Russia
or any other enemy that threatened
us. This isn't said as any defense
of the Negro's loyalty, because any
loyalty that needs defense can't
amount to much in the long run. And
no one has ever questioned my race's
loyalty except a few people who don't
amount to very much.

"What I'm trying to get across is
that the American public is off on
the wrong foot when it begins to
think of radicalism in terms of any
special minority group. It is
thinking of this sort that gets
people scared because one Negro,
speaking to a communist group in
Paris, threatens an organized boycott
by 15,000,000 members of his race.

"I can't speak for any 15,000,000
people any more than any other one
person can, but I know that I've got
too much invested for my wife and
child and myself in the future of
this country, and I and other Americans
of many races and faiths have too much
invested in our country's welfare, for
any of us to throw it away because of
a siren song sung in bass. I am a
religious man. Therefore I cherish
America where I am free to worship as
I please, a privilege which some
countries do not give. And I suspect
that 999 out of almost any thousand
colored Americans you meet will tell
you the same thing.

made available a mimeographed copy of a letter
to this letter was a clipping entitled "Every Time you Buy a Ford
Product," showing a photograph of Ed Sullivan presenting "the NAACP's
highest award, the 'Spingarn Metal,' to Negro agitator Jackie Robinson."

105-55211-229 p. 7
(20)

The "Houston Post" and "Houston Chronicle," Houston, Texas,
contained articles on 6/22/58, and the "Houston Informer," a bi-weekly
newspaper for Negroes, reported on 6/24/58, that Jackie Robinson spoke
to a group of Negro leaders in Houston, Texas, on 6/21/58, and urged
them to continue the fight of equalization of Negroes in all phases of
American life. His appearance was in the interest of the NAACP.

62-101087-46-37 p. 2
(9)

A Bureau memo dated 7/7/58 contained information relating to
Drew Pearson's Radio Broadcast over station WTOP, Washington, DC, on
7/5/58. Pearson stated that Jackie Robinson had promised to campaign
for Adam Clayton Powell (100-51230).

100-51230-204
(15)

advised that there was a discussion
about a children's march on Washington, DC, scheduled to take place
10/11/58. Jackie Robinson was to act as leader of the march. (u)

advised that the integration march scheduled for
10/11/58 had been canceled and re-scheduled for 10/25/58. (u)

62-101087-523 encl. p. 1
(7)
SI 62-101087-554
(7)
SI 62-101087-A "Washington News"
(8) Washington, DC, 9/26/5
SI 100-3-60-1081 p. 21
(11) (Press release 9/15/58)

SECRET

-13-

100-438850-4

A highly confidential source advised that he was present on the evening of 10/15/46 in the hotel room of ███████████ ███████████ CP,USA and ███████████████████ of CP handling Veterans affairs, when they discussed their day's activity. According to this informant ████ advised that Jackie Robinson had offered to appear in Los Angeles to speak in behalf of the veterans. α(u)

100-3-73-107 p. 23
(11)

The "Michigan Chronicle" for December 7, 1946, reported that the Detroit Committee to Fight Racial Injustice and Terrorism was sponsoring a mobilization in Washington, DC, on 1/3/47, in conjunction with the American crusade to end lynching. In connection with this, they scheduled a dance for 12/13/46 and a rally on 12/17/46 at which Jackie Robinson was to be the principal speaker in an effort to raise funds. At the last minute Robinson telegraphed his inability to appear and the rally was not held in Detroit, Mich.

100-135-15-311 p. 9
(13)

The AYD (61-777) planned a gathering for 12/20/46, at Manhattan Center, NYC. This gathering was known as "Salute Young America" and its purpose was to present awards to young Americans who had allegedly done outstanding work in inter-racial-inter-faith unity. (A delicate confidential source) α(u)

Jackie Robinson was among those who was scheduled to receive an award. (A delicate confidential source) α(u)

61-777-756
(3)
SI 61-777-34-213 p. 1
(3) ████████ α(u) b2,b7D

The following references on Jackie Robinson appear in the file captioned "United Negro and Allied Veterans of America" (100-344537) (UNAVA). Robinson attended and spoke at the organizing conference for the New York State chapter of the UNAVA and was appointed Honorary New York State Commander of this organization in June of 1946. In May of 1947 he was one of ten individuals to receive an award for outstanding contributions to the struggle for Negro Rights.

SERIAL	SEARCH SLIP PAGE NUMBER
31 p. 7	(16)
78 p. 4	(16)

(continued)

SIXTT
100-428850-4

-6-

UNITED STATES DEPARTMENT OF JUSTICE

FEDERAL BUREAU OF INVESTIGATION

New Haven, Connecticut

October 16, 1963

CON~~FIDE~~NTIAL

In Reply, Please Refer to
File No.

Re: Jackie Robinson, Stamford, Connecticut
     Board of Directors and Co-chairman
     National Life Membership Committee,
     National Association For The Advancement
     of Colored People

Jack Roosevelt Robinson is a negro male born January 31, 1919,
at Cairo, Georgia. He is employed as the Vice President of
Chock Full O'Nuts Coffee Company, New York City. Prior to
his current employment with the Chock Full O'Nuts Coffee Company he was a star baseball player with the Brooklyn Dodgers.

The November, 1940 issue of "Fraternal Outlook" page 7, column
3, contains an article and a photograph of Jackie Robinson
in connection with the opening of the Solidarity Center of the
International Workers Order in Harlem, New York. The name
of Jackie Robinson, ballplayer, is listed as one of the persons on the Advisory Board.

During 1947, a source who has furnished reliable information
in the past, made available the names and addresses of a
considerable number of past and present officers of the International Workers Order in the New York area. The following
information concerning Jackie Robinson was noted.

     Lodge number 691
          Solidarity House
          124 West 124th Street
          Advisory Board
               Jackie Robinson
               (among others)

On February 15, 1952, a second source who has furnished
reliable information in the past, stated that the Committee
to End Discrimination in Levittown, New York announced that

ALL INFORMATION CONTAINED
HEREIN IS UNCLASSIFIED
EXCEPT WHERE SHOWN
OTHERWISE.

DECLASSIFIED BY
ON 7/28/93
Appeal # 93-1285

67C

3/21/89
Classified by
Declassify on OADR

CON~~FIDE~~NTIAL

100-428850-NOT RECORDED

Re: Jackie Robinson, Stamford, Connecticut CONFIDENTIAL

Jackie Robinson, famous Dodger baseball star, told the committee he would cooperate with them to end discrimination in Levittown, New York and offered them his assistance in the matter. X (u)

The June 1, 1946 issue of "The Peoples Voice" page 10, column 3, contains an article and photograph of Jackie Robinson reflecting that Jackie Robinson, the first negro to break into organized baseball, accepted Chairmanship of the New York State Organizing Committee for United Negro and Allied Veterans of America (UNAVA). Bert Alves, Regional Director for UNAVA made the announcement.

On January 22, 1948, a third source who has furnished reliable information in the past, advised that [ ] was a member of the Communist Party.

The July 9, 1949, "New York Times" contains an article dated "Washington July 8" Jackie Robinson, negro star second baseman for the Brooklyn Dodgers "said today he would fight for the United States against Russia or any aggressor because 'I want my kids to have the same things I have.'"

A name check of the indices and/or printed hearings of the House Committee Un-American Activities (HCUA) on the name Jackie and Jack Roosevelt Robinson, on May 26, 1958, reflected the following references which were not checked against the original source:

1.   "Soviet Russia Today" for December, 1938, page 29, reflected that one J. R. Robinson of N.Y.C. was a contributor.

2.   "Soviet Russia Today" for February, 1942, page 31, reflected that one J. R. Robinson of Pennsylvania was a contributor.

3.   Hearings regarding Communist Infiltration of Minority Groups, July 13, 14, 18, 1949, pages 479-483, reflected that one Jack Roosevelt Robinson was a witness.

2.

CONFIDENTIAL 100-428850 NOT RECORDED

Re: Jackie Robinson, Stamford, Connecticut   CONFIDENTIAL

4.   "The Worker" for 12/19/48, page 11, Magazine
     Section, reflected that one Jackie Robinson was
     the author of "Jackie Robinson", which was
     recommended by "The Worker".

5.   The "Daily Worker" for 8/30/49, page 1 (not in
     this issue), reflected that one Jackie Robinson
     was a writer of a statement in behalf of Paul
     Robeson.

6.   "Youth" for June, 1947, page 18, reflected a
     photo of one Jackie Robinson.

7.   The "Daily Worker" for 6/2/47, reflected that one
     Jackie Robinson, Dodger player, received an award
     given by the United Negro and Allied Veterans of
     America.

8.   ████████████████████████████████████

9.   "The Worker" for 5/25/47, page 8, reflected that
     one Jackie Robinson was Honorary New York State
     Chairman of UNAVA.

10. ████████████████████████████████████

11. Hearings Regarding Communist Infiltration of
     Minority Groups - Part I; Hearings, etc. 81st
     Congress, 1st session, Sworn Testimony of
     George K. Hunton, 7/13/49.

     Page 451:   Hunton stated that conferences
                   held with Monsignor Campion
                   of Brooklyn and his group
                   brought about the hiring of
                   one Jackie Robinson and said

                        3.

                                CONFIDENTIAL

                        100-428850- NOT RECORDED

Re: Jackie Robinson, Stamford, Connecticut   CONFIDENTIAL

that, in his judgment, the
hiring of Jackie Robinson
improved the racial attitude
of hundreds of thousands of
sports lovers in this country.

Page 479
to 483:

Sworn testimony of one Jack
Roosevelt Robinson, 7/18/49,—
he stated he was born in Cairo,
Ga., in 1919. He stated he had
received a great many messages
urging him not to appear before
the Committee and that not all of
them came from communist
sympathizers. He stated, As
I see it there has been a terrific
lot of misunderstanding on this
subject of communism among the
Negroes in this country, and it's
bound to hurt my people's cause
unless it is cleared up.------"
"And one other thing the American
people ought to understand, if we
are to make progress in this
matter: The fact that it is a
communist who denounces injustice
in the courts, police brutality,
and lynching when it happens
doesn't change the truth of his
charges. Just because communists
kick up a big fuss over racial
discrimination when it suits their
purposes, a lot of people try to
pretend that the whole issue is a
creation of communist imagination.

"But they are not fooling anyone
with this kind of pretense, and
talk about 'communists stirring up
Negroes to protest', only makes
present misunderstanding worse than

4.

CONFIDENTIAL
NOT
100-458850-RECORDED

Re: Jackie Robinson, Stamford, Connecticut   CONFIDENTIAL

ever. Negroes were stirred up long
before there was a Communist Party,
and they'll stay stirred up long
after the Party has disappeared--
unless Jim Crow has disappeared by
then as well.

"I've been asked to express my views
on Paul Robeson's statement in Paris
to the effect that American Negroes
would refuse to fight in any war
against Russia because we love Russia
so much. I haven't any comment to
make on that statement except that if
Mr. Robeson actually made it, it
sounds very silly to me. But he has
a right to his personal views, and if
he wants to sound silly when he
expresses them in public, that is his
business and not mine. He's still a
famous ex-athlete and a great singer
and actor.

"I understand that there are some
few Negroes who are members of the
Communist Party, and in the event of
war with Russia they'd probably act
just as any other communist would.
So would members of other minority
and majority groups. There are some
colored pacifists, and they'd act
just like pacifists of any color.
And most Negroes--and Italians and
Irish and Jews and Swedes and Slavs
and other Americans--would act just
as all these groups did in the last
war. They'd do their best to keep
their country out of war; if successful,
they'd do their best to help their
country win the war--against Russia
or any other enemy that threatened
us. This isn't said as any defense
of the Negro's loyalty, because any
loyalty that needs defense can't
amount to much in the long run. And

5.

CONFIDENTIAL
100-428850 - NOT RECORDED

no one has ever questioned my race's
loyalty except a few people who don't
amount to very much.

"What I'm trying to get across is
that the American public is off on
the wrong feet when it begins to
think of radicalism in terms of any
special minority group. It is
thinking of this sort that gets
people scared because one Negro,
speaking to a communist group in
Paris, threatens an organized boycott
by 15,000,000 members of his race.

"I can't speak for any 15,000,000
people any more than any other one
person can, but I know that I've got
too much invested for my wife and
child and myself in the future of
this country, and I and other Americans
of many races and faiths have too much
invested in our country's welfare, for
any of us to throw it away because of
a siren song sung in bass. I am a
religious man. Therefore I cherish
America where I am free to worship as
I please, a privilege which some
countries do not give. And I suspect
that 999 out of almost any thousand
colored Americans you meet will tell
you the same thing.

"But that doesn't mean that we're
going to stop fighting race discrimination in this country until
we've got it licked. It means that
we're going to fight it all the
harder because our stake in the future
is so big. We can win our fight
without the communists and we don't
want their help."

6.

Re: Jackie Robinson, Stamford, Connecticut CONFIDENTIAL

He stated he attended U.C.L.A., and that he took his grade and high school work at Pasadena.

He was asked if, in his school life, he ever noted any attitude on the part of members of his race that would give any support to the alleged statement of Mr. Robeson.

He replied that he had never run across it any time.

He was asked if he had ever been approached to join any of the subversive organizations.

He replied that he was never approached but, when he was a kid, "we" were interested in the way "they" acted to get "us" to join. Young ladies were sent out to see if he and others would join their organization (CP in Pasadena). He said he and the others had enough sense to know what "they" were after, and none of the fellows in his group had any desire to join an organization like that.

7.

CONFIDENTIAL
100-428850-NOT RECORDED

Frank Lloyd Wright
358

Chapter XIV

Frank Lloyd Wright:
The Man Who Dared To Dream of A
Mile High 500 Story Tower

Frank Lincoln Wright was born on June 8,1867 in Richland Center, Wisconsin. He was the first of three children begotten by Richard Cary Wright and Anna Jones, who became his father's second bride. When Frank Lloyd was nineteen years old he changed his middle name from Lincoln to Lloyd. His father had given him the Lincoln moniker to show his personal esteem for the assassinated president. By changing his middle name Frank Lloyd Wright did not believe he was showing disrespect for his father's wishes, he just simply wanted a more visible tie with the Lloyd Joneses who carried the Welsh bloodline of his mother.

Richard Cary Wright's first wife was Permella Holcomb, a woman who bore his first four children. Thus, Frank Lloyd Wright came into this life with three stepsisters and a brother. Frank Lloyd's father was a flashy dresser and a female charmer. He wasa highly sought after individual because of his distinctive looks and his talents in multi-disciplines such as law, ministry, school (superintendent), music (master), and also as a distinguished orator. Frank Lloyd Wright's father taught him piano and musical structure and his mother introduced him to the basics of the Troehel Kindergarten System, which involved the manual handling of simple geometric shaped blocks.

In spite of his preschool training, Frank Lloyd Wright was a recurrent dropout in both elementary and high school. His failure in the school system could very well be attributed to his being bored with the packaging methods of basic public education. On the other hand, Wright's high intelligence quotient showed that he was a better reader than most university juniors, in that he had already absorbed the great ideas of Thomas Jefferson, Thomas Paine, Herman Melville, Oliver Wendell Holmes, Henry Adams, Henry David Thoreau, Nathaniel Hawthrone, Abraham Lincoln, Walt Whitman, Henry James, William Dean Howell, Ralph Waldo Emerson and Emily Dickinson. Moreover, as a result of his early exposure to the printed page he acquired a natural love for reading with the same passion as both his mother and father.

When Wright made the decision to drop out of high school, he maneuvered himself into the University of Wisconsin, in Madison in 1885, under the pretext of being a special student; his work there was marginal. He dropped out of the university at the end of his third semester.

Wright was basically a pathological prevaricator, in that he continued to cover-up lies with additional lies. For reasons known only to him, he wanted his friends to think of him as one who had been distinguished from the day that his head popped out of his mother's womb (there may be more than an ounce of truth in that allegation). The only academic degrees that Frank Lloyd Wright ever received in his lifetime were honorary ones according to his son David.

While at the University of Wisconsin, Wright got a job as a student assistant to Dr. Allan D. Conover, a professor of engineering. The professor paid the boy thirty-five dollars a month to work as his handyman. At the same time he taught Wright the rudiments of civil engineering and draftsmanship. Dr. Conover's hands-on instruction as an employer was superior to the classroom drills, in that it stood for something that Wright could understand and get his teeth into because it was analogous to actions in the real work-a-day world. The training that Wright received in the lap of professor Conover, made him feel like a bee ready to construct a honeycomb in Chicago as an architectural engineer.

Frank Lloyd Wright left Madison, Wisconsin in the spring of 1887 for Chicago without saying goodbye or "dog kiss my foot" to his mother or sisters. His mother had been strongly opposed to him making such a move because she felt that he was too young, too innocent and physically too small to wrestle with the Ragtime music and boisterous temptations of Abraham Lincoln's City by the Lake.

It was in Chicago that young Frank Lloyd Wright saw his first cable streetcar, and witnessed his

A Downtown Chicago Street scene in 1888 looking westward from Madison and State Street.

first ballet performance at the Chicago Opera House for the price of $1.00. Even more spectacular than the Opera performance for him was the sight of the eleven story Rookery Building, which was one of Chicago's pre-eminent early high-rise structures designed by Dan "don't make no small plans" Burnham and John Wellborn Root on the southeast corner of Adams and LaSalle. The edifice still stands bold and beautiful after one hundred and fourteen years. It contained more than 600 offices when its construction was completed in 1886. The people who worked there were labeled the "Cliff Dwellers" by the novelist, Henry B. Fuller.

The Rookery Building on the Southeast corner of Adams and LaSalle Street.

Wright spent four days sightseeing and trudging through the streets of Chicago looking for work and drinking up the sights through his wide angle pupils, the wonders of Chicago- including the 360 acre ill smelling Stockyards on the near west side, where Gustavus Swift and Phillip Danforth Armour had built financial empires slaughtering millions of hogs and cows for the meat markets of the world. On State Street which was just two blocks east of Lake Michigan, he wandered with shifting and glazing eyes through the corridors of Potter Palmer's 225 Room Palmer House Hotel. Upon leaving the hotel, he went north on State Street where he walked up and down the aisles of the Marshall Field's and Levi Zeigler Department Store, which at that time was located on the northwest corner of State and Randolph Street, as opposed to its present site diagonally across the street on the southeast corner. On the fifth day, he went job searching at the office of J.L. Silsbee, the architect who designed his Uncle Jenkins' new church for "All Souls". He approached Mr. Silsbee as a stranger and was hired based on the strength of some of the drawings that he had brought along with him from Madison. The only food that passed through his lips until he actually found employment was one banana a day according to the Book of Wright.

Although Frank Lloyd Wright enjoyed working for the Silsbee firm, he decided to move on up the ladder because he believed he had learned everything of value that they were capable of teaching him within the first ninety

The 1889 Auditorium Hotel and Theater Building located on the Northwest corner of Michigan and Congress Street is currently the home of Roosevelt University and The Auditorium Theater.

days that he had been in their employ. Hence, the hotshot took wings and found another position with the architectural firm of W.W. Clay. It took him exactly one week to realize that his new job assignment with the Clay firm was beyond his depth; thus he made a double time retreat back to the Silsbee firm, where the prodigal son was welcomed back with open arms. As a matter of fact, they were so pleased with his return they gave him a small increase in salary.

When Wright's feet started itching again he beat the pavements and found a new position in the drafting room of Dankmar Adler and Louis Sullivan. The firm had recently been engaged to prepare a design for the Auditorium Hotel Building and Theater (presently the home of Roosevelt University and Auditorium Theater). The sixteen story building was the tallest skyscraper in Chicago and the Auditorium Theater where the international famous Enrico Caruso, the powerful Italian operatic tenor had performed, was

The interior of the Auditorium Theater which is known worldwide for its perfect accoustics.

known worldwide by singers and musicians for its perfect acoustics. The Adler and Sullivan firm was ranked second in Chicago behind Burnham and Root when they hired Frank Lloyd. Sullivan became Wright's mentor in that they both loved to draw. Wright became adept at imitating Sullivan's drawings of ornaments, those infinitely complicated arabesques of natural forms that were never to be found in nature. As time passed, neither of the men could discern by glancing at a worksheet which one of them had actually done the drawing.

Early on, Sullivan was so proud of his 22year old protégé he gave him a five year contract on August 18, 1889 and he subsequently loaned him $5000 to build a home for himself and his young wife Catherine in Oak Park, Illinois, a small suburb on the west border of Chicago. The house that Wright designed as their honeymoon house still stands at the corner of Chicago and Forest Avenue.

At their first meeting Sullivan and Wright saw themselves as companionable. Wright became Sullivan's favorite person. The two men worked side by side in the drafting room. After the office closed for the day, they talked late into the night about common interests. If Sullivan had been less consummately narcissistic, he might have fallen in love with Wright who was beardless and wore his long brown hair in clusters that fell an inch above his shoulders. It is believed that Wright's feelings toward Sullivan were reciprocal in spite of his heterosexual upbringing. A key that opened the door to Wright's feelings about Louis Sullivan can be found in an obituary notice of Sullivan's demise written by Wright for an architectural magazine in 1924. In part it read as follows:

To know him well was to love him well. I never liked the name Frank until I would hear him say it and the quiet breath he gave it made it beautiful in my ears... The deep quiet of his temper had great charm for me. The rich humor that was lurking in the deeps within him and that sat in his eyes whatever his mouth might be saying however the moment might be, was rich and rare in human quality. He had remarkable and beautiful eyes- true windows for the soul of him...

For an architect who had not celebrated his fortieth birthday, Wright had gained an exceptional amount of notoriety. Pencil men many years older than Wright began to take his braggadocio talk seriously on matters dealing with arts and crafts and their relationship to the modern machines.

Daniel H. Burnham known to his colleagues as "Uncle Dan" was the most prominent architect in Chicago during the late 19th century and through the first decade of the 20th century. Among his great works was the general design for the Columbian Exposition (1893 World's Fair) which was held in Chicago's Jackson Park by Lake Michigan on the southeast side of the city. His design partner on the project was John Wellborn Root who died in 1891, at the early age of forty-one. Root's successor Charles B. Atwood died in 1895, at age forty-six from a drug overdose.

A few months and several twists in the road following Atwood's death

"Uncle Dan" offered to bring Wright into his firm as a design partner providing he agree to go to school for three years at the Beaux-Arts in Paris, France. Burnham's offer included traveling and living expenses for Wright's wife Catherine and their three children. "Uncle Dan's" opinion of Frank Lloyd was so high he further sweetened the deal by agreeing to treat Wright and his family to a two year residence in Rome after he graduated from Beaux-Arts. To "Uncle Dan's" surprise and disappointment Wright rejected the offer. After refusing "Uncle Dan's" offer Wright said: " I know how obstinate and egotistical you think I am, but I am going on as I have started. I am spoiled, first by birth, then by training and finally by conviction".

Despite Wright's success as a mid-west architect, he was on the fringe of world-wide recognition. On the other hand, his dual love life with Martha Borthwick Cheney, the wife of one of his best clients was pushing him into a midlife crisis. Wright's temporary solution to his triangle love affair, was to go to Germany in 1908 and take his client's wife along as his companion.

When Wright returned to the United States in 1910, he told his wife Catherine that their separation was permanent and that he wanted a divorce, his wife refused to accommodate him, thinking that when his libido cooled down he hopefully might regain his wits. Rather than hang suspended in mid-air over his marital dilemma, Wright immediately began designing for himself a new love nest which he called Taliesin, a country house outside of Spring Green, Wisconsin. In 1911, he moved there with Martha Brothwick, who had by this time resumed using her maiden name after divorcing her husband the same year.

In August 1914, a mentally challenged servant set Taliesin on fire and murdered Martha Brothwick, her two children and four others. While Wright was still in mourning, he was approached by Miriam Noel, a beautiful long legged self described artist, who in short order became his new ladylove. She accompanied him on his prolonged stays in Japan over the next seven years, earthquake demolished much of Tokyo and Yokohama in September 1923, the Imperial Hotel survived with only minor damage.

In November, 1922, Wright and his first wife were finally divorced after a twelve year separation. Despite his nine year yo-yo type relationship with Miriam Noel, he married her in 1923, but a year later she left him. In 1924, Wright met Olgivanna Lazovich Hinzenberg a married 26 year-old woman of

Frank Lloyd Wright and his third wife Olgivanna Lazovich Hinzenberg at Taliesin in Spring Green, Winconsin.

Montenegrin origin. She divorced her husband in 1925 and moved into Wright's Taliesin with her daughter, Svetiana. Their domestic life was disrupted by a second fire at Taliesin in April 1925, which destroyed their living quarters but spared Wright's studio and drawings. Wright and Olgivanna had a daughter, Iovanna in December, 1925. Threats of financial foreclosure on Taliesin and harrassment by Mariam Noel sent Wright and his new family into hiding until he was arrested for allegedly violating the Mann Act. The Mann Act was passed in June, 1919, by Illinois Congressmen James Robert Mann to prohibit Jack Johnson the first Negro World's Heavyweight Boxing Champion from carrying or inviting white women across state lines for immoral purposes.

By twentieth century standards, Wright was considered a left winger because of his liberal attitude about freedom, race, women and sex. His philosophy about the aforementioned subjects qualified him big time for J. Edgar Hoover's F.B.I. surveillance file. For example, he was observed as a participant at a liberal leaders Freedom Conference in New York City on January 30-31, 1953, by Federal agents. This conference was cited by the Attorney General of the United States as both subversive and communist under Executive Order 9835.

Among the conference sponsors were:
Rabbi Michael Alper, Hebrew Union College
      Prof. Hadley Cantrils, Princeton University
      Dean Frank Carthy of New Jersey Episcopal Diocese
Atty. Earl B. Dickerson, a Negro insurance executive and civil rights activist from Chicago, Illinois

Prof. Albert Einstein- Institute for Advanced Study, Princeton, N.J.
Dr. John A. Mackay, President of the Princeton Theological Seminary
Rev. Gardner C. Taylor- Pastor of the Concord Baptist Church, Brooklyn New York.
Prof. Fowler Harper, Yale Law School.

On an earlier occasion in April, 1951, The House Un-American Activities Committee listed Hollywood Academy Award winners Jose Ferrer and Judy Holiday as being members of five to ten Communist- Front organizations. Others among the better known listed by the committee were Lillian Hellman, the writer, Paul Robeson, the singer, author Dashiell Hammett, writer Dorothy Parker and anthropologist Dr. W.E.B. DuBois. It was the committee's thought that the Reds had devised special appeals and projects directed at artists, union members, women, youth, rural workers, and minority groups.

Guilt by association justifies an ever-expanding investigation: each association widens the circle of suspects and justifies still further investigation of the new suspects' associations. Thus, we have reached the bridge where civil liberties are sacrificed in the name of national security, in spite of the fact there is no clear and present danger. Frank Lloyd Wright died on April 9, 1959.

Federal Bureau of Investigation

Freedom of Information/Privacy Acts Section

Subject: Frank Lloyd Wright

FEDERAL BUREAU OF INVESTIGATION

FREEDOM OF INFORMATION/PRIVACY ACTS SECTION

COVER SHEET

SUBJECT: <u>FRANK LLOYD WRIGHT</u>
<u>PART 1 OF 2</u>

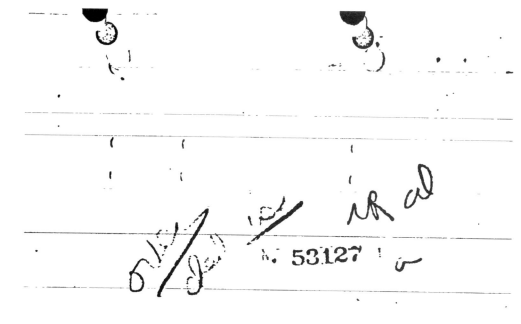

N. 53127

Rally Tomorrow for Russian War Aid

A complete sell-out of all seats for the great Madison Square Garden rally tomorrow night at which outstanding public figures and stars of stage, screen and radio will appear in the benefit given by Russian War Relief, Inc., was seen yesterday.

Contributions in cash to be given at the rally will pass the $100,000 mark, it was indicated by advance information from several organizations.

Special arrangements have been made to have a prominent newscaster bring a summary of President Roosevelt's speech, scheduled for 10:30 P. M. to the Garden au-

Those scheduled to appear include Joseph Davies, former U.S. Ambassador to the Soviet Union; Walter Duranty, former Moscow correspondent of the New York Times; Frank Lloyd Wright, prominent architect; Dr. Henry E. Sigerist, of Johns Hopkins University and medical head of Russian War Relief, Inc.; Genevieve Tabouis, French political journalist; W. W. Waymack, editor of the Des Moines Register-Tribune; Bert Lytell, president of Actors Equity; Mady Christians, now appearing in "Watch on the Rhine"; Paul Draper, leading American dancer, and a group of dancers from the Monte Carlo Ballet.

Garden Rally To Open Russian War Relief Drive

Noted Personalities to Attend Huge Benefit Meeting October 27

Prominent public figures, writers, artists, and stage and screen stars will take part in the Russian War Relief Benefit to be held at Madison Square Garden on Monday evening, Oct. 27.

Announcing that the rally, planned on a gigantic scale, will be the first public meeting of the Russian War Relief, Inc. the organization declared that the benefit will launch its nationwide campaign for civilian aid and medical supplies for the Soviet Union.

With Mr. Gilbert Miller as honorary chairman the relief organization's entertainment division gave out a partial list of famous persons who will take part in the benefit on Oct. 27.

Scheduled to appear so far, are: Walter Duranty, noted correspondent; Frank Lloyd Wright, prominent American architect who will fly here from Wisconsin to attend; Dr. Henry E. Sigerist, of Johns Hopkins University and medical head of Russian War Relief, Inc.; Genevieve Tabouis, French political journalist; W. W. Waymack, editor of the Des Moines Register-Tribune; Bert Lytell, president of Actor's Equity; Mady Christians, now appearing in "Watch on the Rhine"; Paul Draper, the dancer, and a group from the Monte Carlo Ballet. Ira Gershwin and Harold Arlen have written a song entitled "If This Be Propaganda" expressly for the occasion.

the appearance of several choral groups whose homelands are now in the Nazi occupied territory. These are the Norwegian Singing Society of Brooklyn, the Netherlands Zukoor Orpheus; the Czechoslovakian Choral Group and the French Lyric Society.

Tickets for the Madison Square Garden Benefit may be purchased at the Russian War Relief Headquarters, 835 Fifth Ave. and 325 Seventh Ave., and at Brentano's, 586 Fifth Ave.; American Friends of Danish Freedom, 115 Broad St.; Leblang-Gray's 1476 Broadway, the Czechoslovakian Consulate, 1440 Broadway and the Book Fair, 133 West 44th St.

53134

INDEXED

NOT RECORDED
100-37226-A-

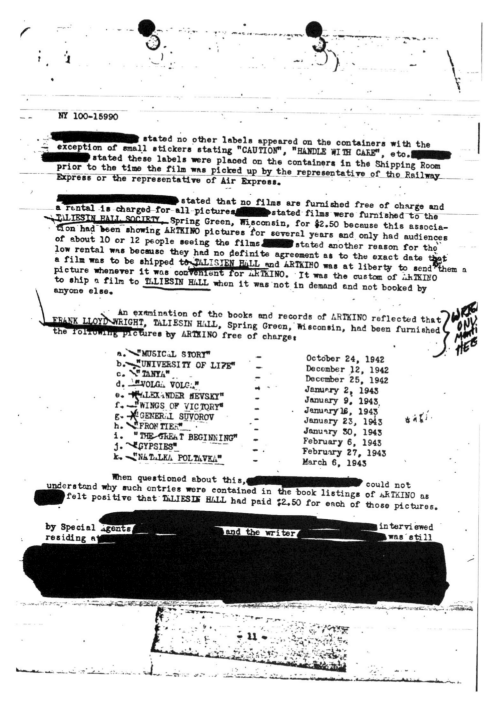

NY 100-15990

████████ stated no other labels appeared on the containers with the exception of small stickers stating "CAUTION", "HANDLE WITH CARE", etc. ████ ████████ stated these labels were placed on the containers in the Shipping Room prior to the time the film was picked up by the representative of the Railway Express or the representative of Air Express.

████████████ stated that no films are furnished free of charge and a rental is charged for all pictures. ████ stated films were furnished to the TALIESIN HALL SOCIETY, Spring Green, Wisconsin, for $2.50 because this association had been showing ARTKINO pictures for several years and only had audiences of about 10 or 12 people seeing the films. ████ stated another reason for the low rental was because they had no definite agreement as to the exact date that a film was to be shipped to TALIESIN HALL and ARTKINO was at liberty to send them a picture whenever it was convenient for ARTKINO. It was the custom of ARTKINO to ship a film to TALIESIN HALL when it was not in demand and not booked by anyone else.

An examination of the books and records of ARTKINO reflected that FRANK LLOYD WRIGHT, TALIESIN HALL, Spring Green, Wisconsin, had been furnished the following pictures by ARTKINO free of charge:

a.	"MUSICAL STORY"	-	October 24, 1942
b.	"UNIVERSITY OF LIFE"	-	December 12, 1942
c.	"TANYA"	-	December 25, 1942
d.	"VOLGA VOLGA"	-	January 2, 1943
e.	"ALEXANDER NEVSKY"	-	January 9, 1943
f.	"WINGS OF VICTORY"	-	January 16, 1943
g.	"GENERAL SUVOROV"	-	January 23, 1943
h.	"FRONTIER"	-	January 30, 1943
i.	"THE GREAT BEGINNING"	-	February 6, 1943
j.	"GYPSIES"	-	February 27, 1943
k.	"NATALKA POLTAVKA"	-	March 6, 1943

When questioned about this, ████████████████ could not understand why such entries were contained in the book listings of ARTKINO as ████ felt positive that TALIESIN HALL had paid $2.50 for each of those pictures.

by Special Agents ████████ ████████ and the writer ████████████ interviewed residing at ██ was still

- 11 -

NY 100-15990

28. By letter dated August 14, 1945, ARTKINO entered into an agreement with LOEW'S INCORPORATED, METRO-GOLDWYN-MAYER PICTURES, whereby ARTKINO secured the right for seven years to use a scene in the Metro-Goldwyn-Mayer production, Assignment In Brittany. ARTKINO agreed to pay $627.00.

29. By letter dated September 4, 1945, ARTKINO entered into a five year contract with VICTOR PAHLAN of the BRANDON PICTURES CORPORATION, 8272 Sunset Boulevard, Hollywood, California, whereby ARTKINO agreed to make available to PAHLAN positive prints or negatives of all ARTKINO's feature films, short subjects, news reels, and documentaries, in order that PAHLAN could produce a full length film on American-Russian friendship. ARTKINO was to receive $5,000 in installments of $1,250 each. It is to be noted that PAHLAN formerly acted as a sub-agent for ARTKINO PICTURES, INC. and he has recently been discharged from the United States Army.

30. A contract entered into on August 31, 1939 between UNIVERSAL PICTURES, INC. and AMKINO whereby UNIVERSAL granted AMKINO the exclusive right to exhibit throughout the U.S.S.R. the picture, "One Hundred Men And A Girl" for five years from the date of the contract, AMKINO agreeing to pay $5,000 for this right. This contract was contained in the ARTKINO contract file.

BOOKING DATES

The books and records of ARTKINO PICTURES, INCORPORATED, were examined by Special Agents ███████████ and ███████████ and the writer, in order to ascertain each booking of each film distributed by ARTKINO PICTURES, INC. from September 1, 1943 to March 31, 1944 and from April 1, 1945 up to and including September 21, 1945. The results of the examination will be set forth and broken down into the classifications, picture, place played, city and state, date played, contract number and amount received. The examination was conducted under the authority of the Foreign Agents Registration Act.

- 28 -

STANDARD FORM NO. 64

Office Memorandum • UNITED STATES GOVERNMENT

TO : Director, FBI (61-7099)   DATE: 5/11/54

FROM : SAC, Los Angeles (105-1636)

SUBJECT: ALBERT EINSTEIN
IS-R
OO: Newark

      The following is a summary of interesting information concerning the subject and members of his household during the period from approximately 1929 to 1939, which was obtained from records of the "morgue" of the Los Angeles "Times" newspaper:

      (An article by HEDDA HOPPER entitled, "Hedda Hopper's Hollywood" in the January 11, 1939, issue of the Los Angeles "Times" states that) EINSTEIN and CHARLIE CHAPLAN were "great friends", their friendship having started "way back in 1931" when they met aboard a boat coming to California; that CHAPLAN later entertained EINSTEIN and took him to the opening of the film entitled, "City Lights."

      EINSTEIN, his wife, and two SECRETARIES (including HELENE DUKAS, his private secretary) arrived in Pasadena, California, from San Diego, California, on New Year's Eve, 1930. He was a guest in the home of ARTHUR FLEMING, member of the Executive Council of the California Institute of Technology (CIT) for a few days until he moved into a bungalow located at 707 South Oakland Avenue, Pasadena. He originally planned six weeks of rest, seclusion and research in Southern California. He was scheduled to visit CHAPLAN's film studio on January 14, 1931. Later it was reported his wife "likes" CHAPLAN. EINSTEIN attended a testimonial banquet of the Los Angeles Jewish Community at the Ambassador Hotel on February 16, 1931, and was honored guest at the annual banquet of the Los Angeles Chamber of Commerce at the same hotel on February 23, 1931. He departed from Los Angeles in the private car of the President of the Santa Fe Railway on February 27, 1931. He was adopted as "great relative" by the Hopi Indian Tribe while en route to the East Coast; and in Chicago, Illinois, he read a prepared speech from the rear platform of the train (on March 4, 1931), during which he advocated resistance to military service "at all times." While passing through Chicago, he was visited by

EX-125   RECORDED: 24   61-7099-82
          INDEXED - 24

REGISTERED
cc: 2 - Newark (100-32986)(REGISTERED)   27 MAY 17 19...
    1 - OKLahoma City (INFO)(100-6135)(REGISTERED)

68 MAY 25 1954

LA 105-1636

"noted architect" FRANK LLOYD WRIGHT. He departed from New York City aboard the liner "Deutschland" on March 5, 1931, having earlier breakfasted with a "Cleveland surgeon", Dr. GEORGE W. CRILE.

On June 26, 1931, he sent a letter to Governor ROLPH of California, condemning the case against TOM MOONEY and WARREN BILLINGS as a miscarriage of justice, and appealing for absolute pardon for them. On July 5, 1931, it was reported that one Dr. GOLDSCHMIDT had obtained the adhesion of EINSTEIN, THOMAS MANN, LION FEUCHTWANGER, GEORGE LEDEBAUR, and others to a "German committee" formed by GOLDSCHMIDT in support of "DREISER's committee", which had been organized to save eight Negroes at Scottsboro, Alabama, from the electric chair. On July 26, 1931, it was reported that according to EINSTEIN, man is here on earth for the sake of other men; that "his God is the God of Spinoza; and that he could not imagine a God who rewards and pensions."

EINSTEIN (apparently accompanied by his wife and stepdaughter, MARGOT MARIANOFF) arrived in California from Germany aboard the steamer "Portland" on December 30, 1931. Almost immediately, he confirmed having written a letter to Governor ROLPH concerning the MOONEY case. Again he was temporarily a guest in the home of ARTHUR H. FLEMING at 1003 South Orange Grove Avenue, Pasadena, until he moved into a two-room suite at the Athenaeum, faculty residence on the campus of CIT. It was reported on February 3, 1932, that EINSTEIN's wife had arranged an exhibit of sculptures by her daughter, Mrs. MARIANOFF, at the Grace Nicholson Art Gallery, 46 North Los Robles Avenue, Pasadena, featuring five small works in bronze and three figures of Russian peasants in ceramics. EINSTEIN and his wife embarked for Germany aboard the Hamburg-American liner "San Francisco" on March 4, 1932.

It was reported on December 6, 1932, that EINSTEIN had been angry at questions put to him at the American Consulate (apparently in Berlin) regarding his "political affiliations" and had threatened to cancel his trip to the United States, and that his wife, also angry, had stated that her husband had no political affiliations but was a "confirmed pacifist." EINSTEIN and his wife arrived in Pasadena, California, from Germany on January 10, 1933, the expenses of their sojourn in the United States being borne by the Oberlaender Trust of the Carl Shurz

- 2 -

62-26

On October 31, 1941, another article appeared in the Baltimore Sun. This article reflected that a meeting was to be held at the Stafford Hotel sponsored by the Baltimore Committee of the American Committee on Soviet Relations. ▓▓▓▓▓▓▓▓ B7C

▓▓▓▓▓▓ Captain SERGEI KOORNAKOFF of the Russian Imperial Army was scheduled to give a lecture.

An article appeared in the Baltimore Sun dated August 10, 1941, which reflected ▓▓▓▓▓▓▓▓▓▓ a club of Baltimore citizens sponsoring a "Stop Hitler" mass meeting at the coliseum, 2200 N. Monroe, to be held August 27, 1941. In this article Mrs. NANETTE CANDEL, Secretary-Treasurer of the Baltimore Committee, American Council on Soviet Relations, announced that the meeting was to be held to organize public sentiment around a program of aid to Great Britain, the Soviet Union and countries fighting Hitler. Other speakers included CORLISS LAMONT and THOMAS L. HARRIS, National Secretary of American Committee on Soviet Relations.

On October 25, 1941, an advertisement from The Nation reflected the Russian War Relief Benefit was to be held October 27, 1941, in Madison Square Garden. The heading of this ad was "A Stirring Testimonial Meeting - JOSEPH E. DAVIES, Former United States Ambassador to Russia." Also appearing on the program were WALTER DURANTY, FRANK LLOYD WRIGHT, Dr. HENRY E. SIGERIST, and VILHJALMUR STEFONSSON. This benefit was sponsored by the Russian War Relief, Inc., 525 Fifth Avenue, New York City. The ad further reflected that tickets would be on sale at the 44th Street Book Fair, 133 W. 44th Street, New York City; the Czech Consulate, 1440 Broadway, New York City; The American Friends of Danish Freedom, 116 Broad Street, New York; Bretanos, 586 Fifth Avenue, New York; and Lablang-Grays, Inc., 1476 Broadway, New York.

The files also contained a copy of a pamphlet issued by the Spanish Intellectual Aid, 381 4th Avenue, Rm. 1114, New York City. The following sponsors were listed: Chairman - LOUIS BROMFIELD; Executive Secretary - FRANKLIN FOLSOM; Treasurers - RICHARD STARRS CHILZS and LELAND REA ROBINSON; and Asst. Secretary - SYLVIA S. ROBERTS. A number of sponsors were listed, ▓▓▓▓▓▓▓▓▓▓▓▓▓

A 30-day mail cover was placed against the ▓▓▓▓▓▓▓▓▓ The results of this mail cover B7C indicated large correspondence, particularly national in character, with some local correspondence in addition to some international correspondence. The cover also indicates that subject has correspondence with numerous universities, medical laboratories, medical societies, organizations and physicians.

- 3 -

ALL INFORMATION CONTAINED
HEREIN IS UNCLASSIFIED
DATE 1 8 63 BY

MAY 17 1945

TELETYPE

CONFIDENTIAL

51413

WASH 16 WASH FIELD 2 FROM NEW YORK 17

DIRECTOR AND SAC URGENT

GREGORY. ESPIONAGE R. REFER FIVE IS. CONFIDENTIAL SOURCE ADVISED THAT

MADE STATEMENT TO ONE
/PHONETIC/ THAT THERE WAS A JOB FOR AN ARCHITECT PAYING SEVEN
THOUSAND DOLLARS OPEN WITH THE UNRRA IN CHINA, AND THAT
PHONETIC/ WAS THE ONE TO SEE FOR THE JOB. FURTHER, THAT THEY, PRE-
SUMABLY UNRRA, WERE INTERESTED ONLY IN " PROGRESSIVES" FOR THE JOB.
SAID HE IS DOING THE SOLICITATION FOR JOBS FOR   SAME
SOURCE ADVISED THAT   CONTACTED   PHONETIC/ WHO
ASKED   OPINION RE ATTITUDE OF ARCHITECT SOCIETIES TO
USE OF FRANK LLOYD WRIGHT-S NAME IN A FILM PROJECT FOR THE STATE DEPT.
SAID THAT WRIGHT WAS OK.   STATED THAT HE HAD
NAME IN WASHINGTON AS A GOOD MAN TO DO SOME PROJECTS FOR OWI. APPARENT.
DID NOT FOLLOW THROUGH WITH EFFORTS FOR JOB.   THEN SAID
" I CAN TALK TURKEY WITH THOSE BOYS   / PHONETIC/ AND
/ PHONETIC/ WHO FORMERLY WAS IN CHARGE OF FILM WORK." NAMES MENTIONED
HEREIN TO BE CHECKED NY INDICES AND BUREAU ADVISED. FROM CONTEXT OF
CONVERSATION IT WOULD APPEAR THAT   ET AL ACTIVE IN PLACING
COMMUNISTS IN GOVERNMENT JOBS IN WASHINGTON AND ELSEWHERE.

CONROY

ANC IN ORDER PLS

WA HCDXX HOLD FOR ANOTHER

CONFIDENTIAL

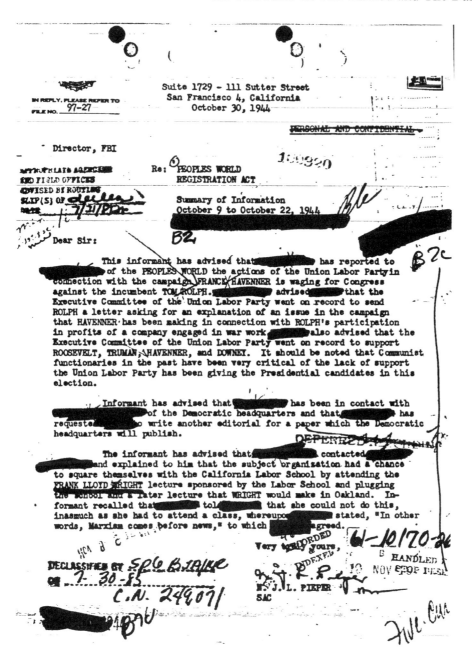

PERSONAL AND CONFIDENTIAL

Suite 1729 - 111 Sutter Street
San Francisco 4, California
October 30, 1944

IN REPLY, PLEASE REFER TO
FILE NO. 97-27

Director, FBI

APPROPRIATE AGENCIES
AND FIELD OFFICES
ADVISED BY ROUTING
SLIP(S) OF
DATE 7/31/72

Re: PEOPLES WORLD
REGISTRATION ACT

Summary of Information
October 9 to October 22, 1944

Dear Sir:

This informant has advised that [redacted] has reported to [redacted] of the PEOPLES WORLD the actions of the Union Labor Party in connection with the campaign FRANCK HAVENNER is waging for Congress against the incumbent TOM ROLPH. [redacted] advised [redacted] that the Executive Committee of the Union Labor Party went on record to send ROLPH a letter asking for an explanation of an issue in the campaign that HAVENNER has been making in connection with ROLPH's participation in profits of a company engaged in war work. [redacted] also advised that the Executive Committee of the Union Labor Party went on record to support ROOSEVELT, TRUMAN, HAVENNER, and DOWNEY. It should be noted that Communist functionaries in the past have been very critical of the lack of support the Union Labor Party has been giving the Presidential candidates in this election.

Informant has advised that [redacted] has been in contact with [redacted] of the Democratic headquarters and that [redacted] has requested [redacted] to write another editorial for a paper which the Democratic headquarters will publish.

The informant has advised that [redacted] contacted [redacted] and explained to him that the subject organization had a chance to square themselves with the California Labor School by attending the FRANK LLOYD WRIGHT lecture sponsored by the Labor School and plugging the school and a later lecture that WRIGHT would make in Oakland. Informant recalled that [redacted] told [redacted] that she could not do this, inasmuch as she had to attend a class, whereupon [redacted] stated, "In other words, Marxism comes before news," to which [redacted] agreed.

Very truly yours,

N. J. L. PIEPER
SAC

DECLASSIFIED BY SP6 BJAYKE
ON 7-30-85
C.N. 249071

L A 100-5377

Variety for the same date stated that General Membership meeting of Sound Technicians Local 695 has been called to hear report of Business Representative HAROLD V. SMITH on New York wage negotiations.

The same issue of Variety stated that members of Screen Cartoonists Guild met to discuss plans for new contract negotiations expected to get under way next week. It is probable that the opening session will be held next Wednesday.

The Hollywood Reporter for April 26, 1944, under the headline "ROBINSON Bound for OWI", stated "EDWARD G. ROBINSON may seek an overseas assignment with the OWI on completion of his starring role in International's 'Once Off Guard.'"

████████ a committee created by the Writers Congress ████████ was endeavoring to establish a department of Arts and Letters in the President's Cabinet.

████████ meeting ████████ was attended by the following parties:

████████ FRANK LLOYD WRIGHT, ████ and some others.

At this meeting it was stated that the matter seeking to have a department of Arts and Letters created in the President's Cabinet be put off until after the November election, otherwise it might be considered a political move and would handicap the movement. It was stated that in the meantime the group would endeavor to interest local people in the creation of such a post in the Writers Congress in cooperation with New York people in their plan to hire three field representatives to arouse interest of this sort all over the country by personal visits to heads of museums, art galleries, schools, etc.

████████ inquiry was made as to how this venture would be financed and what were to be the functions of this proposed cabinet member, nebulous answers were given which considered that the purpose of the group was not to create pressure for a post of this type, but rather to form a group

- 3 -

L A 100-5377

sympathetic to the purposes of the Writers Congress and this group, in turn, was to interest other people until it became a powerful pressure group.

Source stated that the leadership of this committee ███████ was definitely Communist, although ███████████████ had no documentary evidence to prove that they were members of the Communist Party.

███████████████ FRANK LLOYD WRIGHT, a noted architect, who has no sympathies for Communism, was invited to the meeting and during the discussion someone stated that the group was non political. At this juncture WRIGHT stated that the group had to be political if it hoped to be successful and there was only one way to do this and that was to get the President out of the White House first. This remark by WRIGHT caused a furor in the meeting and WRIGHT left before the meeting adjourned.

██████████████████ the meeting came to no conclusion ██████ believed that the move to have a post of Arts and Letters created was at least temporarily abandoned until after the fall election, though it was ████ opinion that the committee will continue to meet just to hold the group intact and form it into a pressure group for whatever its Communist leaders may desire.

THE LEAGUE OF AMERICAN WRITERS PROPOSE POST OF ARTS AND LETTERS IN THE PRESIDENT'S CABINET

DR. GAETANO SALVEMINI

On October 1,2 and 3, 1943, the Hollywood Writers Mobilization sponsored a meeting which was called the "Writers Congress" which was held at the University of California at Los Angeles. When this meeting adjourned a Continuations Committee was formed to carry on the work of the Writers Congress, which was in effect the League of American Writers. This committee set up what they called the "Writers Congress Continuations Forum." This forum was to give programs from time to time to keep up interest in the Writers Congress.

The Writers Congress Continuations Forum prepared a program for April 21, 1944, to be given at the Women's Club of Hollywood. The subject was to be "Europe - Occupied and Free". The forum issued its advertising matter, stating that JOHN HOWARD LAWSON would be the Chairman of the meeting and that Dr. GAETANO SALVEMINI, Italian History Professor at Harvard University and lecturer at the University of California at Berkeley who was designated in the advertising matter as "Noted Italian Anti-Fascist," was to address them.

It appears that JOHN HOWARD LAWSON, ROBERT ROSSEN and others of the Forum Program Committee were not fully or properly advised on the political

-4-

Tom Bradley

Chapter XV

Tom Bradley:
The Uncharted Path
From the Cotton Fields of Texas
to Mayor of Los Angeles

Thomas Bradley was born on December 29, 1917 on a cotton plantation near a place called Calvert, a small, dusty, rural and sparsely populated town in East Central Texas. The town was not big enough to have a court-house, thus no birth records were available except in the family bible. Tom was the second child of seven sired by Lee and Crenner (Hawkins) Bradley. Some of the Bradley offspring died before they reached their first birthday. His parents moved from the cotton plantation in Texas to Los Angeles, California in 1924 in search of a better life for their siblings and themselves. The path they followed to the City of Angels had been paved earlier by Black migrants who had moved west from Texas and Louisiana after World War I in 1918.

The senior Bradley initially found employment in L.A. on a series of low wage hard labor jobs however after approximately a year he struck pay dirt with the help of a boyhood friend who worked for the Pullman Company. His hometown boy vouched to get him hired by Big Mac, a foreman at the George

M. Pullman Sleeping Car Company. His first position with the company was as a waiter in the railroad dining car and then he later got a lateral promotion to Pullman Porter, where the uniform that he wore was a white jacket, blue pants with a cadet cap to match. It was mandatory that all of the Pullman porters kept their shoes spit polished with a black sheen. The salary for nonunion Negro Pullman employees was meager, but the tips for the sleeping car passengers were good. The porters shined the shoes and freshened the clothes of their sleeping passengers. Both the waiter and porter positions were considered high status jobs in the Black community because many of Pullman's car employees were college trained. The white collar positions for which they had been trained at for Colored Only universities such as Fisk, Howard, Morehouse and other land grant institutions run by white missionaries from the North were considered out of the loop because of racism.

Tom Bradley's job opportunities were unrealistically high when he enrolled in the Polytechnic High School in Los Angeles, following his graduation from elementary school with high honors. Neither his father nor his mother went beyond third grade in the plantation owners' schools which were only in session approximately six months a year, to avoid conflict with the child labor jobs of planting and picking cotton. Young Tom Bradley early in life was labeled as an alert go-getter, in that at the age of nine he had his own morning newspaper route which in his time and mine was considered an excellent training ground for young Black boys. The paper boys' success ratio in life, based on a sample of one hundred covering a period of twenty-five years, was sixty-five percent. The tall and skinny Tom ran the 440 yard dash for Polytech and won consistently, he also became an all-city football tackle in high school. He was not a flypaper or groupie kind of individual, in that he did not have a psychic need to be surrounded by close friends and gladhanders to function. As a matter of fact, his favorite companions were his books and they talked back to him in orderly fashion through their printed pages.

When the six feet, four inch youngster graduated from high school in 1937, he was treated like most Black students during that period, in that he was advised not to go to college because he was not considered college material and therefore such a journey would be a waste of his time. He trashed the advice of his white senior counselor and enrolled at the University of California at Los Angeles on athletic scholarship where he continued his track star status.

In 1940, Tom quit college to help his mother who had been deserted by Lee Bradley for another sunburned woman. The wages of a female domestic worker were not enough to support a family of six, even when the breadwinner was permitted to bring leftover food from her employers' table. Hence, Thomas Bradley joined the Los Angeles Police Department, to help fill the food basket and pay rent. He initially regarded the job with the LAPD as a temporary gig but ended up staying there for twenty-one years. He retired in the early nineteen sixties with the rank of lieutenant, which in 1962 was the highest rank in the department that a Black police officer had ever been promoted.

In 1951, he took up the study of law in night school at Southwestern University where he received his L.L.B. in 1956 and passed the state bar examination the following year. He entered the practice of law for five years before deciding to run for a seat in the lily-white City Council. He won a seat in that august body in 1963 and was re-elected in 1967 for a second four year term. He then did a three peat in 1971 from a biracial district. His continued success would not have been possible without the full support of Ethel Mae Arnold, who he married in 1941, shortly after joining the Los Angeles Police Department. She was the wind under his wings and she also joined him in frequent prayers as a fellow member of the African Methodist Episcopal Church.

His next political challenge was to run against the incumbent Republican Mayor Sam Yorty. The Los Angeles mayoral elections are non-partisan, therefore, Democrat Bradley entered the mayoral ring against his Republican opponents on the right in 1969. There were thirteen other mayoral contenders of various political stripes in that contest. In the bloody political battle that followed, Bradley came in second behind Yorty who had played dirty pool and showered Bradley with several false allegations such as accusing him of being a participant in the 1965 Watts Riot in Los Angeles and also of being intrinsically connected to the radical and Black militant movement.

Mayor Sam "Saigon" Yorty used his political stump to exploit the raw racial fears of the white populace. He warned white people that if Bradley was elected it would cause 2,000 L.A. policemen to resign from the force in protest. He shook his finger in their faces as he warned them that Bradley was a puppet on the string for "Black militants and leftwing radicals" who were trying to take over their city, he even stated that the Bradley campaign was a communist conspiracy to gain control of a major American city. As a result of the garbage spewed out of Yorty's propaganda machine, Bradley was defeated.

Like all true troopers Bradley dusted himself off and climbed back into the ring for another bout against Mayor Sam "Saigon" Yorty in 1973. This time, Bradley won the election with 57 percent of the vote in a city where Blacks made up only 15 percent of the electorate. Bradley's majority was composed of solid Black voting block combined with white liberals and the Jewish brothers from the affluent west side of the city. President Richard M. Nixon's Watergate scandal indirectly helped Bradley because the voters considered Bradley honest and Yorty somewhat of a "Tricky Dick" like President Richard M. Nixon. The icing for that allegation was supported when it was revealed that Yorty had bought a $50,000 paid-up life insurance policy with "gifts" given to him by his political right wing friends. Moreover, in the last week of the campaign, a court injunction forced the Yorty machine to modify some racist campaign literature.

An analysis of the election returns revealed that Bradley had nearly half of the citywide vote, making a particularly strong showing in the liberal Jewish districts. He won a very small margin among Chicanos who had heavily supported Yorty in 1969, and he got 95 percent of the Black vote.

Although Mayor Bradley was not a "race flag waving liberal" he was not insensitive to the needs of his core Black constituency, therefore he established contract set-asides and preferential hiring for Blacks and other minorities. Much of this was done without a bugle call or a drum roll but with a muffled calmness which became the hallmark of Bradley's style of dealing with race problems.

In 1982, Tom Bradley won handily the gubernatorial nomination of the California Democratic party. He led his Republican opponent, States Attorney General George Deukmejian, in every major published voter survey. The print and electronic media proclaimed Bradley the winner when the polls closed because of his comfortable lead in exit interviews of voters conducted throughout the state. In spite of what seemed to be, he lost that election. He was edged out Florida style by the closest proportional margin in the history of California gubernatorial races, 49.3 percent to 48.1 percent. Just 93,000 votes out of more than 7.8 million votes cast. He tried again in 1986 but was out of the loop with only 37.4 percent of the vote to Deukmejian's 60.5 percent.

In 1990 Douglas Wilder of Virginia was the first Black to ever be elected governor of any state. P.B.S. Pinchback had been appointed governor of Louisiana in 1873 during the Reconstruction Period (he served only 43 days).

Bradley's hand was on the mayoral wheel when he brought the 1984 Olympics to his city. He cleverly negotiated a contract that protected Los Angeles taxpayers from being held liable for any losses incurred by the event, such as those that saddled the Montreal taxpayers after their Olympics had become history.

Following Mayor Bradley's triumphant fourth election in 1985, the Bradley coalition began to unravel because he had reversed his long standing decision and approved oil drilling at the Pacific Palisades. Many of his comfortable middleclass constituents were more concerned with lifestyle and the environment, and therefore were unhappy campers with the mayor's decision. Bradley made his decision based on the fact that Los Angeles had reached a standstill, the notion of creating growth was a progressive concept in the eyes of liberals, business folk, and Blacks.

Other factors that contributed to the cooling off of Bradley's political alliance with the west side homeowners was the increase in traffic congestion and the smog that it generated. Furthermore, when Bradley ignored the west side Jewish communities' initial request to denounce the Nation of Islam leader Farrakhan in advance of his scheduled appearance in Los Angeles in September 1985, Bradley remained silent until after Farrakhan gave his anti-Semitic speech, he then denounced him but it was too late to satisfy his critics. The Jewish publishers of four of the L.A. weeklies proclaimed: "As far as they were concerned, Bradley was a dead pigeon."

Mayor Bradley's teflon exterior had begun to wear as thin as expensive toilet paper with white homeowners in that they were both nervous and suspicious of his "Managed Growth" program. The "Mr. Clean" frosting melted on his cake when the media discovered that Bradley was on the payroll with two banks that did business with the city of Los Angeles. This finding eroded trust in his administration. The timing of the scandal was bad for Bradley in that it erupted on the eve of his fifth term election. He barely crawled across the finish line with 52 percent of the votes in the election and that was his smallest majority in five elections. Both municipal and federal investigations threw out wide lassoes to catch the culprit, however they both came up empty-handed in that they found no evidence of criminal wrongdoing that would enable them to indict the mayor. On the other hand, he was reprimanded for ethical impropriety for which he paid a fine.

The fat lady did not start to sing the closing number in Mayor Thomas Bradley's Opera until the Rodney King beating by the LAPD. The whole event was captured on videotape by a private citizen visiting Los Angeles in 1991. Bradley was highly criticized for his snaillike pace in calling for the police chief's resignation. An investigating panel headed by former F.B.I. Chief William Webster, singled out former Police Chief Gates and Mayor Bradley for criticism in 1992. The panel found fault with both of them for failing to contain the violence that went on for days. The chief was upbraided for not having a plan ready, and the mayor for fumbling and failing to know and follow the correct procedure in such an emergency which was to call for regional police reinforcements, and not the governor for the National Guard. Bradley saw the handwriting on the wall and a sign in the sky which read the party was over. Therefore, he announced that he would not seek another term in 1993. Bradley told his supporters at a meeting "The time for change has come and I am prepared to pass the torch on to new leadership".

Federal Bureau of Investigation

Freedom of Information/Privacy Acts Section

Subject: Tom Bradley

FEDERAL BUREAU OF INVESTIGATION

FREEDOM OF INFORMATION/PRIVACY ACTS SECTION

SUBJECT: <u>TOM BRADLEY</u>

FILE NUMBER: <u>161-11871</u>

PLAINTEXT   TELETYPE   URGENT

b6,b7C

TO SACS WASHINGTON FIELD - ENC. (4) (BSM)   MAY 11, 1976
        LOS ANGELES
        SAN ANTONIO
        SACRAMENTO
        CHICAGO
        ALEXANDRIA

FROM DIRECTOR FBI

    THOMAS BRADLEY, SPECIAL INQUIRY, BUDED MAY 18, 1976,

WITHOUT FAIL.

    BUREAU HAS BEEN REQUESTED TO CONDUCT VERY EXPEDITE INVESTI-

GATION OF BRADLEY WHO IS BEING CONSIDERED FOR PRESIDENTIAL

APPOINTMENT, POSITION NOT INDICATED.

    BORN DECEMBER 29, 1917, CALVERT, TEXAS, MARRIED TO FORMER

▮▮▮▮▮▮ HAS TWO CHILDREN, RESIDES ▮▮▮▮▮▮▮▮

LOS ANGELES, CALIFORNIA, AND SINCE 1973 HAS BEEN MAYOR OF

THAT CITY.

    SEE WHO'S WHO, 38TH EDITION, PAGE 346, FOR ADDITIONAL

BACKGROUND DATA.

    LOS ANGELES IMMEDIATELY OBTAIN COMPLETE BACKGROUND DATA

COVERING ENTIRE ADULT LIFE, INCLUDING IDENTITIES AND LOCATIONS

FX-112   REC-71   11871

CH 40   MCT-27   7 MAY 12 1976

NOTE: Request received today.

RER:mal

(5)

FEDERAL BUREAU OF INVESTIGATION
COMMUNICATIONS SECTION

MAY 11 1976

TELETYPE
b6, b7C

RETURN TO MR. ▮▮▮▮▮▮ ROOM 3117

MAIL ROOM ☐   TELETYPE UNIT ☑   GPO: 1975 O - 594-120

PAGE TWO

OF ALL CLOSE RELATIVES, AND SET OUT LEADS AT ONCE. FURNISH

SSAN TO WASHINGTON FIELD FOR IRS CHECK. ALSO OBTAIN RELEASE

FOR REVIEW OF EDUCATIONAL RECORDS AND FURNISH COPY TO

SAN ANTONIO.

CHECK RECORDS APPROPRIATE BARS AND BAR ASSOCIATIONS,

INCLUDING ABA.

CONDUCT NO NEIGHBORHOOD INVESTIGATION UNLESS CIRCUMSTANCES

ARISE MAKING SUCH ADVISABLE AT WHICH TIME PRIOR BUREAU APPROVAL

SHOULD BE OBTAINED.

WHITE HOUSE DESIRES ORAL SUMMARY THIS CASE, A.M., MAY 19,

1976. CONSEQUENTLY, BUDED MUST BE MET WITHOUT FAIL. NO

DELAY WILL BE TOLERATED.

SPIN.

END

The records of the American Bar Association,
Chicago, Illinois, were checked and disclosed

☐ No record

✗ Current member

☐ Former member

NCBE Records contain no unfavorable information.

PAGE TWO (161-3016)

L967; BROTHER - HOWARD BRADLEY, DECEASED 1972; SISTER -

WILLA MAYE BRADLEY MORRAH, DECEASED 1961; BROTHER -

███████████ BORN ████████████ RESIDES ████████████

████████ LOS ANGELES, CALIFORNIA. APPOINTEE STATES

HE HAS NO ADDITIONAL BROTHERS OR SISTERS LIVING OR DECEASED.

WIFE - ████████████ AGE ███ RESIDENCE WITH APPOINTEE;

DAUGHTER - ████████████ AGE ███ RESIDES ████████████

████████ LOS ANGELES; DAUGHTER - ████████████ AGE ███

RESIDES ████████████ LOS ANGELES. APPOINTEE STATES

HE HAS NO OTHER CHILDREN LIVING OR DECEASED.

$b7C$

    EDUCATION.

    SOUTH WESTERN UNIVERSITY LAW SCHOOL, LOS ANGELES,

CALIFORNIA, 1951 - 1956 - LLB.

    UNIVERSITY OF CALIFORNIA AT LOS ANGELES, FEBRUARY

1937 - JUNE 1940.

    POLYTECHNIC HIGH SCHOOL, WASHINGTON AND GRAND,

LOS ANGELES, FEBRUARY 1934 - 1937.

    EMPLOYMENT.

    MAYOR OF LOS ANGELES, 1973 - PRESENT

FEDERAL BUREAU OF INVESTIGATION
COMMUNICATIONS SECTION

MAY 1 8 1976

TELETYPE

Assoc. Dir.
Dep.-A.D.-Adm.
Dep.-A.D.-Inv.
Asst. Dir.:
Adm. Serv.
Ext. Affairs
Fin. & Pers.
Gen. Inv.
Ident.
Inspection
Intell.
Laboratory
Legal Coun.
Plan. & Eval.
Rec. Mgmt.
Spec. Inv.
Training
Telephone Rm.
Director Sec'y

LA 573

NR 01 LA PLAIN

11:31AM NITEL 5-13-76 TSM

TO : DIRECTOR

SACRAMENTO

WASHINGTON FIELD

b6, b7C

RM. 3821

FROM : LOS ANGELES (161-3216)

THOMAS BRADLEY, SPECIAL INQUIRY, BUDED MAY 18, 1976, WITHOUT

FAIL.

RE LOS ANGELES TEL TO BUREAU, MAY 12, 1976.

SACRAMENTO, REQUESTED TO INTERVIEW ████████████████

AND ████████████████████ CONCERNING APPOINTEE.

WASHINGTON FIELD, REQUESTED TO INTERVIEW CALIFORNIA ████

████████████████████ AS WELL AS ████

████████████████████ CONCERNING APPOINTEE.

b7C

SPIN.

END

161-11871-4

NOT RECORDED

3 JUN 22 1976

LA -643

NR 037 LA PLAIN

1056 PM NITEL 5-14-76 CEE

TO DIRECTOR

FROM LOS ANGELES (161-3716) (P)

THOMAS BRADLEY, SPECIAL INQUIRY, BUDED: MAY 18, 1976,

WITHOUT FAIL.

RE LOS ANGELES TELETYPES TO BUREAU, MAY 12, 1976,

AND MAY 14, 1976.

EMPLOYMENT.

MAYOR OF LOS ANGELES, 1973 - PRESENT.

ON MAY 14, 1976, ███████████████████████ **b7C**

DISTRICT OF LOS ANGELES, LOS ANGELES, CALIFORNIA, ADVISED

AS FOLLOWS:

HE HAS KNOWN APPOINTEE SINCE 1963, BOTH AS FELLOW

COUNCILMAN AND AS MAYOR. HE HAS ENJOYED EXCELLENT PERSONAL

RELATIONSHIP, POLITICAL, AND PROFESSIONAL ASSOCIATION WITH

APPOINTEE. HE CONSIDERS BRADLEY TO BE AN EXCELLENT MAYOR

WHO HAS BEST INTEREST OF THE POPULACE AT HEART. HE STATED

THAT THERE IS NO QUESTION CONCERNING THE HONESTY,

SOBRIETY, MORALITY, INTEGRITY OR CHARACTER, ASSOCIATES,

REPUTATION AND LOYALTY (CARL) OF THOMAS BRADLEY. BRADLEY

ENJOYS THE CONFIDENCE OF MANY HIGH RANKING POLITICIANS

NOT RECORDED

JUN 22 1976

PAGE TWO (LA 161-3715)

IN THE LOS ANGELES AREA. ▮▮▮▮▮▮ HAS NOTHING BUT

FAVORABLE INFORMATION TO FURNISH CONCERNING APPOINTEE

AND IS HAPPY TO RECOMMEND HIM FOR A FEDERAL POSITION OF

TRUST.

ON MAY 14, 1976, ▮▮▮▮▮▮▮▮▮▮▮▮▮▮▮▮

DISTRICT OF CITY OF LOS ANGELES, FURNISHED APPROXIMATELY

THE SAME INFORMATION AS ▮▮▮▮▮▮▮▮ ADDING THAT

APPOINTEE IS MAN OF FEW WORDS BUT WHEN HE SPEAKS, HE

MAKES HIS WORDS COUNT. HE RECOMMENDS APPOINTEE

AS A GOOD SOLID EXECUTIVE POSSESSING EXCELLENT LEADERSHIP

AND GUIDANCE ABILITIES WHOM HE RECOMMENDS FOR FEDERAL

POSITION OF TRUST.

ON MAY 14, 1976, FOLLOWING INDIVIDUALS, WHO HAVE KNOWN

APPOINTEE FOR LISTED PERIOD OF TIME, ALL ADVISED THEY

CONSIDER HIM TO BE A FINE MAYOR, AN EXCELLENT ADMINISTRATOR,

AND ONE WHO CERTAINLY RELATES WELL TO HIS EMPLOYEES. ALL

BELIEVE HIM TO BE A GENTLEMAN, WHO IS ARTICULATE, NEAT,

DEDICATED, OF HIGH MORAL CHARACTER AND ASSOCIATES, REPUTATION,

LOYALTY, AND ONE WHO LISTENS WELL TO INDIVIDUALS WITH

b7c

LA 639

NR 231 LA PLAIN

9:53PM NITEL MAY 14, 1976 DLA

TO DIRECTOR

FROM LOS ANGELES (161-3016)

THOMAS BRADLEY, SPECIAL INQUIRY, BUDED: MAY 18, 1976,

WITHOUT FAIL.

RE LOS ANGELES TELETYPE TO BUREAU MAY 12, 1976.

THE FOLLOWING INVESTIGATION CONDUCTED BY LOS ANGELES

DIVISIONEDUCATION.

SOUTH WESTERN UNIVERSITY LAW SCHOOL, LOOS ANGELESN

CALIFORNIA, 1951 - 1956.

ON MAY 13, 1976, ███████████

█████████ SOUTH WESTERN UNIVERSITY LAW SCHOOL,

LOS ANGELES, MADE AVAILABLE THE SCHOLASTIC RECORD OF THOMAS

BRADLEY. THIS RECORD REFLECTS BRADLEY ATTENDED FROM FEBRUARY

5, 1951, UNTIL JUNE 22, 1956, WHEN HE GRADUATED AND WAS

AWARDED AN LLB DEGREE. HE COMPLETED 81 UNITS, MAINTAINED

GRADE POINT AVERAGE OF 1.75 ON 3.0 GRADE SCALE, AND RANKED

AS 19 IN CLASS OF 63. RECORDS REFLECT APPOINTEE'S DOB AS

DECEMBER 29, 1917, AT CALVERT, TEXAS, AND RESIDENCE AS ██████

█████████ LOS ANGELES. PREVIOUS EDUCATION LISTED AS

NOT RECORDED

3 JUN 22 1976

FEDERAL BUREAU OF INVESTIGATION
COMMUNICATIONS SECTION

TELETYPE

PAGE TWO (LA 161-3216)

(7) ████ SAID FURTHER THAT APPOINTEE HAS BEEN SUPPORTIVE
IN HIS POLITICAL CAMPAIGN BY INDIVIDUALS OF QUESTIONABLE
CHARACTER AND ALL OF THIS INFORMATION CAN BE OBTAINED
THROUGH A READING OF THE NEWSPAPER DURING THE PERIODS OF
THE CAMPAIGN WHEN HE OPPOSED THE APPOINTEE.

DURING THE LAST MAYORAL CAMPAIGN WHICH RESULTED IN
APPOINTEE'S VICTORY, IT IS A PUBLIC FACT THAT APPOINTEE
SPENT TWICE AS MUCH MONEY ON HIS CAMPAIGN ████ DID.
████ AND BRADLEY
WAS COUNCILMAN, SOMEONE PETITIONED THE CITY COUNCIL FOR
A ZONING VARIANCE TO ALLOW A GAS STATION TO BE BUILT AT THE
CORNERS OF WEST ADAMS STREET AND HOOVER STREET IN LOS ANGELES.
BRADLEY WAS OPPOSED THIS WHEN IT WAS FIRST PRESENTED AND THEN
SUDDENLY CHANGED HIS MIND AND GAVE IT HIS FULL SUPPORT. AN
INDIVIDUAL NAMED ████ CAME TO HIM ONE DAY AND TOLD HIM
THAT HIS BROTHER HAD GIVEN BRADLEY SEVERAL THOUSAND
DOLLARS IN CASH AND DELIVERED IT TO BRADLEY AT HIS LAW OFFICE
AND AS A RESULT OF THIS CASH PAYMENT, BRADLEY CHANGED HIS
MIND. ████ ASKED THE LOS ANGELES POLICE DEPARTMENT TO

b7C

b7C

PAGE FOUR (LA 161-3016)

MADE PUBLIC, BRADLEY REFUSED TO DISMISS THE INDIVIDUAL
FROM HIS CAMPAIGN.

(6) ████████ THAT APPOINTEE HAS ALWAYS BEEN ANTI-LAW
ENFORCEMENT AND HAS "HATED THE POLICE." ████████
THAT HE HEARD RUMORS TO THE EFFECT THAT APPOINTEE,
WHILE WATCH COMMANDER AT THE WILSHIRE DIVISION WOULD
INTERVENE IN THE BOOKING OF BLACK PRISONERS.

████████ HE BELIEVES APPOINTEE IS LOYAL, ALTHOUGH
HE PERSONALLY BELIEVES APPOINTEE JOINED THE POLICE FORCE TO
AVOID SERVICE IN THE MILITARY. HE SAID ALL OF HIS THOUGHTS
ABOUT APPOINTEE ARE NEGATIVE AND THAT HE WOULD HAVE NOTHING
TO DO WITH HIM AND LET ALONE, RECOMMEND HIM FOR AN IMPORTANT
POSITION.

ON MAY 17, 1976, ████████████████████████
WAS CONTACTED AT HIS HOME IN LOS ANGELES, CALIFORNIA, AND
ADVISED HE IS A ████████████ OF APPOINTEE WITHIN THE
DEMOCRATIC PARTY. HE SAID HE DOES NOT CONSIDER HIM TO
BE A CAPABLE MAYOR IN THAT HE CANNOT ARTICULATE HIS FOUR OR
FIVE MOST IMPORTANT PROGRAMS IN ORDER TO GAIN THEIR ACCEPTANCE.

b7C

FD-36 (Rev. 2-14-74)

FBI

Date: 5/18/76

Transmit the following in _____
(Type in plaintext or code)

Via AIRTEL _____
(Precedence)

- -

TO: DIRECTOR, FBI

FROM: SAC, WFO (161-11297) (P)

THOMAS BRADLEY
SPECIAL INQUIRY

ReButel 5/11/76; LA nitel 5/12/76; LA nitel 5/13/76;
Sacramento nitel 5/13/76 and LA nitel 5/14/76.

LEADS: WFO: IRS, ▆▆ and U. S. Secret Service

EMPLOYMENT

White House Office (WHO)

b6, b7C

The following investigation was conducted by SA
▆▆▆▆▆▆▆▆ on 5/13/76:

A search of the files of the Personnel Office and
Records Office, WHO revealed the following information concerning
THOMAS BRADLEY

9/9/68   Appointed by President to be a member of Peace Corps
          National Advisory Council.

12/30/74 Presidential Commission to be a member of the National
          Commission on Productivity and Work Quality.

161-11871-14

① - Bureau
1 - WFO
JCS:jcs
(2)

NOT RECORDED

3 JUN 22 1976

Approved: _____   Sent _____ M Per _____
          Special Agent in Charge

U.S. Department of Justice

Federal Bureau of Investigation

Los Angeles, California   90024

In Reply, Please Refer to
File No.

June 30, 1989

FREE THROW
BRIBERY

On May 3, 1989, ████████████████████ ███████ Los Angeles, related that his office has uncovered information concerning Los Angeles Mayor TOM BRADLEY's purchase of stock via DREXEL BURNHAM LAMBERT on companies who were the subjects of corporate takeovers. Following the purchase of stock, BRADLEY would sell the stock within 30 days following completion of the takeover. ████████ stated that he did not have any information at this time to indicate that BRADLEY received "insider information" concerning the stock purchases.

BRADLEY was instrumental in applying pressure on the SECURITIES EXCHANGE COMMISSION (SEC) to drop its demand that DREXEL BURNHAM LAMBERT relocate its junk bond operations to New York. BRADLEY contacted ████████████████████ to arrange what ██████ described as "some coordinated effort" to persuade the SEC to drop its demand. Specifically, BRADLEY persuaded ████████████████████████████████████ ██████████████████████████████ to intervene on behalf of DREXEL in negotiations with the SEC. Consequently, the SEC agreed to permit DREXEL to maintain its junk bond department in Beverly Hills, California. According to campaign statements, BRADLEY has received approximately $72,000.00 in campaign contributions from DREXEL since 1983.

In recent years, DREXEL has received lucrative municipal and junk bond business from various Los Angeles city departments. Specifically, ████████ pension system have invested $35 million in junk bonds and within the last four years, $981 million of trades in high yield bonds. It is noted that ████████████████ are BRADLEY appointees.

This document contains neither recommendations nor conclusions of the FBI. It is the property of the FBI and is loaned to your agency; it and its contents are not to be distributed outside your agency.

b7C

- 1 -

FREE THROW

with the stock and bond market. In order to purchase the bond, ▓▓▓▓ received a $50,000.00 loan from COLUMBIA SAVINGS and LOAN and two $25,000.00 unsecured loans from WELLS FARGO and SECURITY PACIFIC NATIONAL BANKS. Initially, ▓▓▓▓▓▓ was unaware of the total bond price and that COLUMBIA SAVINGS and LOAN, specifically ▓▓▓▓ had loaned ▓▓▓▓▓ the $50,000.00 to purchase the bond. ▓▓▓▓ stated that he primarily discussed the purchase of the bond with ▓▓▓▓

With respect to reporting the wrong purchase and sale date of the bond, ▓▓▓▓▓▓ stated that it was an oversight ▓▓ and he was not asked by anyone to purposely falsify disclosure statements regarding the bond purchase.

On May 15, 1989, the facts in this matter were discussed with Assistant United States Attorney (AUSA) GEORGE B. NEWHOUSE, JR., Los Angeles. AUSA NEWHOUSE suggested the initiation of a full field investigation in this matter and advised that his office would fully dedicate the necessary resources to prosecute this matter. The case has subsequently being assigned to AUSA JEFF EGLASH, Los Angeles and he is fully supportive of this investigation.

b7C, b7D, b3

AIRTEL

5/31/89

Director, FBI

SAC, Los Angeles (58C-LA-102113) (WCC-4)
Attention: SSA █████████

█████████████████ (CALIFORNIA);
THOMAS BRADLEY, MAYOR OF LOS ANGELES, CALIFORNIA;
BRIBERY/CONFLICT OF INTEREST - UNITED STATES CONGRESS;
CORRUPTION OF STATE AND LOCAL PUBLIC OFFICIALS;
OO: LOS ANGELES

Reference is made to FBIHQ teletype to Los Angeles dated 5/24/89, captioned as above and telcal of SSA ██████████ Los Angeles Division, to SSA ████████████ Public Corruption Unit, FBIHQ, 5/31/89.

Enclosed is one copy each of Ethics in Government Act - Financial Disclosure Statements for 1985 through 1987 as filed with United States House of Representatives, Committee on Standards of Official Conduct concerning ████████████

In referenced telcal Los Angeles requested copies of Ethics in Government Act/Financial Disclosure Statements for the years 1985 through 1988 as filed with the United States House of Representatives, Committee on Standards of Official Conduct, for ████████████████████

These records are a matter of public source information and are maintained by the Clerk of the House of Representatives, Committee on Standards of Official Conduct, Office of Records and Registration, Room 1036, Longworth House Office Building, Washington, D.C., telephone number (202) 225-1300. For your information the Office of Congressional and Public Affairs, FBIHQ, maintains copies of these filings for all members of the United States House of Representatives and, therefore, no inquiry with the Clerk of the House of Representatives was required to obtain these records.

Since filing for the 1988 year did not occur until 5/15/89, FBIHQ does not anticipate receiving copies regarding the 1988 year until approximately July, 1989. One copy of the enclosed documents have also been provided to James Cole, Deputy Chief, Public Integrity Section, Criminal Division, Department of Justice, as of 5/31/89.

ENC. BEHIND FILE

Enclosures (3)

Exec AD Adm ——
Exec AD Inv ——
Exec AD LES ——
Asst Dir. ——
Adm Serv. ——
Crim Inv ——
Ident ——
Insp ——
Intell ——
Lab. ——
Legal Coun ——
Off. Cong. &
  Public Affs. ——
Rec. Mgnt. ——
Tech Servs ——
Training ——
Off. Liaison &
  Int Affs ——
Telephone Rm ——
Director's Sec'y ——

1 — ████████
1 — ████████
JTD:bja (5)
MAIL ROOM ☐   Federal Express
5/31/89

APPROVED:

Director _____
Exec AD-Adm _____
Exec AD-Inv _____
Exec. AD-LES _____

Adm Servs. _____
Crim Inv _____
Ident _____
Inspection _____
Intell. _____

Laboratory _____
Legal Coun. _____
Off. of Cong.
  & Public Affs. _____
Rec. Mgnt. _____
Servs. _____
Training _____

b7C

Mr. Gerald E. McDowell, Chief
Public Integrity Section   May 31, 1989
Attention: Mr. James Cole

Larry A. Potts, Chief
White-Collar Crimes Section

██████████████████████████ (CALIFORNIA);
THOMAS BRADLEY, MAYOR OF LOS ANGELES, CALIFORNIA;
BRIBERY/CONFLICT OF INTEREST - UNITED STATES CONGRESS;
CORRUPTION OF STATE AND LOCAL PUBLIC OFFICIALS;

INFORMATION MEMORANDUM

     Reference is made to a telephone conversation between
James Cole of your staff and Supervisory Special Agent ████
████ of my Public Corruption Unit on May 31, 1989.

     Enclosed is one copy each of Ethics in Government Act -
Financial Disclosure Statements for 1985 through 1987 as filed
with United States House of Representatives, Committee on
Standards of Official Conduct, concerning ████████████

     These records are a matter of public source information
and are maintained by the Clerk of the House of Representatives,
Committee on Standards of Official Conduct, Office of Records and
Registration, Room 1036, Longworth House Office Building,
Washington, D.C., telephone number (202) 225-1300. For your
information the Office of Congressional and Public Affairs,
FBIHQ, maintains copies of these filings for all members of the
United States House of Representatives and, therefore, no inquiry
with the Clerk of the House of Representatives was required to
obtain these records.

     Since filing for the 1988 year did not occur until May
15, 1989, FBIHQ does not anticipate receiving copies regarding
the 1988 year until approximately July, 1989. One copy of the
enclosed documents have also been forwarded to our Los Angeles
Office as of May 31, 1989.

Enclosures (3)

    1 - Mr. Potts
    1 - ████████████
    JPO:bja (6)

HAND CARRIED
6/1/89
58-12268-16X2

Exec AD Adm.
Exec AD Inv
Exec AD LES
Asst Dir
Adm Servs.
Crim Inv
Ident
Insp
Intell
Lab
Legal Coun.
Off. Cong. &
  Public Affs.
Rec Mgnt
Tech Servs.
Training
Off Liaison &
  Int Affs
Telephone Rm
Director's Sec'y — MAIL ROOM ☐

b7C

APPROVED:
Director
Exec AD-Adm
Exec AD-Inv
Exec AD-LES

Adm. Servs
Crim Inv
Ident
Inspection
Intell

Laboratory
Legal Coun.
Off of Cong
  & Public Affs.
Rec Mgnt
Tech Servs.
Training

6/6/89

Mr. Baker

RE: ████████████████████ (CALIFORNIA);
THOMAS BRADLEY, MAYOR OF LOS ANGELES, CALIFORNIA;
BRIBERY/CONFLICT OF INTEREST - U.S. CONGRESS;
CORRUPTION OF STATE AND LOCAL PUBLIC
OFFICIALS; OO: LOS ANGELES

The following is a chronological list of events in captioned matter:

o   On 4/13/89, "The Washington Post" ran a front-page story questioning Representative Coelho's purchase of a $100,000 junk bond through Drexel Burnham Lambert (DBL) Inc., in 1986, and suggested the purchase may have been improperly financed with campaign funds. ████████████ subsequently directed his attorney, ███████████ to reconstruct the transaction and prepare a report.

o   During late April and early May, 1989, "The Los Angeles Times" reported that Thomas Bradley, Mayor of Los Angeles, was involved in questionable stock transactions with DBL Inc., along with other allegations concerning Mayor Bradley's involvement with two Savings & Loan (S & L) Associations in Los Angeles.

o   By teletype dated 5/3/89, the Los Angeles Division reported the essence of the news articles concerning Mayor Bradley for information. These matters were under investigation by Los Angeles City Attorney ███████████ The U.S. Attorney's Office (USAO), Central District of California (CDC), recommended that the Los Angeles Division establish contact with ███████ office and monitor his investigation. An informational note was prepared dated 5/5/89 (attached).

o   By teletype dated 5/10/89, the Los Angeles Division reported on additional newspaper articles concerning Mayor Bradley and Representative Coelho. This information included reports that Mayor Bradley was instrumental through Representative Coelho, to apply pressure on the Securities Exchange Commission to drop its demand that DBL Inc., relocate its junk bond operations from Beverly Hills, California, to New York, New York. This teletype requested FBIHQ to determine if this information had any bearing on the securities case against ████████████ and if the Bureau's interests would be served by FBI inquiry.

1 - Mr. Ahlerich
1 - Mr. Baker
1 - Mr. Walton
1 - Mr. Daniels

1 - ██████████
1 - Mr. Potts
1 - Special Assistants, CID

JPO:bja (9)   (CONTINUED - OVER)

DocID: 259148

FD-36 (Rev. 2-14-74)

F B I

Date: 5/19/76

Transmit the following in _____
(Type in plaintext or code)

Via _____ AIRTEL _____
(Precedence)

Assoc. Dir.
Dep.-A.D.-Adm.
Dep.-A.D.-Inv.
Asst: Dir.:
  Adm. Serv.
  Ext. Affrs.
  F.. & Pers.
  Gd. Inv.
  Iden.
  Ins....:..n
  Int...
  Le.'. :..ury
  Le.:l. Cun.
  Plan. & Eval.
  Pay Mgmt.
  Spec. Inv.
  Training
  Telephone Rm.
  Director Sec'y

TO: DIRECTOR, FBI

FROM: SAC, ALEXANDRIA (161-3736) -RUC-

THOMAS BRADLEY
SPECIAL INQUIRY
BUDED: 5/18/76

        Re Bureau teletype to WFO, 5/11/76, and
Los Angeles teletype to Bureau, 5/12/76.

b6, b7C   SC [   ] caused a search to be made
of the files of the Central Intelligence Agency (CIA),
Langley, Va., and was advised on 5/19/76, that the files
contained no pertinent identifiable information concerning
the appointee or spouse, ETHEL ARNOLD BRADLEY.

APPROVED FOR RELEASE - CIA INFO
DATE: OCT 1999

1 - Bureau
1 - Alexandria
SW:sw
(2)

161-11871. 1(

NOT RECORDED

3 JUN 22 1976

): 259148

(ev. 2-14-74)

F B I

Date: 5/19/76

. the following in _____
(Type in plaintext or code)

AIRTEL
_____
(Precedence)

| Assoc. Dir. |
| Dep.-A.D.-Adm. |
| Dep.-A.D.-Inv. |
| Asstt Dir.: |
| Adm. Serv. |
| Ext. Affairs |
| Fi l & Pers. |
| Gel. Inv. |
| Ident. |
| In ... |
| La ... |
| Lef ... |
| Le ... un. |
| Plan. & Eval. |
| P ... ment. |
| Spec. Inv. |
| Training |
| Telephone Rm. |
| Director Sec'y |

TO: DIRECTOR, FBI

FROM: SAC, ALEXANDRIA (161-3736) -RUC-

THOMAS BRADLEY
SPECIAL INQUIRY
BUDED: 5/18/76

        Re Bureau teletype to WFO, 5/11/76, and
Los Angeles teletype to Bureau, 5/12/76.

b6, b7C   SC [redacted] caused a search to be made
of the files of the Central Intelligence Agency (CIA),
Langley, Va., and was advised on 5/19/76, that the files
contained no pertinent identifiable information concerning
the appointee or spouse, ETHEL ARNOLD BRADLEY.

1 - Bureau
1 - Alexandria
SW:sw
(2)

161-11871. 11

NOT RECORDED

3   JUN 22 1976

_____ Sent _____ M   Per _____

FREE THROW

   In an article appearing in the LOS ANGELES TIMES on May 14, 1989, COELHO admitted to allowing SPIEGEL to buy a hundred thousand dollar BCI holding corporation, 12.5% senior subordinated debenture (junk bond) for him in 1986. The formation of BCI was for the purpose of a leverage buy-out of BEATRICE FOODS. COELHO later repaid SPIEGEL with money borrowed partly from COLUMBIA SAVINGS and LOAN, however, COELHO failed to disclose the $50,000.00 from COLUMBIA on his annual report.

   When the bond became available on April 10, 1986, COELHO was unable to purchase the bond. Consequently, SPIEGEL purchased the bond for COELHO with the understanding COELHO would reimburse him with interest.

   On or about June 3, 1986, COELHO took possession of the bond and by that time, the bond had increased substantially in value from its initial price. Instead of paying SPIEGEL the higher price, COELHO paid him the initial offering price and $1,667.00 in interest. COELHO sold the bond in October, 1986, and profited approximately $6,800.00.

   A review of BRADLEY's statements of Economic Interest Form 721 dated March 25, 1987, disclosed that BRADLEY purchased preferred stock of BEATRICE FOODS sometime in March, 1986 and sold the stock August, 1986. In addition, BRADLEY purchased common stock in WICKES CORPORATION and WORLDS of WONDER in June, 1985 and April, 1986, respectively which along with BEATRICE FOODS, were the subjects of corporate takeovers.

   DREXEL's Political Action Committee (PAC) has contributed to BRADLEY's campaign fund. ███████████ ██ ████████████████████ It is noted that ██████ was not known to make such investments prior to this instance and junk bonds are not normally available to the average individual investor.

   On June 1, 1989, ████████ was interviewed concerning ████████ purchase of a hundred thousand dollar BCI junk bond. █████ related that in the beginning of 1986, ████████████████████████████ ██████████████████████████ relating to ███████████ purchase of the bond. ████████ considered the purchase of the bond a good investment, although he was not that familiar

b7C. - 2 - b7D

FREE THROW

with the stock and bond market. In order to purchase the bond,
████████ received a $50,000.00 loan from COLUMBIA SAVINGS and LOAN
and two $25,000.00 unsecured loans from WELLS FARGO and SECURITY
PACIFIC NATIONAL BANKS. Initially, ████████ was unaware of the
total bond price and that COLUMBIA SAVINGS and LOAN, specifically
████████ had loaned ████████ the $50,000.00 to purchase the bond.
████████ stated that he primarily discussed the purchase of the
bond with ████████

With respect to reporting the wrong purchase and sale
date of the bond, ████████ stated that it was an oversight
████████ and he was not asked by anyone to purposely falsify
████████ disclosure statements regarding the bond purchase.

On May 15, 1989, the facts in this matter were
discussed with Assistant United States Attorney (AUSA) GEORGE B.
NEWHOUSE, JR., Los Angeles. AUSA NEWHOUSE suggested the
initiation of a full field investigation in this matter and
advised that his office would fully dedicate the necessary
resources to prosecute this matter. The case has subsequently
being assigned to AUSA JEFF EGLASH, Los Angeles and he is fully
supportive of this investigation.

```
        AIRTEL
                                                    5/31/89


    Director, FBI

    SAC, Los Angeles (58C-LA-102113) (WCC-4)
        Attention:  SSA
```
█████████████████ (CALIFORNIA);
THOMAS BRADLEY, MAYOR OF LOS ANGELES, CALIFORNIA;
BRIBERY/CONFLICT OF INTEREST - UNITED STATES CONGRESS;
CORRUPTION OF STATE AND LOCAL PUBLIC OFFICIALS;
OO: LOS ANGELES

        Reference is made to FBIHQ teletype to Los Angeles
dated 5/24/89, captioned as above and telcal of SSA █████
████████ Los Angeles Division, to SSA ███████████ Public
Corruption Unit, FBIHQ, 5/31/89.

        Enclosed is one copy each of Ethics in Government Act -
Financial Disclosure Statements for 1985 through 1987 as filed
with United States House of Representatives, Committee on
Standards of Official Conduct concerning ████████████

        In referenced telcal Los Angeles requested copies of
Ethics in Government Act/Financial Disclosure Statements for the
years 1985 through 1988 as filed with the United States House of
Representatives, Committee on Standards of Official Conduct, for
██

        These records are a matter of public source information
and are maintained by the Clerk of the House of Representatives,
Committee on Standards of Official Conduct, Office of Records and
Registration, Room 1036, Longworth House Office Building,
Washington, D.C., telephone number (202) 225-1300. For your
information the Office of Congressional and Public Affairs,
FBIHQ, maintains copies of these filings for all members of the
United States House of Representatives and, therefore, no inquiry
with the Clerk of the House of Representatives was required to
obtain these records.

        Since filing for the 1988 year did not occur until
5/15/89, FBIHQ does not anticipate receiving copies regarding the
1988 year until approximately July, 1989. One copy of the
enclosed documents have also been provided to James Cole, Deputy
Chief, Public Integrity Section, Criminal Division, Department of
Justice, as of 5/31/89.

    Enclosures (3)

    1 -
    1 -
    JTP:bja (5)

AIRTEL

5/31/89

Director, FBI

SAC, Los Angeles (58C-LA-102113) (WCC-4)
Attention: SSA ████████
████████████████████ (CALIFORNIA);
THOMAS BRADLEY, MAYOR OF LOS ANGELES, CALIFORNIA;
BRIBERY/CONFLICT OF INTEREST - UNITED STATES CONGRESS;
CORRUPTION OF STATE AND LOCAL PUBLIC OFFICIALS;
OO: LOS ANGELES

Reference is made to FBIHQ teletype to Los Angeles
dated 5/24/89, captioned as above and telcal of SSA ████
████████ Los Angeles Division, to SSA ████████████ Public
Corruption Unit, FBIHQ, 5/31/89.

Enclosed is one copy each of Ethics in Government Act -
Financial Disclosure Statements for 1985 through 1987 as filed
with United States House of Representatives, Committee on
Standards of Official Conduct concerning ████████████

In referenced telcal Los Angeles requested copies of
Ethics in Government Act/Financial Disclosure Statements for the
years 1985 through 1988 as filed with the United States House of
Representatives, Committee on Standards of Official Conduct, for
██

These records are a matter of public source information
and are maintained by the Clerk of the House of Representatives,
Committee on Standards of Official Conduct, Office of Records and
Registration, Room 1036, Longworth House Office Building,
Washington, D.C., telephone number (202) 225-1300. For your
information the Office of Congressional and Public Affairs,
FBIHQ, maintains copies of these filings for all members of the
United States House of Representatives and, therefore, no inquiry
with the Clerk of the House of Representatives was required to
obtain these records.

Since filing for the 1988 year did not occur until
5/15/89, FBIHQ does not anticipate receiving copies regarding the
1988 year until approximately July, 1989. One copy of the
enclosed documents have also been provided to James Cole, Deputy
Chief, Public Integrity Section, Criminal Division, Department of
Justice, as of 5/31/89. ENC. BEHIND FILE

Enclosures (3)

APPROVED:

Adm Servs. _____ Laboratory _____
Crim Inv. _____ Legal Coun. _____
Director _____ Off. of Cong.
Exec AD-Adm _____ _____ & Public Affs. _____
Rec. Mgnt. _____

1 - ████████
1 -

6/6/89

Mr. Baker

RE: ████████████████ (CALIFORNIA);
THOMAS BRADLEY, MAYOR OF LOS ANGELES, CALIFORNIA;
BRIBERY/CONFLICT OF INTEREST - U.S. CONGRESS;
CORRUPTION OF STATE AND LOCAL PUBLIC
OFFICIALS; OO: LOS ANGELES

The following is a chronological list of events in captioned matter:

o   On 4/13/89, "The Washington Post" ran a front-page story questioning Representative Coelho's purchase of a $100,000 junk bond through Drexel Burnham Lambert (DBL) Inc., in 1986, and suggested the purchase may have been improperly financed with campaign funds. ████████ subsequently directed his attorney, ████████████ to reconstruct the transaction and prepare a report.

o   During late April and early May, 1989, "The Los Angeles Times" reported that Thomas Bradley, Mayor of Los Angeles, was involved in questionable stock transactions with DBL Inc., along with other allegations concerning Mayor Bradley's involvement with two Savings & Loan (S & L) Associations in Los Angeles.

o   By teletype dated 5/3/89, the Los Angeles Division reported the essence of the news articles concerning Mayor Bradley for information. These matters were under investigation by Los Angeles City Attorney ████████████ The U.S. Attorney's Office (USAO), Central District of California (CDC), recommended that the Los Angeles Division establish contact with ████ office and monitor his investigation. An informational note was prepared dated 5/5/89 (attached).

o   By teletype dated 5/10/89, the Los Angeles Division reported on additional newspaper articles concerning Mayor Bradley and Representative Coelho. This information included reports that Mayor Bradley was instrumental through Representative Coelho, to apply pressure on the Securities Exchange Commission to drop its demand that DBL Inc., relocate its junk bond operations from Beverly Hills, California, to New York, New York. This teletype requested FBIHQ to determine if this information had any bearing on the securities case against ████████████ and if the Bureau's interests would be served by FBI inquiry.

1 - Mr. Ahlerich
1 - Mr. Baker
1 - Mr. Walton
1 - Mr. Daniels

1 - ████████
1 - Mr. Potts
1 - Special Assistants, CID

JPO:bja (9)

(CONTINUED - OVER)

6/6/89

Mr. Baker

    RE: ██████████████████████ (CALIFORNIA);
           THOMAS BRADLEY, MAYOR OF LOS ANGELES, CALIFORNIA;
           BRIBERY/CONFLICT OF INTEREST - U.S. CONGRESS;
           CORRUPTION OF STATE AND LOCAL PUBLIC
           OFFICIALS; OO: LOS ANGELES

        The following is a chronological list of events in
captioned matter:

    o   On 4/13/89, "The Washington Post" ran a front-page
story questioning Representative Coelho's purchase of a $100,000
junk bond through Drexel Burnham Lambert (DBL) Inc., in 1986, and
suggested the purchase may have been improperly financed with
campaign funds. ██████████████ subsequently directed his
attorney, ████████ to reconstruct the transaction and
prepare a report.

    o   During late April and early May, 1989, "The Los Angeles
Times" reported that Thomas Bradley, Mayor of Los Angeles, was
involved in questionable stock transactions with DBL Inc., along
with other allegations concerning Mayor Bradley's involvement
with two Savings & Loan (S & L) Associations in Los Angeles.

    o   By teletype dated 5/3/89, the Los Angeles Division
reported the essence of the news articles concerning Mayor
Bradley for information. These matters were under investigation
by Los Angeles City Attorney ████████ The U.S. Attorney's
Office (USAO), Central District of California (CDC), recommended
that the Los Angeles Division establish contact with ████████
office and monitor his investigation. An informational note was
prepared dated 5/5/89 (attached).

    o   By teletype dated 5/10/89, the Los Angeles Division
reported on additional newspaper articles concerning Mayor
Bradley and Representative Coelho. This information included
reports that Mayor Bradley was instrumental through
Representative Coelho, to apply pressure on the Securities
Exchange Commission to drop its demand that DBL Inc., relocate
its junk bond operations from Beverly Hills, California, to New
York, New York. This teletype requested FBIHQ to determine if
this information had any bearing on the securities case against
████████ and if the Bureau's interests would be served by
FBI inquiry.

1 - Mr. Ahlerich   1 - ████████
1 - Mr. Baker   1 - Mr. Potts
1 - Mr. Walton   1 - Special Assistants, CID
1 - Mr. Daniels

JPO:bja (9)   (CONTINUED - OVER)

o   By teletype dated 5/24/89, the Los Angeles, New York,
and WMFO Divisions were advised of the above decision of PIS.
The Los Angeles Division was instructed to open a preliminary
investigation and the NYO was instructed to serve as an auxiliary
office to the Los Angeles investigation.

o   On 5/25/89, "The Los Angeles Times" reported in a
front-page article, quoting unnamed sources, that a preliminary
criminal investigation of both Mayor Bradley and Representative
Coelho had been opened by the PIS/DOJ. This article reported
detailed information concerning internal DOJ decisions in this
matter (article attached).

I will keep you advised of pertinent developments.

K. ?/ Walton

- 3 -

o   By teletype dated 5/24/89, the Los Angeles, New York, and WMFO Divisions were advised of the above decision of PIS. The Los Angeles Division was instructed to open a preliminary investigation and the NYO was instructed to serve as an auxiliary office to the Los Angeles investigation.

o   On 5/25/89, "The Los Angeles Times" reported in a front-page article, quoting unnamed sources, that a preliminary criminal investigation of both Mayor Bradley and Representative Coelho had been opened by the PIS/DOJ. This article reported detailed information concerning internal DOJ decisions in this matter (article attached).

I will keep you advised of pertinent developments.

K. ⫻ Walton

- 3 -

b7C

5/5/89

Director Sessions:

> RE: TOM BRADLEY, MAYOR, CITY OF LOS ANGELES,
> CALIFORNIA; POSSIBLE CORRUPTION OF STATE
> AND LOCAL PUBLIC OFFICIALS - LOCAL LEVEL;
> OO: LOS ANGELES

SAC, Los Angeles, advised that they have been made aware of a possible public corruption matter that is currently under investigation by the Los Angeles City Attorney concerning allegations of possible impropriety and conflict of interest violations on the part of Democratic Mayor Tom Bradley. Mayor Bradley, a very popular, conservative, 5th term Mayor, has not been touched by prior allegations of corruption.

According to recent newspaper articles, Mayor Bradley has allegedly been involved in a possible conflict of interest matter relating to his personal financial dealings with the Far East National Bank (FEB), Los Angeles, California. Mayor Bradley is one of a 46-member advisory board, and in 1988, was the only board member who received a consultant fee ($18,000) from FEB. The city of Los Angeles has recently deposited two million dollars with FEB, giving rise to the allegations. Mayor Bradley has also served as a board member with the Valley Federal Savings and Loan Association for a number of years, and was paid a total of $150,000, presumably for consultant fees. According to the California Fair Political Practices Commission, Mayor Bradley is not covered by the California Political Reform Act, which prohibits a public official from making a Government decision in which he has a financial interest.

As noted above, this matter is currently under investigation by the Los Angeles City Attorney's Office and the Office of the U.S. Comptroller with whom our Los Angeles Office has established liaison in order to follow any areas of interest we might have as to FBI jurisdiction arising out of these initial allegations. The U.S. Comptroller is investigating the FEB for compliance with banking laws and regulations to include the possible misapplication of bank funds in the relationship between the FEB and Mayor Bradley with respect to the $18,000 payment.

This matter is continuing to receive the very close attention of our Los Angeles Office, and I will keep you advised of any further significant developments.

W. M. Baker

1 - Mr. Revell
1 - Mr. Ahlerich
1 - Mr. Baker
1 - Mr. Walton

1 - ▓▓▓▓▓
1 - Mr. Potts   b7C
1 - ▓▓▓▓▓
1 - Special Assistants, CID

Chapter I
FBI Documents
1,275 preprocessed pages on Frank Sinatra released under the (Freedom of Information Act) pursuant to Title 5, United States Code 552 and/or 552 a (Privacy Act).

Books

Brashler, William. The Don, The Life and Death of Sam Giancanna. New York: Harper and Row Publishers, 1977.

Editor's of Time - Life Books. This Fabulous Century 1940 to 1950. New York: Time - Life Books, 1969.

Kelly, Kitty. His Way: The Unauthorized Biography of Frank Sinatra. New York: Bantam Books, 1986.

Koskoff, E. David and Kennedy, P. Joseph. A Life and Times. New Jersey: Prentice-Hall, Inc. Englewood Cliffs, 1974.

Kuntz, Tom and Kuntz, Phil, Editors. The Sinatra Files: The Secret FBI Dossier. New York: Three River Press, 2000.

Lasky, Victor. JFF: The Man And The Myth, A Critical Portrait . New York: The Macmillan Company, 1963.

Sinatra, Nancy. Frank Sinatra An American Legend. Great Britain: Virgin Books, 1995.

Magazines

His Kind of Town. Midwest Magazine, May 9, 1976.
Black's Mourn Death of The Frank Sinatra That Nobody Knew. Jet Magazine, June 1998.

The Lost Rat Packer. GQ, October 1998.

Newspapers

A Career In Three Acts: Skinny Kid 1945, Smooth Operator 1956, Old Pro 1967. Chicago Tribune, May 17, 1998.

Well Outfitted: The Mob and Sinatra Took Good Care of Each Other. Chicago, Tribune, May 17, 1998.

Remembering Sinatra: The Memory of All That. Chicago Tribune, May 17, 1998.

What Would Frank Do? Chicago Tribune, May 17, 1998.

'The Voice Is Stilled' His Kind of Town Mourns. Chicago Sun-Times, May 17, 1998.

Frank Sinatra Dies at 82; Matchless Stylist of Pop. New York Times, May 16, 1998.

Frank Sinatra Opens and Then Cancels. New York Times, May 17, 1990.

He Did It His Way - Under Ceaseless Scrutiny. The Wall Street Journal, June 13, 2000.

FBI Dossier On Sinatra. Chicago Sun-Times, June 18, 2000.

FBI Releases It's File, With Tidbits Old and New. New York Times, December 8, 2000.

Chapter II
FBI Documents
8 preprocessed pages on Ella Fitzgerald released under the (Freedom of Information Act) pursuant to Title 5, United States Code 552 and/or 552 a (Privacy Act).

Author Interviews
Author interviews with Ella Fitzgerald, Louis Jordan, Clark Terry, Lonnie Simmons, Viola Jefferson, Dorothy Donegan, John Young, Jimmy Jones, Eddie Johnson, Louis Armstrong, Billy Eckstine, "Dizzy" Gillespie, Earl Hines, Duke Ellington, Cab Calloway, Nancy Wilson, Maxine Sullivan, George Kirby, and Nat Cole.
Books
Bogle, Donald. Brown Sugar: Eighty Years of America's Black Female Superstars. New York: Harmony Books, 1980.

Colin, Sid. Ella: The Life And Times of Ella Fitzgerald. New York: Elm Tree, 1986.
Fidelman, Geoffrey Mark. The First Lady of Song Ella Fitzgerald For the Record. New York: Birch Lane Press Book, 1994.

Fox, Ted. Show Time At the Apollo. New York: DaCappo Press, 1983.
Gourse, Leslie. Louis' Children: American Jazz Singers. New York: Morrow, 1984.
Kliment, Bud. Ella Fitzgerald: A Biography. New York: Scribner's, 1994.
McHenry, Robert, ed. Famous American Women. New York: Dover, 1980.
Pleasants, Henry. The Great American Popular Singers. New York: Simon & Schuster, 1974.

Schiffman, Jack. Apollo Uptown: The Story of Harlem's Theater. New York: Cowles Book Company, 1971.

Simon, George T. The Big Bands. New York: Schirmer, 1981.
Stuart, Nicholson. Ella Fitzgerald A Biography of the First Lady of Jazz. New York: Charles Scribner's Sons, 1993.

Torme, Mel. It Wasn't All Velvet. New York: Viking, 1988.
Travis, Dempsey J. An Autobiography of Black Jazz. Chicago: Urban Research Press, 1983.

Travis, Dempsey J. The Duke Ellington Primer. Chicago: Urban Research Press, 1996.
Travis, Dempsey J. The Louis Armstrong Odyssey: From Jane Alley to America's Jazz Ambassador. Chicago: Urban Research Press, 1997.

Chapter III

FBI Documents

2,027 preprocessed pages on Howard Hughes released under the (Freedom of

Information Act) pursuant to Title 5, United States Code 552 and/or 552 a (Privacy Act).

Books

Barlett, L. Donald and Steele B. James. Empire: The Life, Legend, and Madness of Howard Hughes. New York: W.W. Norton and Company, 1979.

Burns, MacGregor James, Roosevelt. The Soldier of Freedom. New York: Harcourt Brace Javanovich, 1970.

Cassini, Igor and Molli, Jeanne. I'd Do It All Over Again: The Life and Times of Igor Cassini. New York: Putnam, 1977.

Craven, Frank Wesley and Cate Lea James. The Army Air Forces in World War II. Chicago: University of Chicago Press, 1955.

Daniels, Jonathan. White House Witness. Garden City: Doubleday, 1975.

Davies, Marion. The Times We Had. Indianapolis: Bobbs - Merrill, 1975.

Higham, Charles and Greenberg, Joel. The Celluloid Muse. London: Augus and Robertson Publishing, 1969.

Hoffman, Paul. Lions In The Street: The Inside Story of The Great Wall Street Law

Firms. New York: Saturday Review Press, 1973.

Thomas, Bob. Selznick. Garden City: Doubleday, 1970.

Walsh, Raoul. Each Man In His Own Time. New York: Farrar Straus and Giroux, 1974.

Wilcox, Herbert. Twenty-five Thousand Sunsets. New York: A.S. Barnes, 1967.

Zeckendorf, William and McCreay, Edward. New York: Holt Rhinehart and Winston, 1970.

Magazines

Movie Magician. Colliers, March 19, 1932.

A Boy Who Began At The Top. American, April 1932.

Howard Hughes Record Breaker. Liberty, February 6, 1937.

The Problems of Howard Hughes. Fortune, January 1959.

The Bankers and The Spook. Fortune, March 1961.

Riddle of An Embattled Phantom. Life, September 7, 1962.

Howard Hughes Is Battling for Control of a Billion-Dollar Empire. Saturday Evening Post, February 9, 1963.

The View From Inside Hughes Tool. Fortune, December 1973.

I Remember Hughes. New York Times Magazine, May 2, 1976.

Chapter IV

FBI Documents
967 preprocessed pages on Roy Wilkins released under the (Freedom of Information Act) pursuant to Title 5, United States Code 552 and/or 552 a (Privacy Act).

Books

Branch, Taylor. Parting The Waters: America In The King Years 1954-63. New York: Simon and Schuster, 1988.

Farmer, James. Lay Bare The Heart, An Autobiography of The Civil Rights Movement. New York: Arbor House, 1985.

Garrow, J. David. Bearing The Cross: Dr. Martin Luther King, Jr., and the Southern Leadership Conference. New York: William Morrow and Company, Inc., 1986.

King, L. Martin Jr. Stride Toward Freedom: The Montgomery Story. New York: Harper and Brothers, 1958.

Morris, D. Aldon. The Origins of The Civil Rights Movement. Black Communities Organizing For Change. New York: The Free Press, a division of Macmillan, Inc., 1984.

Reed, R. Christopher. The Chicago NAACP and The Rise of Black Professional Leadership 1910-1966. Bloomington: Indiana University Press, 1997.

Travis, J. Dempsey. An Autobiography of Black Chicago. Chicago: Urban Research Press, 1981.

Travis, J. Dempsey. An Autobiography of Black Politics. Chicago: Urban Research Press, 1987.

Travis, J. Dempsey. I Refuse To Learn To Fail. Chicago: Urban Research Press, 1992.

Wilkins, Roy and Matthews, Tom. The Autobiography of Roy Wilkins - Standing Fast. New York: DaCappo Press, 1994.

Wilson, Q. James. Negro Politics: The Search For Leadership. The Free Press of Glencoe, Illinois, 1960.

Chapter V
FBI Documents
80 preprocessed pages on Marilyn Monroe released under the (Freedom of Information Act) pursuant to Title 5, United States Code 552 and/or section 552 a (Privacy Act).
347 preprocessed pages on Joe DiMaggio released under the (Freedom of Information Act) pursuant to Title 5, United States Code 552 and/or section 552 a (Privacy Act).
Books
Griffith, Richard and Mayer, Arthur. The Movies. New York: Simon and Schuster, 1970.
Miller, Arthur. Time Bends A Life. New York: Harper & Row Publisher, 1991.
Nass, Herbert E. Wills of The Rich & Famous. New York: Gramercy Books, 1991.
Summers, Anthony. Goddess: The Secret Lives of Marilyn Monroe. New York: Penguin Books, 1986.

Summers, Anthony. Official and Confidential: The Secret Life of J. Edgar Hoover. New York: G.P. Putnam's Sons, 1993.

Magazines
Joe's Last Words: I'll Finally See Marilyn. Examiner Magazine. August 29, 2000.
The Final Days of Joe DiMaggio. Vanity Fair. September 2000.
Marilyn Monroe: Tragic and Timeless. Biography Magazine. September 2000.
Newspapers
Joe's Deathbed Wish. Chicago Sun-Times. August 9, 2000.

Chapter VI
FBI Documents
210 preprocessed pages on Sammy Davis Jr. released under the (Freedom of Information Act) pursuant to Title 5, United States Code 552 and/or 552 a (Privacy Act).
Books
Baker, Jean Claude and Chris Chase. Josephine; The Hungry Heart. New York: Random House, 1993.

Branch, Taylor. Parting The Waters: America In The King Years 1954-63. New York: Simon and Schuster, 1988.

Davis, Jr., Sammy, Jane Boyar and Burt Boyar. Yes I Can. New York: Farrar, Straus and Giroux, 1965.

Davis, Miles with Quincy Troupe. Miles. The Autobiography. New York: Simon and Schuster, 1989.

Epstein, Daniel Mark. Nat King Cole. New York: Farrar, Straus and Giroux, 1999.
Feldman, Geoffrey Mark. First Lady of Song Ella Fitzgerald, For The Record. New York: A Birch Lane Press Book, 1994.

Fox, Ted. Show Time At The Apollo. New York: DaCappo Press, 1983.
Garrow, David J. Bearing The Cross: Martin Luther King, Jr., And The Southern Leadership Conference. New York: William Morrow and Company, Inc., 1986.

Hampton, Lionel with James Haskins. Hamp An Autobiography. New York: Amistad, 1989.

Kuntz, Tom and Phil Kuntz, Editors. The Sinatra Files. New York: Three Rivers Press, 2000.

Murray, Albert. Good Morning Blues: The Autobiography of Count Basie. New York: Donald I. Fine, Inc., 1985.

Schiffman, Jack. Uptown: The Story of Harlem's Apollo Theater. New York: Cowles Book Company, Inc., 1971.

Sinatra, Nancy. Frank Sinatra: An American Legend. Great Britain: Virgin Books, 1995.

Stearns, Marshall and Jean. Jazz Dance! The Story of Americans Vernacular Dance. New York: Schirmer Books, 1968.

Travis, Dempsey J. An Autobiography of Black Chicago. Chicago: Urban Research Press, Inc., 1981.

Travis, Dempsey J. An Autobiography of Black Jazz. Chicago: Urban Research Press, Inc., 1983.

Watkins, Mel. The Real Side. New York: Simon and Schuster, 1994.
Magazines
Sammy Davis Jr. The Kid Turns 50. Ebony Magazine. February, 1976.
Like Deaths In The Family: Fans of All Ages Mourn Sammy Davis Jr. U.S.A. Today. May 17, 1990.

The World of Sammy Davis Jr. In Retrospect. Chicago Defender. May 17, 1990.
'Last Trooper' Davis Is Dead. Chicago Sun Times. May 17, 1990.
Legendary Entertainer Sammy Davis Jr. Chicago Tribune. May 17, 1990.
Sammy Davis Jr., Showman Dies At 64. The New York Times. May 17, 1990.
A Final Ovation For Sammy Davis Jr. Chicago Sun Times. May 19, 1990.
An Entertainer Should Entertain, And Davis Did. Chicago Tribune. May 20, 1990.
So Long, Sammy, The Amazing Life of The Showbiz Pioneer Who Did It All. People Weekly. May 28, 1990.

Fond Memories of Sammy. By Hermene D. Hartman Publisher of N'Digo. June, 1990.
Sammy Davis Jr. Drive Formally Dedicated. Chicago Defender. October 6, 1990.
Sammy Davis Jr. Drive Dedicated in Chicago. Jet Magazine. October 22, 1990.
Nixon Meets Sammy Davis Jr. As Oval Office Titters. Chicago Tribune. September 24, 2000.

Chapter VII
FBI Documents
60 preprocessed pages on Helen Keller released under the (Freedom of Information Act) pursuant to Title 5 United States Code 552 and/ or 552 a Privacy Act.
Books
French, Richard Slayton. From Homer to Helen Keller: A Social and Educational Study of the Blind. New York: American Foundation of the Blind, 1932.

Goodwin, Doris Kearns. No Ordinary Times. New York: Simon and Schuster, 1994.

Harrity, Richard, and Ralph G. Martin. The Three Lives of Helen Keller. Garden City: Doubleday, 1962.

Herman, Dorothy. Helen Keller: A Life. University of Chicago Press, 1998.
Keller, Helen. Light In My Darkness. New York: Chrysalis Books, 1994.

Lash, Joseph P. Eleanor: The Years Alone. New York: W.W. Norton & Company, 1972.

Lash, Joseph. Helen and Teacher: The Story of Helen Keller and Anne Sullivan Macy. New York: Delacarte Press, 1980.

Leblanc, Georgette. The Girl Who Found The Blue Bird. New York: Dodd, Mead, 1914.

Ridley, Peter. Helen Keller: Revolutionary Socialist. New York: Touchstone, Simon and Schuster, 1979.

Villey - Demeserets Pierre. The World of the Blind. New York: Macmillan, 1930.

Magazines

"Helen Keller As She Really Is". Ladies Home Journal. November 1902.

"Helen Keller at Radcliffe College". Youth's Companion. June 2, 1905.

Chapter VIII
FBI Documents
2564 preprocessed pages on Coleman Young released under the (Freedom of Information (Act) pursuant to Title 5, United States Code 552 and/or section 552 a (Privacy Act).
Books
Davis, Allison. Leadership, Love and Aggression. New York: Harcourt Brace Jovanovich, 1983.

Keeran, Roger. The Communist Party and Auto Unions. Bloomington: Indiana University Press, 1980.

Lee, Alfred McClung and Norman D. Humphrey. Race Riot Detroit, 1943. New York: Octagon Books, 1968.

Leinen, Stephen. Black Police, White Society. New York: New York University Press, 1984.

Rich, Wilbur C. Coleman Young and Detroit Politics: From Social Activist to Power Broker. Detroit: Wayne State University Press, 1989.

Stolberg, Benjamin. The Story of The CIO. New York: Viking Press, 1938.
Travis, Dempsey J. Views From The Back of The Bus During WWII And Beyond. Chicago: Urban Research Press, Inc., 1995.

Widick, B.J. Detroit: City of Race and Class Violence. Chicago: Quadrangle Books, 1972.

Wilson, James Q. Varieties of Police Behavior. New York: Atheneum Press, 1976.

Chapter IX
FBI Documents
18 preprocessed pages on Dorothy Dandridge released under the (Freedom of Information Act) pursuant to Title 5, United States Code 552 and/or section 552 a (Privacy Act).
30 preprocessed pages of Nat King Cole released under the (Freedom of Information Act) pursuant to Title 5, United States Code 552 and/or section 552 a (Privacy Act).
Books
Bogle, Donald. Toms, Coons, Mulattoes, Mammies and Bucks. New York: Continuum Press, 1989.

Dandridge, Dorothy and Earl Conrad. Everything And Nothing. New York: Abelard Schuman, 1970.

Mills, Earl. Dorothy Dandridge. New York: Holloway House, 1989.
Rampersad, Arnold. Hughes, Langston The Life of Langston Hughes: Volume II: 1941-1967. I Dream A World. New York: Oxford University Press, 1988.

Watkins, Mel. On The Real Side. New York: Simon and Schuster, 1994.
Periodicals
Life Magazine. November 5, 1951, March 23, 1953, November 1, 1954.
Time Magazine. February 4, 1952, May 2, 1955.
The Private World of Dorothy Dandridge. Ebony. June 1962.
Dorothy Dandridge Hollywood Tragic Enigma. Ebony Magazine. March 1986.
The Real Life Tragedy of Dorothy Dandridge. Ebony Magazine. September 1986.
The Last Days of Dorothy Dandridge. Ebony Magazine. August 1997.

Newspapers
Those Dapper Tappers by Howard Reich. Chicago Tribune. December 22, 1991.
The Fallen Star Smolders in Memory. The New York Times. June 19, 1997.
Francine Everett, Striking Star of All-Black Movies Is Dead. The New York Times. June 20, 1999.

Hollywood's First Black Goddess and Casualty. The New York Times. August 15, 1999.

Harold Nicholas, Dazzling Hoofer, Is Dead At 79. The New York Times. July 4, 2000.

Chapter X
FBI Documents
340 preprocessed pages on Groucho Marx released under the (Freedom of Information Act) pursuant to Title 5, United States Code 552 and/or section 552 a (Privacy Act).
Books
Crichtor, Kyle. The Marx Brothers. Garden City: Doubleday, 1970.
Griffith, Richard and Arthur Mayer. The Movies. New York: A Fireside Book Published by Simon and Schuster, 1970.

Hecht, Ben. A Child of the Century. New York: Simon and Schuster, 1954.
Edited by Stephan Kanfer, Writings by, for and about Groucho Marx. New York: Vintage Books, 2000.

Kanfer, Stefan. The Life and Times of Julius Henry Marx. New York: Alfred A. Knopf, 2000.

Lauvish, Simon. The Lives and Legends of the Marx Brothers: Groucho, Chico, Harpo, Zeppo with added Gummo. New York: Thomas Dunne Books/ St. Martin's Press, 2000.

Nass, Herbert E. Wills of The Rich and Famous. New York: Random House, 2000.
Stolair, Steve. Raised Eyebrows. Los Angeles: General Publishing Group, 1996.
Newspapers
There Ain't No Sanity Claus. Review by Gary Giddins. New York Times. June 18, 2000.

Duck Soup. A Review by Roger Ebert. Chicago Sun Times. July 9, 2000.
Magazine
Groucho's Club. By Terrence Rafferty Critic At Large. Gentlemans Quarterly. June 2000.

Chapter XI

FBI Documents

123 preprocessed pages on Marian Anderson released under the (Freedom of Information Act) pursuant to Title 5, United States Code 552 and/or section 552 a (Privacy Act).
Books
Adams, L. Russell and Jr. Ross, P. David. Great Negroes Past and Present. Chicago: Afro-American Publishing Company, 1963.

Anderson, Marian. My Lord, What A Morning. New York: Viking Press, 1956.
Duberman, B. Martin. Paul Robeson. New York: Alfred A. Knopf, 1988.

Goodwin, K. Doris. No Ordinary Time - Franklin and Eleanor Roosevelt: The Home Front in World War II. New York: Simon and Schuster, 1994.

Lash, P. Joseph. Eleanor and Franklin: The Story of Their Relationship, Based on Eleanor Roosevelts' Private Papers. New York: W.W. Norton and Company, 1971.

Lash, P. Joseph. Eleanor: The Years Alone. New York: W.W. Norton and Company, Inc., 1972.

Rampersad, Arnold. The Life of Langston Hughes, Volume II: 1941-1967 I Dream A World. Oxford: Oxford University Press, 1988.

Waters P. Enoch. American Diary. Chicago: Path Press, Inc., 1987.

Woman's Almanac, by the editors of the World Almanac. The Good Housekeeping. New York City: Newspaper Enterprise Association, 1977.

Newspapers

Hail Marian Anderson In Met Opera Debut. New York Times, January 7, 1955.

A Carnegie Hall Tribute To Marian Anderson at 80: She Broke Classical Music's Color Barrier. Chicago Tribune, January 17, 1982.

A Musical Tribute to a Legend. New York Times, August 15, 1989.

Marian Anderson's Life of Unfailing Dignity. New York Times, May 8, 1991.

Marian Anderson, 95, Off To West. Sun Times, June 28, 1992.

Marian Anderson Is Dead At 96; Singer Shattered Racial Barriers. New York Times, April 9, 1993.

Humanity Made Anderson More Than A Great Artist. Chicago Sun Times, April 11, 1993.

Marian Anderson, America's Great Singer, Remembered. Chicago Defender, April 12, 1993.

Grounded In Faith, Free to Fly. New York Times, April 18, 1993.

D.A. R. and Marian Anderson: Fresh Perspective On A Rebuff. New York Times, May 18, 1993.

Chapter XII
310 preprocessed pages on Orson Welles released under the (Freedom of Information Act) pursuant to Title 5, United States Code 552 and/or section 552 a (Privacy Act).
Books
Writings By Orson Welles
 Citizen Kane. New York: Simon and Schuster, 1969.
 Everybody's Shakespeare. New York: Harper and Brother, 1933.
 Mercury Shakespeare. Woodstock: Todd Press, 1934.
 The Trial. New York: Simon and Schuster, 1970.
 Books By Others
Carringer, Robert L. The Making of Citizen Kane. Berkeley: University of California Press, 1985.

Fowler, Roy. Orson Welles, A First Biography. London: Pendulum Publications, 1946.

Gottesman, Roland, ed. Focus On Orson Welles. New Jersey: Prentice-Hall. Englewood Cliffs, 1976.

Griffith, Richard and Arthur Mayer. The Movies. A Fireside Book. New York: Simon and Schuster, 1970.

Maremore, James. The Magic World of Orson Welles. New York: Oxford University Press, 1978.

McBride, Joseph. Orson Welles. New York: Viking Press, 1972.
Noble, Peter. The Fabulous Orson Welles. London: Hutchinson Press, 1956.
Newspapers
'Kane' At 50 Dazzles Yet With His High Spirits. New York Times, April 28, 1991.
Citizen Kane A Masterpiece At 50. By Roger Ebert (Film Critic). Chicago Sun-Times, April 28, 1991.

Even After 50 Years, 'Citizen Kane' Resonates With A Clarity Both Technical and Allegorical. Chicago Tribune, May 1, 1991.

Chapter XIII
FBI Documents
152 preprocessed pages on Jackie Robinson released under the (Freedom of Information
Act) pursuant to Title 5 United States Code 552 and/ or 552 a Privacy Act.
Interview
Truman K. Gibson Jr. July 6, 1994, December 4, 1994.
Books

Ashe Jr., Arthur. A Hard Road To Glory: The History of The African-American Athlete Since 1946. New York: Warner Books, 1988.

Duberman, Martin Bauml. Paul Robeson. New York: Alfred A. Knopf, 1988.

Branch, Taylor. Parting The Waters. New York: Simon & Schuster, 1988.
Falkner, David. Great Time Coming, From Baseball to Birmingham. New York: Simon & Schuster, 1995.

Frommer, Harvey. Jackie Robinson. New York: Franklin Watts, 1984.
Garrow, David J. Bearing The Cross. New York: William & Company, 1986.
Goldstein, Richard. Spartan Seasons. New York: Macmillan, 1980.
Henderson, Edwin Bancroft. The Negro In Sports. Washington: The Associates Publisher, Inc., 1949.

Kahn, Roger. The Boys of Summer. New York: Harper & Row, 1972.
Peterson, Robert. Only the Ball Was White. New York: McGraw-Hill, 1984.
Ritter, Lawrence S. The Glory of Their Times. New York: Morrow, 1984.
Robinson, Jackie. I Never Had It Made. New York: G. P. Putnam's Sons, 1972.
Rogosin, Donn. Invisible Men. New York: Atheneum, 1985.
Scott, Richardson. Jackie Robinson. New York: Chelsea House Publishers, 1987.
Travis, Dempsey J. Views From The Back of The Bus During World War II and Beyond. Chicago: Urban Research Press, 1995.

Travis, Dempsey J. An Autobiography of Black Politics. Chicago: Urban Research Press, 1987.

Travis, Dempsey J. An Autobiography of Black Chicago. Chicago: Urban Research Press, 1981.

Tygiel, Jules. Baseball's Great Experiment. New York: Oxford University Press, 1983.
Voigt, David Quentin. American Baseball. 3 volumes. University Park and London: Pennsylvania State University Press, 1983.

Newspapers and Other Media
"Chicago Defender Lists Ben Davis on Honor Roll". Daily Worker. December 27, 1945.

"Dodger Farm Signs Negro Hurler". Daily Worker. January 30, 1946.

"119th Anniversary of Negro Journalism". The Worker. March 3, 1946.

"Jim Crow Will Strike Out". Daily Worker. March 8, 1946.

Article with Photo of Robinson. "Fraternal Outlook". November 1946.
Jackie Robinson Was New York State Chairman of The UNAYA. "The Worker". May 25, 1947.

"Dodger Player Received Award." Daily Worker. June 2, 1947.
"Cleveland's Larry Doby". Daily Worker. July 4, 1947.

Letters to the Editor Re: Jackie Robinson. Peoples Voice. September 20, 1947.

"Jackie Robinson's Day". Daily Worker. September 23, 1947.

"Michigan Battled Jim Crow in '47". Michigan Herald. February 8, 1948.

"Jim Crow Wins Another Round in Pix". Daily Worker. February 24, 1948.

"Robbie Jittery As Club Opens KKK Belt Tour". NY Post and Home News. April 7, 1949.

Book Parade "Jackie Robinson's Own Story of a Negro Ballplayer". Daily Worker. April 19, 1948.

"Protest by KKK is Disregarded". Washington Post. January 16, 1949.

"Sports of the Times" "Jackie Robinson and the Ku Klux Klan". New York Times. January 18, 1949.

"KKK Won't Demonstrate". NY Daily Mirror. April 9, 1949.

"Jackie Robinson Would Fight For The United States Against Russia." New York Times. July 9, 1949.

"Jackie Robinson and the Un-American Committee". Daily Worker. July 11, 1949.

"Robinson Appeared Before HCUA on July 18, 1949." New York Times. July 14, 1949.

Articles Re: Robinson's Appearance Before HCUA. Daily Worker. July 18, 1949. Washington Daily News - July 18, 1949. Daily Peoples World. July 24, 1949.

Articles regarding "Daily Worker" editorial concerning Robinson and the Ku Klux Klan. Daily Worker. July 21, 1949.

Article concerning HCUA Hearings, Robinson Appeared Before HCUA. Daily Worker. August 2, 1949.

Article Relating to a Communist Inspired Move to Create a National Jim Crow Incident in Baseball. Journal American. September 27, 1949.

Robinson participates in WLIB Broadcast from Hotel Theresa in New York City. April 29, 1950.

Jackie Robinson's Life Threatened; FBI Called - Cincinnati Inquirer. May 17, 1951.

Drew Pearson Broadcast From Washington, D.C. Mentioned Robinson. November 14, 1951.

"Map Fight on Eviction of Whites Who Fought Levittown Jim Crow". Daily Worker. February 11, 1952.

Jackie Appears On T.V. Program "We The People", NBC, NYC. May 30, 1952.

"Jackie Robinson to Keynote Parley on Met Bias". Daily Worker. January 9, 1953.

"Jack Robinson Hails Meet to End in Parkchester". Daily Worker. January 12, 1953.

"NAACP Aid Hits Tyranny in South". New Orleans States. New Orleans, La. January 16, 1957.

"Robinson Heads Anti-Bias Fund". NY Herald Tribune. January 18, 1957.

"Jackie Draws Crowds on Tour for NAACP". Daily Worker. January 18, 1957.

"Atlanta Pastors Praised". Pittsburgh Courier. January 19, 1957.

"Jackie Robinson on Look Magazine Payroll". White American News Service. February, 1957.

"Jackie Robinson Visits NAACP Official Walter Reuther". White Sentinel. February, 1957.

"A Worthy Purpose". The Worker. February 10, 1957 & April 1, 1957.

"Virginia Fund Drive Opened by NAACP". Washington Star. April 1, 1957.

"Jackie Robinson Says NAACP Shuns Force". Washington Post and Times Herald. April 1, 1957.

"Robinson Lauds Nixon, Adams at NAACP Rally". Washington Star. April 15, 1957.

"Honored in Rights Issue". NY Times. May 27, 1957.

Jackie Robinson & Dr. Martin Luther King Received Honorary Law Degrees From Howard University. Washington Star - June 8, 1957. Washington Post & Times Herald June 8, 1957.

"Ribicoff Appoints Jackie Robinson to New 3 Member Parole Board". NY Herald Tribune. June 9, 1957.

World Watches Prayer Protest. Pittsburgh Courier. May 18, 1957.
"Major Issues Go Before NAACP Meeting Here. Detroit News. June 23, 1957.

"1,000 Delegates Here for NAACP Parley". Detroit Times. June 23, 1957.

"1,000 Delegates Due at NAACP Parley Tomorrow". Daily Worker. June 24, 1957.

"NAACP Chief Sets 1963 As Integration Date". Washington Star. June 26, 1957.

"NAACP Urges Ike Speak Out on Dixie Bias". NY Post. July 1, 1957.

"13 Sign for 'Life' with the NAACP". The Chicago Defender. July 20, 1957.

Jackie Robinson Spoke at Membership Meeting of the NAACP on October 6, 1957, Camden, NJ. Evening Bulletin, Philadelphia. October 7, 1957.

"Nat King Cole Supports NAACP Freedom Dinner". Daily Worker. October 9, 1957.

"Mrs. Bates Will Speak in N.Y." Daily Worker. October 30, 1957.

"NAACP Honors 2 at Dinner - Scrolls Given to Rickey, Ellington". NY Herald Tribune. November 23, 1957.

"NAACP Asks "Moderation End". Washington Post and Times Herald. January 7, 1958.

"NAACP Urges Southerners Be Fair on Rights". Washington Star. January 7, 1958.

"3 New Members on NAACP Board". Pittsburgh Courier. January 18, 1958.

"1957 Was Biggest Year in History of Natl. Organization". NY Courier. January 18, 1958.

"Jackie and NAACP Denied Use of School Auditorium". Pittsburgh Courier. February 1, 1958.

"NAACP to Host Jackie". New Orleans States. February 5, 1958.

"NAACP Schedules Meeting Monday". The Times Picayune. February 6, 1958.

"Robinson Tells Road to Right". The Times Picayune. New Orleans, La. February 17, 1958.

"People". Washington News. February 17, 1958.

"1500 Negroes Turn Out for Speech by Robinson". The Clarion Ledger, The State Times & Washington News. Jackson, Miss. February 17, 1958.

"Jackie Robinson, Rev. Sullivan Threatened by Local Hoodlums". Philadelphia Tribune. February, 28,1959.

"Robinson Talks at South Carolina Negro Rally". Charlotte Observer. October 26, 1959.

"Threaten Jackie Robinson with Jail at S.C. Airport". NY Post. October 26, 1959.

"Jackie Robinson". NY Post. October 28, 1959.

"Justice Department is Studying Incident at Greenville Airport". Greenville News. October 30, 1959.

Article relating to Incident Greenville, SC, Airport Involving Jackie Robinson. Greenville News. October 27, 1959 & November 4, 1959.

Article relating to a March on the Airport in Greenville, SC, in Protest of a Racial Incident Involving Robinson. Charlotte Observer. December 1, 1959.

"No Action Taken on Jan. 1 Airport March". The Greenville News. Greenville, SC. December 16, 1959.

"Nothing Finer Than Courage of This Kind". The Worker. April 3, 1960.

"Jackie Robinson Says Aides Told Nixon to Shun Harlem". NY Herald Tribune. March 10,1961.

"Bobby Kennedy- Guy With Style". NY Amsterdam News. June 9, 1962.

Harlem Pickets Switch Tactics - Threaten A Demonstration Against Jackie Robinson. New York Times. July,14, 1962.

"Powell Hit by Jackie Robinson. NY Post. March 28, 1963.

"Egg Throwing and Dr. King". Amsterdam News. July 13, 1963.

"Chock Full Bias Charges A Headache for Robinson." New York Herald Tribune. October 4, 1963.

Equality Must Apply to All, Robinson Says. Columbus Citizens Journal. January 20, 1964.

"Lawmakers Little Affected by Civil Rights March". Louisville Courier- Journal. March 6, 1964.

"Philly's Antidote". Washington Daily News. September 16, 1964.

Newark NAACP Strikes Out Don Newcombe". NY Herald Tribune. November 29, 1964.

Jackie Still Has Doubts. Detroit Free Press. December 12, 1964.
Rachel Robinson: A Profile Of Courage. Chicago Sun-Times. January 17, 1982.

Chapter XIV

FBI Documents

450 preprocessed pages on Frank Lloyd Wright released under the (Freedom of Information Act) pursuant to Title 5 United States Code 552 and/ or 552 a Privacy Act.
Books
Alofsin, Anthony. Frank Lloyd Wright - The Lost Years, 1910-1922: A Study of Influence. Chicago: University of Chicago Press, 1993.

Banham, Reyner. Age of the Masters: A Person View of Modern Architecture. New York: Harper and Row, 1975.

Bardeschi, Marco Dezzi. Frank Lloyd Wright. London: (Twentieth Century Masters) Hamlyn, 1972.

Bolon, Carol R., Robert S. Nelson, and Linda Seidel. The Nature of Frank Lloyd Wright. Chicago: University of Chicago Press, 1988.

Brooks, H. Allen. Frank Lloyd Wright and the Prairie School. New York: George Braziller, 1984.

Eaton, Leonard K. Two Chicago Architects and Their Clients: Frank Lloyd Wright and Howard Van Doren Shaw. Cambridge: MIT Press, 1969.

Frank Lloyd Wright: The Early Work. New York: Horizon Press, 1968.

Frank Lloyd Wright: The Guggenheim Correspondence. Carbondale: The Press at

Photo Credits

Photo Credits

PAGE 367- ASSOCIATED PRESS/ WIDE WORLD PHOTO, INC.

PAGE 382- JOINT CENTER FOR POLITICAL STUDIES

Index

Index

Index

Index

Index

Index

Index

Index